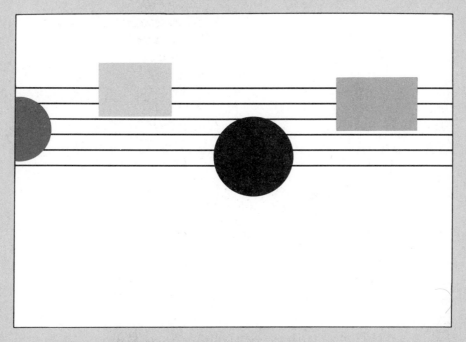

COMPARATIVE ECONOMIC SYSTEMS

FOURTH·EDITION

MARTIN C. SCHNITZER

Professor of Management
College of Business
Virginia Polytechnic Institute
and State University

Published by

H78 **SOUTH-WESTERN PUBLISHING CO.**

CINCINNATI   WEST CHICAGO, IL   DALLAS   LIVERMORE, CA

ISBN: 0-538-08781-1
Library of Congress Catalog Card Number: 85-63401

 2 3 4 5 6 6 7 FG 3 2 1 0 9 8 7
Printed in the United States of America

P R E F A C E

Several major changes have been made in this book since the third edition. The most important change is the addition of a section on the less developed countries of the world. Seventy percent of the world's population lives in these countries. Three representative countries—China, Nigeria, and Mexico—are discussed in separate chapters. China is the largest country in the world and one of the poorest. To modernize its economy, China's current leaders have introduced elements of a market economy to go along with state direction and control. Nigeria is the largest country in Africa. It achieved its independence from England in 1960, but still retains many of the institutions of British colonial rule. It depends on oil exports for its economic development. Mexico, one of the oldest countries in Latin America, is of extreme importance to the United States in many ways. Its economic problems are representative of those of most Latin American countries, but may be more serious.

The book also includes more first-hand statistical and economic data and is as up-to-date as possible. There is more reliance on economic analyses to compare countries and economic systems. To facilitate comparison, the book includes separate chapters on the economies of important industrial countries—both market and centrally planned. These countries cannot be rigidly classified by ideology. How they allocate resources varies from country to country. In the market economies, there is some government ownership of industry and extensive participation by government in the economy. In the centrally planned economies, market arrangements are used to some degree to supplement planning. Again, the degree varies from one country to the other.

The book is divided into six sections. Part 1 explains the difference between capitalism, socialism, and communism. A frame of reference for comparing the market and centrally planned economies of today is also provided. Part 2 discusses the economy of the United States, taking into consideration the relationship between the government and the market mechanism. Part 3 presents the mixed economic systems of three highly developed industrial democracies: France, Japan, and the United Kingdom. Part 4 pertains to the centrally planned economies. The Soviet Union, Poland, and Yugoslavia, three countries with considerable variation in their economies, are examined. Part 5 covers the less developed countries. China, Mexico, and Nigeria are discussed in terms of their approaches to resource allocation and economic growth. Part 6 summarizes the performance of the market and centrally planned economies in the 1980s.

I would like to thank Dr. Scott E. Masten of the University of Michigan and Dr. Shirley J. Gedeof on the University of Vermont for their helpful comments on the manuscript. Thanks and appreciation are also expressed to individuals at the World Bank, the Population Reference Bureau, Inc., the National Defense University, the Central Intelligence Agency, and the U.S. State Department for their assistance in providing data, and to my graduate assistant, Josh Fox, for his help in data collection. I also wish to thank Dr. Kalman Toth of the Karl Marx University in Budapest, Hungary, for providing information on the Hungarian reforms and a number of people in Poland who provided information on the post-Solidarity period. Thanks also go to Rhonda G. Dunn for her assistance in typing the manuscript.

Martin C. Schnitzer

ABOUT THE AUTHOR

Martin C. Schnitzer received his PhD in economics from the University of Florida. He teaches courses in government and business, and international business at Virginia Polytechnic Institute. Dr. Schnitzer is the author of ten books, including one on the Swedish economy and one concerning East and West Germany. He has lectured in Hungary and Poland and served on the U.S. East-West Trade Commission and the Virginia Export Council. He has served as an economic consultant to the U.S. Joint Economic Committee and has published a number of monographs on European economic policy.

CONTENTS

v

PART 1

INTRODUCTION TO ECONOMIC SYSTEMS

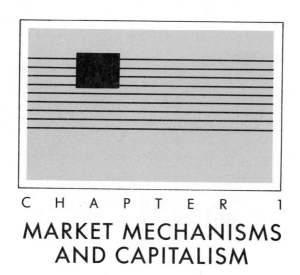

C H A P T E R   1

MARKET MECHANISMS
AND CAPITALISM

A fundamental dilemma of any economic system is a scarcity of resources relative to wants. Decisions are necessary to determine how a given volume of resources is to be allocated to production and how the income derived from production is to be distributed to the various factors—capital, labor, and land—that are responsible for it. Human wants, if not unlimited, are at least indefinitely expansible. But the commodities and services that can satisfy these wants are not, and neither are the factors of production that can produce the desired goods and services. These productive factors usually have alternative uses; that is, they can be used in the production of a number of different goods and services. The system must allocate limited productive resources, which have alternative uses, to the satisfaction of great and growing human wants.

Large amounts of capital will not be available for use in production unless there is a process of saving and capital formation. This process is fundamentally the same in all types of economic systems. It cannot operate unless the available productive resources are more than adequate to provide a bare living for the people of the system. When it *is* able to operate, the process involves spending part of the money income of an economy, directly or indirectly, for capital goods rather than for consumer goods. In a nonmonetary sense, saving and capital formation require the allocation of a part of the productive resources of a country to producing capital goods rather than consumer goods. The cost of obtaining capital goods is

the same in all economic systems: It is going without, at present, the qualities of consumer goods and services that could have been produced by the
factors of production.

In general, societies have endless ways of organizing and performing
their production and distribution functions. In economic and political
terms, the possible range is from laissez-faire capitalism through totalitar-
ian communism. The economy of the United States today by no means
represents a pure laissez-faire capitalist system. It is, rather, a mixed economic system. There are public enterprises, considerable government regulation and control, and various other elements that hinder the unrestrained functioning of market forces. However, to understand how a capitalist system works, it is necessary to know something about its institutional arrangements. For practical purposes, an *institutional arrangement*
is a practice, convention, or custom that is a material and persistent element in the life or culture of an organized group. *Economic institutions*
are ways of reacting in certain economic situations and with respect to certain economic and social phenomena. Some economic institutions rest on
custom, while others are formally recognized through legislative enact-
ment.

■ CAPITALISM ■
AS AN ECONOMIC SYSTEM

A number of institutional arrangements characterize a capitalist economic
system. These arrangements reflect a set of basic beliefs that define how a
society should be organized, how goods and services should be produced,
and how income should be distributed. In the United States these beliefs
are incorporated into the institutional arrangements that typify a capitalist
system—private property, the profit motive, the price system, freedom of
enterprise, competition, individualism, consumer sovereignty, the work
ethic, and limited government. Each of these institutions will be discussed
in some detail.

PRIVATE PROPERTY

Under capitalism there is private ownership of the factors of production—
land, labor, and capital. There are also certain rights concerning property.
An individual has the right to acquire property, to consume or control it,
to buy or sell it, to give it away as a gift, and to bequeath it at death. Private property ownership is supposed to encourage thrift and wealth ac-

cumulation and to serve as a stimulus to individual initiative and industry, both of which are considered essential to economic progress.

However, private ownership of property is subject to certain limitations. In practice, even under capitalism, property rights are often restricted by the actions of social groups or government units. Also, a good deal of the private wealth of capitalist systems, such as the United States, is owned not by individuals, but rather by business firms. There is actually a good deal of publicly owned property within a capitalistic system. Where public property exists, the exclusive control of wealth is exercised by a group of individuals through some political process.

THE PROFIT MOTIVE

The kinds of goods produced in an economy that relies on market arrangements are determined in the first instance by managers of business firms or by individual entrepreneurs. They are directly responsible for converting resources into products and determining what these products will be, guided by the actions of consumers in the marketplace. The profit motive is the lodestar that draws managers to produce goods that can be sold at prices that are higher than the costs of production. In private enterprise, profit is necessary for survival; it is the payment to owners of capital. Anybody who produces things that do not, directly or indirectly, yield a profit will sooner or later go bankrupt, lose the ownership of the means of production, and so cease to be an independent producer. There can be no other way. Capitalism, in other words, uses profitability as the test of whether any given item should or should not be produced, and if it should, how much of it should be produced.

THE PRICE SYSTEM

Individuals and businesses under capitalism are supposed to make most types of economic decisions on the basis of prices, price relationships, and price changes. The function of prices is to provide a coordinating mechanism for millions of decentralized private production and distribution units. The prices that prevail in the marketplace determine the kinds and quantities of goods and services that shall be produced and how they shall be distributed. Price changes are supposed to adjust the quantities of these goods and services available for the market.

It is through the mechanism of prices that scarce resources are allocated to various uses. The interaction between the price system and the pursuit of profits is supposed to keep economic mistakes down to a reasonable level. Profit, which depends upon the selling price of goods and the cost of making them, indicates to businesses what people are buying. A product that commands high prices relative to costs draws businesses into that industry, whereas low prices relative to costs check production by causing businesses to drop out.

PRICE DETERMINATION   In a free market economy, demand and supply determine the price at which a purchase or sale of a good is made. Demand originates with the consumer. It involves a desire for a good or service expressed through a willingness to pay money for it in the marketplace. Market demand is the sum of all individual consumers' demands for a particular good or service. There is an inverse relationship between market demand and the price of a good or a service. The higher the price, the lower the quantity of the good or service demanded; the lower the price, the greater the quantity of the good or service in demand.

Supply originates with the producer. It is the quantity of a good or service that a producer is willing to offer at any given price. Market supply is the sum of all the supplies that individual producers will offer in the marketplace at all possible prices over a given period. There is a direct relationship between market supply and price—the higher the price, the greater the supply of goods or services that will be provided.

The interaction of demand and supply determines the price for a good or service in the marketplace. The equilibrium price is the price that equates the quantity demanded with the quantity supplied in a market. It is the one price that will clear the market. At any price above the equilibrium price, supply is greater than demand, and the price must fall. At a price below the equilibrium price, demand is greater than supply, and the price must rise. In the example, the equilibrium price is $3 per pound.

Market Demand	Price Per Pound	Market Supply
180 pounds	$ .50	40 pounds
140	1.00	50
100	2.00	65
80	3.00	80
60	4.00	100
40	5.00	120

The forces of supply and demand acting through the price mechanism can send effective signals to the marketplace. For example, an increase in demand means that buyers will be willing to purchase more at any price than they were formerly. An increase in demand, with supply remaining constant, would result in an increase in price. The increased price would cause producers to supply more so quantity would increase also. A decrease in demand would have the opposite effect.

Conversely, an increase in supply, with demand remaining constant, would result in a decrease in price. The lower price would lead to an increase in the quantity purchased. A decrease in supply would have the opposite effect. Consumers have to pay more for a smaller amount of a good or service.

Figure 1-1 illustrates the determination of prices and output in a free market. Both are determined at the intersection of the demand and supply curves. The equilibrium price is p_0, and q_0 is the quantity supplied. At any price above p_0 the quantity supplied is greater than the quantity demanded, and the price will fall. At any price below p_0, demand is greater than the quantity supplied, and prices will rise.

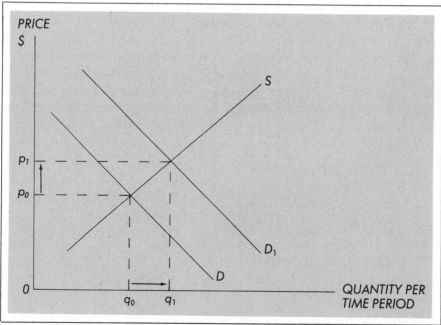

FIGURE 1-1   DETERMINATION OF EQUILIBRIUM
                    PRICE AND OUTPUT

An increase in demand to D_1 with supply remaining constant will result in an increase in both price and quantity. The new equilibrium price will be p_1, and the quantity will increase to q_1. The increase in demand to D_1 will eventually result in an increase in supply (the supply curve shifts to the right) as producers react to the potential for higher profits. New producers will enter the market, and resources will be shifted from other areas into the market in anticipation of a greater rate of return.[1]

FREEDOM OF ENTERPRISE

Freedom of enterprise is another basic institution of capitalism. It refers to the general right of each individual to engage in any appealing line of economic activity. However, there are limits placed on the choice of an activity. People cannot engage in activities that are deemed socially immoral (e.g., child pornography) or that may harm others (e.g., driving while intoxicated). As far as the government is concerned, the individual is free to move to any part of the country, work in any chosen occupation, and find and operate a business unit in virtually any field of lawful economic activity. By comparing market indicators—namely prices and costs—the individual is supposed to be able to select a field of activity that promises to be remunerative. The institution of private property furnishes the social sanctions necessary for the use and control of the factors of production vital to the chosen field of activity.

The theory used to justify the existence of freedom of enterprise is quite simply one of social welfare. That is, individuals, in choosing fields of economic activity in which they will be the most successful from the point of view of private gain, will also be selecting fields in which they presumably will be most productive to society.

COMPETITION

The attempts of individuals to further their economic self-interest, given the institutions of private property and freedom of enterprise and given the scarcity of resources and reliance on a market to allocate them, result in competition. Competition is an indispensable part of a free enterprise sys-

---

1. For example, as student enrollment in a college town increases, the demand for housing will increase. Townspeople will be willing to rent more rooms and existing housing will be fully used. Rents will increase and someone will decide to build apartments for students. The supply of housing will increase as available resources are shifted into housing construction.

tem. In economic life, self-reliant individuals must struggle and compete for economic rewards—good jobs, high pay, promotions, desirable goods and services, and security in old age. There is the element of social Darwinism in competition: Life is a competitive struggle in which only the fittest, in terms of resources, get to the top.

Certainly, *competition* is one of the "good" words in the American vocabulary. From a very early age, school children are told that the distinguishing characteristic of the historically successful U.S. economic system is competition and that other economic systems have inefficiencies because, in some degree, they lack that magic ingredient in the particular and unique context in which it exists in our economy. It is, therefore, not surprising that by statute and common law our legal system has been actively concerned with the maintenance of a competitive system.

Certain benefits are thought to be derived from competition in the marketplace. A competitive market will

1. Allow the price mechanism to reflect actual demand and cost and thus maximize efficiency in the use of capital and other resources;

2. Encourage product innovation and long-run cost reduction;

3. Result in the equitable diffusion of real income;

4. Provide consumers with a wide variety of alternative sources of supply.

INDIVIDUALISM

Individualism is linked to a set of related institutional values of capitalism. Again there is social Darwinism—life is a competitive struggle where the fit survive and those who are unfit do not. Individualism also involves competition, which, when combined with social Darwinism, is supposed to provide some guarantee of progress through the inexorable process of evolution. Individualism is also related to equality of opportunity—the right of each person to succeed or fail on his or her own merit or lack of it.

The institutions of private property ownership and individualism are related from two standpoints. First, private property ownership provides the spur for individual initiative, a reward to be gained through competition and hard work. Second, it provides some guarantee of individual rights against the encroachments of the state. It follows that a necessary requisite for individualism is a limited state role. The individual would have preference over the state, for the latter is a fictitious body composed of individual people considered to represent its members. The idea of individualism can therefore be a safeguard against the tyranny of the state.

To some extent, individualism is linked to the philosophical roots of capitalism.[2] Individualism itself is a distinctive achievement of human consciousness—a mark of high civilization. It is consistent with the principles of a libertarian society in that it carries with it the concept of freedom to live and work as one prefers. There is a sense of privacy in individualism, privacy as something sacred in its own right. Under classical liberalism the individual is the center of society and the fulcrum that makes a free enterprise system work. Through energy applied to the fulfillment of personal needs, the individual pushes society forward. This does not result from charitable motives, but from the inexorable logic of the system— Adam Smith's "invisible hand." Stated simply, if all people are motivated to work at full capacity, whether they work as laborers, artisans, or executives, the net supply of goods and services available for consumption by all will be increased.

CONSUMER SOVEREIGNTY

In a capitalistic market economy, consumer sovereignty is an important institution because consumption is supposed to be the basic rationale of economic activity. As Adam Smith said, "Consumption is the sole end and purpose of all production; and the interest of the producer ought to be attended to only as far as it is necessary for promoting that of the consumer."[3] Consumer sovereignty assumes, of course, that there is a competitive market economy. Consumers are able to vote with their money by offering more of it for products that are in greater demand and less of it for products that are not in demand. Shifts in supply and demand will occur in response to the way in which consumers spend their money.

In competing for consumers' dollars, producers will produce more of those products that are in demand, for the prices will be higher, and less of those products that are not in demand, for the prices will be lower. Production is the means; consumption is the end. Those producers that effectively satisfy the wants of consumers are encouraged by large monetary returns, which enable them in turn to purchase the goods and services they

2. George Lodge, *The New American Ideology* (New York: Alfred A. Knopf Inc., 1975), Chapter 1.

3. Adam Smith, *An Inquiry Into The Nature and Causes of The Wealth of Nations* (Indianapolis: Liberty Classics, 1981), p. 660.

require in their operations. On the other hand, those producers who do not respond to the wants of consumers will not remain in business very long.

Freedom of choice is linked to consumer sovereignty. In fact, one defense of the market mechanism is the freedom of choice it provides to consumers in a capitalistic economy. Consumers are free to accept or reject whatever is produced in the marketplace. Thus the consumer is king, because production ultimately is oriented toward meeting the wants of consumers. Freedom of choice is consistent with a laissez-faire economy. It is assumed that consumers are capable of making rational decisions, and in an economy dominated by a large number of buyers and sellers this assumption has some merit. Since the role of the government is minimal, the principle of *caveat emptor*, "let the buyer beware," governs consumer decisions to buy.

THE PROTESTANT WORK ETHIC

The Protestant work ethic is an ideological principle stemming from the Protestant Reformation of the sixteenth century and is associated with the religious reformer John Calvin. Calvin preached a doctrine of salvation that later proved to be consistent with the principles of a capitalist system.[4] According to Calvin and the Puritan ministers in early New England, hard work, diligence, and thrift are earthly signs that individuals are using fully the talents given to them by God for His overall purposes. Salvation is associated with achievement on this earth. Thus work and economic gain have come to have a moral value. According to this view, it is good for the soul to work; rewards on this earth go to those who achieve the most. Salvation in the world to come is a reward that is in direct proportion to a deceased person's contribution during life.

The Calvinist doctrine of work and salvation became an integral part of the ideology of capitalism. The hard work of merchants and traders often produced profits, and their thrift led to saving and investment. Saving is the heart of the Protestant work ethic. With Adam Smith's idea of parsimony (or frugality) and Nassau Senior's idea of abstinence, it was established that saving multiplied future production and earned its own reward through interest.

---

4. Richard H. Tawney, *Religion and the Rise of Capitalism: A Historical Study* (New York: Harcourt, Brace, and World, 1926); and Max Weber, *The Protestant Ethic and the Spirit of Capitalism* (New York: Charles Scribner's Sons, 1930).

Carried into American society in the nineteenth century, the Protestant work ethic came to mean rewards for those who were economically competent and punishment for those who were incompetent or unambitious. Work was put at the center of American life. Most of the industrial capitalists of the last century belonged to fundamentalist Protestant churches. John D. Rockefeller, who became the then-richest man in the world, attributed his success to the "glory of God." (Skeptics, however, attributed his success to much more mundane factors than God's beneficience.[5])

LIMITED GOVERNMENT

For many years, the idea prevailed that the government in a capitalist system, however it might be organized, should follow a policy of laissez-faire with respect to economic activity. That is, activities of the government should be limited to the performance of a few general functions for the good of all citizens, and government should not attempt to control or interfere with the economic activities of private individuals. Laissez-faire assumes that individuals are rational and better judges of their own interests than any government could possibly be.[6] The interests of individuals are closely identified with those of society as a whole. It is only necessary for government to provide a setting or environment in which individuals can operate freely. This the government was supposed to do by performing only those functions that individuals could not do for themselves: provide for national defense, maintain law and order, carry on diplomatic relations with other countries, and construct roads, schools, and public works.

In a free enterprise market economy competition is regarded as a virtue rather than a vice. The proper use of resources in a free enterprise system is assured by the fact that if a firm does not use resources efficiently, it goes broke. If the market is to function effectively, it must operate freely. If there is intervention in any form, then there is no effective mechanism

5. See, for example, Matthew Josephson, *The Robber Barons* (New York: Harcourt, Brace, and World, 1934); and Ida M. Tarbell, *The History of the Standard Oil Company* (New York: McClure, Phillips, 1904).

6. The term *laissez-faire* originated in France, possibly as early as the first half of the eighteenth century, and was later developed by Adam Smith as a rule of practical economic conduct. In particular, see Adam Smith, *The Wealth of Nations*, Book IV, especially p. 630. Laissez-faire was a reaction to the stringent government restrictions imposed on all phases of economic activity by mercantilism. Under mercantilism, the state controlled all businesses, and one could engage in a particular activity only by receiving a monopoly from the state.

for weeding out inefficient enterprises. Nevertheless, government has always participated to some extent in business activity of capitalist countries. From the very beginning, the government of the United States was interested in the promotion of manufacturing, and it passed tariff laws very early to protect American business interests. Subsidies were used to promote the development of canals, roads, and railroads. Business was a direct beneficiary of those subsidies.

■ INCOME DISTRIBUTION ■ IN A CAPITALIST ECONOMY

Once goods and services have been produced, the next important question in any economic system is the manner in which these goods and services are to be divided or apportioned among the individual consumers of the economy. The distribution of income does not refer to the processes by which physical goods are brought from producers to consumers, but rather to the distribution of the national income, first in money and then in goods and services, among the owners of the factors of production—land, labor, and capital.

Income distribution in a market economy is based on institutional arrangements, such as the pricing mechanism, associated with this type of system. The demand for a factor of production is derived from the demand for the good the factor helps to produce. High prices are set on scarce factors of production and low prices on plentiful factors. In terms of rewards to labor, those persons whose skills are scarce relative to demand enjoy high income, while those persons whose skills are not scarce relative to demand do not. Professional football and baseball players receive high salaries because they possess a scarce talent and people are willing to pay to see them perform.

MEASUREMENTS OF INCOME INEQUALITY

There are various measures of income inequality, including the Lorenz curve and the Pareto and Gini coefficients. Of these measures, the Lorenz curve is most commonly used. The starting point for the Lorenz curve involves the use of an arithmetic scale that begins with an assumption of income equality as a starting point. Equality in the distribution of income is found when every income-receiving unit receives its proportional share of the total income. If incomes were absolutely uniformly distributed, the lowest 20 percent of income earners would receive exactly 20 percent of the total income; the lowest 80 percent would get exactly 80 percent of the total income; and the highest 20 percent would get only 20 percent of the income. In using a Lorenz curve, the curve of absolute equality would actually be a straight line extending upwards at a 45° angle from left to right, showing that 20 percent of income earners on the horizontal axis receive 20 percent of the income on the vertical axis, 40 percent of income earners receive 40 percent of the income, and so on. Any departure from this line is a departure from complete income equality.

Figure 1-2 illustrates the Lorenz curve. The straight line *OAF* is the line of perfect equality. The line *OBF*—the Lorenz curve—shows a departure from equality. The further *OBF* is from *OAF*, the greater the inequality. There are certain weaknesses in the use of the Lorenz curve as a measure of income distribution. First, one cannot tell by inspecting a curve how unequal the distribution of income is. The use of percentages conceals

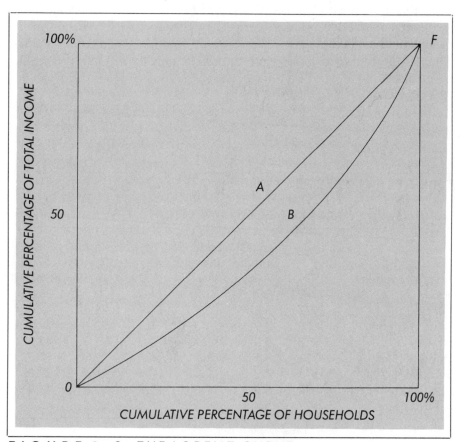

FIGURE 1-2   THE LORENZ CURVE

the number of income-receiving units in the different income brackets. It is also true that the slope of a curve at various points gives no more information than the curve itself. On the other hand, the Lorenz curve is an excellent device for visual presentation of inequalities in the distribution of income. It also can illustrate the effects of changes in taxes and government spending on the distribution of income.

It is possible to avoid relying solely on visual comparisons of Lorenz curves to draw inferences about various income distributions. This method uses the Gini concentration coefficient. In a Lorenz diagram the Gini concentration coefficient is the ratio of the area between the diagonal and the Lorenz curve to the total area below the diagonal. For a perfectly equal distribution, the Gini coefficient is zero. The size of the Gini coefficient is tied to the concavity of the Lorenz curve—the greater the concavity, the greater the coefficient. The coefficient, however, is basically an average, and does not tell anything about the extent to which inequality of distribution may be marked in various segments of the income distribution.

Table 1-1 presents the distribution of household income by quintiles for several market economies. Perfect equality in the distribution of income would mean that each quintile would contain 20 percent of income. None of the countries comes close to perfect equality in income distribution.

TABLE 1-1   PERCENTAGE SHARES OF HOUSEHOLD INCOME BY QUINTILES FOR SELECTED MARKET ECONOMIES

		Lowest Quintile	Second Quintile	Third Quintile	Fourth Quintile	Highest Quintile
United Kingdom	1979	7.0%	11.5%	17.0%	24.8%	39.7%
Japan	1979	8.7	13.2	17.5	23.1	36.8
Canada	1977	3.8	10.7	17.9	25.6	42.0
West Germany	1978	7.9	12.5	17.0	23.1	39.5
France	1978	5.3	11.1	16.0	21.8	45.8
United States	1979	4.6	8.9	14.1	22.1	50.3
Sweden	1979	7.2	12.8	17.4	25.4	37.2
Italy	1977	6.2	11.3	15.9	22.7	43.9
Australia	1977	5.4	10.0	15.0	22.5	47.1

Source: The World Bank, World Development Report 1985, p. 229.

The major socialist countries are not included in Table 1-1. If they were, it would appear that their distribution of income is more equal. However, there is a gap between rhetoric and reality in the socialist countries; it separates claims of egalitarianism from the facts of special privileges for a small elite. These privileges include, among other things, automobiles, country homes, and special shops in which party officials, scientists, technicians, and other members of the elite can buy products not available to the average worker.

SOURCES OF INCOME

Income in a market economy emanates from two sources: (1) earned income from wages and salaries or self-employment and (2) property income. Property may be regarded as a stock of claims on the value of wealth, including natural resources, capital, and consumer durable goods. The structure of property claims in a capitalist economy is complex. The claims on wealth owned by corporations, for example, may be represented by common or preferred stock, by corporate bonds, and by notes and mortgages. In national income accounting, labor income consists of wages, salaries, and entrepreneurial income, while property income takes the form of rent, interest, and profit. Thus there is a fundamental dichotomy in a capitalist system between labor and nonlabor income.

INCOME DISTRIBUTION AND MARGINAL PRODUCTIVITY

The most basic theory underlying income distribution in a market economy involves the concept of marginal productivity. This concept can be applied to the distribution of both labor and property income. Under competitive conditions, individuals' incomes are determined by (1) the amount of resources they can command and (2) the market evaluation of these resources. Thus the income received by a worker tends to be determined by supply and demand, so that the income received equals the contribution the worker is able to make to the value of goods and services. The contribution to total product made by the worker is known as the *marginal physical product (MPP)* of labor. The dollar value of the contribution is the *marginal revenue product (MRP)* of labor. It is found by multiplying the *MPP* by the selling price of the product. The same reasoning is also applied to the distribution of property income. Resource owners tend to be remunerated according to the marginal revenue products of the resources they own.

■ SAVING AND CAPITAL FORMATION ■
UNDER CAPITALISM

In a capitalistic system, large amounts of savings are made by individuals on the basis of the relationship between interest rates and other prices. The necessary condition for such savings is that the interest rate be sufficient to overcome the time preference of the savers. Time preference is the desire to consume income in the present as opposed to some time in the future. A certain amount of savings, however, is independent of the interest rate. Some savings are made to provide for certain financial emergencies or to obtain the power an accumulation of income can bring. People with very large incomes may save almost automatically because of the difficulties involved in finding enough consumption uses for their incomes.[7] Other savings, such as those that result when corporations retain their earnings instead of paying dividends to stockholders, do not depend on the voluntary decisions of those individuals (stockholders) whose earnings are being saved. Finally, there may be forced savings in the form of taxes that government may use directly or indirectly for capital purposes.

The use of capital goods in production clearly involves the existence of savings. Savings are translated into investment in a capitalist system through the market mechanism of supply and demand, with interest rates performing an allocative function. To be able to afford to pay interest on a loan and ultimately to repay the principal, the borrower must be able to put the funds to good use. This tends to exclude less productive uses and thus ration savings to more productive uses.

Under capitalism, saving and investment, in large part, are carried out by different sets of people for different reasons. Investment is the purchase of capital goods and as such is largely undertaken by businesses. The act of saving is undertaken by both individuals and businesses. With large numbers of scattered savers and borrowers who want to obtain funds for investment purposes, there is clearly a need for some type of intermediary or go-between to bring the savers and borrowers together. This function is performed to a large extent by commercial and investment banks that are privately owned and operated for a profit. They underwrite securities issues for governmental units as well as businesses. The investment bankers

---

7. However, human psychology, as pictured by Hobbes, is an appetitive drive that drives people ferociously to achieve their desires. In a modern society, the engine of appetite is an increased standard of living, with an emphasis on display. Thorsten Veblen made a similar point when he contended that people are driven by an impulse for status. See Thomas Hobbes, *Leviathan* (Oxford: Blackwell, 1946); also Thorsten Veblen, *The Theory of the Leisure Class* (Boston: Houghton Mifflin, Co., 1973).

bring together the business and government units that desire short- and long-term funds and individuals and institutions that have these funds to invest.

■ THE HISTORICAL DEVELOPMENT ■
OF CAPITALISM

The roots of capitalism go back to the Middle Ages, where the search for profit was the dominant motive in the lives of many, especially the merchants of the Italian city-states of Genoa and Venice.[8] In fact, the discovery of America in 1492 can be attributed to the search for new markets. The Catholic church and other molders of public opinion came to accept the concept of profit, in part because they too found good use for money. Earlier Catholic church thought had held that money was sterile in that it did not reproduce itself and that it was morally wrong to lend money to earn interest. However, there was nothing wrong in using money to buy something. But when it was seen that, if invested in productive enterprises, money could indeed make more money for the benefit of all, and that payment for the use of money (interest) would alone persuade the owners of money to invest it, the earlier concept was abandoned.

No pronounced break can be discerned between the growing capitalistic practices of the later Middle Ages and those of modern times. The influx of gold and silver from the New World had major political and economic consequences in Europe, contributing to the rise of the nation-states. The new wealthy classes, who engaged in trade everywhere, needed a stable national government to guarantee commerce, protect sea routes, and assure the arrival of merchant ships. Monarchs, who needed the financial support of wealthy merchants to pay for their wars, were expected to support home commerce. One method of supporting home commerce was by ensuring that only ships of the home country could be used in transporting goods from, and sometimes even to, home ports.

MERCANTILISM

It became accepted theory during the sixteenth to eighteenth centuries that a country was wealthy when it had a large reserve of gold and silver

---

8. The merchants of the Italian city-states invented almost all of the commercial devices that made a profit-seeking society possible. One such device was double-entry bookkeeping, which showed merchants that they were supposed to show a balance on the right side of the ledger.

bullion. To obtain bullion, the country had to have what was known as a favorable balance of trade, gained by exporting more than was imported. Thus it was in the country's own interest to support home industry to enable it to export as many products as possible. This policy of supporting home industry came to be called *mercantilism*. It meant government intervention everywhere, but particularly in foreign trade. It also meant regulation of commercial relations between the mother country and her colonies; the colonies existed to furnish the mother country with raw materials and goods that could not be produced at home. The colonies were also expected to furnish the mother country with a favorable balance of trade, as represented by an inflow of precious metals into the country. It was against the policy of mercantilism that the thirteen colonies of North America arose and fought for their independence.

THE INDUSTRIAL REVOLUTION

The Industrial Revolution changed national attitudes from the policy of mercantilism to a policy of laissez-faire. Scientific breakthroughs, inventions, and the factory system encouraged specialization and the concentration of production. These, in turn, encouraged a movement from national self-sufficiency to a doctrine of free trade, which was supported by classical economists Adam Smith and David Ricardo and the philosopher John Locke. During the nineteenth century, the amount of world trade increased rapidly while the pattern of world trade changed.

The Industrial Revolution consisted mainly of the application of machinery to manufacturing, mining, transportation, communication, and agriculture, and of the changes in economic organization that attended these applications.[9] Fundamental in the new industrial order was the development of a cheap, portable source of power. James Watt's invention of the condenser and of a practical method for converting the reciprocating motion of the piston into rotary motion made the steam engine a practical prime mover for all kinds of machinery.

The Industrial Revolution probably represented the hallmark of capitalism. The old method of small-scale production in the home with one's own tools could not meet the competition of machine production. The cost of machinery was prohibitive to individual workers. Hence, the factory

---

9. The Industrial Revolution began in England between 1770 and 1825 and in continental Europe after 1815. Some scholars contend that we are in a new period of postindustrial development. See, for example, Daniel Bell, *The Coming of Post-Industrial Society* (New York: Basic Books Inc., Publishers, 1976).

system arose, with large-scale production in factories using machinery owned by the employer. The factory system stimulated the growth of division of labor and mass production through the standardization of processes and parts. Old industries began to produce on a much larger scale than previously, and new industries developed, offering new goods to satisfy new demands.

Industrial capitalists were created, and it was they who shaped the course of future industrialization by reinvesting their gains in new enterprises. The Industrial Revolution also enormously accentuated the movement toward international economic interdependence. As the people of Europe became more and more engaged in urban industry, they raised less food and became heavy importers of wheat, meat, and other food products. In exchange for food, Europe exported manufactured goods, and the entire world became a marketplace.

The doctrine of laissez-faire fit in with the development of capitalism. It carried with it a sense of independence, personal initiative, and self-responsibility. If individual initiative is respected, it gives free play to entrepreneurs to create products for those who want and will pay for them. A necessary requisite for individualism is a limited state role. The individual should have preference over the state, for the latter is, again, only a fictitious body composed of individual people who are considered to be its members. The ideas of individualism and laissez-faire were therefore regarded by Adam Smith and others as a safeguard against the tyranny of the state.

FINANCE CAPITALISM

Constant growth in the use of machinery, and especially mass production, made it increasingly necessary for individual entrepreneurs to raise large amounts of capital. As raising capital became more difficult, the control of industry passed more and more into the hands of a few large investment banking houses. This system became known as *finance capitalism*. Banks became professional accumulators of capital. Corporations, which by the latter part of the nineteenth century had become the dominant form of business unit, were able to obtain large quantities of long-term capital funds by selling their securities with the assistance of investment banks. The banks underwrote and distributed the securities, eventually getting them in the hands of insurance companies, banks, investment trusts, and individual investors. These banking houses were able to acquire an inordinate amount of economic power through the ownership of securities and through the device of the interlocking directorate.

■ MODIFICATIONS ■
OF PURE CAPITALISM

Various elements have combined over time to transform pure market capitalism to what might be called "state-guided" capitalism. In fact, the term *mixed economic system* is used in later chapters to describe countries that were at one time purely capitalistic. Part of this transformation has been the development of the welfare state, which resulted from the extremely unequal distribution of income that developed during the Industrial Revolution. A growing concentration of economic power in the hands of a few people created extremes of wealth and poverty. In the United States during the 1890s, for example, the department store magnate Marshall Field had an income calculated at $600 per hour; his shopgirls, earning salaries of $3 to $5 a week, had to work three to five years to earn that amount.[10] Working conditions for most workers in the Western industrial world were deplorable: The twelve-hour work day and seven-day work week were not uncommon. There were no child labor laws; children of eight and even younger worked in the coal mines and textile mills in the United States and England.

THE DECLINE OF THE PROTESTANT WORK ETHIC

Other factors influenced the transformation of capitalism as well. Thrift, which at one time was a linchpin of the Protestant work ethic, began to decline. Traditional morality, as represented by Puritanism, was challenged by the automobile, movies, and credit cards. A mass production society could not tolerate thrift. Why save when you could buy an automobile on credit? Since the 1920s credit has become the passport to instant gratification. American culture is no longer concerned with how to work and achieve, but with how to spend and enjoy.

THE DECLINE OF INDIVIDUALISM

The idea of rugged individualism has always been a greatly romanticized part of the American frontier spirit. This individualism, as epitomized by John Wayne in the movie *True Grit*, carried with it a sense of independence, personal initiative, and self-responsibility.[11] Life was a series of con-

---

10. Cited in Otto Bettman, *The Good Old Days—They Were Terrible* (New York: Random House Inc., 1974), p. 67.

11. Henry Hathaway, director, *True Grit*, Paramount Pictures, 1969.

stant challenges to be met head on, as did John Wayne when, at the end of *True Grit*, he went charging into the four bad men, reins in teeth and guns blazing. It was the individual rather than the state who did the punishing, and moralizing was left to the preachers. There was in individualism the idea of a "just meritocracy."[12] Individuals should be left free to achieve what they can through their own abilities and efforts. Naturally, there will be winners and losers, but this is the inevitable end result in a libertarian society.

To some extent, individualism in the Western world has been superceded by egalitarianism. The decline of individualism is largely a result of urban industrialized life. Individual desires often clash with the wishes of groups. There is frequent disharmony as the individual pulls in one direction while the group wants to go in the other direction. Claims on a community have come to be decided on the basis of group membership rather than individual attributes.[13] Social life has increasingly become organized on a group basis.

Egalitarianism has meant different things during different periods. In the United States, the Jeffersonian concept of equality was an equality of the elect (those eligible to vote).[14] The Jacksonian idea of equality was somewhat simpler. In essence, Jackson felt that any man was just as good as the next one. Equality has come to be defined in terms of equity; hence the emphasis on equality of result, which is defined as a group right rather than an individual right. This equality is not to be achieved through upward mobility or merit, but through government action. The rules of the game must be changed so as to reduce the rewards of competition and the cost of failure. Or, as the Dodo said to Alice in Wonderland when explaining the results of the Caucus race, "Everybody has one and all must have prizes."[15]

GOVERNMENT AND THE DECLINE OF LAISSEZ-FAIRE

Government has always played some role in Western society, even during the zenith of capitalism. In the historical development of the United

12. Daniel Bell, "On Meritocracy and Equality," *The Public Interest* (Fall 1972), pp. 18-32.

13. Daniel Bell, *The Cultural Contradictions of Capitalism* (New York: Basic Books Inc., Publishers, 1976) pp. 141-145.

14. To Jefferson, equality meant giving each person an equal opportunity, before the law and under God. He said, "There is a natural aristocracy among men. The grounds of this are virtue and talents. ... The natural artistocracy I consider as the most precious gift of nature." See Thomas Jefferson, *Notes on the State of Virginia*, ed. Thomas Abernethy (New York: Harper & Row, Publishers Inc., 1964), pp. 1-10.

15. Lewis Carroll, *Alice's Adventures in Wonderland* and *Through the Looking Glass* (New York: Airmont Publishing Co., Inc., 1965), p. 27.

States, government policy was primarily a mixture of measures that provided equality of opportunity for the common man, such as public education, and generous favors for those who knew how to help themselves,
such as railroad and canal builders. Tariffs were enacted to protect American business firms from foreign competition. In France, where state participation in the economy had always been important, much of the railroad
system was state-owned by the 1850s, and the state also had a monopoly
over the sale of such products as alcohol, tobacco, and tea. State ownership of certain industries also existed in Prussia.

The Depression of the 1930s was probably the catalyst for increasing
the role of government. On the basis of experience during the Depression,
organized labor, farmers, business firms, and consumer groups turned to
government for assistance in improving their incomes and assuring economic security. The satisfaction of these demands made for a new concept
of government. An increase in the power of the state has become the central fact of modern Western society. Crucial decisions about production
and distribution have come to be made through the political process rather
than through the marketplace.

RESTRICTIONS ON COMPETITION

Competition is one of the basic institutions of capitalism. Its justification,
like that of other institutions, is found in the notion that it contributes to
the social welfare. It is a regulator of economic activity and is thought to
maximize productivity, prevent excessive concentration of economic
power, and protect consumer interests. *Competition* may be used to describe the economic structure of a nation, applicable to all economic
units—individuals, farmers, and business firms. Economic success goes to
efficiently operated firms, and failure eliminates inefficiently and waste-
fully operated firms. The impersonal market system does not lock in products or skills that have become obsolete and therefore nonproductive.

But competition is a hard taskmaster, for there are losers as well as
winners. Since losers don't think they should lose, they take action to prevent losing and thus the rules of the game are altered. The market system
has been changed in many ways by government action to prevent or cushion the effects of losing. Through subsidies and restraints on foreign competition, uneconomic production and job skills have been maintained by
governmental intervention.

Business firms have formed into various forms of combinations, cartels, trusts, and holding companies to prevent competition. Workers have
joined labor unions to avoid individual competition, and obsolete job skills

have been preserved. In the United States obsolete jobs have been preserved in the construction industry and elsewhere through federal building codes, and inefficient firms, such as Chrysler, have received financial support from the government when otherwise they would have been eliminated by the forces of competition.

SUMMARY

Capitalism is an economic system characterized by a set of institutional arrangements. The centerpiece of capitalism is a freely competitive market where buyers satisfy their wants and sellers supply those wants in order to make a profit. The price mechanism determines resource allocation, and freedom of enterprise and private property ownership provide incentives to save and produce. Individualism is also at the core of the capitalist or free market ideology. It was assumed by Adam Smith and others that people were rational and would try at all times to promote their own personal welfare. The individual, in promoting his or her self-interest, works in the interest of society.

Competition is an indispensable part of a free enterprise system. In economic life, self-reliant individuals must compete for economic rewards (good jobs, high pay, and promotions), and business must compete for consumer incomes. The Protestant work ethic stressed rewards in this life, not in the hereafter. Hard work included thrift, which could provide the savings necessary for investment. The role of government is minimal in a capitalist economy.

The advanced capitalist countries of today have modified the institutions of capitalism. In the operation of capitalist economies, problems arose that seemed impossible for private individuals to solve. Their impact brought a demand for government intervention. As a result, government intervention and regulation is a very common feature of life under capitalism. Consumers are not left to depend solely on competition to furnish them with foods and drugs of acceptable quality and purity; there are laws that provide certain standards in these matters. Capitalistic societies have never been willing to extend complete freedom of enterprise to any individual. That is, it has always been recognized that an individual, in selecting the most profitable field of activity, might well choose something that would be clearly antisocial. In such cases, government has not hesitated to step in with restrictions. But government has also altered the economic institutions of capitalism through, for example, subsidies to farmers and protection of inefficient business firms from competition.

REVIEW QUESTIONS

1. What is meant by the term **institutions** as applied to an economic system?
2. Explain the concept of economic scarcity. Are there things that are not scarce?
3. Apply the concept of scarcity to life in the United States today. Is scarcity still present in the United States? How does scarcity affect an American's life?
4. What are the three factors of production? Why do economists classify resources in this way?
5. What is the function of profit in a market economy?
6. What is the function of the price mechanism in a market system?
7. How are incomes distributed in a market economy?
8. What are some of the factors responsible for the breakdown of a true market economy?
9. The United States economy has diverged from pure market capitalism. Why?

RECOMMENDED READINGS

Bell, Daniel. *The Coming of the Post-Industrial Society*. New York: Basic Books Inc., Publishers, 1976.

Bell, Daniel. *The Cultural Contradictions of Capitalism*. New York: Basic Books Inc., Publishers, 1976.

Hacker, Louis M. *The Triumph of American Capitalism*. New York: Simon & Schuster Inc., 1940.

Heilbroner, Robert L. *The Making of Economic Society*. 4th ed. Englewood Cliffs, N.J.: Prentice-Hall, 1962.

Hofstadler, Richard. *Social Darwinism in American Thought*. Rev ed. Boston: Beacon Press, 1955.

Polanyi, Karl. *The Great Transformation*. New York: Rinehart, 1944.

Smith, Adam. *The Wealth of Nations*. Indianapolis: Liberty Classics, 1981.

Tawney, R.H. *Religion and the Rise of Capitalism*. New York: Harcourt, Brace, and World, 1926.

Toynbee, Arnold. *The Industrial Revolution*. Boston: Beacon Press, 1956.

Weber, Max. *The Protestant Ethic and the Spirit of Capitalism*. New York: Charles Scribner's Sons, 1930.

C H A P T E R   2

MARKET MECHANISMS, ECONOMIC PROBLEMS, AND GOVERNMENT POLICIES

The United States, Great Britain, and other countries of European culture have had decades of experience with free market economies. One important principle of free enterprise economies is that if individuals are permitted to pursue their own interests, without interference from public authority, they will, in pursuit of their own selfish interests, promote the well-being of all. This will not result from charitable motives, but from the inexorable logic of the system—Adam Smith's "invisible hand." Stated simply, if all people are motivated to work at full capacity—whether as laborers or executives—the net supply of goods and services available for consumption by all will be maximized.

However, there is no ubiquitous human nature that guarantees that, if just allowed to do so, all persons will always pursue profits, income, and satisfaction, and will always benefit each other in the process. The pursuit of profits, income, and satisfaction does not occur innately; it is learned behavior. It is learned by some people from their environments and it is not learned by others at all. The pursuit of individual self-interest is socially beneficial only when the environment is appropriate. But the environment is not always appropriate; the cultural heritages of many societies do not contain the necessary requisites for the development of a successful market system.

Some government intervention is necessary for the establishment of even a free type of economic system. The very atmosphere for the conduct of a free market economy is created by the ability of government to establish and maintain private property, freedom of enterprise, money and credit, and a system of civil laws for adjudicating the private disputes of individuals. However, the role of government has increased enormously in the market economies over the last 50 years. One reason is the failure of the market mechanism to allocate resources properly. A breakdown in competitive market forces allows monopoly, oligopoly, and otherwise imperfectly competitive market structures to cause inefficient resource allocation. A second reason is unemployment. The Great Depression of the 1930s created a fundamental shift in government policy away from laissez-faire to direct government intervention. Third, an unequal distribution of income and wealth created social frictions that threatened to undermine the social and political structure of many capitalist countries. A final reason for government intervention is economic insecurity, which results from the operation of a market system. Each of these reasons will be discussed in some detail.

■ GOVERNMENT REGULATION ■ OF MARKET STRUCTURES

For a market system to work well and to adjust to changing conditions, the prices of goods, services, and resources must be allowed to rise and fall. Changes in prices are the means by which consumers, producers, and resource owners are induced to make adjustments beneficial to others. Thus, if consumer preferences change in favor of some good and its price rises as a result, the higher price induces producers to supply more of the good. If a technological innovation reduces the demand for a particular type of labor, a fall in the relevant wage rate is called for. That fall would encourage employers to reemploy their labor elsewhere.

RESTRAINTS ON COMPETITION

The United States and many other industrial countries have long depended on competition to provide the discipline that is necessary for efficient allocation of scarce resources. A competitive market will allow prices to reflect actual demand and costs and thus maximize efficiency in the use of capital and other resources. There is also a relationship between a competitive market economy and a democratic political structure: Competition is expected to prevent the development of excessively powerful economic units. When firms find ways to limit competition, the public welfare is adversely affected. Companies have found many ways to restrict competition within their industries. Collusion among companies to limit output results in higher prices.[1] Large enterprises can dominate an industry and provide barriers to entry by other firms.

MONOPOLY   A monopoly exists when there is only one seller of a commodity that has no close substitutes. A monopoly market is the direct antithesis of a competitive market in that a monopolist can fix prices through control of the supply of the commodity. The individual firm and the industry are, in effect, identical, and the market demand curve for the industry is the same as the average revenue or demand curve for the monopolist. Monopoly prices are also frequently higher than prices that would prevail under competition because a monopolist can charge different prices to different consumers. There are no competing sellers to whom buyers may go to avoid price discrimination.

Resource allocation is also less efficient under monopoly. There is no incentive for a monopoly to organize its plant in the most efficient manner because a successful monopolist is able to make a profit by merely restricting supply. Modernization of facilities, experimentation with lower prices and larger output, and managerial incentives may be retarded by the lack of competition.

PRICE AND OUTPUT UNDER MONOPOLY   A monopolist's price and output determination are shown in the accompanying example.[2] Remember that in a monopoly, unlike pure competition, the average revenue is not constant because the price declines as the output increases. The average revenue *(AR)* column shows the prices at which various quantities of output can be sold, and the marginal revenue *(MR)* column shows the increments to total revenue *(TR)* that result from selling additional units of output. In the short run, some costs are fixed and others are variable. In the example, total fixed costs *(FC)* are assumed to be $500, regardless of the volume of output, and total variable costs *(VC)* have been given assigned values.

The same analysis is presented graphically in Figure 2-1, which shows the monopolist's average revenue or demand curve *(D)*, marginal revenue

1. An example is a cartel such as OPEC, the oil cartel, which attempts to limit the output of producers for the purpose of raising the price of the product and the profits of the producers.

2. The example is for the short run. In the long run, a monopolist is able to adjust its scale of operations because all costs are variable, whereas in the short run it can determine the most profitable rate of operation limited by its existing fixed factors of production.

Quantity of Output	AR Price	TR	MR	FC	VC	TC	MC	Profit
10	$100	$1,000	—	$500	$483	$ 983	—	$17
11	99	1,089	89	500	544	1,044	61	45
12	98	1,176	87	500	598	1,098	54	78
13	96	1,248	72	500	659	1,159	61	89
14	94	1,316	68	500	725	1,225	66	91
15	90	1,350	34	500	802	1,302	77	48
16	85	1,360	10	500	890	1,390	88	− 30

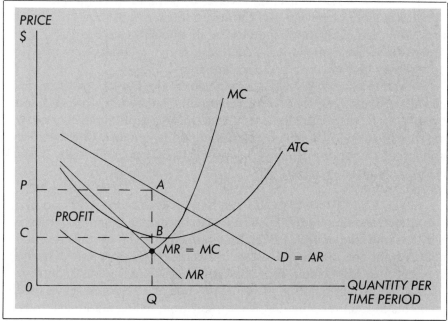

FIGURE 2-1   COST AND REVENUE CURVES FOR A MONOPOLIST

curve (MR), short-run marginal cost curve (MC), and average total cost curve (ATC). ATC equals TC divided by output. The marginal revenue curve shows the increment to total revenue that results from selling an additional unit of output while the marginal cost curve shows the cost to produce the additional unit. MR equals MC at an output of 0Q. It would be profitable for the monopolist to expand up to this point, because at all smaller volumes MC lies below MR. Beyond this point, however, MC rises above MR. The price at which this quantity can be sold can be determined from the AR curve, which is also the monopolist's demand curve.

- $0Q$ equals output that will be produced to maximize profits. It is 14 units of output in the example.

- $0P$ equals price that will maximize profits. It is $94 in the example.

- $0PAQ$ equals total revenue, which is $1,316 in the example.

- $0CBQ$ equals total cost, which is $1,225 ($500 + $725) in the example.

- $PABC$ equals total profit, which is $91 ($1,316 − $1,225) in the example.

OLIGOPOLY   Oligopoly refers to a market situation in which there are a few sellers of a basically similar product. Many industries in the Western capitalistic countries have oligopolistic qualities: for example, the steel, automobile, and cigarette industries. In fact, oligopoly seems to be a characteristic of industries to which modern methods of production apply. The pattern of oligopolistic industries is for a few giant firms to account for one-half or more of the total industry output, followed by smaller firms that produce the rest. For example, General Motors and Ford account for at least two-thirds of the domestic output of automobiles by American car manufacturers. In West Germany, three chemical companies produce more than 90 percent of domestic chemical products. Typical of most oligopolistic industries is differentiation, which means distinguishing a firm's products from those of its competitors by means of brands and trademarks and creating a preference for the brand through advertising.

Oligopoly markets have several important characteristics:

1. No one firm can increase its revenue through price competition. For example, if one firm raises its prices and other firms do not follow suit, its sales will usually suffer. If one firm lowers its prices, all the others will follow and all the firms will have lower revenue.

2. Prices are identical or almost identical in oligopoly markets.

3. Without price competition, firms are often able to reach some sort of agreement, tacitly or otherwise, as to what the set price will be.

The economic and social losses under oligopoly are similar to those under monopoly. Output in such industries is restricted, prices can be maintained at levels above marginal cost, and too few resources are employed when compared with competitive sectors of the economy.

Nonetheless, oligopoly itself does not always contradict the social interest, since it may be based on economies of scale that can be maintained only by large-sized firms. These economies may be so great in relation to the size of the market served that there is room for only a few firms in the industry. An industry of many small firms with higher costs would not be any more efficient. When, however, oligopoly results from the exclusion of new, potentially efficient firms by such means as collusion, the situation is clearly contrary to the public interest.

ANTITRUST LAWS

In a market economy, competition is necessary to provide the discipline needed for efficient allocation of resources. Any departure from competition can work against the public welfare. A prime example was the development of trusts and other forms of business combinations in the United States in the last century. The trusts were aimed at eliminating competitors and many industries fell under the control of a single trust. Discriminatory pricing practices were numerous, and companies colluded to restrain competition.[3] Some competition took the form of social Darwinism—the "survival of the fittest" principle applied to the business world. However, one outcome of this social Darwinism was cutthroat competition where the field of industry became a battleground between rival firms, each intent upon destroying the other.

For these reasons, governments in the United States and other countries passed antitrust laws to protect the public against anticompetitive business practices. These laws are designed to maintain competition by limiting monopoly power, whether achieved through internal growth or by mergers. They also are directed at specific anticompetitive business practices: price fixing, price discrimination against buyers or sellers, tying agreements, interlocking directorates, and other coercive practices. Each device can be used to restrain competition. For example, the aim of a price-fixing agreement, if effective, is the elimination of price competition. The power to fix prices, whether reasonably exercised or not, involves power to control the market.

---

3. One example was the basing point system. To avoid giving mills located near a consuming center a price advantage in getting business because of lower transportation costs, steel companies adopted a policy of selling all steel and iron products from a base point, which was Pittsburgh, regardless of the origin of the shipment.

■ UNEMPLOYMENT ■

Probably the most important basis for the increased role of governments in market economies has been their explicit assumption of responsibility for the general economic health of their countries. The Depression of the 1930s was the catalyst for the transformation of the role of the government from passive to active in its use of economic policy measures to achieve the goal of prosperity. The Depression was unprecedented in both size and duration, and its impact on the Western industrial countries was enormous. It did more to reshape the American economy than any other event; there was massive government intervention in many areas of the economy. In Germany, the Depression was a prime contributing factor to the rise to power of Adolf Hitler. The Depression contributed to the rise of militarism in Japan, which resulted in the eventual confrontation with the United States. To many it appeared that the capitalistic system was in a state of collapse and the demise of capitalism predicted by Marx was about to begin.

CLASSICAL ECONOMIC THEORY AND UNEMPLOYMENT

Until the 1930s, no market economy had experienced a deep and prolonged depression. Everything about the past supported the classical economic theory that full employment of labor and other resources could be the norm.[4] There could be lapses from full employment, but self-correcting market forces would pull the economy back to the normal state. Classical economic theory was based on two important assumptions.

1. There was a competitive market system in which resources were mobile. There were many buyers and sellers in both the product and resource markets, and prices were free to move either upward or downward.

2. Income was spent automatically at a rate always consistent with full employment. There could not be too much saving, for saving was channelled into investment through the mechanism of the interest rate. If there was excessive saving, the interest rate would fall and investment would increase. Conversely, if there was too little saving, the interest rate would rise and in-

---

4. The term *classical economies* was used by Karl Marx to refer to the writings of David Ricardo and his predecessors, including Adam Smith. Later the term was applied to the writings of John Stuart Mill, A.C. Pigou, and Alfred Marshall.

vestment would decline. An equilibrium point would always be reached at full employment. Both saving and investment were functions of the interest rate. Since saving was first of all another form of spending, according to classical theory, all income was either spent on consumption or investment.

The basis for classical economic theory was Say's Law of Markets.[5] This law states, in effect, that supply creates its own demand. Supply is the catalyst: Whatever is produced represents the demand for another product. Additional supply creates additional demand; hence, any increase in production is an increase in demand, and therefore overproduction is impossible. This assertion is supported by the argument that goods really exchange for goods, money being merely a medium of exchange. Say reasoned that whenever workers and other resources are used to create goods and services, a demand equal in value to the incomes paid to the factors of production is created automatically. Because the purpose of earning income is to spend it on goods and services, income will automatically equal that output. In an exchange economy, Say's Law means that there will always be a rate of spending sufficient to maintain full employment.

KEYNESIAN ECONOMIC THEORY

An economic theory is valid until events prove otherwise, and economic life simply did not correspond to the way market economies were supposed to act in the classical system. The automatic adjustment toward a level of full employment did not occur; to the contrary, as the Great Depression continued, serious and prolonged unemployment became the normal condition of the market economies. Under these conditions, not even the staunchest defenders of classical theory could seriously maintain that there were forces in the economy that automatically generated full employment. The classical theory offered little help to policymakers who were responsible for devising measures to combat unemployment. Also, it was no consolation to those who were unemployed to be told that unemployment was temporary and that eventually market forces would lead to the conditions necessary for full employment. What was needed was a new theory that would explain the causes of unemployment and offer solutions for policy-

---

5. Jean Baptiste Say was a French economist who lived during the time of Adam Smith. His major work, *Treatise on Political Economy*, was the first popular book on economics produced in Europe.

makers to follow. This theory was provided by the British economist John Maynard Keynes in his book *The General Theory of Employment, Interest, and Money.*[6]

In Keynesian theory, the level of employment is linked to the total production of goods and services. The volume of production, in turn, depends on the level of spending or aggregate demand. The catalyst in the Keynesian economic framework is aggregate demand, for it determines, at least in the short run, the extent to which an economy's productive capacity will be used. It is at one time both the source of total national income and the basis on which the level of employment is determined. If aggregate demand is not sufficient to employ all available resources, national income will be lower than it need be. If aggregate demand falls, so will income; as national income falls, so will output and employment. When aggregate demand increases, so will national incomes, and output and employment will follow. The key to economic stability is to maintain aggregate demand and national income at levels consistent with high employment of labor and other resources.

COMPONENTS OF DEMAND   The two major components of aggregate demand in the Keynesian system are consumer demand for goods and services and investment demand by private business firms for capital goods. Both consumer and investment demand are based on certain determinants. Disposable income, or income after taxes, is the prime determinant of consumption expenditures. As disposable income increases, so will consumption, but not at the same rate. The marginal propensity to consume is the fraction of any change in income that is consumed. The functional relationship is called the *consumption function.*

Investment in the Keynesian framework is determined by the marginal efficiency of capital in conjunction with the interest rate. The former is the expected rate of yield on a capital good, and the latter is the cost of borrowing money. A functional relationship can be expressed as follows: $I = f(n,i)$ where n = marginal efficiency of capital and i = rate of interest.

AN EXAMPLE OF THE KEYNESIAN MODEL   The Keynesian framework can be presented in a basic model. Both national income and employment are determined by aggregate demand, which in turn depends on the marginal propensity to consume and the level of investment. This relationship can be expressed by the equation $Y = C + I$, where Y = total output,

---

6. John Maynard Keynes, *The General Theory of Employment, Interest, and Money* (New York: Harcourt, Brace & Co., Inc., 1936).

C = consumption expenditures, and I = investment expenditures. Y is referred to as aggregate supply and is determined mainly by aggregate demand, $C + I$. Aggregate supply and aggregate demand interact to determine an equilibrium level of national income and output. At any level below the equilibrium point $Y = C + I$, aggregate demand is greater than aggregate supply; at any level above the point of equilibrium, aggregate supply is greater than aggregate demand. The equilibrium level is at 400, for aggregate supply and aggregate demand are equal, and savings of 40 equals investment of 40. Savings represents a withdrawal from income and investment represents an injection into it. Total goods and services produced, Y, is equal to total demand, $C + I$.

Y	C	S	I	$C + I$
0	120	− 120	40	160
100	180	− 80	40	220
200	240	− 40	40	280
300	300	0	40	340
400	360	40	40	400
500	420	80	40	460
600	480	120	40	520
700	540	160	40	580

The determination of income and output can also be shown through the use of algebraic equations. In the example, as income increases by 100, consumption increases by 60. The marginal propensity to consume, which is $\Delta C \div \Delta Y$, or $60 \div 100$, is 0.6. Since saving is $Y - C$, each increase in Y of 100 results in an increase in S of 40. The marginal propensity to save is $\Delta S \div \Delta Y$, or $40 \div 100$, or 0.4. The formulas can be written as follows:

$Y = C + I$ Y = income

$S = Y - C$ C = consumer expenditures

$C = C_0 + aY$ I = investment expenditures

$I = I$ C_0 = consumption when Y is zero

$S = -C_0 + (1 - a)Y$ a = marginal propensity to consume

$1 - a$ = marginal propensity to save

Solving for Y:

$$Y = C + I$$
$$= C_0 + aY + I$$
$$= 120 + .6Y + 40$$
$$Y - .6Y = 160$$
$$.4Y = 160$$
$$Y = 400$$

Solving for S:

$$S = Y - C$$
$$= Y - (C_0 + aY)$$
$$= -C_0 + (1 - a)Y$$
$$= -120 + (1 - .6)Y$$
$$= -120 + .4(400)$$
$$S = 40$$

This basic macroeconomic model is illustrated in Figure 2-2. The vertical axis measures aggregate demand, or $C + I$, and the horizontal axis

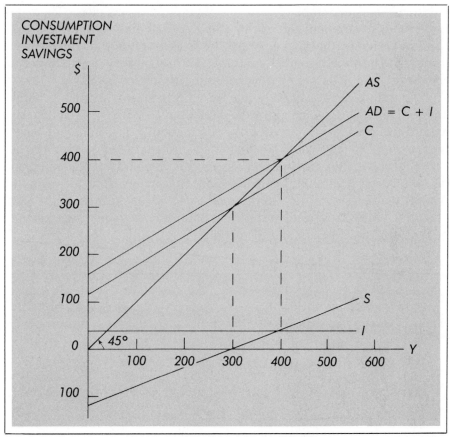

FIGURE 2-2   THE KEYNESIAN MODEL

measures output, or real gross national product. The 45° line is the aggregate supply schedule that shows, in effect, that total cost of national output must be matched by an equivalent amount of sales proceeds if producers as a whole are to justify total output. The line implies that there must always be an equal vertical amount of expenditure for each horizontal cost of national output. The aggregate demand line is a schedule associating spending decisions with different levels of real income. Given the aggregate supply and aggregate demand schedules for the economy, the equilibrium level of income and employment will be determined by the intersection of the two schedules. Saving and investment are also equal at this point. There are two fundamental identity equations: $Y = C + I$ and $S = I$.

IMPLICATION FOR GOVERNMENT POLICY   Keynesian economic theory rejects laissez-faire and accepts government intervention as the prime requisite for economic stability. The policy implications are clear: There has to be more government intervention in economic life. Keynes held that classical economic theory was wrong in its assumption that full employment is the norm in a market economy. To the contrary, unemployment could exist for a long period of time, as it did during the 1930s.

The goal of Keynesian economic theory is to create a better economic and social milieu in which industrial capitalism can survive. The first step toward that better environment is the elimination of mass unemployment. High unemployment would be eliminated through use of government fiscal and monetary policies to stimulate consumption and investment expenditures. Government policies are necessary to increase aggregate demand. Assume that in the example above, mass unemployment exists at the level of output of 400. Government spending is introduced to increase total output. Assume that the amount of spending is 80.

Y	C	S	I	G	C + I + G
0	120	− 120	40	80	240
100	180	− 80	40	80	320
200	240	− 40	40	80	360
300	300	0	40	80	420
400	360	40	40	80	480
500	420	80	40	80	540
600	480	120	40	80	600
700	540	160	40	80	660

The equilibrium level is now 600. Aggregate demand is 600 and aggregate supply is 600. Total saving of 120 is equal to the sum of private investment and government spending. The equations may now be written as follows:

$$Y = C + I + G \qquad\qquad S = I + G$$
$$C = C_0 + aY \qquad\qquad S = -C_0 + (1 - a)Y$$
$$Y = C_0 + aY + I + G \qquad\qquad = -120 + .4(600)$$
$$= 120 + .6Y + 40 + 80 \qquad\qquad = -120 + 240$$
$$Y - .6Y = 240 \qquad\qquad = 120$$
$$.4Y = 240 \qquad\qquad 120 = 40 + 80$$
$$Y = 600 \qquad\qquad 120 = 120$$

STABILIZATION POLICIES   Keynesian economics provided the basis for economic policy in most Western capitalistic countries after World War II.[7] The role that governments played in the economies of the capitalist countries increased. They came to act as the main stabilizing force by using policies that influenced an economy's overall expenditure level. Fiscal policy and monetary policy became the two chief instruments used by central governments to attain expenditure levels consistent with economic growth, stable prices, and high employment.

FISCAL POLICY   Fiscal policy refers to the tax and expenditure policies of a government. The objective of fiscal policy is to increase or decrease the level of aggregate demand through changes in the level of government expenditures and taxation. An expansionary fiscal policy would stimulate employment and economic growth through an increase in government spending, decrease in taxes, or both. Conversely, fiscal policy can be used to contract the level of aggregate demand. Taxes can be raised, government expenditures can be reduced, or a combination can be used. A government can also run a surplus in its budget.

MONETARY POLICY   Monetary policy is used by government central banks to control the level of national output and the price level through

---

7. It is a common misconception that Keynesian economics, or the "new economics" as it came to be called by many, was introduced in the United States during the Kennedy administration.

variations in the money supply.[8] An increase in the money supply will lower interest rates and stimulate private and public spending; a decrease in the money supply will raise interest rates and reduce private and public spending. Central banks cannot fix the amount of credit and its cost independently. If they want to restrain the rate of growth in the money supply, they must allow interest rates to rise as high as possible; if they want to keep interest rates low, they have to accept the consequences in terms of an increase in the money supply. Monetary policy has become an increasingly important economic tool used by governments to achieve given economic objectives. It differs from fiscal policy in that *total* control over it is not always in the hands of government.[9]

■ EQUITY AND ■
INCOME DISTRIBUTION

It is difficult to reach agreement on the optimum distribution of income. Each individual and group views an economic system from its own position in society. Unanimity of opinion is therefore impossible, and it is highly doubtful if an agreed-upon concept of optimum distribution can be achieved. If so, the actual effect of taxes and government expenditures on the distribution of income will not be determined on the basis of a particular theory of optimum distribution, but rather as a result of a struggle between the dominant political forces at a particular moment. The results will be strongly modified, of course, by political decisions made in the past. This does not mean that theories will play no role whatever, for each group must have a rationale for its position.

The question of what constitutes an equitable distribution of income is hard to answer. It is difficult to justify on purely ethical grounds the position that those persons who contribute the most to output should receive the most income, which would happen in a market economy. (This is the basis of marginal productivity analysis, as mentioned in chapter 1.) Problems arise because individuals and families differ with respect to age, health problems, and in many other ways, and therefore have different needs in an objective sense. There are no accepted ethical standards for de-

---

8. The money supply is the total quantity of money existing in an economy at a particular time. It consists of coins and currency, demand deposits, and other checkable account balances. It includes $M1$, which represents the more liquid types of money. Then there is $M2$, which includes assets that are less liquid. Savings accounts and certificates of deposit are examples. $M2$ equals the more broadly defined money supply.

9. The Federal Reserve System of the United States is an example. The twelve Federal Reserve Banks are under the direction of policies set by its Board of Governors, which operates independently from government influence.

termining the degree to which contributions to output should be rewarded, nor are there any accepted economic standards for determining how much effort any individual is making. The result is that the Western market-oriented countries have accepted the idea that income distribution is much too important to be left solely to market forces. Many governments have accepted the idea that income ought to be redistributed in favor of those with lower incomes at the expense of those with higher incomes.

THE INTERACTION OF WEALTH AND INCOME

Inequality of income interacts with and mutually reinforces inequality of wealth. Those with large incomes have a greater ability to save part of their income and accumulate it in the form of wealth or property than do those with small incomes. A family that possesses property or wealth derives more income than just its labor income in wages and salaries. It receives, in addition, rent, dividends, interest, or profits. It can afford to take risks in choosing its occupations and in using its wealth. If these choices are successful, they will augment the wealth and income further.[10] A poor family is usually without a cushion of wealth or discretionary income on which to rely in case a risky venture fails. That family cannot undertake the risky venture for fear of jeopardizing essential income. So it is that in a market system inequality of income and wealth may be cumulatively self-enforcing.

In general, the development of the modern welfare state stems from a dissatisfaction with the distribution of income. One result of market capitalism, as mentioned above, has been an extreme inequality in the distribution of income. This inequality can be attributed primarily to receipts of income from property. The methods that governments have used most widely to distribute income more equitably are progressive income and inheritance taxes, and transfer payments. Policies directed toward a high level of employment also have an effect on the distribution of income.

TAX POLICIES

The progressive income tax affects the distribution of income in two ways. First, the tax directly reduces the disposable income of individuals. The progressive income tax redistributes income in the direction of greater equality because the share of the total disposable income received by upper-income groups is reduced and the share received by lower-income groups is raised. The progressive income tax structure brings about this re-

10. The wealthy also do the bulk of saving in a capitalist country. Saving provides the basis for capital formation.

sult because the effective rate of taxation—the ratio of total taxes paid to incomes received—increases with the size of the income. Second, there is an indirect effect on incentives. It may be presumed that highly progressive income taxation has a restraining influence on the creation of income. Not only would high marginal rates cause people to think twice before adding to their work output, but they might well have an injurious effect on savings and investment.

TRANSFER PAYMENTS

Transfer payments are different from other government expenditures in that no equivalent value in goods or services is received in exchange. Their chief effect is to redistribute income between individuals, economic and social groups, or geographic regions. Transfer payments normally can be classified in one of two categories. First are transfers of money that go to individuals. Most transfer payments of this type are linked to welfare programs. This kind of transfers has the most direct effect upon the distribution of income in a society. Second, there are transfer payments in the form of subsidies to certain economic sectors, such as agriculture or business, designed to bring about a greater production of a particular commodity than would be forthcoming if the regulation of production was left to market forces. Sometimes, too, subsidies are designed to supply goods or services to particular groups at a cost below the market prices, for example, low-cost lunch programs for poor children.

■ ECONOMIC INSECURITY ■

The very nature of a market system provides for a certain amount of economic insecurity. A free enterprise system means the freedom to fail as well as the freedom to gain. Competition in the market place carries with it an element of social Darwinism—the efficient survive and the inefficient do not. The concept of individualism carried with it self-responsibility. A person was responsible for his or her own actions.[11] The Protestant work

---

11. This attitude was epitomized by W.E. Henley's poem "Invictus," one verse of which is as follows:
"It matters not how strait the gate,
Nor charged with punishment the scroll.
I am the master of my fate;
I am the captain of my soul."

ethic stressed thrift and hard work. Life's vicissitudes, such as unemployment and old age, were the responsibility of the individual, not the state; and savings were to be set aside to cover them. Life was for the venturesome—people who enjoyed the excitement of not knowing what the future had in store for them and who welcomed the challenge of adjustment. It can be said the United States was settled by venturesome souls who were not interested in economic security, but in the challenge of opening up new frontiers.

CAUSES OF INSECURITY

The virtues of the free market are many. It is an affair of many buyers and many sellers, each insistent on getting his or her terms. And if either is not satisfied, that person can go elsewhere and seek to do better. From a societal point of view, one virtue of the market is that it disperses responsibility. If a company introduces a product and finds that the public won't buy it, the loss is its own. If there is a change in buying habits so that a particular industry loses jobs (the U.S. textile industry is an excellent example), the problem is the industry's. If there is a change in demand for the skills of a particular worker, the problem is the worker's. All of this introduces an element of insecurity into a market system.

As the United States and other Western societies developed as industrial nations, new risks developed. Paramount among those risks was unemployment. Industrial accidents were a second risk, and then came other risks, such as the loss of income when one became too old to work. Market capitalism carried with it the idea that incomes were determined by impersonal forces outside of human control. Life was a competitive struggle in which victory went to the swift and resourceful. However, in life's competitive struggle, most people did not fare well. Toward the end of the nineteenth century, working conditions for most workers were deplorable; twelve-hour days and seven-day weeks were not uncommon.

GOVERNMENT RESPONSE

In a very short period of time—just a little more than 100 years—changes have taken place in Western society that mandate some type of institutional protection for the individual who in many cases can no longer provide adequate self-protection. Technological change is rapid, posing a constant threat that workers may lose their old jobs and need to undergo expensive and psychologically distressing retraining and education. Consumer preferences may shift away from some product or production may be moved to other countries, causing a loss of jobs and a shutdown of plant facilities.[12] In addition, improved health care means that more people are living longer and many are not able to accumulate the resources needed to support themselves during retirement. Finally, the modern industrial economy brought with it the business cycle, which introduced an element of insecurity into the market system. Not only did workers lose their jobs, but business firms and banks failed.

All Western governments have now become heavily involved in altering the distribution of market resources directly or indirectly. With this commitment came the responsibility to provide a minimum income if a family is, for whatever reason including unemployment, unable to take care of itself. There has been in Western societies what sociologist Daniel Bell calls a "revolution of rising expectations," which can be translated into entitlement. It means that anyone who is old should have a pension, anyone who is sick should have medical care, and anyone who wants an education should have it. In addition, minimum wage laws set a floor under workers' wages and labor laws limit the number of hours that workers can work each day. Safety laws protect workers from hazardous working conditions and child-labor laws prohibit the employment of children until they reach a certain age.

GOVERNMENT SUPPORT OF INDUSTRY AND AGRICULTURE

Competition is the cornerstone of a free market economy. The whole rationale for a competitive market economy is to maximize productivity by channeling resources into the most efficient uses. In a free market economy, government intervention is inappropriate because it tends to lessen the efficiency of the market in fulfilling its objectives. Also, central to the operation of a free market economy is a flexible system of prices determined by supply and demand. Above all else, government should not intervene in market pricing, for that action would strike a mortal blow to the heart of the market system.

However, governments have come to intervene in the marketplace when the results of competition appear undesirable to society. An excellent example is the Chrysler bailout by the U.S. government. Chrysler, on the verge of bankruptcy in 1979, asked the U.S. Congress for financial assis-

---

12. The decline of the U.S. steel industry is a good example.

tance, which was eventually provided in the form of a loan guarantee.[13] If the rules of a competitive market economy had prevailed, Chrysler would have gone broke.[14] It can be argued that if government bails out businesses that fail in the competitive race, it compromises the discipline of the marketplace. Yet it also can be argued that if Chrysler had failed, there would have been an immediate loss of several hundred thousand jobs, which would have created a ripple effect throughout the American economy, creating more unemployment and the loss of tax revenues. Chrysler is only one example of how Western governments have intervened to protect firms and industries that are adversely affected by competition.

AID TO INDUSTRY   Governments not only aid businesses with loans and subsidies, they also protect domestic businesses from the competition of firms in other countries through the use of trade restrictions. A basic premise of a market economy is that free trade between countries is desirable. By specializing in the commodities for which it has the greatest comparative advantage and trading a part of its total output with other countries, a nation can produce a greater volume of goods and services than if it tried to be self-sufficient. Conversely, other countries do the same. In a free world market each country would specialize in what it does best and trade would take place on the basis of specialization. Japanese cars would be exchanged for American farm products, and consumer well-being would be maximized in both countries. However, in reality, the Japanese government protects its agriculture from the competition of American farm products, and the United States protects its automobile industry from the competition of Japanese cars.

AID TO AGRICULTURE   Agriculture, probably more than any other area of economic activity, fits the economist's concept of pure competition, which is the ideal market situation.[15] There are a large number of buyers and sellers of farm products, and price and output are determined by sup-

13. See U.S. Congress, House Committee on Banking, Finance, and Urban Affairs, *The Chrysler Corporation Financial Situation: Hearings on the Chrysler Corporation Loan Guarantee Act*, 96th Cong., 1st Sess. 1979, parts 1 and 2.

14. Chrysler has become profitable and has repaid its loans. Nevertheless, it is necessary to point out that import quotas were imposed on Japanese cars. Restricting imports of Japanese cars had the effect of increasing market shares of auto sales for the U.S. auto companies. They were able to increase prices, and profits increased.

15. Pure competition has the following characteristics: (1) The products of all sellers are exact substitutes for each other; (2) no seller produces more than a negligible share of market supply; (3) new firms can enter the industry with the same costs as existing firms; (4) there is the absence of collusion; and (5) there is no outside interference in the marketplace.

ply and demand operating in the markets for those products. However, prices for farm products can fluctuate widely and prices are subject to factors over which farmers have no control. Economic insecurity is the result. One type of government action to protect farmers from the vagaries of the market is through the use of price supports, which assure farmers of a price for their product no matter what the actual market price is. The purpose of price supports is the same as minimum wage laws: to provide a floor below which incomes cannot fall.

Price supports have been used in the United States for fifty years. They circumvent the market determination of both price and output of a product by supply and demand. An example will suffice. Assume that the market-determined price of wheat is $4.50 a bushel. However, farmers contend that the price is too low and want the government to guarantee a higher price. The government sets a support price of $5.25 a bushel for wheat. Figure 2-3 shows the market-determined price and the support price. There is a market-determined output and a support price output. Assume that output under the market price is 1 million bushels and under the support price, 1.2 million bushels. The difference between the two adds to the surplus the government buys to maintain the support price.

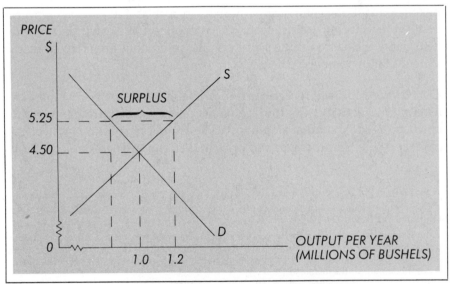

FIGURE 2-3   EFFECT OF A SUPPORT PRICE
SET HIGHER THAN
THE MARKET-DETERMINED PRICE

■ S O C I A L   R E G U L A T I O N ■

Social regulation is broad based in its objectives and enforcement. It encompasses such areas as occupational health and safety, employment opportunities for women and minorities, consumer product safety, and environmental protection. The government's role in social regulation has increased in the United States and other market economies. Pollution, which is a prime external effect of industrial progress, has become a problem in the market economies.[16] Government regulation requiring air and water standards have been imposed on society.

INABILITY TO EXPRESS NEGATIVE WANTS AND PREFERENCES

In a market economy, the price mechanism gives individuals no opportunity to bid against the production and sale of commodities and services that they regard as undesirable. To the contrary, the price mechanism will provide goods and services that people are willing to pay for, no matter how frivolous or undesirable they are. They may be many people who would be happier if they could prevent the production and sale of, for instance, alcoholic beverages or the emission of noxious fumes from a chemical plant, and would gladly pay the price if given the opportunity to do so. But there seems to be no way that the market-price mechanism can take these negative wants or preferences into consideration. The only way this can be done is through government action that controls the output of both public and private goods deemed undesirable.

EXTERNALITIES

Externalities are costs society must bear. Pollution is an externality because one individual can impose its cost on others without having to compensate them. The other individuals then demand government protection in the form of regulation that prohibits or limits the actions of the first individual. As society has become more technologically advanced and congested, one group's meat has become another group's poison. Airports are necessary to facilitate rapid transportation, but their creation brings attendant noise that damages the environment of people who live near them. Thus

---

16. Pollution transends ideology—the Soviet Union has pollution; the Danube river at Budapest, Hungary, is polluted.

these persons will coalesce into a group demanding noise abatement measures. Coal is an important source of fuel, but there are externalities in its mining—black lung disease for the miners plus the despoliation of the environment. Competitive markets provide no solution to these externalities; a competitive firm will generate as much, or more, smoke than a noncompetitive one does.

CONSUMER PROTECTION

A pure market economy assumes that consumers are knowledgeable about products and can make rational choices. However, the average person (in fact even the most intelligent) has neither the ability, time, nor the inclination to become an expert in the intricacies of the many products that industry produces today. Consumer protection regulation has evolved because buying decisions have become more complex as technology has become more sophisticated.

SUMMARY

Government intervention in market economies has increased over time for a number of reasons. In the market system the distribution of income and wealth can become quite uneven. Governments have redistributed both income and wealth through the use of progressive income and inheritance taxes and through transfer payments. Business fluctuations have created mass unemployment, and governments have used fiscal and monetary policies to stimulate aggregate demand. Concentration of business activities in the hands of a few firms and anticompetitive business practices have resulted in the creation of antitrust laws to regulate business. Economic insecurity in a market economy has been reduced by government action designed to help both individuals and groups. Governments have introduced social security measures to protect individuals from the loss of income resulting from unemployment or old age. Groups such as farmers are protected against fluctuations in market prices through price supports and subsidies. Finally, governments have intervened to provide regulation when the negative wants of consumers cannot be expressed in the market.

R E V I E W   Q U E S T I O N S

1. What are negative wants? Why are they difficult to express in the marketplace?
2. Compare the classical and Keynesian views of unemployment.
3. Monopolies are generally considered as undesirable in a free market economy. Discuss.
4. What are the objectives of antitrust laws?
5. Keynesian economics increased the importance of government in the Western market economies. Discuss.
6. What are transfer payments?
7. Distinguish between fiscal and monetary policy.
8. In what ways have governments altered the allocation of resources by the price mechanism?
9. What was Say's Law of Markets? What relevance did it have to classical economic theory?
10. In what ways have governments protected business firms from competition?

R E C O M M E N D E D   R E A D I N G S

Baumol, William J., John C. Panzar, and Robert D. Willig. *Contestable Markets and the Theory of Industry Structure*. San Diego, Calif.: Harcourt Brace Jovanovich Inc., 1982.

Bronfenbrenner, Martin, Werner Sechel, and Wayland Gardner. *Economics*. Boston: Houghton Mifflin Co., 1984. Chapters 11 and 12.

Gilder, George. *Wealth and Poverty*. New York: Basic Books Inc., Publishers, 1981.

Heilbroner, Robert J. *The Worldly Philosophers: The Lives, Times and Ideas of the Great Economic Thinkers*. 6th ed. New York: Simon & Schuster Inc., 1984.

Keynes, John Maynard. *The General Theory of Employment, Interest, and Money*. New York: Harcourt, Brace & Co., 1936.

Schnitzer, Martin C. *Contemporary Government and Business Relations*. 2d ed. Boston: Houghton Mifflin Co., 1983. Chapters 2 and 18.

Steiner, George A., and John P. Steiner. *Business, Government & Society: A Managerial Perspective*. 4th ed. New York: Random House Inc., 1985.

Thurow, Lester. *The Zero-Sum Society*. New York: Penguin Books, 1981.

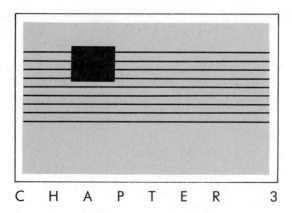

C H A P T E R 3

NONMARKET MECHANISMS: SOCIALISM AND COMMUNISM

Differences in economic and political institutions are one way to compare economic systems. Capitalism is an economic–cultural system, organized economically around the institutions of private property and the production of goods for profit and based culturally on the idea that the individual is the center of society. Other economic systems can be defined in terms of the modifications they would make in these institutions. For example, in a capitalist economy the agents of production—land, labor, and capital—are privately owned. In a socialist system, the agents of production are owned by a public authority and operated not with a view of profit by sale to other people, but for direct service of those whom the authority represents.

However, one caveat is in order. There are many definitions of socialism, and it is necessary to differentiate between socialism as the concept is applied to the governments of France and Greece and socialism used as a self-description of the countries controlled by communist parties—the Soviet Union, China, the Eastern European countries, Cuba, North Korea, and Vietnam. To the West these countries are communist.

To avoid confusion, in Marxist terminology there are two stages of communism. The first stage, or *socialism*, is a transitional stage during which some elements of capitalism are retained. The second stage, or *communism*, is a higher stage to be marked by an age of plenty, distribution according to needs, the absence of money and the market mechanism, the disappearance of the last vestiges of capitalism, and the withering away of the state. The Soviet Union calls itself a socialist country (Union of Soviet Socialist Republics—USSR). It is a state-directed society that has sought to fuse all realms into a single monolith and to impose a common direction, from economics to politics to culture, through a single institution, the Communist Party. Bureaucratic collectivism characterizes the Soviet economy.

In a non-Marxist form, socialism is an economic system that would modify, but not eliminate, many of the institutions of capitalism. The extent of modification is something that has never been completely delineated by socialists because there are many variations of socialism. Some socialists favor the complete elimination of private property with replacement by public property ownership. Other socialists favor placing maximum reliance on the market mechanism while supplementing it with government direction and planning in order to achieve the desired economic and social objectives.

Socialism today has also come to be associated with the concept of a welfare state, where the state, through a wide variety of transfer payments, assumes responsibility for protecting its citizens against all of the vicissitudes of life. Private ownership of the agents of production is permitted, with state ownership of those facets of production and distribution considered vital to the interests of society. In reality Western society has incorporated many of the principles of both capitalism and socialism.

■ HISTORICAL DEVELOPMENT ■ OF SOCIALISM

The words *socialist* and *socialism* are relatively new concepts. They first came into use in England and France in the early part of the last century and were applied to the doctrines of certain writers who were seeking a transformation of the economic and moral basis of society by the substitution of social for individual control of life and work.[1] The word *socialism* was popularized as the antithesis of *individualism*, However, precursors of socialism can be found among the medieval writers and even going back as far as Plato. For example, Thomas Aquinas believed that property ownership should be private, but that the use of goods should be in common.

---

1. *Socialist* seems to have been used first in England to describe the followers of Robert Owen. The word *socialism* was used in France to describe the writings of Saint-Simon and Fourier.

Whatever goods a man possessed should be shared with the poor. He considered poverty undesirable because it led to sin, and he proposed that both church and state should help poor people to bring healthy children into the world.

THE RENAISSANCE UTOPIAS

During the Renaissance a number of scholars turned their attention to the construction of imaginary communities or utopias in which society was so organized as to remove all of the evils of the day. These utopias were primarily economic and social, rather than religious. For the most part, they formed a definite pattern, the authors placing a group of regenerated people on an isolated land area where they could be free from contamination by the rest of the world. Rigid conditions would then be set up by means of which an ideal state would be attained. For example, in Sir Thomas More's *Utopia*, everything is owned in common and there is no money.[2] In the middle of each city is a marketplace to which each family takes the things it produces; from these central marketplaces products are distributed to central warehouses from which each family draws what it needs. Women and men have equal rights, and the households are so arranged that the women are relieved of some of their most time-consuming domestic duties.

FRENCH UTOPIAN SOCIALISTS

French utopian socialism was associated with the French Revolution and later with the Industrial Revolution. The French Revolution created a great economic and political upheaval, the impact of which was felt all over Europe. In France every political and social division became rooted in the alignment of the revolution. Commercial business interests, as represented by a merchant class, replaced the aristocracy, who had gone to the guillotine. A large class of urban workers who had helped make a revolution found that their living conditions were largely unchanged. The fact that a great political revolution had taken place in France and that socially the results of this revolution were largely unsatisfactory set the stage for a new group of reformers, the French utopian socialists.

In general, the ideas of the utopian socialists were based on the theory that nature had ordained all things to serve the happiness of humankind

---

2. Lewis Mumford, *The Stories of Utopias* (New York: Boni and Liveright, 1922), pp. 23-37.

and that every person had natural rights due at birth.[3] Furthermore, it was believed that human beings were perfect in the original state. However, at various times in the past, people had tampered with the natural order of things by establishing customs and institutions that ran contrary to it. As a result, people in the existing state were not happy, enjoyed few if any rights, and certainly were far from being perfect. Having discovered the cause of human difficulties, the utopian socialists proceeded to the obvious solution of the problem of social regeneration. If people had been rendered bad by unnatural customs and institutions, the thing to do was to discover the nature of the original state of goodness and then reorganize society so as to give nature's forces full play, unhampered by the conventions and institutions of the existing social environment.

However, the French utopian socialists could not agree on how to reorganize society. Some advocated the elimination of private property, considering it the main reason for human degeneracy. Others favored complete income equality. Babeuf proposed that production be carried out in common, distribution be shared in common, and children be brought up in such a way as to prevent the growth of individual differences. Saint-Simon, one of the better known early French utopian socialists, rejected the whole idea of equality, arguing instead that people were naturally unequal and that any attempt to make them equal would involve greater injustices than actually existed at the time. However, differences were to be based on talent, rather than the inheritance of wealth. Saint-Simon favored an economic mechanism that would require each person to labor according to his or her capacity and would provide rewards on the basis of service. Charles Fourier worked out a plan for cooperative living in small communities, which he hoped would lead to a transformation of society. These communities were called *phalanxes*, and each phalanx was to be self-sufficient. The highest pay would go to those performing the most necessary work, as determined by the members of the phalanx.

SOCIALISM AND THE INDUSTRIAL REVOLUTION

The Industrial Revolution was in due course to revolutionize the economic life of the whole Western world. The availability of new technology encouraged the formation of real capital with which the technology might be put into widespread use. The availability of resources for use in capital for-

---

3. Richard T. Fly, *French and German Socialists in Modern Times* (New York: Harper, 1883), pp. 37-51.

mation encouraged the search for new technology that, once discovered, could be embodied in the real capital. The new technology enabled gross national product to be large enough to provide sufficient consumer goods to satisfy the minimum subsistence needs of the population and still have some resources left over. Population growth provided labor to use the enlarged amounts of real capital to increase total national output.

However, there was a darker side to the Industrial Revolution. Working conditions in factories were unpleasant. Equipment was sometimes dangerous and caused workers to have serious accidents. Average wages of industrial workers were low, largely because the rapid expansion of population provided a large number of workers for the labor force. These workers concentrated in the industrial cities and competed with each other for jobs.

The cities that grew up or expanded to house the workers were unattractive and unpleasant. Many of them consisted of slums with houses of poor quality when constructed and in a constant state of disrepair thereafter. Charles Dickens, that great chronicler of English society in the nineteenth century, has a rather graphic description of the squalor of the London slums in his book *Bleak House*.

> Jo lives—that is to say that Jo has not yet died—in a ruinous place known to the like of him by the name of Tom-all-Alone's. It is a black, dilapidated street, avoided by all decent people, where the crazy houses were seized upon, when their decay was far advanced, by some bold vagrants who after establishing their own possession took to letting them out in lodgings. Now, these tumbling tenements contain by night, a swarm of misery. As on the ruined human wretch vermin parasites appear, so these ruinous shelters have bred a crowd of foul existence that crawls in and out of gaps in walls and boards; and rocks itself to sleep in maggot numbers, where the rain drips in; and comes and goes, fetching and carrying fever and sowing more evil in its every footprint.[4]

MODERN SOCIALISM

Modern socialism, as opposed to utopian socialism, had its genesis during the Industrial Revolution. It developed as a social reform movement to protest the seamy side of the Industrial Revolution. Robert Owen, an early English socialist, was considered a utopian socialist in that he developed a scheme for social regeneration; change society, you change the person. He

---

4. Charles Dickens, *Bleak House* (New York: Signet Books, 1964), pp. 232-233.

believed that true happiness is found in making others happy.[5] Owen, un-like many other social reformers, had the money to carry out his plan of so-cial regeneration. He created a textile mill at New Lanark in Scotland in 1800, reducing the hours of work to 10½ hours per day and raising wages.[6] He did not employ children under the age of 10. Education and playgrounds were provided for the children of mill workers. The experi-ment made money, and Owen was able to get a factory reform bill intro-duced in Parliament. However, other mill owners were not willing to adopt similar measures. Subsequent experiments by Owen were unsuc-cessful. He came to the United States and created a community called New Harmony in Indiana. His attempts to create a perfect community there failed too.

Socialism coalesced into a political movement in England around the middle of the last century. A contributing factor in its development was mass unemployment created by business recessions. One of the basic de-fects of capitalism was the constant recurrence of recessions. In England and in other countries, unemployment and labor unrest began to occur more frequently, and a working class movement developed in these coun-tries.

The movement found its support in labor unions and in intellectuals who were not of the working class but who felt that the political and eco-nomic structure of society had to be reformed for the benefit of the work-ers. A split developed between Marxist and non-Marxist socialists, with the former preaching class revolution and the overthrow of the existing politi-cal and social order, and the latter believing in the attainment of econom-ic, political, and social reforms by working within the existing system. Po-litical parties representing both the Marxist and non-Marxist points of view had been formed in France and Germany by 1900.

■ INSTITUTIONS OF SOCIALISM ■

Socialism, as mentioned above, developed into a viable political force in Western Europe around the latter part of the last century and has contin-ued to develop during this century. Socialist parties captured control of the governments of France and Greece in elections held in 1981. Socialism is

---

5. Or, in the words of Paul, "remember the words of the Lord Jesus, how He said, it is more blessed to give than to receive" (Acts 20:35).

6. By the standards of those days, these provisions were not harsh.

an important political force today, but, like capitalism, it has lost much of its original meaning. There are certain institutional arrangements that set socialism apart from capitalism and communism. These arrangements represent a modification in most of the institutions of capitalism, since socialism developed in opposition to some of the worst abuses of capitalism.

PRIVATE PROPERTY

Under ideal socialism, the rights of private property would be limited to consumption goods; productive wealth, land, and capital would in general be owned by society as a whole. Socialists today say that the social ownership of the means of production would be limited to the land and capital used in large-scale production. For example, the socialist government of François Mitterand proposed the nationalization of some French banks (the more important ones have already been nationalized) and some key industries, such as aluminum. In France, one car company (Renault) is state-owned, but another car company (Peugeot) is not.

Most socialists would permit private individuals to own and operate small farms, stores, and repair shops. Some even contend that certain industries, which operate satisfactorily under private ownership and which are not suited to government ownership and operation, be left alone to function in the hands of individuals. Modern socialists thus do not adhere to ideal socialism when it comes to the right of private property ownership.

THE PRICE SYSTEM

According to many socialists, the ideal socialist system would retain money and the price system, but it would not rely on price movements and price relationships in making important economic decisions to nearly as great an extent as does a capitalist system. Decisions as to the kinds and quantities of goods, particularly public goods, would be made by the government. A major socialist criticism of the price mechanism in a market economy is that prices do not reflect nonmarket wants of the people, such as the desire for economic security. Nor can negative wants be expressed through the price mechanism.[7] Also, individuals with large sums of money can express

---

7. For example, there may be a number of people whose total satisfaction would be much increased if they could prevent the publication and sale of pornographic books or the production and sale of cigarettes. They might well be glad to pay a price to obtain that satisfaction of their negative preferences if the opportunity could be given them to do so. But there seems to be no way, short of government edict, in which the market mechanism can take these negative preferences into account.

their wants through prices and thus cause resources to be used in producing goods that the mass of consumers cannot afford. Socialism would divert productive resources to satisfy basic wants of all of the people before the relatively less important wants of the few with large incomes are satisfied.

SOCIALISM AND GOVERNMENT

Perhaps because various noncapitalistic economic systems have so often operated under dictatorial governments, there is a tendency in popular discussion to link capitalism with democracy and to link socialism and communism with dictatorship. However, this is not the case with socialism. European social democratic parties have operated within the framework of democracy. The 1981 elections of socialist governments in France and Greece illustrate the point.

By the early 1960s, many of the European social democratic parties severed completely whatever remaining ideological ties they had with Marx and communism.[8] They abandoned their traditional opposition to private property and their goal of social ownership and turned their attention to improving the public mix of total goods and services. Thus, what have developed in Western Europe are mixed capitalist-socialist economies. When socialists come into power, the tilt is toward socialism; there is still reliance on a market economy, but also heavy government direction and planning to achieve desired social and economic objectives.

■ COMMUNISM ■

Early hints of communism can be found in Plato's *Republic*.[9] Plato's criticisms of the economic and social structure of his time led to his proposal for an ideal state. The state described in the *Republic* is a city-state, a type of political organization quite common in Greece at the time (431-351 B.C.). Among other things, Plato's ideal republic is a communist society in which all things are held in common, at least as far as the upper classes are con-

8. The staunchest European supporter of President Reagan's attempts to attain military parity with the Soviet Union is the socialist president of France, François Mitterand. Even though there are communists in his government, Mitterand is in opposition to the Soviet Union, regarding it as a threat to the security of Western Europe. It is interesting to note that massive anti-nuclear missile demonstrations against U.S. policy were held in Holland, the United Kingdom, and other European countries, but not in France. In fact, the French were busy with construction of their own nuclear warheads.

9. In Irwin Edman, ed., *The Works of Plato* (New York: Modern Library, Inc., 1956), pp. 397-481.

cerned. The upper classes, or guardians of the state, eat in common dining rooms and live in common quarters, receiving their support from contributions made by the citizens at large.[10] Members of this group never consider their own personal interests but always work for the good of the whole state. To insure their disinterest, Plato does not have any private interest, not even a private family life. However, Plato's communism was not for the masses, who were excluded from political life in his republic. Instead, it was communism of the select.

KARL MARX AND DAS KAPITAL

Both modern communism and socialism began in England and were reactions against capitalism. As mentioned previously, unequal incomes, squalor, and poverty were characteristic of industrial life in England. The winds of revolution that had blown in from France had died away, and rank and privilege were firmly entrenched. The upper class was all-powerful over a tenantry for the most part unenfranchised.

Flattered, adulated, deferred to, the English aristocracy reigned supreme, with incomes enormously increased by the Industrial Revolution and as yet untaxed. The aristocracy was subject to no ordinary laws and held the government firmly in its hands. However, an entrepreneurial class had begun to emerge as a result of the Industrial Revolution, and the two classes clashed over government control. This conflict did very little to ameliorate the working conditions of the industrial masses.

This was the general economic and social milieu within which Karl Marx wrote *Das Kapital*. It is necessary to remember that Marx was a product of his time and that the activities of other persons in England, as well as in other countries, had attracted widespread attention to the problem of poverty. Marx is important because in *Das Kapital* he presented a dynamic theory of economics that still serves as the basis of much of communist dogma. The most important elements of the theory are summarized as follows.

THE MARXIST THEORY OF INCOME DISTRIBUTION   At any given time, according to Marx, the way in which people make a living is conditioned by the nature of the existing productive forces. There are three productive

---

10. In Plato's republic there are three social classes, the rulers or guardians, the auxiliary guardians, and the artisans. The ruling class is selected from the auxiliary class and is composed of philosophers who have been selected after a long course of study. The artisans comprise the largest group of the republic, but have little status.

forces: natural resources, capital equipment, and human resources. Since people must use these productive forces in the process of making a living, some sort of relationship between people and the productive forces is necessary. Specifically, the property relation is involved. People may own certain productive forces individually, as in a capitalist society, or they may own them collectively, as in a socialist society. Under capitalism, there were people who owned property or capital and there were people who owned only their own labor. Marx called the former the capitalists or the *bourgeoisie* and the latter the *proletariat* or the workers.

THE LABOR THEORY OF VALUE   Many economists of the eighteenth and nineteenth centuries, including Adam Smith and David Ricardo, believed that labor supplied the common denominator of value.[11] Marx adopted this idea and made it the basis for his own theory of income distribution. He stated that the one thing common to all commodities is labor and that the value of a commodity is determined by the amount of socially necessary labor requied for its production. *Socially necessary labor,* as defined by Marx, is the amount of time necessary to produce a given product under existing average conditions of production and with the average degree of skill and intensity of labor.[12] The relative prices of two products will be in the same proportion as the amount of socially necessary labor required to produce them. If two hours of labor are required to make a pair of shoes and five hours of labor are required to build a cart, the price of shoes in the market will be two-fifths that of the cart.

The price of labor is the wage rate. The wage rate determines the income of those who own their own labor. Marx asserted that the wage rate itself is determined by the labor theory of value. How much a worker receives in income in return for working for an employer depends on how many labor hours are required to produce the necessities of life for that worker. If the necessities can be produced with five hours of labor per day, a worker can produce and be available to the employer for work if five hours wages are paid to the worker each day. Even if the worker actually works twelve hours each day for an employer, the pay will only be for five hours because that is all it takes to sustain the worker. That is all the pay can be, under a labor theory of value. In effect, Marx believed in a subsistence theory of wages in a system of market capitalism.

11. *Value* may be defined as the worth of a commodity or service as measured by its ability to command other goods and services in return. It is, in short, exchange value, which is the power to command exchange in the market.

12. Karl Marx, *Das Kapital* (New York: Modern Library, Inc., 1906), pp. 198-331.

THEORY OF SURPLUS VALUE   Although all value is created by the workers, it is expropriated by employers in the form of *surplus value,* which can be defined as the difference between the value created by the workers and the value of their labor power. When a worker sells labor power to an employer, the worker gives up all title and claim to the products of that labor. Income in the Marxist scheme is divided into two categories—surplus value, which is the source of all profit, and labor income. Value in the Marxist rubric can be expressed in the formula $C + V + S$, where C represents raw materials and capital consumption, V represents various outlays in wages, and S represents surplus value in the form of rent, interest, and profit. The C component, raw materials and capital, although clearly not labor, is explained away by Marx, who regarded it as stored-up labor from past periods. Thus the remainder, $V + S$, represents net output, which consists of the two basic income shares, wages and profit.

How much a worker gets as a wage is based on the amount of labor time socially necessary to produce subsistence or maintenance for the worker and the worker's family. Assume that this subsistence only requires five hours of socially necessary labor time for its production. If the worker only worked five hours for the employer, the worker would be fully paid and there would be no surplus value. However, it is the employer's right to set the length of the working day, and it will normally be set at a number of hours greater than that required to produce the worker's subsistence. The difference between the actual hours worked and the labor time needed for subsistence is surplus value.

THE DYNAMIC WEAKNESSES OF MARKET CAPITALISM   The market distribution of income between workers and property owners was bound, according to Marx, to be a source of increasing difficulty for capitalist economies.

CRISIS AND DEPRESSIONS   For one thing, it would sometimes be difficult to sell the output being produced. The workers received money income enough to buy only part of the total output. This part would necessarily take the form of subsistence or consumer goods. The capitalists received the rest, an amount sufficient to buy the remainder of the output of goods and services. But would they buy it? Of course they would buy some of it to satisfy their own consumption desires. The rest they might purchase in the form of capital goods with which to carry on production and to expand productive capacity if they found such a purchase profitable. However, from time to time there would be periods of months or even years when they would not find it profitable to expand capacity. These would be periods of crisis and depression. During these times there would be sharply increased financial losses for business, unsold output, business bankruptcies, falling prices, and unemployment.

WORSENING TRENDS   Marx suggested that these crises and depressions would become increasingly severe. In each successive crisis, the weakest firms would disappear, being absorbed or replaced by a smaller number of larger firms. In the long run the number of firms and the number of capitalists would decline both absolutely and relative to the size of the economy and of the population. The proletariat would be absolutely and relatively enlarged.

The capitalist employers would be impelled by competition among themselves to substitute machinery or capital for labor, even though it was labor that provided surplus value and profits. The capitalists would be impelled to discover and introduce into use new technology because it would reduce the cost of subsistence needs for labor and thereby enlarge the amount of surplus value and profit. The increasingly severe crises, the substitution of capital for labor, and the introduction of new technology would create a larger and larger volume of unemployment among the workers. There would be an ever-increasing *industrial reserve army* of the unemployed.

Marx felt that the rate of profit on capital would fall continually lower, primarily because of the replacement of laborers with machines. The laborers were the source of all surplus and hence of all profits. Machines produced no surplus and, therefore, did not contribute to profits. The capitalists, desperately seeking to sustain profits, would seek ways to increase the surplus value by greater exploitation of the workers. They would resort to longer working hours, more intense work, and the employment of children.

There would be more and more severe crises, fewer and fewer capitalists, larger and larger unemployment, lower and lower profit rates, bigger and bigger amounts of unsold goods, and ever more outrageous exploitation of the workers by the capitalists. These trends would ultimately lead, in the Marxist view, to the end of market capitalism. It would be replaced with a new economic system, or rather, with a whole new society. In Marx's view, economic arrangements were causally determinant of all else in society, and capitalism's inevitable demise would mean a complete change of everything else in society.[13] Because Marx felt that the character

---

13. A clear, entertaining, and brief explanation of Marx's theories appears in Sir Alexander Gray, *The Development of Economic Doctrine: An Introductory Survey* (New York: John Wiley & Sons, Inc., 1931), chap. 11. A more technically difficult account, which assumes more knowledge of economic analysis, can be found in Mark Blaug, *Economic Theory in Retrospect*, Rev. ed. (Homewood, Ill.: Richard D. Irwin, Inc., 1968), chap. 7.

of a society wholly depended upon its economic system, his philosophy is labeled one of *materialism*.

ECONOMICALLY DETERMINED HISTORY   To reiterate, Marx contended that economic conditions were the basic causal forces shaping the nature of society. All other aspects of society—political, religious, and philosophical—depended upon the economic system of the society.

MATERIALISM   For example, in a primitive nomad society where horses might be of particular importance in enabling the people to gather food and to exist in general, the ownership of horses would also be important to the people. Those persons who owned the horses would be able to control the others. That is, those who possessed the principal means of production would also possess the ability to rule. The religion and philosophy of the nomad society would center about horses and those who owned them. The patterns of marriage and inheritance would be heavily influenced by considerations regarding the use and ownership of horses.

In a society that had amassed considerable real capital and technology, the capital would be the principal means of production. The society would be organized around the existence, ownership, control, and use of the capital. Political power would reside with the owners and controllers of capital, the capitalists. Religion and philosophy would sanctify the ownership and rationalize the social dominance of the owners.

In some advanced societies with great real capital, all ownership and control might be exercised by the government. It would act on behalf of all the people. Political power would rest with all the people. A philosophy of altruism would develop among them.

In the most advanced society, so much capital and such advanced technology would exist that enough goods and services would be produced to more than completely satisfy the desires of everyone. The ownership of the means of production would cease to matter. Political control over others would cease to have significance. Interpersonal animosity, based on the covetousness of each for the material goods and services of others, would disappear. Government, no longer necessary as the instrument by which some controlled others or by which some were protected from others, would gradually wither away.

THE DIALECTIC   Marx's view of philosophy and history is called a *dialectic*. From the philosopher Hegel, Marx adopted the notion that everything that happened in the world could be explained by the clash of opposites. In simple terms, Hegel claimed that a proper understanding of the world could be achieved if all change were viewed as the result of clashing ideas. First, there is an idea, such as scarcity. Then there emerges an opposite idea, such as abundance. Finally, the two opposing ideas are combined into a new and superior idea, such as *economy*, which is a means to achieve abundance out of scarcity.

Marx adopted the notion of the clashing of opposites to produce a successor synthesis. However, he rejected the view that this clashing and synthesis took place basically and most significantly in the realm of ideas. Rather, according to Marx, the essentially basic and causal conflict and synthesis took place, as his philosophy of materialism suggests, in the real world of economic events, economic classes, and economic systems.

DIALECTICAL MATERIALISM   Marx welded together his views of the primacy of economic arrangements and of history as progressive conflict into the doctrine of *dialectical materialism*. According to this doctrine, a society, such as that of Europe during the Middle Ages, is based on an economic system, such as manorial agriculture. A political structure, such as feudalism, and a philosophical and religious structure, such as medieval Catholicism, grow up in harmony with the economic base. There are several socioeconomic classes: landed nobility, clergy, and serfs. The economic system is successful in filling the material needs of the people. In fact, it is too successful for its own permanence.

The increasing productive ability of the manorial system makes its possible for some people to leave agriculture and become traders or craftsmen. Others have sufficient time to make economically useful discoveries and innovations. Gradually the techniques of production and other economic arrangements change. Local economic self-sufficiency decreases as trading increases. First guilds and then factory workers carry on production in place of the manorial serfs or craftsmen. There begins to grow up a new socioeconomic class made up of the shopkeeping proprietors, the factory managers and owners, and the merchant traders.

In the meantime, the political power remains, in an increasingly outmoded way, with the hereditary landed aristocracy. The religious rules grow more and more inappropriate for the economic system. For example, doctrines against usury and in favor of just prices become obsolete. Finally, the economic system and the seat of real power have changed enough that the new class, the bourgeoisie, is able to wrest political power from the landed nobility. They do so either by forceful revolution, by new laws, or by influence with the sovereign. They also reshape the religious code, perhaps by replacing Catholicism with Protestantism.

Capitalism thereby replaces feudalism. Then, because of its inherent nature, capitalism under the bourgeoisie unintentionally promotes its own replacement. Capitalism brings together the working proletariat and infuses in them a unity born of misery and exploitation. The class conflict between the proletariat and the bourgeoisie sharpens with conditions increasingly favorable to a proletarian victory. The political superstructure of government is in the hands of the bourgeoisie, who use it to perpetuate their power. However, it fails to reflect the underlying economic reality of bourgeoisie weakness and proletarian strength. Religion has been used as a device for cowing the workers, for justifying their exploitation, and for drugging them with visions of heaven so that they will accept their earthly misery. However, religion becomes more and more obviously a sham.

Eventually, the workers topple the bourgeoisie government, seize the means of production, abolish private property, and set up a socialist state under the dictatorship of the proletariat. The economic system is thus converted to socialism. Then, because all else follows from economic change, the society becomes ultimately a communist one, with neither government, scarcity, conflict, nor classes.[14]

THE WEAKNESSES OF MARXISM

What is wrong with Marx's views? Each of Marx's main ideas can be attacked on a number of grounds.

THE LABOR THEORY OF VALUE   The labor theory of value, as an explanation of what determines relative prices of goods and services, is extremely vulnerable to criticism. Marx anticipated some of these criticisms and tried to deal with them.

EXCEPTIONS TO THE THEORY   A piece of fertile land may exist and command a high price without any human labor at all having been expended on its creation. Such nonreproducible goods, Marx said, fall in a special category. The prices or values of this category are determined without reference to amounts of labor. Then what of a durable good that was produced some time ago and for whose production a technological improvement has been discovered in the meantime? The value of such a good will fall, Marx would say, in the meantime. It is not the amount of original labor expended but the amount necessary to replace a good that is the determining variable.

What of a unit of a good much like many other units of the same good except that it embodies a much greater amount of labor because it was

14. A readable account of world history, including the Industrial Revolution, as seen by a modern Marxist, is Leo Huberman, *Man's Worldly Goods: The Story of the Wealth of Nations* (New York: Monthly Review Press, 1952).

turned out by a very slow, inept worker? Will it on that account be much more valuable than the other units? No, it will not, because it is the actual amount of *socially necessary* labor that determines values and prices, Marx would answer. What of a good, like a hideous piece of sculpture, on the production of which a great amount of labor has been expended but which cannot be sold for any price because no one wants it? Can it, all in all, be said to be of great value? No, Marx might answer, because labor expended on a useless product is not socially necessary labor. What of a good produced by a monopolist and sold at a high price? Is its price in proportion to the labor in it? Admittedly it is not, for monopoly may distort prices from true values.

THE PROBLEM OF DIVERSE KINDS OF LABOR What of two goods, one of which embodies four hours of unskilled labor and the other, four hours of skilled labor? Will the two goods sell at the same price? Do they have equal value? No, in creating and determining value, one hour of skilled labor counts for more than one hour of unskilled labor. To compute value, one must convert skilled labor into unskilled labor by multiplying the number of hours of skilled labor by an appropriate conversion number. How can the appropriate number be known? It is determined, in part, by the number of hours of labor socially necessary to produce the goods and services needed to sustain the skilled laborers through the period of training. It is also determined, in part, by the number of hours required for every laborer, skilled or unskilled, to produce the goods needed to rear that person from infancy and for subsistence during working years.

Unfortunately, too many qualifications and exceptions spoil the attraction of a generalization. There is little left of the labor theory of value after all the obviously necessary modifications are taken into account. Furthermore, the modifications suggested above are incomplete. In the last case, for example, the number of labor hours necessary to sustain a worker consists itself of some hours of unskilled labor and some of skilled labor. To add the two together, a conversion number must be available. Of course, it is not available, for it is precisely what the whole procedure is set up to find.

ALTERNATIVE MODERN THEORY Modern economic theory, developed since Marx, explains values or prices in terms of degree of scarcity. According to this theory, the value of a thing in exchange for something else depends on how scarce it is. Its scarcity in turn depends on the state of its supply and the state of demand for it. Behind supply and demand lie a great many interdependent determinants. The scarcity theory is a complicated one, but it provides a more satisfactory explanation than the labor theory of value. The scarcity theory treats not only labor but also capital and natural resources as productive and value-creating.

Marx's labor theory of value is weak. His use of it as a basis for attacking the capitalistic market society's distribution of income makes that attack weak. One might still condemn market capitalism or market capitalism's distribution of income. However, one would probably do so for some reason other than because one believed that only labor had the power to create value and all value was in proportion to labor used.

THE SUBSISTENCE THEORY OF WAGES   Another element in Marx's theory of market capitalism is the subsistence theory of wages. Marx vacillated between two alternative explanations of this theory. One is that the wage rate will tend to fall until workers receive only enough income to provide a minimum physical existence for themselves. The other is that the wage rate will tend to fall until workers receive only enough to provide a psychologically or culturally determined minimum level of living for themselves.[15] The latter minimum might change as attitudes changed. It might vary from place to place, depending upon the attitudes prevailing in the society of each place. Marx did not give a satisfactory causal explanation of why the wage rate under market capitalism tended toward a subsistence minimum, however defined.

THE MALTHUSIAN EXPLANATION   Marx rejected the explanation offered by such people as Thomas Malthus. Malthus had argued that any wage higher than subsistence would reduce the death rate or raise the birth rate. These changes would cause the population and the supply of labor to increase. The increase would depress the market for labor and force the wage rate down. Perhaps Marx rejected the Malthusian explanation because it seemed to place the blame on the workers or to suggest that any economic system, not just market capitalism, would produce the same undesirable result.

LOPSIDED BARGAINING POWER   Marx did contend that the bargaining power of each individual worker would be small relative to that of a capitalist employer in the negotiations on wage rates. A worker sometimes has no real alternative, other than unemployment, to accepting a job from one accessible employer. On the other hand, most employers either can offer work to any one of a number of different workers who are competing with each other for jobs or can withhold work entirely by shutting down operations.

---

15. See Thomas Sowell, *Marxism* (New York: William Morrow & Co. Inc., 1985), pp. 136-137.

Critics of Marx have pointed out that, at least sometimes, workers have considerable bargaining power. Their power arises because of their unusual skills, because they band together in labor unions, because there is competition among employers for their services, or because without their labor real capital is unprofitable. Even with weak bargaining power, there is no proof that the wage rate will fall to the subsistence level.

THE RESERVE ARMY OF THE UNEMPLOYED   Marx also contended that there usually would be substantial numbers of unemployed workers. They would always be ready to compete with those who had jobs. They would also furnish an inexhaustible suply of labor at a minimum subsistence wage rate, no matter how strong the demand for labor.

Critics of this argument emphasize that Marx never really convincingly demonstrated that capitalism creates unemployment. Indeed, if Marx was right that only labor creates surplus value and profits, capitalist employers would seek out and employ every available worker because, by so doing, profits could be maximized. Actually, real wages in countries heavily dependent upon market capitalism have risen substantially in the long run. A Marxist may choose to dismiss this evidence by claiming that it merely reflects a rising psychological minimum subsistence level. But one can reasonably rejoin that capitalism is performing well, not badly, in this respect. It has raised both aspirations and the means to fulfill them.

THE THEORY OF SURPLUS VALUE   The theory of surplus value asserts that workers usually produce more goods and services than are needed for their subsistence. This assertion seems acceptable. It is probably equally acceptable, however, to assert that land is capable of producing more crop than that needed to reseed the land adequately in the next growing season. Likewise, a labor-saving machine may spare more labor hours than were required to make it. As the basis for an attack on market capitalism, the theory of surplus value is no attack at all unless supplemented by a labor theory of value and a subsistence theory of wages. If these latter two ideas are not valid, the theory of surplus value loses its sting for market capitalism.

Actually, land, labor, and capital cooperate in most production activities, regardless of the economic system. The complete removal of any one of these three factors would cause production to cease almost entirely. So long as they do cooperate, the productive output is usually more than enough to replace the worn equipment, maintain the natural resources, and provide for the subsistence needs of the workers. The excess may take the form either of suprasubsistence consumer goods or of capital goods that increase the society's stock of real capital.

THE THEORY OF CRISES AND TRENDS   Another element in Marx's attack on market capitalism is the crisis or business cycle. These do occur in many forms of capitalistic economic systems. They had been the object of economists' inquiries and theories before Marx and they have continued to be afterward. Marx's explanation of them was incomplete and faulty, and we have not yet achieved a complete understanding of them. However, most economists believe, as a result of economic studies undertaken since the Great Depression, that mixed economic systems can avoid severe crises and cycles by accepting rather modest government economic intervention. In any case, crises and cycles have not yet forced the complete collapse of market capitalism and its replacement with Marxist socialism or communism.

Many of the trends Marx predicted would carry capitalism to its doom have not been corroborated by subsequent history. Most striking has been the failure of the capitalist owners to become a smaller and smaller percentage of the population and the proletariat a larger and larger percentage. An increasingly greater portion of the people of Western Europe and North America possess property in the form of savings accounts, shares of corporate stock, government bonds, houses, automobiles, and durable consumer goods. The proletarian proportion of the populace has diminished as skilled white-collar and service workers have come to outnumber unskilled, manual workers.

The percentage of the labor force unemployed has not increased in the long run, as Marx predicted it would. The quality of life of the majority of the population has not become increasingly miserable. Working conditions have improved, not deteriorated, on the average at least. In the long run the rate of profit on capital has not fallen as much as Marx predicted. Technological and social changes have provided new, profitable opportunities for the use of machinery and other capital goods. The governments of most capitalist countries have not resolutely blocked every attempt by the majority of the people to obtain legislation to improve their lot. It would be laughable to contend that for most noncommunist, developed countries the government is used as the instrument by which an increasingly small number of capitalists keep subjugated an ever more preponderant working class.

THE THEORY OF ECONOMIC DETERMINISM AND DIALECTICAL MATERIALISM   Marx's emphasis upon the economic system of a society as determinant of all else about society is also easily criticized.

ECONOMICS AS ONLY ONE OF MANY INTERDEPENDENT FORCES
The economic system is as much a result as a cause of the general character of society. Religion and philosophy, for example, help to determine eco-

nomic organization. A people's religion may emphasize the evil of the accumulation of material goods and the virtue of asceticism. In consequence, the economic system is likely to remain a traditional one, and economic growth will not occur. Alternatively, religion may lay stress upon individual responsibility and upon working hard, saving much, and investing productively. As a result, the economic system is likely to become a market one with rapid change. A people's philosophy may accord great prestige to those who are very successful in military, spiritual, or governmental affairs and little prestige to those who are economically successful. Then the economic system of the people is likely to remain organized around the principle of tradition, and what modern Westerners regard as economic progress will probably be slow.

The political system of a society may place and keep in power those who wish to maintain the status quo. Then economic change will probably occur only slowly. The cultural heritage of a people may include a great accumulated stock of technological knowledge. The economic system of that people will probably be very different from that of a people with little such knowledge. The physical environment of a people is also likely to shape their economic system. The tropics may offer no challenge to traditional economic organization, which remains primitive. The arctic may offer too great a challenge, which prevents economic organization from being anything but traditional and primitive.

MONOCAUSAL THEORIES OF HISTORY It is implausible that human history is simply a sequence of economic changes that bring about other changes. Such a theory of history probably deserves the same derision as every other monocausal explanation of history. For example, one other such theory is the *hero theory*, which claims that the shape of history is the result of the appearance from time to time of extremely influential people such as Plato, Jesus, Caesar, Charlemagne, Columbus, Luther, Marx, and Lenin. Another is the *idea theory*, which stresses the great historical influence of ideas such as monotheism, asceticism, altruism, capitalism, democracy, and communism. Another is the *war theory*, which claims that conflicts of arms provide the key to the understanding of history. There is also the *political theory*, which claims that history is the sequence of governments.[16]

Marx's selection of struggles between economic classes as the vehicle of historical progress is also not convincing. People generally have not thought of themselves primarily as members of an economic class, but as

16. A brief elaboration of this kind of criticism of Marx can be found in William Ebenstein, *Today's Isms: Communism, Fascism, Capitalism, and Socialism*, 7th ed. (Englewood Cliffs, N.J.: Prentice-Hall Inc., 1973), chap. 1.

members of a family, an occupation, a tribe, a race, a district, or a nation, or simply as individuals. A theory of history that explains behavior as arising out of a loyalty that people do not have does not explain much.

THE MERITS OF MARX

Marx's theory was not totally without merit. He did indicate some of the weaknesses of the market capitalism of his time and place. The inequality of income, wealth, and power of nineteenth-century European capitalism was too great to be permanently tolerated by the populace and too great by twentieth-century Western standards. Marx correctly predicted some of the trends in market capitalism. Recurrent and sometimes severe business fluctuations have taken place. Unemployment has been a persistent problem. Inordinate political and social power has accrued to the economically most successful. Control, if not ownership, has been concentrated in the hands of those who guide the great private corporations.

Marx was perhaps the first to try to explain why history had occurred as it had rather than merely to describe what had occurred. He attempted to integrate economic theory with history. He was undoubtedly one of the few of his time to do so.

Perhaps Marx's greatest achievement was as a propagandist or as an inspiration for revolution and reform. It is ironic that Marx denied the influence of ideas on history and claimed instead the ascendancy of events—his own ideas have inspired and provoked people ever since he propounded them. Perhaps half the earth's people either are led by or want to be led by those who proclaim their allegiance to Marxism. This is not to say, of course, that the world today is markedly different than it would be had Marx never lived. It is entirely possible that events subsequent to Marx's time, such as the Russian and Chinese communist revolutions, would have taken place whether or not Marx had ever existed. People like Lenin and Mao, bent on seizing power and on changing society, are likely to pluck from the pages of previous history one name if not another to sanctify their actions and increase the probability of their success. Historical speculation aside, however, it is easy to claim for Marx that no other person did as much as he to besmirch the reputation of market capitalism.

■ INSTITUTIONS OF COMMUNISM ■

Communism, in Marxist ideology, is supposed to be the final stage of historical development. It is the end result of a classless society with the withering away of the state, and production from each according to ability and distribution to each according to need. However, modern communism is far removed from ideal or pure communism, nor can it be considered a transitory stage through which a country passes on its way to pure communism. There are variations in communism as practiced today, ranging from the bureaucratic collectivism of the Soviet Union to a supplementary market economy in Yugoslavia. All communist countries subscribe, or at least pay lip service, to Marxism-Leninism, which provides an ideological guideline for various institutional arrangements that distinguish modern communism from other economic systems.

ECONOMIC PLANNING

The role of economic planning in the communist countries is to allocate resources through the setting of economic targets by a central planning agency. The state, as represented by the planning agency, rather than the market mechanism, determines both output and its distribution. A rationale for central planning is the elimination of the wasteful use of resources that often occurs in a capitalist system. This waste is exemplified by planned product obsolescence, the duplication of goods and services, unnecessary product differentiation, and conspicuous consumption. Since the state has control over resource allocation in a communist system, presumably planning can make better use of resources.

The primacy of social over private preference is ensured by planning. The state, through the mechanism of the plan, is supposed to be in a better position to study social costs and benefits of resource allocation, which the market mechanism in a capitalist system cannot do. However, a weakness of planning is that prices, which are an integral part of the market mechanism under capitalism, have never been integrated into planning and do not perform a rational allocative function. This makes decision making under economic planning highly arbitrary.

STATE OWNERSHIP OF PROPERTY

Most property is owned by the state under communism. Included under property is land and capital. Labor is in a somewhat different position. It is supposed to be the only factor of production capable of creating value. As the means of production are owned by the state, owners and workers are supposed to be the same people, so there should be no antagonism between the employer (the state) and the employees (the workers).[17]

---

17. This would make it impossible for workers to strike against the state, because they would be striking against themselves. The strikes by labor in Poland have put an end to this fiction.

The purpose of state ownership of property is simple. Of all of the capitalist institutions, private property ownership was regarded as being the one institution most responsible for the evils of capitalism. It was responsible for the division of society into two opposing classes—the bourgeoisie and the proletariat. The bourgeoisie controlled land and capital and exploited the workers by appropriating their surplus value. Property inheritance contributed to a widening income division between rich and poor and provided the former with unearned income. Interest and dividend payments accrued only to those few persons who had a claim on the ownership of capital.

CONCENTRATION OF POWER IN THE COMMUNIST PARTY

The Communist Party is supposed to represent the interests of the working class. It is the sole proprietor of political power and is involved in all phases of economic activity. For example, the election of trade union officials is usually arranged by the Communist Party, and higher union positions are mostly occupied by party members. In all factories, collective farms, military units, or organizations, the Communist Party maintains local units or cells. Under the supervision of higher party organizations, they attempt to improve the discipline and political education of the workers and spur them on to the fulfillment of planned economic goals.

In spite of the democratic facade some communist countries maintain (such as the German Democratic Republic), the government is a complete dictatorship, with the leaders of the Communist Party in complete control. The Communist Party controls the armed forces and the electoral process. All candidates for office must have the approval of the party if they hope to be successful. The Communist Party maintains party officials and agencies to match the various officials and agencies of government. For all practical purposes party and state are one and the same.

COOPERATION

Individualism, which is one of the basic institutions of capitalism, is replaced by cooperation. Individualism is supposed to foster acquisitive ambitions, which are contrary to the ideal of the "communist person" free of such antisocial instincts. In a communist country, the interests of the individual are subordinate to those of society. Communism has the conception of regenerated people in a regenerated society, acting in tandem with their fellow human beings rather than in competition against them. This cooperation is supposed to lead to the development of the perfect society or, as the placards say in May Day parades in communist countries, "We are building for socialism." Competition is directed toward the attainment of political and social goals. In the Olympic games, the communist countries do quite well because success in sports is one way to tout the superiority of the communist system.

SUMMARY

Although the philosophical roots of socialism and communism go back thousands of years, modern socialism and communism are products of the Industrial Revolution. The Industrial Revolution, although it produced many benefits, also had its seamy side: squalor, poor working conditions, low wages, and income insecurity. Both socialism and communism promised a new economic and social order, but they differed in degree as to how the new order would be achieved. The socialists believed in the attainment of a new society through an evolutionary process; the communists believed in class revolution, with the ultimate dictatorship of the proletariat. Socialism in the latter part of the twentieth century has come to be equated with the democratic process as socialist parties have won major elections in France and Greece. Socialists advocate nationalization of certain key industries and increased welfare measures, but leave such capitalist institutions as private property and the price mechanism pretty much intact. Communism has come to mean bureaucratic collectivism, with the state, as represented by the Communist Party, making the decisions concerning production and distribution of goods and services.

REVIEW QUESTIONS

1. What role did market conditions have in creating the bad conditions for the working classes of Britain in the last century?
2. What was utopian socialism?
3. Marx is said to have had an interpretation of history and explanation of social existence in his "dialectical materialism." What is dialectical materialism?
4. In the Marxist framework, what is the difference between socialism and communism?
5. What was Marx's labor theory of value? How can this theory be criticized?

6. What was Marx's theory of surplus value? Is it a valid theory?
7. What were the causes and consequences, according to Marx, of the distribution of income under market capitalism? What was Marx's theory of income distribution?
8. What are some of the institutions of modern socialism?
9. What was the difference between socialism in France today and socialism in England in the eighteenth and nineteenth centuries?

RECOMMENDED READINGS

Balinsky, Alexander. *Marx's Economics: Origin and Development*. Lexington, Mass.: D.C. Heath & Co., 1970.

Dickens, Charles. *Hard Times*. New York: Signet Books, 1962. [A novel protesting working conditions and education in 19th-century England.]

Gray, Alexander. *The Development of Economic Doctrine: An Introductory Survey*. New York: John Wiley & Sons, Inc., 1931.

Hammond, John L., and Barbara Hammond. *The Rise of Modern Industry*. New York: Harper & Row, Publishers, Inc., 1969.

Harrington, Michael. *Socialism*. New York: Monthly Review Press, 1972.

Hill, Christopher. *Reformation to Industrial Revolution*. Baltimore: Penguin Books, 1969.

Marx, Karl. *Des Kapital*. New York: Modern Library, Inc., 1906.

Taylor, Philip A.M., ed. *The Industrial Revolution in Britain: Triumph or Disaster?* Rev. ed. Lexington, Mass.: D.C. Heath & Co., 1970.

Toynbee, Arnold. *The Industrial Revolution*. Boston: Beacon Press, 1956.

Tucker, Robert C. *The Marxian Revolutionary Idea*. New York: W.W. Norton & Co., Inc., 1969.

C H A P T E R   4

GOALS OF ECONOMIC SYSTEMS

The countries of the world can be divided into three categories: (1) the developed market economies, including the United States, Japan, Western Europe, Australia, and New Zealand; (2) the developed socialist economies of the Soviet Union and Eastern European countries; and (3) the developing and less developed countries, which are far more numerous and comprise most of the world's population. Included in the last category are countries that rely on the market mechanism to allocate resources and countries that rely on central economic planning to allocate resources. An example of a country that relies on the market mechanism as a resource allocator is Taiwan, while Cuba allocates resources through central economic planning. Most less developed and developing countries have some mixture of a market and a planned economy. China, a less developed communist country, is using both economic planning and the market mechanism to allocate resources.

Figure 4-1 presents a breakdown of world gross national product and population by three categories—developed noncommunist countries, less developed noncommunist countries, and communist countries—for 1984.[1] The United States accounted for 26.2 percent of world GNP and the developed noncommunist countries accounted for 59.4 percent. The less developed noncommunist countries accounted for 16.7 percent of world GNP, and the communist countries for 23.9 percent. The United States and the other developed noncommunist countries have by far the smallest

1. The countries are referred to as communist and their economies as centrally planned socialist.

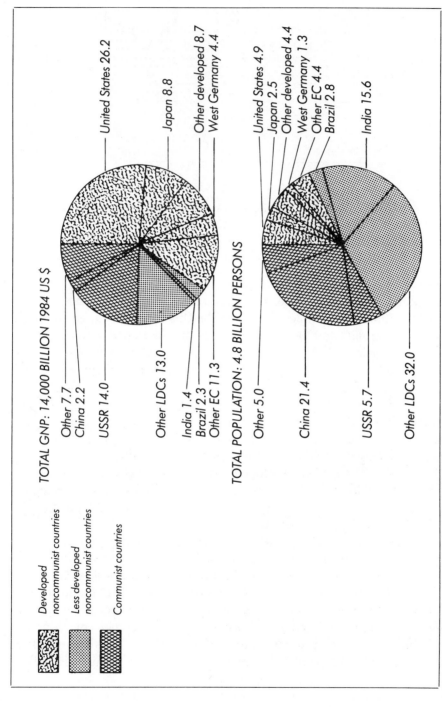

Developed
noncommunist countries

Less developed
noncommunist countries

Communist countries

TOTAL GNP: 14,000 BILLION 1984 US $

United States 26.2

Japan 8.8

Other developed 8.7
West Germany 4.4

Other 7.7
China 2.2

USSR 14.0

Other LDCs 13.0

India 1.4
Brazil 2.3
Other EC 11.3

TOTAL POPULATION: 4.8 BILLION PERSONS

United States 4.9
Japan 2.5
Other developed 4.4
West Germany 1.3
Other EC 4.4
Brazil 2.8

India 15.6

Other 5.0

China 21.4

USSR 5.7

Other LDCs 32.0

FIGURE 4-1 WORLD GROSS NATIONAL PRODUCT AND POPULATION, 1984

Source: Central Intelligence Agency, *Handbook of Economic Statistics, 1985* (Washington: USGPO, 1985), p. 4.

percentage of the world population, accounting for 17.5 percent of the total in 1984. The less developed noncommunist countries accounted for 50.4 percent, with India alone having a population almost equal to the combined totals for the developed noncommunist countries. The communist countries, including China, the largest less developed country in the world, have 32.1 percent of the world's population. When China is added to the population of the other less developed countries, the combined total is equal to 71.8 percent of the world's population.[2]

■ ECONOMIC GOALS ■

All economic systems have economic and social goals and can be evaluated on the basis of their goal attainment. These goals include maximum employment and economic security, price stability, and economic growth. To these three, a fourth goal, equitable distribution of income, may also be added. The results of production must be shared among members of society in a way that is considered just and equitable. However, no absolute standard of income distribution can satisfy everyone. In addition, noneconomic goals, such as the political freedom of the individual in society, are very important. Recent events in Poland and South Africa illustrate that, to many people, individual freedom is as important as full employment and a high rate of economic growth and should be factored into any comparison of economic systems. Social welfare goals, such as a clean environment, can also be included.

Conflicts often arise among accepted economic and social goals, so that choices and tradeoffs are necessary at the most general policy levels. For example, there can be a conflict between the reduction of income inequality and reduction of incentives to work. There can be a conflict between economic growth and protection of the environment. The opportunity cost of production can also be expressed as a trade-off—how much of one good or service must be given up to gain a certain quantity of another good or service. Resources are limited in any society and choices must be made as to what can be produced.

■ MAXIMUM EMPLOYMENT AND ■
ECONOMIC SECURITY

The Depression of the 1930s led most Western countries to assume national responsibility for the human tragedy and economic waste of involuntary

---

2. In chapter 16 a distinction will be made between less developed and developing countries. Brazil is a "developing" country, but China and India are "less developed" countries.

unemployment. Unemployment had previously been regarded as almost solely the responsibility of the individual, who was to look out for himself or herself within the market mechanism. Unemployment carried with it economic insecurity, for family savings vanished when it was prolonged. Poverty was also an end result of unemployment. Moreover, unemployment was the *bete noire* of capitalism, the situation that Marx predicted would bring down capitalism. Capitalist countries had a vested interest in the amelioration of unemployment, for it carried with it the potential for social unrest.

Economic security involves more than just having a job. The Western countries decided that they could not in good conscience permit their citizens to be inadequately nourished, clothed, or housed; their sick to be denied medical care; or their young to be deprived of schooling. Unemployment insurance and public assistance recognize this social obligation. This protection can assume many forms. Old-age pensions benefit those who have retired from work, many of whom have been unable to accumulate sufficient savings during their working lives to support them when they retire. Family allowances benefit families who have children and reduce the cost of their maintenance. Housing allowances and food programs generally benefit low-income families. Workers' compensation provides income for those workers injured on the job. National health insurance, which most countries have, protects workers against the cost of major illnesses.

One way to compare different economic systems is on the basis of how well they protect their citizens from economic insecurity. A supposed strength of socialist countries is that, through central planning, unemployment is eliminated. At first glance, the capitalist countries suffer by comparison. The unemployment rate in the United States in January 1986 was 6.7 percent; in the United Kingdom, 13.2 percent. Conversely, there is full employment in the Soviet Union and the other socialist countries. However, a *caveat* is in order. There are many ways to disguise unemployment. The military is one way to create employment for many youths. There is also underemployment of labor, with workers in jobs that require little or no skills.

■ PRICE STABILITY ■

Price stability is another economic goal. Inflation results in arbitrary and regressive changes in the distribution of wealth and income. It retards economic growth by diverting resources and energy from the production of goods and services to attempts by both businesses and individuals to lessen the impact of inflation on their own economic positions.

Attempts to protect individual positions from the effects of inflation can give rise to social, economic, and political strife just as quickly as mass unemployment can.[3] In fact, inflation is probably a greater evil today than mass unemployment. Countries such as Argentina, Israel, and Mexico have experienced price-level increases greater than 100 percent a year. These price increases are not only bad for domestic economics, but also contributed to balance of payments problems because the price increases are greater than those experienced by other countries.

In a modern economy, the government actively tries to regulate the money supply, either through its treasury or its central bank. One frequent cause of inflation, therefore, is government monetary policy itself. For one reason or another, the state may wish to increase the money supply. A government's own fiscal deficit is one common reason. Thus, a period of high government spending, like a war, is almost always a period of inflation. In themselves, of course, government deficits are not always inflationary. When resources are idle, a governmental deficit can stimulate an economy without fostering inflation. If taxes do not cover expenditures, the government may borrow all the funds it needs from the existing pool of savings in the domestic capital market. The borrowed funds are thereby used for government spending rather than private purposes. If the supply of savings is adequate to satisfy the borrowing needs of both government and private borrowers, inflation does not occur.[4] Deficits create inflation when central banks regularly create extra money to cover them.

SOCIAL AND POLITICAL CONSEQUENCES OF INFLATION

The impact of inflation is felt unevenly by different groups in an economy. One of the social consequences of inflation is the redistribution of income and wealth between economic groups. Debtors as a group fare well during inflation, because they are not only in a better position to repay their debts but also to pay them in money whose purchasing power is lower than

---

3. The rate of inflation in Argentina increased at an annual rate of 1,010 percent during the 1980s. In 1985, Argentina issued a new national currency called the *austral*. To maintain its value, the government vowed that it would no longer print money to cover expenses. A similar chain of events happened in Germany in 1923. Inflation reached astronomical proportions and contributed to social unrest. The German government issued a new currency with a new value.

4. Japan has a larger deficit in its budget than does the United States. However, the pool of saving is much larger in Japan than in the United States and interest rates are lower. Inflation has been lower in Japan than in the United States.

when they borrowed. Creditors, on the other hand, stand to lose since they receive less in real terms than if they had received the repayments during a period of low prices. Those on fixed incomes usually lose during a period of inflation in that their real income declines while the cost of living increases. Wealth in the form of savings accounts, bonds, and cash drops in real value when prices rise, but wealth held in the form of property or common stocks will generally increase when prices rise.

Inflation became a problem during the 1970s in the Western countries for several reasons. One reason was the burgeoning spending policies of Western governments.[5] Keynesian economics has a built-in inflationary bias. An emphasis on full-employment policies led Western governments to stimulate aggregate demand whenever there was an economic downturn. This led to expectations on the part of both business firms and unions that an increase in government spending would always bail out an economy from a recession. Keynesian demand-management that smoothes out the business cycle also eliminates many of the incentives for business and labor to be efficient. An economic policy that mitigates the effect of the business cycle can also reduce its benefits. Providing full employment without inflationary fiscal and monetary policies became a problem that governments found more difficult to resolve.

INFLATION AND BALANCE OF PAYMENTS PROBLEMS

Inflation has both an internal and external effect on a country's balance of payments. Internal inflation can cause domestic products to become more expensive than imported products. Exports decrease and imports increase, which creates a deficit in the balance of payments and a loss of foreign exchange reserves. If this continues to happen, it becomes less likely that a country can continue to convert its own currency into foreign currencies. Inflation also encourages capital outflows. The result is the imposition of austerity measures including anti-inflation monetary policy, policies to restrict imports, and price increases or currency devaluation. Devaluation is a downward adjustment of a currency's official par value or exchange rate relative to other currencies. Protection of domestic industries by tariffs and other restrictions on imports can also be used to correct balance of payments problems.

The problem of price stability is different in a centrally planned economy because pricing is not merely a question of economics but also of ideology and politics. Pricing policy is the responsibility of the government

---

5. Another was the rise in oil prices during 1973 and 1974.

through various administrative agencies. Prices are determined within the framework of important economic and social goals. For example, prices for food and other necessities are kept low for consumers through government subsidies. Wages are also regulated by the government, so on an *a priori* basis it would appear that inflation is impossible. In reality, centrally planned economies are not immune to inflation. For one thing, the prices of consumer goods are not indicative of their value. In Poland, for example, almost half of government budget expenditures are committed to subsidizing food prices at a low level. Inflation is suppressed because the price of food is set below its value. The suppressed inflation is demonstrated in the long lines of people waiting to purchase the limited supply.

■ ECONOMIC GROWTH ■

Economic growth can be defined most simply and directly as the expansion of a nation's capability to produce the goods and services its people want. It is the measure of the rate of increase in an economy's real output or income over time. Continued increases in the output of goods and services form the basis for an increase in the standard of living for families and individuals in a society. Moreover, it is not difficult to reconcile the goals of maximum employment and economic security with economic growth, for the latter is necessary to absorb new entrants into the labor force and to accommodate those workers who become unemployed because of changes in technology. Rising levels of output are also needed to improve the social well-being of society. If a nation does not have economic growth, it will not be able to obtain the resources to expand its schools, medical care, hospitals, and other things it needs. A dynamic, expanding economy eases the social and economic transitions required by a society that is experiencing technological change and demands social improvements.

The heart of all modern industrial societies, capitalist or socialist, is the ability to set aside a portion of total output for savings and capital formation—fundamental requisites for economic growth. Economic growth has become important to both the developed and developing countries as the source of individual motivation, the basis of political solidarity, and the grounds for the motivation of a society for a common purpose, namely, the promise of a better life for all of its citizens.

ECONOMIC GROWTH IN A MARKET ECONOMY

Recall the process by which economic growth is brought about in a market economy. The basic decisions regarding growth are made by individual households and businesses. Each of these individual units decides such things as how much to save, how much to invest, how much education to purchase, and how much research and exploration to undertake on the basis of a comparison of the benefits and costs of these activities. For example, in a market economy each business firm decides for itself the amount of research it will undertake. It does this on the basis of the marginal cost and benefits of the research. The main cost is the expense of the research. The main benefit is the greater profit from reduced costs for existing production or from new products that provide an advantage over competitors and enable profits to be larger.

Saving is a prime requisite for economic growth, for without it, there would be no capital formation. In a market economy, decisions to save are made by households out of their disposable incomes. There is a cost in saving: the sacrifice of the goods and services a household could buy and enjoy now if it did not save. The principal benefit to a household from saving is the goods and services it will be able to enjoy in the future as well as the earnings from savings. In a market economy, savings are transmitted through financial institutions and loaned to business firms. The firms use the borrowed funds to purchase the use of resources to create capital goods. The capital goods so created make possible thereafter a larger real output and real gross national product.

THE ROLE OF GOVERNMENT IN ECONOMIC GROWTH

In the market economies, government policies have come to play a strong role in the process of economic growth. Fiscal policy measures can be directed toward influencing the level of aggregate demand so as to bring it into line with an economy's changing productive capacity. Government expenditures, transfers, and taxes also can operate on the supply side and thus influence productive capacity. For example, government tax policy can be used to increase the rate of saving.[6] Government expenditures on improving the health, education, and training of the labor force also have an impact on economic growth, as do expenditures on research and development. In the less developed countries, governments also have to participate directly in the formation of capital because the rate of saving is low; the market system is ineffective and the entrepreneurial class, undeveloped.

---

6. The Individual Retirement Accounts (IRAs) are a good example. People are allowed to defer the income tax on income of up to $2,000 per year for individuals and $2,250 for married couples ($4,000 if both work) if they put their money in IRA accounts.

ECONOMIC GROWTH IN A CENTRALLY PLANNED ECONOMY

In a centrally planned economy, the state is the prime determinant of economic growth. The economic plan determines the rate of economic growth to be achieved, as well as the allocation of resources to the attainment of that rate. Saving is done by the state by controlling the amount of resources allocated to consumption. This is, in effect, forced saving in that consumers must do with less so that resources can be diverted into capital formation. The planned economy has an advantage over a market economy when it comes to the goal of a high growth rate: The state can allocate resources into those areas that contribute to high growth rates. Economic growth is never allowed to be hampered by a lack of money. If there are physical resources available and if the production has priority under the economic plan, the means of financing will be available. Figure 4-2 presents trends in real economic growth in the same three categories presented earlier in this chapter.

■ INCOME DISTRIBUTION ■

It was mentioned in chapter 2 that most governments have become involved in altering the distribution of market resources both directly and indirectly. This represents a departure from the free market idea that an individual's income is determined by the impersonal forces of supply and demand operating in the marketplace. However, this idea had to be modified because it was easy to see that large incomes accrued to some persons not on the basis of their contribution to total output, but through inherited wealth or other accidents of birth or through the exercise of special privileges. Moreover, capricious economic and social changes often worked hardships even on the most productive persons. The result of free market capitalism was extreme inequality in the distribution of income and wealth. This inequality has been reduced over time by government use of progressive income and inheritance taxes and transfer payments to redistribute income.

EQUITY IN INCOME DISTRIBUTION

The issue of equity concerns the disparities in income distribution among people and the role of the government in reducing these disparities or at least containing their undue influence. However, we cannot insist that

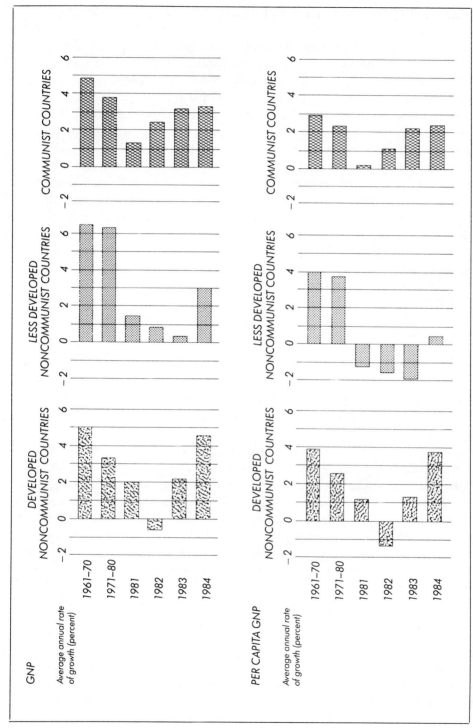

FIGURE 4-2 REAL GROSS NATIONAL PRODUCT TRENDS

Source: Central Intelligence Agency, *Handbook of Economic Statistics, 1985* (Washington: USGPO, 1985), p. 5.

perfect equality in the distribution of income and wealth would be necessary for the existence of an economic optimum. There is no objective way to compare satisfaction or utility between persons.[7] There is also no way to measure aggregate satisfaction for the whole population of an economy because of differences among individuals in their capacities to experience satisfaction. The assumption that all individuals have equal capacities for satisfaction cannot be proven scientifically. Thus, it is necessary to know more about the psychological basis of human wants before a given condition can be considered an economic optimum. To what extent is it possible for income to measure the magnitude of human needs and wants?

INCOME DISTRIBUTION UNDER SOCIALISM

Income distribution under socialism refers to the allocation of national income by distributive shares, primarily in the form of wages paid to workers. Interest does figure in the national income to some extent, as a part of the income received by individual producers may be considered a return on the relatively small amounts of capital they own. Interest is also used as a device to encourage personal savings, which is regarded as necessary to put a brake on excess consumer demand, and there are interest-rate differentials in favor of long-term deposits. Profits, which are distributed in the form of dividends or retained by corporate shareholders in a capitalist system, occupy a different role under socialism. They are used as a criterion of enterprise performance and, up to a point, of the efficiency of production.

Income distribution is determined by the state within the framework of the economic plan. The total amount of wages to be paid depends on the division of the national income between accumulation and consumption, and further, the division of consumption between the social consumption fund and the wage fund. The total wage fund is partitioned into wage funds for all economic fields. In its economic planning the state is able to determine the total wages for the economy by multiplying the planned number of workers by the wage rates it has set. Wages are changed as seems necessary to achieve government policy and particular production ends. For example, in order to attract more workers to a given industry, the wages it pays may be raised while other wages remain constant or are allowed to decline. Direct pressure from workers would in general have little or no effect on wage determination.

7. The theory of utility analysis assumes that a person's additional satisfaction or marginal utility grows less as he or she consumes more and more units of the same product. It also holds that the marginal utility for a rich person is less than that for a poor person. For example, a rich person would assign less additional satisfaction to consuming another steak than would a poor person. However, it is not valid to compare the utility that two different individuals receive from the same good or service.

■ FREEDOM AND THE INDIVIDUAL ■

In Western society over the last 200 years, the individual has assumed precedence over the state. Before this time, the king, lord, or any ruler had precedence over the individual. The individual ethic is also the ethic of personal freedom. Individual freedom means minimizing the obligations society imposes on the individual. Beginning with the Industrial Revolution, the private individual's economic interest in accumulation was pursued in the market, and the enhancement of self-interest became the free choice of a personal life-style. This was linked to the concept of freedom—to be free from the ties of community or state; to be responsible for oneself; and to handle one's life in accordance with one's ambition and personal merit.

RATIONALE FOR PERSONAL FREEDOM

The idea of personal liberty as an individual right is a relatively new phenomenon. It was not a part of the legal conceptions of the Romans and Greeks; this seems also to hold true of the Jewish, Chinese, and other ancient civilizations. The dominance of the ideal of personal liberty has been the exception rather than the rule, even in the West. The desire not to be impinged upon, to be left to oneself, has become a mark of high civilization in Western society. The freedom to live and to do as one prefers is supported by a number of economic and philosophical justifications. For Adam Smith, an economic system in which each individual pursued his or her own self-interest was the basis for freedom, self-satisfaction, and mutual advantage. When rationally pursued through the division of labor, it became the basis for the accumulation of wealth. Smith insisted that social well-being is the outcome of individual activity and that individual activity becomes greater the less it is hampered by government interference.

The philosopher John Locke held that individuals have a ready-made body of rights that are the responsibility of government to preserve. The primary assumption of Locke's argument is that freedom and government are opposites. Locke assumes an individual who, outside of society, has reason; Locke does not suppose that the state can do more than protect the individual in the consequences of its exercise. Central to Locke's philosophy was the doctrine of individual property rights. Property is the extension of labor and provides protection against exploitation by others. He was writing a defense of the right of persons who own property to enjoy its fruits without constant interference from the arbitrary actions of government. Government was the enemy; liberty of the individual and government were opposites. This, above all, is the postulate from which liberty begins.

CAPITALISM AND DEMOCRACY

Democracy is a socio-political system in which legitimacy lies in the consent of the governed, where the political arena is available to various contending groups, and where fundamental liberties are safeguarded. The beginnings of the idea of democracy are associated with the city-states of ancient Greece. Greek democracy was direct in that all of the male citizens of a city-state formed the legislature and had the right to vote.[8] After the decline of the Greek city-state, democracy went into a period of eclipse for about 2,000 years, only to be revived by the American and French revolutions. Both gave rise to ideas and institutions that did much to determine the distinctive characteristics of modern democratic governments. The basic organ of government is the representative legislature or parliament. Their underlying ethical basis is the conception that all persons are created equal and that governments exist for the purpose of protecting people in the exercise of certain basic rights.

Although capitalism and modern democracy historically have arisen together and have been commonly justified by philosophical liberatism, there is nothing that makes it theoretically or practically necessary for the two to be yoked.[9] Actually, the government of a capitalist system does not have to be democratic in the strict sense of the term, which would presumably involve direct and equal participation in the government by all citizens. In a large and heavily populated capitalistic system, it would be impossible for all citizens to participate directly in the government. In modern society, the political system has become increasingly autonomous, and fiscal management has become increasingly independent of capitalism. However, the government of a capitalist system could scarcely be a dictatorship, for it is difficult to image a dictatorial government that would not restrict economic life to an extent that would be inconsistent with the operation of capitalist institutions.

INDIVIDUAL FREEDOM IN THE MODERN DEMOCRACIES

The United States, Canada, and the countries of Western Europe are all democracies. Japan, Australia, and New Zealand can be added to them.

---

8. Women were disenfranchised and there was a large class of slaves who enjoyed no rights at all. Ancient Greek democracy was not only compatible with slavery, it presupposed slavery, which alone permitted the necessary leisure for the citizens to devote themselves to public affairs. It recognized the equality of all male citizens, but failed to develop a general conception of the equality of all mankind.

9. France and Greece are democracies with socialist governments, with a mixture of public and private enterprise.

These countries have free elections and have two or more political parties that compete for elective offices. They guarantee certain rights to their citizens. One is the freedom to live as one prefers. The sense of privacy is regarded as sacred, for it guards against the tyranny of the community. Freedom of speech is a second right. It means that the state, or for that matter individuals, cannot restrict people either in the views they hold or the views they express. A third right is freedom of the press, which is regarded as one of the great bulwarks of liberty.[10] This freedom preserves the people's right to know and to be informed. Freedom of religion is a fourth right. In most modern democracies there is a separation of church and state. Some of the democratic countries have one religion;[11] others, such as the United States, have a variety of religions, all of which are tolerated. There is also the right not to participate.

INDIVIDUAL FREEDOM UNDER SOCIALISM

The relationship between the individual and the state is different in the socialist countries. To put it simply, the individual is subservient to the interests of the state. Power is concentrated in the communist party, which is supposed to represent the working classes. The system of government is based on monoparty rule. No opposition parties are allowed unless the party permits some form of opposition. Elections are held to ratify the choices that the party makes. It provides the continuity of economic policy and it makes overall value judgments. For example, any outside influence, particularly something like rock music, is considered decadent.

The fundamental freedoms that individuals take for granted in democracies either do not exist or exist in varying degrees in the socialist countries. Freedom of the press does not exist, for the press is the mouthpiece of the state. The press may criticize or report negatively on some result of party action, but it rarely criticizes the party itself. There is no freedom of speech, at least in public.[12] Freedom of religion varies from country to country. In the Soviet Union, religion is at best barely tolerated. Poland, which is a Catholic country, allows freedom of religion, but the state is not happy about it. Hungary and East Germany tolerate some religious free-

10. The Virginia Bill of Rights states that the freedom of the press is one of the great bulwarks of liberty and can never be restrained but by despotic governments.

11. Sweden is an example; 99 percent of its citizens are Lutheran. Italy, on the other hand, is a Catholic country.

12. Private speech is another matter. The author heard much criticism of the Polish economy, its leaders, and the Russians from a number of Poles when he was in Poland.

dom. The freedom to live as one prefers is a rather limited option in the socialist countries. The state, as represented by the party, attempts to impose a common direction, from economics to culture, on everyone.

■ SOCIAL GOALS ■

There are certain social costs that result from the operation of any industry or business. The operation of a business may be injurious to the health of its workers. It may discharge wastes that pollute streams and kill fish, or it may emit smoke, soot, and grime that will be costly to its neighbors in a number of ways. Consumption of certain products can also increase social costs. Excessive alcohol consumption results in job absenteeism and a loss of productivity that is a disadvantage to society. If production decisions are based solely on the relationship of prices and costs in the market, many goods may be produced and sold that would not be produced if their prices included the full social costs of production.[13] The production of alcohol and cigarettes is an example.

THE ENVIRONMENT

The quality of the environment has emerged as one of the more important economic and social issues of this century. It is common to all advanced industrial countries, regardless of their ideologies. In the Soviet Union, inadequately treated industrial effluents have polluted rivers and lakes. In Poland, the Vistula river is polluted, and Warsaw was recently without water for several days because a chemical plant dumped mercury into it. Unlike the famous waltz of Johann Strauss, "The Blue Danube," the Danube is not blue, but a dirty brown at Budapest and Vienna. Of all the major industrial countries, given its small land area and crowded cities, Japan has had the worst pollution problem. In West Germany, the famous Black Forest is in danger of being destroyed by cars' exhaust fumes.

The desire for a clean environment represents an extension of human wants; it increases as a country's standard of living increases. Poor countries cannot afford the luxury of being concerned about clean air, clean water, and the preservation of the snail darter. Both money and real incomes are low, and people are only interested in physiological survival.

---

13. The costs to society are not created by business alone. Increasing urbanization creates social costs. The desire for higher living standards creates social costs.

Food and shelter constitute their main demands. As countries become more wealthy, the wants of their citizens are upgraded toward more and better goods and services. Physiological survival is no longer a categorical imperative. Meanwhile, pollution increases along with a rising real standard of living. It represents a blockage that causes various needs to remain unsatisfied, such as the need for clean recreational facilities. People cannot achieve a higher real standard of living unless something can be done about the condition of the environment.

CONSUMER WELFARE

In a capitalist economy, consumer sovereignty is an important institution because consumption is the basic rationale for economic activity. As Adam Smith said, "Consumption is the sole end and purpose of all production; and the interest of the producer ought to be attended to only as far as it is necessary for promoting that of the consumer."[14] Production is the means, consumption is the end. Those producers that effectively satisfy the wants of the consumers are rewarded by large monetary returns, which in turn enable them to purchase the goods and services they require in their operations. On the other hand, those producers that do not respond to the wants of consumers will not remain in business for very long. Supply and demand will shift in response to the way in which consumers spend their money.

Consumer welfare under capitalism is subject to several criticisms. First, producers take the initiative to increase the volume and variety of consumer goods.[15] Are consumers better off with a proliferation of breakfast cereals or is it a waste of scarce resources?[16] Second, producers use sophisticated marketing methods, including advertising, that influence the consumer's choice of goods. Marketing people argue that the purpose of advertising is to provide product information for the consumer. But it also can be argued that the purpose of advertising is to entice consumers into buying products that, for the most part, they do not need or that could even prove injurious to their health.[17] Third, the market and price me-

---

14. Adam Smith, *The Wealth of Nations* (Indianapolis: Liberty Classics, 1981), p. 660.

15. Henry Ford revolutionized the automobile industry with the production of the Model T. It came in one style and one color (black), and it was cheap and durable. General Motors came along with planned obsolescence, with new models and style changes every year. The purpose was to make the consumer unhappy with his or her car, even though it was perfectly good.

16. Do sugar-laden cereals and other breakfast foods with exotic names really contribute to consumer welfare?

17. A very good example is cigarette smoking. Many young people begin smoking cigarettes because advertising makes it appear sophisticated and grown up.

chanisms never ask consumers to specify for which commodities and services they would like the scarce resources of society used. Consumers are not totally passive, however; they can exercise a considerable degree of selectivity despite the persistent advertising aimed at them. So there is some freedom of choice though it is limited to the range of available alternatives.

In a planned socialist economy, consumer sovereignty hardly exists. The state reduces choice to a minimum by presenting only a narrow and biased range of alternatives. There is one major advantage to state control over consumption: Resources are not wasted on the production of a wide variety of frivolous goods that are not necessary to basic survival. However, there are also disadvantages. First, in the absence of the price mechanism to allocate resources in a market economy, the production of goods in a socialist economy is often arbitrary. The result is that often some goods are overproduced, and others, underproduced. Queueing up to purchase consumer goods is a common phenomenon in many socialist countries. Second, in the absence of competition between producers, there is no incentive to be efficient. Many consumer goods are poorly made and consumer welfare is not maximized.

EDUCATION AND HEALTH

Improved education and health are important goals in any society because they both have an impact on the development of human capital. Human capital is the productive power of individuals and is developed through expenditures for education and health care. Society as a whole depends on educated people to carry on the research and development leading to new products and new processes that raise the nation's standard of living. How productive people are and how much they earn affects a society's rate of economic growth and its distribution of income. Health, both physical and mental, is also important in that it affects the quantity and quality of the labor force in a society. Poor health standards will lower labor's capacity to produce; excellent health standards will increase labor productivity.

Table 4-1 presents a comparison of education indicators for three categories of selected countries: less developed countries, developed countries, and communist countries. Many countries, such as Brazil and Mexico, are considered developing countries and are not included in the table. Sudan and Chad are among the poorest countries in the world. The level of human capital is low because few persons have an education above primary school level. China, which is also a less developed country, but a communist one, would also have low human capital. The more developed capitalistic and communist countries have higher quality human capital because a large percentage of their population has had a secondary school

TABLE 4-1   A COMPARISON OF EDUCATION INDICATORS FOR SELECTED COUNTRIES
(number of students enrolled as a percentage of age group)

	Primary School	Secondary School	Higher Education
Less developed			
Haiti	69%	13%	1%
India	79	30	9
Sudan	52	18	2
Pakistan	44	14	2
Chad	34	1	1
Developed			
Italy	100%	74%	25%
United Kingdom	100	83	19
Japan	100	92	30
France	100	87	27
West Germany	100	50	30
United States	100	97	58
Communist			
Hungary	100%	73%	14%
Poland	100	75	18
East Germany	94	88	30
Cuba	100	72	19
China	100	35	1
Soviet Union	100	97	21

Source: The World Bank, *World Development Report 1985,* pp. 222-223.

or higher education. The table, however, does not compare the quality of education, which varies from country to country. Japan is regarded by many experts as having the best educational system in the world.

Table 4-2 presents a comparison of health-related indicators for the same selected less developed countries, developed countries, and communist countries. The number of physicians and nurses relative to the size of the population is very low in the less developed countries, and the daily calorie intake is below the normal requirement. In the developed market countries and communist countries, the health-related indicators indicate that both types of countries are adequately served by physicians and nurses, and the daily calorie supply per capita is above the normal daily requirement. The table does not indicate the quality of medical service or the number of hospitals available for the population. In the great majority

TABLE 4-2   A COMPARISON OF HEALTH-RELATED INDICATORS FOR SELECTED COUNTRIES

| | Population per | | Daily per Capita Calorie Intake | |
	Physician	Nurse	Total	Percent. of Daily Requiremt.
Less developed				
Haiti	8,200	2,490	1,903	84%
India	3,690	5,460	2,047	93
Sudan	8,930	1,430	2,250	96
Pakistan	3,480	5,820	2,277	99
Chad	47,640	3,860	1,620	68
Developed				
Italy	340	—	3,520	140%
United Kingdom	650	140	3,232	128
Japan	780	240	2,891	124
France	580	120	3,572	142
West Germany	450	170	3,382	127
United States	520	140	3,616	137
Communist				
Hungary	400	150	3,520	134%
Poland	570	240	3,288	126
East Germany	520	180	3,787	145
Cuba	720	370	2,997	130
China	1,740	1,710	2,562	110
Soviet Union	270	100	3,400	132

Source: The World Bank, *World Development Report 1985*, pp. 220-221.

of countries, medical care is either provided free as a part of a national health plan, or there is some form of shared payment by the government and the patient.

SUMMARY

Both capitalist and socialist economies have specific economic and social goals and can be judged on the basis of how those goals are fulfilled. There are three major economic goals: full employment, price stability, and economic growth. These goals cannot be precisely defined and the attainment of one may not necessarily lead to the attainment of the others. Another goal is an equitable distribution of income. This goal, too, does not lend itself to a precise definition. What is the right degree of income inequality? Considerable government intervention is an indispensable requisite for the attainment of all of these goals. In the capitalist countries, the government coordinates the direction of economic policy and participates in the economy through expenditures that affect the allocation of resources and through the use of taxation and transfer payments to redistribute income. In socialist countries, the state is the employer and distributor of income.

There are also other goals that should be considered in comparing economic systems. One is individual rights and freedom. In some countries, democracy has become the prevailing socio-political system. There are certain guarantees of individual rights that democracy carries with it, such as freedom of speech, freedom of religion, and freedom of the press. The relationship between the individual and the state is different in socialist countries—the rights of the individual are subservient to the interests of the state.

Finally, there are social goals that can be used in comparing economic systems. These goals center around what can be referred to as the quality of life. A very important problem that confronts all industrial societies today, regardless of their ideology, is pollution of the environment.

REVIEW QUESTIONS

1. Democracy could exist only in a capitalistic country. Do you agree?
2. Capitalist and socialist countries have similar economic goals. Discuss.
3. Centrally planned economies generally do a better job of creating full employment than market economies. Discuss.
4. Do socialist countries have more equality in the distribution of income than capitalist countries?
5. The concept of individual freedom is relatively new. Discuss.
6. What is the philosophical justification for freedom of the individual in a capitalist society?
7. What is the relationship of the individual to the state in a socialist economy?
8. Compare the role of the consumer in market and centrally planned economies.

9. How is income distributed in a centrally planned economy?
10. Why are environmental problems of importance in comparing capitalism and socialism?

■ ——————————— R E C O M M E N D E D   R E A D I N G S ——————————— ■

Barro, Robert J. *Macroeconomics*. New York: John Wiley & Sons Inc., 1984.

Bell, Daniel. *The Cultural Contradictions of Capitalism*. New York: Basic Books Inc., Publishers, 1976.

Brittain, John H. *The Inheritance of Economic Status*. Washington: Brookings Institution, 1978.

Locke, John. *The Second Treatise of Government*. Edited by C.B. Macphearson. Indianapolis: Hackett Publishing Co. Inc., 1980.

North, Douglas C. *Structure and Change in Economic History*. New York: W.W. Norton & Co. Inc., 1982.

Nozeck, Robert. *Anarchy, State, and Utopia*. New York: Basic Books Inc., Publishers, 1974.

Okun, Arthur. *Equality and Efficiency: The Big Tradeoff*. Washington: Brookings Institution, 1976.

Olson, Mancur. *The Rise and Decline of Nations*. New Haven, Conn.: Yale University Press, 1982.

Wiles, Peter J.D. *Distribution of Income: East and West*. Amsterdam: North-Holland Publishing Co., 1974.

Williamson, Jeffrey, and Peter Lindert. *American Inequality*. New York: Academic Press Inc., 1981.

P A R T 2

THE MODIFIED MARKET ECONOMY OF THE UNITED STATES

C H A P T E R   5

THE ECONOMIC SYSTEM
OF THE UNITED STATES

The American economic system is dominated by three major institutions—
business, labor, and government. Although the market mechanism allocates resources, it cannot be said that the United States conforms to the
model of a pure market economy. Instead, the rules of the game have been
modified over time as various groups or individuals sought protection
against the results of a free market economy. Many changes have occurred
over time to supplement and modify the effects of the market mechanism
so that the consequences are other than they would be with a market system. Thus, it is more appropriate to call the United States a modified market economy in which the role of government is of considerable importance.

One part of the institutional arrangement is the large corporation. The
original impetus for the emergence of the large corporation was partly
technological—economies of scale become available with bigness—and
partly monopolistic—bigness provides control over markets and over
rivals. These large corporations helped to modify the market system.
Moreover, large corporations have also in part been responsible for the development of the two other institutions that have also served to modify the
market mechanism—labor unions and big government. Both of these have
become major features of the U.S. economic system and in other countries
still relying heavily on the market system. Both have become major means

for counteracting some of the undesirable results of large business firms and for mitigating some of the undesirable effects of a pure market system.

Of the two, government is by far the more important institution. It has intervened in the U.S. economy in several ways: to redistribute income between groups through taxes and transfer payments, to manage the economy through fiscal and monetary policy, and to protect various special interest groups against such things as discrimination and foreign competition.

■ LARGE CORPORATIONS ■

The concentration of industry in the hands of a few firms is a fact of life in the United States and other major industrial countries, regardless of their political ideology. The trend toward industrial concentration in the United States began in the last century, when many industries came to be dominated by a few relatively large firms or even by only one firm. In the 1920s largeness was stimulated by changes occurring in the economy as a whole, in particular the mass production of the automobile and the development of the electrical appliance and broadcasting industries. General Motors became the leader in the automobile industry through a series of mergers with other auto firms. Size became an advantage when using modern marketing and production methods.

World War II contributed to the trend toward largeness. The industrial might of the United States was probably the decisive factor in contributing to the Allied victory over the Axis powers. Large corporations produced the airplanes and tanks used by the United States and its allies in the war.[1] During the 1960s and 1970s the trend toward largeness was facilitated by the development of a new type of merger called the *conglomerate* merger, a union of disparate companies.

CONCENTRATION BY FIRM SIZE

Table 5-1 presents payrolls, value added by manufacturing, and capital expenditures for a distribution of firms based on number of employees. The data are for 1982. Firms employing 1,000 or more workers accounted for 0.6 percent of all firms, but accounted for 25.2 percent of total employment in manufacturing, 33.1 percent of total value of payrolls, 31.5 per-

---

1. The author saw some old destroyed Sherman tanks rusting on a farm in Poland. They represented part of the thousands of tanks sent by the United States to the Soviet Union in World War II.

TABLE 5-1 DISTRIBUTION OF INDUSTRY IN THE UNITED STATES BY EMPLOYMENT SIZE FOR 1982
(establishments and employees in thousands; money in millions of dollars)

	Total	Under 20	Employment Size 20–99	100–249	250–999	1,000 and over
Establishments	348	230	84	21	1	2
Employees	17,818	1,405	3,662	3,287	4,977	4,486
Payroll	341,406	20,404	59,103	55,708	93,125	113,068
Value added by manufacturing	824,117	45,997	135,932	134,379	247,729	260,081
New capital expenditures	74,562	3,639	9,469	12,323	23,331	25,800

Source: U.S. Department of Commerce, Bureau of the Census, *1982 Census of Manufactures: General Summary* (Washington: USGPO, 1986), pp. 1-3.

cent of value added by manufacturing, and 34.6 percent of new capital expenditures. However, these percentages show a decline when compared to statistics for 1977. The respective percentages for 1977 were as follows: employment in manufacturing, 28 percent; total value of payrolls, 35.4 percent; value added by manufacturing, 34.2 percent; new capital expenditures, 35.8 percent. However, it can be said that approximately 2 percent of all industrial firms in the United States produced about half of the value added by manufacturing and of all new capital expenditures for 1982.

THE EXTENT OF CONCENTRATION BY INDUSTRY

The extent of concentration in the United States varies considerably by industry. In some industries, one large firm is clearly dominant, in that it contributes 50 percent or more of total output. General Motors, with more than 60 percent of U.S. domestic output of automobiles, is an example. In other industries, a few firms may account for the bulk of sales, with no one firm clearly dominant over the others. The tobacco industry, with Reynolds Industries, Philip Morris, and American Brands, is a case in point. There are some industries that have little or no concentration, and thus approximate the market situation called *pure competition* in which no seller produces more than a negligible share of market supply. The shoe and clothing industries afford examples. The degree of concentration by industry is shown in Table 5-2, which compares the output of the four largest firms in a number of high- and low-concentration industries. However, a high degree of concentration alone does not necessarily mean there is a monopoly or a general lack of competition.

ISSUES INVOLVING INDUSTRIAL CONCENTRATION

In a number of industries, a certain amount of industrial concentration is apparently inevitable. Some types of business organizations lend themselves to large-scale production. For example, there are industries in which the product itself is highly complex and can be constructed only by a large and diversified organization. Automobiles and computers are a case in point. There are industries in which the product is large in size, requiring complex equipment for construction and large capital investments—for example, shipbuilding and locomotives. Then there are industries that require a large capital investment, particularly in plant and equipment. For example, there are many good reasons for manufacturing iron and steel on a large scale. One of the most important is the tremendous outlay neces-

**TABLE 5-2   THE EXTENT OF CONCENTRATION
BY INDUSTRY IN THE UNITED STATES**
(output measured by value of shipment)

High Concentration	Shipment Percentage of Four Largest Firms
Motor vehicles	93
Cereal breakfast foods	87
Cigarettes	82
Sewing machines	80
Metal cans	79
Tires	72
Soap	70
Aircraft	75
Low Concentration	
Oil refining	30
Meat packing	24
Machine tools	21
Book publishers	18
Concrete products	10
Women's dresses	9
Fur goods	8

Source: U.S. Bureau of the Census, *1982 Census of Manufactures: Concentration Ratios in Manufacturing* (Washington: USGPO, 1986), pp. 12-65.

sary to secure blast furnaces, steel furnaces, and other equipment. Finally, there are industries in which a natural resource is required and in which the natural resource is available only in limited amounts and in specific geographic locations. Examples of this are the lead and petroleum industries.

Moreover, industrial concentration may well be an inevitable result of advancing technology in all industrial countries, regardless of their ideologies. Data show that for the same industries, concentration ratios are generally higher in other Western countries than in the United States; foreign industries in which concentration is high are generally the same as those in which concentration is high in the United States; and industries that are not highly concentrated in foreign countries are generally not concentrated industries in the United States also. In West Germany, three chemical companies produce 80 percent of all chemical products.[2] The French

2. Statistiches Bundesant, *Statistisches Jahrbuch für die Bundesrepublik Deutschland, 1980* (Wiesbaden: Kohlhammer, 1984), p. 235.

aluminum firm Pechiney Ugine Kuhlmann produces 90 percent of French aluminum products, specialty steels, and nonferrous metals such as titanium and zirconium.[3] In Japan two automobile companies account for 60 percent of all Japanese automobile production.[4] These data strongly suggest that fundamental technological and economic factors determine to some extent the degree of concentration of industries in all market economies.

The extent of industrial concentration is even higher in the advanced socialist economies than in the United States.[5] To some extent the centralized planning characteristic of socialist economies necessitates the concentration of output into large production units. The organization of industry has to be considered a basic part of the economic and political organization of the state. There is a constant effort to combine industrial and agricultural enterprises into larger units to increase output to supply the population and to export to world markets. In Poland the tractor combine URSUS produces 100 percent of all tractors made in the country, and in Hungary the combine RABA produces all the heavy-duty trucks, tractors, and railroad equipment made there.[6] The high degree of concentration in centrally planned economies may be used as evidence that large-scale operations and the concentration that accompany them do yield economies of scale.

Industrial concentration also can transcend national boundaries. Large American firms acquire foreign firms and large foreign firms acquire American firms. As competition becomes global, additional economies of scale may be effected. For example, it is conceivable that, by the end of the century, only a handful of automobile companies will be left in the world. Perhaps this is the final extension of an evolutionary process that began with the creation of the automobile industry when there were literally hundreds of firms turning out autos for the populace who could afford them. This world trend may be irreversible, regardless of the product; and laws, antitrust and otherwise, will have to be restructured within a global frame of reference.

ADVANTAGES OF CONCENTRATION There are certain advantages to large-scale production. An expansion in output often permits a firm great-

---

3. Ministerie de l'Economie et des Finances, *Statistiques Francais 1984* (Paris, 1984). The greatest degree of industrial concentration in all Western countries may be in France. This also holds true in banking.

4. *Japan Statistical Yearbook, 1984* (Tokyo: Office of the Prime Minister, 1984), p. 33.

5. Frederick L. Pryor, "An International Comparison of Concentration Ratios," *Review of Economics and Statistics* (May 1972), pp. 130-140.

6. Martin Schnitzer, *U.S. Business Involvement in Eastern Europe* (New York: Praeger Publishers, 1980), pp. 81 and 103.

er specialization in the use of both labor and capital equipment. Overhead costs can be spread over a larger output, which results in a lower unit cost. Economies can result from new combinations of the factors of production (land, labor, and capital), which result in lower minimum costs. Economies of scale result when more of all factors are used, and the total output increases at a rate greater than the increase in the production factors. Highly specialized labor and capital equipment frequently can be added to a production unit only in large, indivisible amounts and cannot be used profitably in small-scale operations. In fact, smaller business units may well result in higher unit costs in many industries, and therefore the best answer to the problems of concentration may not be breaking up large firms. Market power can be based on underlying economies of scale and technological or managerial leadership. In some cases, large firms are the price of efficiency and innovation.[7]

PROBLEMS OF CONCENTRATION However, industrial concentration also carries with it certain problems. In a competitive market economy, the interests of producers and consumers coincide because the way to larger profits for producers is through greater efficiency, price reductions, and increased sales volume, all of which naturally benefit consumers, too. In a monopolistic market, or one approaching this state, profits may be maximized at the expense of the consumer by selling a smaller quantity of goods at a higher price than under competitive conditions. The existence of monopoly power also means that the spur to efficiency and technical progress that competition provides is often lacking.

There is evidence that small- or medium-sized firms are often more innovative than large firms. A case in point is Apple Computer Company, which was created in the 1970s by two men in their twenties, who started their operations in a garage. The computer-data processing industry was and is still dominated by IBM. In 1980, when Apple was just getting started, IBM's total sales amounted to $25.9 billion, in comparison to total industry sales of $52 billion. But IBM had grown somewhat complacent during the 1970s, and Apple came out with a line of personal computers that were inexpensive and easy to use. Apple became the leading exponent of technology for the masses. In 1985, Apple's total sales amounted to around $2 billion.

Small firms are often put in the position of having to innovate in order to survive. From this comes a willingness to take risks. Big firms, like big

---

7. In a case involving Alcoa, the U.S. Supreme Court was unwilling to split up the company for fear of losing substantial economies of scale in production and in research and development.

governments, can be so encrusted with bureaucracy that they have more desire to maintain the status quo than to be experimental. Besides, experimentation usually requires approval from someone in the hierarchy of the organization. This can be disturbing, for often no one in the hierarchy wants to be held responsible in the event of failure. Often it is much easier to go out and absorb a smaller company that has already made the innovation and has survived the risk of failure.

Finally, large firms in certain situations can exercise discretionary power over prices and entry into markets. It is the power to engage in restrictive practices that provides one of the bases of American antitrust policy.

INDUSTRIAL CONCENTRATION AND COMPETITION

Although few American industries operate under the textbook definition of perfect competition, we should not jump to the conclusion that there is no competition at all. Competition can exist in a number of forms. Firms in an industry can compete against each other on the basis of quality and product differentiation. Coca-Cola and PepsiCo wage war with each other for the hearts and minds of the soft drinkers of the world.[8] The war is fought through advertising that creates an image for Coca-Cola, Pepsi-Cola and their offspring. Firms in any given industry also compete on the basis of technology. That is, they try to develop improved machines and production methods that will lower their production costs and render obsolete the machines and methods of competitors. Moreover, firms in an industry compete for customers with firms in industries that produce other products intended for the satisfaction of the same general consumer want. They also can compete with firms in completely unrelated industries for the limited incomes of consumers in general.

GLOBAL COMPETITION   Most major corporations do not confine themselves to domestic operations, but participate widely in business outside of the continental limits of their respective countries through the ownership of foreign subsidiaries. These companies are called *multinational* corporations and are limited to no one country or ideology. They transcend natural boundaries and produce more and more of the world's GNP. Some

---

8. The decision of Coca-Cola to introduce a new Coke is regarded as a major marketing fiasco. Whether it is or not remains to be seen. Coca-Cola and PepsiCo dominate the U.S. soft drink market. An increase in one percentage point in market shares represents an increase of $100 million in soft drink sales. Coca-Cola and PepsiCo compete through advertising and control over counter space in supermarkets.

of the current multinational corporations have sales volumes larger than the GNPs of many middle-sized European countries, and considerably larger than the GNPs of typical less developed African and Asian countries. Competition between multinational corporations for international markets is fierce. One battleground is the American automobile market, where Japanese automobile companies have increased their share of the market at the expense of the U.S. auto companies.[9]

■ LABOR UNIONS ■

The workers in many capitalistic countries, the United States in particular, have not been content to rely entirely on government intervention to improve their economic status. Instead, they have banded together into labor unions to bargain collectively with employers. The individual worker is usually at a disadvantage in bargaining with an employer—lack of financial resources requires an earned income. On the other hand, while an employer must have employees, one worker more or less doesn't mean much. Under collective bargaining, the worker's disadvantage is greatly reduced. The worker's need for a job is not reduced, but the question facing the employer becomes one of having or not having a complete labor force rather than one of having or not having a particular worker. The workers, gathered together in a union and delegating the task of bargaining with the employer to an official or agent of the union, can often obtain much better terms of employment than the individual workers could obtain for themselves.

DEVELOPMENT OF LABOR UNIONS

Labor unions are a product of the last century. Those unions that existed before the Civil War were generally temporary bodies established to redress certain grievances and dissolved when either successful or defeated. The labor movement accelerated after the Civil War. The development of large impersonal business units seemed to many workers to place them at the mercy of employers. In 1869 the first major U.S. labor union, the Knights of Labor, was organized in Philadelphia. The union did not last

---

9. In 1981 import quotas were imposed on Japanese cars shipped to the United States. This limitation probably saved Chrysler from going bankrupt. The U.S. automobile industry, which lost $4 billion in 1981, made a $10 billion profit in 1984.

long, in part because of poor leadership. In 1881 the American Federation of Labor (AFL) was created. As a federation of craft unions, the AFL made no effort for many years to enroll unskilled labor. Under Samuel Gompers, the AFL adopted a policy of political neutrality. Its main thrust was economic—more pay and an 8-hour work day. Other unions, in particular the International Workers of the World (IWW), were more militant. They believed in class conflict and resorted to violent means, including general strikes and sabotage, to achieve their goals.

The labor movement declined in importance during the 1920s. The AFL lost more than a million members during the decade, and efforts to unionize new industries proved unsuccessful. There were several factors responsible for the decline of unionism in the 1920s. The "Red scare" after the end of World War I was one factor. Some unions, particularly the IWW, had been sympathetic to the Bolshevik Revolution in Russia. There was public concern that somehow communists were infiltrating the United States, and all unions were lumped in with the IWW. The sensational murder trial and execution of Sacco and Vanzetti, both of whom were anarchists, convinced many employers that bomb throwers and communists were lurking behind every lamppost.

Another factor responsible for the decline of unionism was the unsympathetic attitude of the government. Government opposition helped to break up strikes in the coal and steel industries in 1919, and conservative court decisions hampered union activity during the 1920s. Laissez-faire was advocated as public policy; unions were blamed for rising prices. Finally, business firms organized an attack on unionism by popularizing the open shop and organizing company unions.

The halcyon days of organized labor occurred during the New Deal of Franklin D. Roosevelt. In 1935 the National Labor Relations Act was passed. This law required employers to bargain collectively with representatives of their employees and prohibited employers from carrying on unfair labor practices or interfering in the organization of unions. The act was intended to stimulate the growth of organized labor, and it did just that. Union memberships more than tripled during the 1930s, and many plants and industries that had previously escaped unionization were organized.

A split within the ranks of labor itself occurred in 1935, when union leaders within the AFL left it to form the Congress of Industrial Organization (CIO). The CIO was interested in organizing workers in the mass production industries. It was highly successful in securing recognition of unions for employees in the automobile and steel industries. Labor achieved at least a parity with management by the end of the 1930s and also gained in terms of social welfare. The Fair Labor Standards Act of 1938 man-

dated minimum wages and maximum hours for labor engaged in interstate commerce.

During the latter part of World War II and in the immediate postwar
period, a series of labor strikes convinced Congress that new legislation in
the field of labor relations was needed. The Labor-Management Relations
Act (Taft-Hartley Act) was passed in 1947 to eliminate some specific
abuses on the part of labor unions and to equalize bargaining conditions
between labor and management. The closed shop was outlawed and the
union shop was permitted only under strict regulation. A notice was required 60 days before a strike or a lockout could be called, and the government could obtain an injunction against a union, postponing for 80 days
any strike that would affect the national interest. Unions could be sued for
breach of contract if they participated in jurisdictional strikes and boy-
cotts. The pendulum, which had swung in favor of labor unions, swung
back to a more centrist position.

THE DECLINE OF UNIONS

As reflected in Table 5-3, union membership peaked in the 1950s and has
fallen since then. A major reason is the shift from a goods-producing to a
service society. The United States has entered a postindustrial age with a
change in the type of work people do—from physically intensive to knowledge-intensive labor. In 1945, 43.4 percent of all workers were employed
in manufacturing; by 1984 the percentage of workers employed in
manufacturing had decreased to 27.8 percent of the labor force. Conversely, the number of persons in the service jobs increased from 56.6 percent of
the labor force in 1945 to 71.2 percent in 1984. In 1945, 38.5 percent of all
workers employed in manufacturing belonged to unions; by 1984, union

TABLE 5-3	UNION MEMBERSHIP AS A PERCENTAGE OF THE U.S. LABOR FORCE, 1945–1984		
	Union Membership		Union Membership
1945	21.9%	1970	22.6%
1950	22.3	1975	21.7
1955	24.7	1980	21.2
1960	23.6	1984	20.6
1965	22.4		

Source: U.S. Bureau of Labor Statistics, *Handbook of Labor Statistics 1984* (Washington: USGPO,
1985), p. 502.

workers employed in manufacturing decreased to 21.8 percent of the total manufacturing labor force.

Unionism has never been strong in the service area. White-collar workers tend to identify more with management than blue-collar workers do. There is also a certain snob appeal about white-collar jobs, which is coupled with a tendency to look down on blue-collar manufacturing workers. By 1990 even more people will be employed in miscellaneous service-type jobs such as data processing, hotels, and restaurants.[10]

■ GOVERNMENT ■

Government intervention and participation in the U.S. economy can be divided into four areas. First there is public finance, where government is a purchaser of goods and services as well as a tax collector. Government economic stabilization policies may also be considered a part of this area. Second, government regulation and control prescribe specific conditions under which private economic activity can or cannot take place. Government may interpose itself as a part of management of certain industries, such as public utilities, and regulate rates and the provision of services. It may also affect the character of private business operations both directly and indirectly through antitrust and other laws. Third, government (at all levels) is the single largest employer in the American economy, and as such it competes directly with private industry for labor. The government also affects the level of wages and salaries. Fourth, government owns and operates certain types of business enterprises and is a major provider of credit. In fact, a shift in emphasis from market to political decisions has taken place in the American economy in recent years, in great measure in response to increased demands from a wide variety of special interest groups.

PUBLIC FINANCE

Public finance is the most straightforward example of the extent of government participation in the "mixed" economy of the United States. Taxes provide the government with control over the nation's resources and also affect the distribution of income and wealth. Government expenditures for goods and services divert resources from the private to the public sector

---

10. Bureau of Labor Statistics, *Occupational Outlook Handbook, 1980–81* (Washington: USGPO, 1981).

of the economy. Through its own expenditures, the government has literally created whole industries. It has conducted much of the basic research in certain industries, and it has given impetus and direction to technological change. Government transfer payments redistribute income from one economic group to another. The direct subsidies and indirect benefits offered by government to special interest groups, such as farmers and shipbuilders, are too numerous to mention. In addition, preferential tax treatment is accorded to some firms and industries to achieve desired economic goals. Examples of special tax treatment include the investment credit, depletion allowance for mineral extraction companies, and accelerated depreciation.

GOVERNMENT SPENDING   The economic influence of the public sector has grown steadily throughout this century and has become particularly pervasive during the last 20 years. To some extent, this increase in influence can be attributed to a growing acceptance of the role of government in public welfare. Increased industrial development of the U.S. economy has resulted in changes in the size and complexity of business enterprises, and the regulatory operations of the government have been stepped up. Government spending for national defense is also large; it accounts for around 30 percent of total government purchases of goods and services.

Economic growth has spurred a trend toward urban living. As more of the nation's population has become concentrated in urban areas, the inevitable result has been an increase in demand for a variety of services provided through the public sector. But regardless of the causes, the growth in both absolute and relative importance of the public sector to the U.S. economy is clear, as Table 5-4 indicates. Government spending on goods and services accounted for around 21 percent of the gross national product in 1984. If transfer payments are added to government spending on goods and services, total government expenditures amount to one-third of gross national product.

TAXES   The composition of taxes is also important in analyzing the role of government in the U.S. economy. Government expenditures are, at least in part, covered by taxes on business firms and individuals. Thus the type of taxes levied determines who ultimately pays for government expenditures. Taxes also have an income redistribution effect. When government extracts taxes, it lowers someone's income; but when that money is spent, it also raises someone's income.

Many public policy theorists believe that variations in the rate of economic growth can be attributed to different tax systems. Many feel that the reason the Japanese growth rate is far superior to that of the United

TABLE 5-4   U.S. GOVERNMENT SPENDING COMPARED TO GROSS NATIONAL PRODUCT FOR SELECTED YEARS
(billions of dollars)

	Gross National Product	Government Spending on Goods and Services		
		Total	Federal	State and Local
1929	$ 103.4	$ 8.8	$ 1.4	$ 7.4
1933	55.6	8.0	2.0	6.0
1939	90.8	13.5	5.1	8.3
1945	211.9	82.3	74.2	8.1
1950	284.8	37.9	18.4	19.5
1960	506.0	100.3	53.7	46.6
1970	982.4	218.9	95.6	125.2
1980	2,631.7	537.8	197.0	340.8
1981	2,957.8	596.5	228.9	367.6
1982	3,069.3	650.5	258.9	391.5
1983	3,304.8	685.5	269.7	415.8
1984	3,661.3	748.0	295.5	452.4

Source: *Economic Report of the President, 1985* (Washington: USGPO, 1985), pp. 232-233.

States is that Japanese tax policy favors saving and investment. The economic policies of the Reagan administration center heavily on tax-cutting measures designed to promote capital formation by increasing the rate of saving. Special incentives have been given to certain persons, corporations, or activities to influence shifts in saving behavior.

ECONOMIC STABILIZATION POLICIES The acceptance of economic policies designed to promote stability and the use of the tax/transfer payment mechanism to promote income redistribution tend to characterize the economic role of Western governments, including the United States, in much of the twentieth century. Economic stabilization policies include fiscal and monetary devices. Fiscal policy in the United States is effected through the federal budget, which can be used to change the level of economic activity in the economy. Taxes represent a withdrawal of income from the income stream, while government expenditures represent an injection of income into it. When the government's revenue, as represented by taxes and other revenues, exceeds expenditures, the net effect is to dampen the level of activity in the economy. On the other hand, when government expenditures exceed revenues, the net effect is to stimulate the economy. Budget surpluses or deficits, then, can be used to change the level of economic activity.

Monetary policy is another economic stabilization tool used in the United States and other Western countries. It involves operations by the central banking authorities to change the stock of money, its rate of turnover, and the volume of close money substitutes. The Federal Reserve is technically a privately owned corporation, but is actually an independent government agency subject to control by Congress and the president. It may be regarded as the central bank of the United States, comparable, for example, to the Bank of England in the United Kingdom and the Deutsche Bundesbank in West Germany.

The Federal Reserve may take action to counteract either inflation or deflation. It effects monetary policy in the United States through open market operations and control over discount rates[11] and legal reserves that commercial banks have to maintain against demand deposits. Raising discount rates and legal reserve requirements are anti-inflation measures; lowering them achieves the opposite result. The Federal Reserve also may either buy or sell U.S. government bonds in the open market. If it buys bonds from commercial banks, demand deposits are increased and banks have more money to lend. Conversely, if it sells bonds to commercial banks, the reverse is true.

TRANSFER PAYMENTS   The composition of the federal budget has been altered considerably since 1960. Transfer payments have increased more rapidly than any single component in the budget, as Table 5-5 indicates. Total outlays for transfer payments and for other social welfare programs amounted to around 42 percent of the federal budget in 1985. When state and local government expenditures on social welfare programs are also taken into consideration, total government expenditures on social welfare programs amounted to $400 billion in 1985. In the state of California, on any given day, about 40 percent of the people received some form of state transfer payment.

There are a wide variety of transfer programs, ranging from food stamps to Medicare to welfare payments. Money spent on entitlement programs has risen at a rate three times as fast as the U.S. gross national product. These funds are provided from general taxes or government borrowing. For example, unemployment compensation provides aid to unemployed workers and is financed by a payroll tax on employers.

---

11. The discount rate is the interest rate charged when commercial banks borrow from the Federal Reserve. In turn, the discount rate affects the interest rate commercial banks charge their customers.

TABLE 5-5   MAJOR CATEGORIES OF FEDERAL GOVERNMENT EXPENDITURES
(billions of dollars)

Fiscal Year	Transfer Payments	Purchases of Goods and Services
1960	$ 20.6	$ 52.9
1965	28.4	65.6
1970	55.0	87.1
1975	131.4	117.9
1980	234.6	189.3
1981	273.7	218.4
1982	304.5	250.6
1983	338.3	273.2
1984	340.7	285.2
1985	361.0	326.8
1986	377.6	354.9

Source: Office of Management and Budget, *Budget of the United States Government, Fiscal Year 1986* (Washington: USGPO, 1985), p. 40.

There are also regular social security programs, created under the Social Security Act of 1937. The most important of these is the old age, survivors, and disability insurance program, which is financed by a payroll tax on both employer and employee.[12] The tax receipts are placed in a reserve fund, and payments are made to workers who have retired or who are disabled and to the spouses and young children of workers who have died. The program was expanded in the mid-1960s when hospital care coverage began to be provided for older persons and voluntary medical insurance become available to them.

GOVERNMENT REGULATION AND CONTROL

Government regulation, particularly of business, is a second area in which government has become firmly entrenched in the U.S. economy. This sphere of public sector influence has developed by fits and starts. In the 1880s the trust movement threatened to envelop much of American industry. This brought about a public demand for control over the monopolies, with the result that the Sherman Anti-Trust Act was passed in 1890.

12. The combined rate in 1986 was 14.3 percent on incomes up to $42,000.

The Depression, which began with the stock market crash of 1929 and continued until the wartime mobilization of the early 1940s, was a severe crisis. In response to that crisis, many new government agencies were created, most of which impinged in some way on business firms. By the end of the Depression, the federal government exercised extensive regulation and control over business. There was little additional government intervention until the late 1960s and early 1970s, when environmental protection, minority employment, and consumer protection became dominant issues.

ANTITRUST REGULATION   One important area of government regulation is antitrust activity to prevent anticompetitive business practices. This activity generally has sprung from the concept that concentration interferes with the efficient operation of a competitive market economy and that the most effective method of regulation is to prevent concentration from developing in the first place. Antitrust laws are designed to promote and maintain competition in industry. There is a fundamental social interest in the efficacy of the competitive market system. Society wants competition in order to get the maximum output of the goods and services at the lowest possible prices, using the most efficient production techniques.

Anticompetitive practices can be divided into several categories. First, there could be an industry in which a few firms are dominant and price competition is therefore minimal. Second, mergers between business firms can create an imperfectly competitive market situation. Third, anticompetitive business practices may involve certain types of market abuses such as price fixing and market sharing.

PUBLIC UTILITY REGULATION   Certain industries vitally affect the public interest by providing a service that is considered too important to society to be left to the vagaries of the market or to private enterprise to provide as it sees fit. In other countries with systems similar to our own, industries directly affecting the public interest are owned and operated by their governments. In the United States, however, when one or both of two conditions exist in an industry, a *natural monopoly* is usually created and regulated by the government. First, economies of scale can occur if output is concentrated in one firm, with the result that one firm can supply the market more efficiently than two or more firms; second, unrestrained competition between firms in the industry is deemed by society to be undesirable. Included under the category of natural monopolies are electricity, gas, local telephone service, and broadcasting.

SOCIAL REGULATION   During the 1970s the federal government extended its participation in the market system. More and more effort was directed toward cushioning individual risks and regulating personal and institutional conduct. Social regulation is broad-based in terms of objectives. It encompasses such areas as occupational health and safety, equal employment opportunity, consumer product safety, and environmental protection. These areas have specific social goals—a cleaner environment, safer consumer products, employment of minorities, and so forth. A number of important regulatory commissions, most of which were created during the 1970s, enforce the laws designed to achieve these social goals.

The Consumer Product Safety Commission, the Occupational Safety and Health Administration, the Equal Employment Opportunity Commission, and the Environmental Protection Agency are examples of regulatory agencies. For these relative newcomers to the federal government hierarchy of administrative agencies and commissions, jurisdiction extends to most of the private sector and at times to productive activities in the government itself. However, each of these newer agencies has a rather narrow range of responsibility. For example, the Equal Employment Opportunity Commission is responsible only for employment policies in a given firm, whereas the Federal Aviation Administration (FAA) is responsible for all the activities of anyone who flies.

GOVERNMENT AS AN EMPLOYER

One measure of the magnitude of the public sector is the number of persons employed directly by one or another governmental unit. When the armed forces are included, some 16 percent of the total labor force is employed directly in the public sector. It is likely that this percentage will increase in the future, particularly at the state and local levels, since the demand for social services is expected to increase. In addition, numerous other jobs are related indirectly to government employment. An army base, defense plant, or state university often supports the economy of a whole area. The public sector sets wage standards in many areas and competes against the private sector for labor resources. However, the productivity of the public sector is often low in comparison to productivity in the private sector; as the public sector expands relative to the private sector, productivity in general will decline.[13]

13. U.S. Congress, Joint Economic Committee, *Productivity in the Federal Government* (Washington: USGPO, May 31, 1979), pp. 1-12.

In the private sector, the profit-and-loss system produces an incentive to stimulate efficiency. Competition between business firms also encourages maximum efficiency in the use of capital and other resources, including labor. Both factors are lacking in government, for it is not in business to make a profit, nor is there a need to be competitive, because there is no competition between government units. There is no rationale to be productive because the stimulus is not there. No government agency has ever gone broke. In fact, some observers have argued that agency managers have strong disincentives to improve production if such gains lead to budget cuts. The prestige of an agency manager is often measured by the number of employees the agency has; thus, the fewer the employees, the lower the prestige. The disincentive possibility means that Congress or state legislatures must in effect fill the role played by the profit-and-loss system.

GOVERNMENT OWNERSHIP OF BUSINESS

Government ownership of business is quite limited in the United States in comparison to other major Western industrial countries. In France, for example, the railroads, coal mines, and most of the banking system, airlines, electric power facilities, and insurance companies are state-owned. The government also has a large interest in the petroleum and natural gas industries and is involved in the production of motor vehicles and airplanes. In the United Kingdom, the coal mines, steel industry, railways, trucking, and electricity and gas industries are state-owned. In West Germany, government ownership is limited to the railroads, airlines, public utilities, and coal mines. However, in all three countries, private enterprise is still dominant in that it employs by far the greater percentage of workers and contributes the greater part of the gross national product.

In the United States, all levels of government own and operate productive facilities of many kinds. Airports, but not railway terminals, are usually government-owned. Governmental units own and operate the plants that provide water, gas, and electricity to thousands of cities and towns, as well as owning local transportation systems, warehouses, printing companies, and a wide variety of other facilities. Government also produces, either directly or indirectly, atomic power and many other goods. It carries on projects connected with reforestation, soil erosion control, slum clearance, rural electrification, and housing. This does not mean that government ownership and operation is necessarily preferred to private. In many cases, the resources required are too large and risks too great, or the likelihood of profit too small to attract private enterprise, and government is compelled to perform the tasks instead.

One illustration of this point is the Tennessee Valley Authority (TVA), a major public enterprise for the production and distribution of electrical power in the southeastern United States. At one time, the area adjacent to the Tennessee River was one of the most impoverished in the United States. Flooding and soil erosion were common, and most homes in the area were without electricity. The area was also generally unattractive to industry. The TVA was created to erect dams and hydroelectric plants to provide electric power, to improve navigation on the Tennessee River, to promote flood control, to prevent soil erosion, to reforest the area, and to contribute to the nation's defense through the manufacture of artificial nitrates. It was opposed by private companies, in particular the utility companies, because it was empowered to sell electricity in direct competition with them. However, the utility companies in the Tennessee Valley area had never considered it profitable to provide anything more than minimal service. The TVA was also supposed to serve as a yardstick of efficiency, but government ownership and operation of power facilities does not always mean lower rates or greater efficiency. Opinion on TVA's efficiency is mixed. The TVA is efficient when compared to other government agencies, but when compared to private business it does not look as good.

Government credit programs constitute a gray area in that they do not involve outright state ownership of industry. However, federal credit programs have an impact on private industry that should be mentioned. Direct, insured, and federally sponsored agency loans passed the $500 billion mark in 1980 and have continued to increase. These programs have three main functions: to eliminate gaps in the credit market, to provide subsidies that stimulate socially desirable activity, and to stimulate the economy. The first two of these functions are microeconomic in effect in that they are supposed to affect the types of activity for which credit is made available, the geographical location of those activities, and the types of borrowers who have access to credit. For example, Federal Housing Administration (FHA) and Veterans' Administration (VA) mortgage insurance programs have resulted in an increased demand for housing. The third function is macroeconomic in nature in that federal lending affects the level of economic activity on a large scale—in particular, the gross national product and employment.

SUMMARY

Three important types of economic organizations have developed in the United States—big business, big labor, and big government. The three have developed partly in response to the needs and deficiencies of the market mechanism. Big business, as represented by large corporations, developed first, and pervades all areas of economic activity ranging from manufacturing to banking and from communications to retailing. Whether this is good or bad is a matter of opinion. Large-scale production and distribution can effect economies of scale and the result can be lower prices for consumers. However, largeness can result in a lessening of innovation and price competition. In all advanced industrial countries, regardless of their political and economic ideologies, large industrial organizations are a fact of life.

Labor unions in part offset the power of corporations and also reduce the power of market forces in labor markets by creating a monopoly for certain types of workers. Unions gained in popularity and strength during the Great Depression. However, union membership began to peak during the 1950s and has been declining as a percentage of the total labor force. There has been a decline in employment in the manufacturing sector of the economy, where union membership has been the highest, and an increase in employment in the service sector, where union membership has never been strong. The increased education and mobility of American workers has also tended to work against an increase in union membership.

Undoubtedly, the most important modification of the U.S. market system has been achieved through an increase in the role of the public or government sector. Public education has been provided, business monopolies have been curbed, and taxes and transfer payments have been used to redistribute incomes. Fiscal and monetary policies have been used, albeit with limited success, to attain full employment and price stability. A variety of government regulations have been adopted to achieve various social goals such as a cleaner environment and the employment of minorities. The social security program has been expanded over time to reduce economic insecurity. Government purchase of goods and services now amounts to around 21 percent of the gross national product. It is clear that government intervention in the economy has become large enough to justify the classification of the United States as a mixed rather than a strictly market system. How successful this mixture has been is the subject of the next chapter.

REVIEW QUESTIONS

1. In what ways can the development of large corporations be regarded as a departure from a market system?
2. What is a multinational corporation?
3. In what ways can the development of labor unions be regarded as a departure from a market system?
4. What is meant by the term "entitlements"?
5. What are some of the factors responsible for the increase in the role of government in U.S. society?
6. Discuss the purpose of U.S. antitrust regulation.
7. What are some of the factors responsible for the decline of unionism in the United States?

RECOMMENDED READINGS

Bell, Daniel. *The Coming of Post-Industrial Society*. New York: Basic Books Inc., Publishers, 1976.

Dunlop, John. *Business and Public Policy*. Cambridge: Harvard University Press, 1981.

Kristol, Irving. *Two Cheers for Capitalism*. New York: Basic Books Inc., Publishers, 1982.

Lodge, George. *The American Disease*. New York: Alfred A. Knopf, Inc., 1984.

Peters, Thomas J., and Robert H. Waterman. *In Search of Excellence*. New York: Harper & Row, Publishers, Inc., 1982.

Reynolds, Lloyd. *Labor Economics and Labor Relations*. 8th ed. Englewood Cliffs, N.J.: Prentice-Hall Inc., 1982.

Schnitzer, Martin C. *Contemporary Government & Business Relations*. 2d ed. Boston: Houghton Mifflin Co., 1983.

Steiner, George A., and John F. Steiner. *Business, Government, and Society*. 4th ed. New York: Random House Inc., 1985.

C H A P T E R 6

AN APPRAISAL
OF THE
UNITED STATES ECONOMY

The 1970s was a decade which few people will remember with any feeling of nostalgia. The most disruptive decade since the Depression of the 1930s witnessed the contradiction of economic growth accompanied by inflation, a condition called *stagflation* by economists. Stagflation was accompanied by an energy shortage in the land of supposedly limitless resources, the depreciation of the dollar, and a decline in real incomes and productivity. A new division of labor developed, as the United States moved on its inexorable way toward a service economy. Newly industrialized countries such as Brazil, Mexico, South Korea, and Taiwan begun to take over the traditional routinized manufacturing activities—shipbuilding, steel, textiles, and so forth. Conversely, Japan adopted a strategy of high value-added production of sophisticated technology and began to obtain an ever-increasing share of the world's markets for automobiles and electronic equipment.

The 1980s represent a considerable improvement over the 1970s. Inflation is way down from its double-digit level of 1979 and 1980, and the rate of economic growth, which was negative during several years in the 1970s, has rebounded to levels achieved during the early 1960s. Unemployment increased during the first part of the 1980s, but in 1985 was around 7.2 percent of the labor force. The automobile industry, in particular Chrysler, which was once considered an endangered species, rebounded with government help to make the highest profits in its history in 1984.

Perhaps, above all, there has been a resurgence of popular optimism about the present and the future. Former President Jimmy Carter talked about an economy of limits where the individual would have to expect to make do with less. President Reagan, with his characteristic ebullience, talked about an economy without limits, where each individual can "go for the gold."[1]

However, there are still flies in the American ointment, the largest and most important of which is the deficit in the federal budget. Bringing it under control will require an extremely bitter and divisive struggle over the domestic component of the budget and, inevitably, a struggle for priority between domestic and foreign goals. To put its fiscal affairs in order, the United States will have to sacrifice more at home to pay for its international position, or it will have to scale down its world commitments. A second problem, which is connected to the federal deficit, is a deficit in the U.S. balance of payments accounts with the rest of the world. This deficit increases the potential for protectionist measures, particularly against Japan. Finally, there is the competition that comes with a rapidly developing world economy—a competition that pits the United States against not only Japan, but also against the developing countries of Asia.

■ ECONOMIC GROWTH ■

A high standard of living today is the result of the economic growth of the past. A rising standard of living is made possible by continued economic growth. The size of the U.S. labor force is constantly expanding, with a million and half new workers entering annually. Thus, it is necessary to provide more job opportunities to absorb these new entrants into the labor force. If the economy does not grow, there is no way in which unemployment can be reduced and new job seekers absorbed into the labor force. Further, the nation will not be able to provide the resources needed to solve its social problems and to provide schools, medical care, hospitals, and other social needs.

Table 6-1 presents U.S. real gross national product in 1982 dollars. A good measure of economic growth is the rate of change in real GNP, either total or per capita, over time. The rate of change from year to year during

---

1. The author stated in the last edition of this book, which was published in 1983, that there was not much room for optimism as far as the U.S. economy was concerned, with inflation high and growth rates low, and U.S. industry taking a beating in international competition. But times have changed. The rate of inflation has been more than cut in half, economic growth has increased, and U.S. industry has become more competitive. The U.S. economy has proved to be quite viable.

TABLE 6-1   REAL GROSS NATIONAL PRODUCT,
             UNITED STATES: 1970–1985

	Billions of 1982 Dollars	Change from Previous Year		Billions of 1982 Dollars	Change from Previous Year
1970	$2,416.2	−0.3%	1978	$3,115.2	5.3%
1971	2,484.8	2.8	1979	3,192.4	2.5
1972	2,608.5	5.0	1980	3,187.1	−0.2
1973	2,744.1	5.2	1981	3,248.8	1.9
1974	2,729.3	−0.5	1982	3,166.0	−2.5
1975	2,695.0	−1.3	1983	3,277.7	3.5
1976	2,826.7	4.9	1984	3,492.0	6.5
1977	2,958.6	4.7	1985	3,573.5	2.3

Source: *Economic Report of the President, 1986* (Washington: USGPO, February 1986), pp. 254-255.

the 1970s was the lowest for any decade since the 1930s. The result was a slippage in the U.S. standard of living relative to other countries. The rate of change in real GNP was a negative 2.5 percent for 1982, but increased to a positive 6.5 percent by 1984, which was the largest increase for any year since 1951. In 1985 the growth of the American economy slowed somewhat; the rate of change in real GNP was 2.3 percent.

PRODUCTIVITY

Productivity is the amount of output produced by a unit of input during a given period. Growth in productivity has long been recognized as one of the most important determinants of national economic growth and price stability. A nation's ability to consume ultimately depends upon its capacity to produce goods and services. If money incomes increase but productivity does not, real purchasing power will fall and living standards will decline. Increased productivity will also help reduce inflation by tempering the growth of per-unit labor costs. Generally, productivity is expressed in terms of product output per unit of labor input. Of course, labor uses capital and natural resources to produce output, so that this measure also captures the productivity of other inputs used.

Table 6-2 presents the productivity performance of the United States during the period 1970–1985, with 1977 used as the base year. Average

TABLE 6-2   PRODUCTIVITY IN THE UNITED STATES:
             1970 – 1985

	Real Output per Worker Hour (1977 = 100)	Change from Preceding Year
1970	88.3	0.7%
1971	91.2	3.2
1972	94.1	3.2
1973	95.9	2.0
1974	93.9	−2.1
1975	95.7	2.0
1976	98.3	2.8
1977	100.0	1.7
1978	100.8	0.8
1979	99.6	−1.2
1980	99.2	−0.3
1981	100.7	1.5
1982	100.3	−0.4
1983	102.9	2.6
1984	105.0	2.1
1985	105.3	0.3

Source: *Economic Report of the President, 1986* (Washington: USGPO, February 1986), pp. 302-303.

real output per worker hour is used as the measure of productivity. The productivity slowdown during the 1970s contributed to a decline in the ability of American industry to compete in the world market. Although all the industrialized Western countries experienced a decline in productivity, the U.S. decline was greater.

INTERNATIONAL COMPARISONS OF ECONOMIC GROWTH

The performance of the United States must be placed in a global perspective. No longer is it possible for the United States to ignore the rest of the world. In an increasingly interdependent world, no economy operates in a vacuum. Japan has already surpassed the United States as the world's leading producer of automobiles and steel products. Other developed countries have caught up to the United States in terms of living standards. In many industries, the United States lags behind other countries in the introduction of new technology. However, there have been wide variations among industrial countries in economic performance levels. Real economic growth is one basic measure of economic performance. Another measure is the rate of employment/unemployment, and a third measure is the stability of the purchasing power of earnings.

Table 6-3 compares the average annual rates of real economic growth for the industrialized market economies of the world. The percentage change in gross domestic product is used as the measure of economic growth. The table indicates that the performance of the United States relative to the other countries is somewhat mixed. For the period 1965–1973, the U.S. growth rate ranked next to last among the nine countries. The growth rate was less than a third of that for Japan. However, the U.S. growth rate for the 1973–1983 period, though lower compared to the previous time period, actually was better than most of the other countries. There was less of a decline—3.2 percent to 2.3 percent—compared to the drop in the Japanese growth rate from 9.8 percent to 4.3 percent.

The real rate of economic growth in the Western European countries during the early 1980s was very low. Some countries, notably France, had negative rates of growth in at least one year during this period. Even West Germany, which had a very high rate of economic growth during the 30 years following World War II, experienced a growth rate that averaged less than 2 percent a year during the early 1980s. Moreover, the real rate of economic growth in Japan showed a decline during the early 1980s, and in 1984 was lower than the U.S. growth rate. The growth rate of the United States, at least for the 1983–1985 period, has been the best of all major industrial countries.

TABLE 6-3   AVERAGE ANNUAL GROWTH OF REAL GROSS DOMESTIC PRODUCT FOR INDUSTRIAL MARKET ECONOMIES

	1965–1973	1973–1983
Italy	5.2%	2.2%
United Kingdom	2.8	1.1
Japan	9.8	4.3
France	5.5	2.5
West Germany	4.6	2.1
Canada	5.2	2.3
Sweden	3.6	1.3
Norway	4.0	3.7
United States	3.2	2.3

Source: The World Bank, *World Development Report 1985*, p. 177.

▪ INFLATION ▪

The 1970s witnessed the worst combination of unemployment and inflation in modern U.S. experience. The unemployment rate for the decade was above 6 percent—the highest rate since the 1930s.[2] During the same decade, the inflation rate was the worst in this century. In fact, the rate of inflation was 11.0 percent in 1974, the highest peacetime rate since just after the Civil War. The inflation rate decreased to less than 6 percent by 1976, but was back to double-digit levels in 1979. In 1980 the misery index, a term used by President Carter during his successful 1976 presidential campaign, was in excess of 20 percent—an unemployment rate of 7.1 percent plus a rate of inflation of 13.5 percent.

Both unemployment and inflation have deleterious effects on the American economy—unemployment in terms of a loss of income that can never be regained and inflation in terms of its impact on consumer purchasing power, saving, and business investment. In 1979 median family income rose by 11.6 percent over 1978, but the price level increased by 11.3 percent.[3] The median family purchasing power rose at an annual average rate of only 0.7 percent during the 1970s.[4]

Table 6-4 presents the average annual rate of increase in the consumer price index for the period 1970–1985. The rate of increase varied widely during the 1970s, ranging from a high of 11.3 percent in 1979 to a low of 3.3 percent in 1972. The rate of inflation, as measured by the consumer price index, remained high in 1980, and was a major reason for the defeat of Jimmy Carter by Ronald Reagan. An important policy goal of the Reagan administration was a reduction in the rate of inflation. The Federal Reserve, under the policies of chairman Paul Volcker, continued a tight money policy, which had originally started during the last year of the Carter administration. The money supply was decreased and interest rates were allowed to increase. The result was a "wringing out" of inflation. In 1983 the rate of inflation was lower than 4 percent.

INTERNATIONAL COMPARISONS OF INFLATION

Given the experience of the United States with inflation during the 1970s and early 1980s, it may be somewhat surprising to learn that our inflation

---

2. *Economic Report of the President, 1981* (Washington: USGPO, February, 1981), p. 244.

3. Ibid., p. 198.

4. Ibid., p. 202.

TABLE 6-4   CHANGES IN THE U.S. CONSUMER PRICE INDEX: 1970–1985

	Year-to-Year Change		Year-to-Year Change
1970	5.9%	1978	7.7%
1971	4.3	1979	11.3
1972	3.3	1980	13.5
1973	6.2	1981	10.4
1974	11.0	1982	6.1
1975	9.1	1983	3.2
1976	5.8	1984	4.3
1977	6.5	1985	3.6

Source: Economic Report of the President, 1986 (Washington: USGPO, 1986), p. 320.

experience compared to other industrial market economies has not been bad. As Table 6-5 indicates, the U.S. average annual rate of inflation (expressed as a percentage increase in consumer price indexes) was one of the lowest of the nine countries for the period 1965–1973, averaging 4.7 percent. During the 1973–1983 period, the average annual rate of inflation for the United States was 7.5 percent, a rate which was exceeded by all of the other countries except Japan and West Germany. When both time periods are taken into consideration, West Germany ranked first, Japan second, and the United States third. However, for 1984 and 1985, the rate of inflation declined in the United States and increased in West Germany and Japan.

TABLE 6-5   AVERAGE ANNUAL INFLATION RATES FOR INDUSTRIALIZED MARKET ECONOMIES

	1965–1973	1973–1983
Italy	5.1%	17.4%
United Kingdom	6.2	14.3
Japan	6.0	4.7
France	5.3	10.8
West Germany	4.7	4.3
Canada	4.4	9.4
Sweden	5.3	10.3
Norway	6.3	9.7
United States	4.7	7.5

Source: The World Bank, World Development Report 1985, p. 175.

■ EMPLOYMENT ■
AND UNEMPLOYMENT

The most popular post-World War II economic policies in the Western industrial countries have been Keynesian economic policies that stress the stimulation of aggregate demand. These policies are a response to Keynes's preoccupation with unemployment, the prevailing economic problem during the Depression of the 1930s, in England as well as elsewhere. This meant that the United States and other Western governments have increased spending and allowed higher budget deficits when unemployment rises. In due course, policies designed to stimulate aggregate demand set in motion inflationary pressures in the United States and other Western countries. Stagflation became endemic as government policies oscillated between concern for unemployment and concern for inflation.

An inflation–unemployment dilemma began in the United States in the late 1960s. As inflation increased, so did unemployment. A goal of full employment with price stability was becoming more difficult to achieve. The attitudes of various administrations are reflected in the *Economic Report of the President*.[5] In the Kennedy administration of the early 1960s, 4 percent unemployment was set as the goal consistent with full employment. The fact that a certain amount of unemployment would always occur for one reason or another was recognized.[6] By the time of the Johnson administration, an unemployment rate of 4.5 percent was accepted as a norm for full employment and price stability. By the end of the Ford administration, the *Economic Report of the President* was listing a goal of 5 percent unemployment as being consistent with full employment. During the Carter administration, 6 percent became the implied target for full employment. The major concern of the Reagan administration when it assumed office in 1981 was inflation; little emphasis was placed on full employment goals.

UNEMPLOYMENT RATES FOR THE UNITED STATES

Table 6-6 presents the average annual rates of unemployment in the United States for the period 1970–1985. These rates (which are by no means comparable to the very high unemployment rates that prevailed

---

5. Lester C. Thurow, *The Zero-Sum Society* (New York: Basic Books Inc., Publishers, 1980), p. 73.

6. There is frictional unemployment that occurs when workers are between jobs, and structural unemployment that occurs when industries decline or become automated. An example would be the decline of employment in the U.S. auto and steel industries resulting from foreign competition and automation.

TABLE 6-6   UNEMPLOYMENT RATES IN THE UNITED STATES BY DEMOGRAPHIC CHARACTERISTICS: 1970–1985

	All Workers	White		Black	
		Male	Female	Male	Female
1970	4.9%	4.0%	5.4%	7.3%	9.3%
1971	5.9	4.9	6.3	9.1	10.8
1972	5.6	4.5	5.9	9.3	11.8
1973	4.9	3.8	5.3	8.0	11.1
1974	5.6	4.4	6.1	9.8	11.3
1975	8.5	7.2	8.6	14.8	14.8
1976	7.7	6.4	7.9	13.7	14.3
1977	7.1	5.5	7.3	13.3	14.9
1978	6.1	4.6	6.2	11.8	13.8
1979	5.8	4.5	5.9	11.4	13.3
1980	7.1	6.1	6.5	14.5	14.0
1981	7.6	6.5	6.9	15.7	15.6
1982	9.7	8.8	8.3	20.1	17.6
1983	9.6	8.8	7.9	20.3	18.6
1984	7.5	6.4	6.5	16.4	15.4
1985	7.2	6.1	6.4	15.3	14.9

Source: Economic Report of the President, 1986 (Washington: USGPO, 1986), p. 296.

during the Depression) are higher than those rates that prevailed during the 1950s and 1960s. However, the economy has changed considerably since the 1960s. There are many more women in the labor force, which has increased overall by some 40 million workers since 1960. The economy is also much more subject to foreign competition than it was 25 years ago. Unemployment in the smoke-stack industries has increased as competing countries, such as Japan, have increased their U.S. market shares of automobile and steel sales. The table also compares unemployment rates by demographic characteristics such as race and sex. Unemployment rates are higher for blacks than for whites. The rate of unemployment is highest for teenagers 16 to 19, with black teenagers almost three times as likely to be unemployed as white teenagers. There is less difference based on sex, with the unemployment rates for males and females, white or black, somewhat similar.

JOB CREATION

One way to measure the performance of an economy is by its ability to create jobs to absorb new entrants into the labor force. The United States has achieved remarkable success when it comes to providing more jobs for its workers, because a million and a half new workers enter the labor force each year. The United States creates more jobs each year than all of Western Europe created during the decade of the 1970s.[7] Moreover, population growth in Western Europe is static, with birth rates and death rates in most countries approximately the same. This means that the number of new entrants into the European labor force annually is relatively small and is offset by retirements. Yet, as shown in Table 6-7, the unemployment rates for West Germany, France, and the United Kingdom for 1984 and 1985 were higher than those for the United States.[8] The ability of the U.S. economy to create new jobs has been the envy of Western Europe.

■ ECONOMIC INEQUALITY: ■ INCOME DISTRIBUTION

The United States is experiencing a period of rapid economic and social change. The traditional family unit, headed by one breadwinner who is male, is no longer typical of American society. The family of today is more likely to be headed by a single parent, male or female, or by two bread-

TABLE 6-7   UNEMPLOYMENT RATES FOR INDUSTRIALIZED MARKET ECONOMIES: 1980–1985

	1980	1981	1982	1983	1984	1985[a]
U.S.	7.1%	7.6%	9.7%	9.6%	7.5%	7.2%
Canada	7.5	7.5	11.0	11.9	11.3	10.5
France	6.4	7.5	8.4	8.6	10.1	10.5
Italy	3.9	4.3	4.8	5.3	5.9	6.1
Japan	2.0	2.2	2.4	2.7	2.8	2.5
U.K.	6.8	10.4	11.8	12.8	13.0	13.5
W. Germany	2.9	4.1	5.9	7.5	7.8	7.9

[a]Estimate

Source: *Economic Report of the President, 1986* (Washington: USGPO, 1986), p. 377.

7. The U.S. labor force increased by 20 million workers during the 1970s. There was actually a decrease in the Western European labor force during the same decade.

8. The August 1985 unemployment rate in the United Kingdom was 13.5 percent; in West Germany, 7.9 percent; in France, 10.5 percent; and in the United States, 7.2 percent.

winners. Birth rates have declined and the United States is in the process of becoming an aging society. The numbers of minority workers are increasing, but their educational background is lower and unemployment rates higher than for the rest of the population. The result of these social changes has been an increased demand for public goods and services —child care, medical care, housing, education, and training. Because of the costs of social and transfer programs, there has been a constant tendency for government expenditures to increase, requiring more borrowing to pay for services and stimulating more inflation because of an imbalance in productivity.

The new "class struggles" of the United States, and for that matter Western society, are less a matter of conflict between management and labor in the workplace than the push and pull of various organized segments to influence outlays from the national budget.[9] This conflict is all related to the distribution of income, which is an important issue in both market and nonmarket economies.

TRENDS IN INCOME DISTRIBUTION

Recent decades have witnessed no real movement toward greater equality in the distribution of income in the United States. There is an apparent conflict between the goals of an egalitarian society and the existence of marked income inequality. However, in a market economy there is bound to be inequality because income distribution is based on institutional arrangements, such as the pricing process, associated with this type of system. High prices are set on scarce factors of production and low prices on plentiful factors.

In terms of rewards to labor, those persons whose skills are scarce relative to demand enjoy a high level of income, while those persons whose skills are not scarce do not. In a market economy people are supposedly rewarded on the basis of their contribution to marketable output which, in turn, reflects consumer preferences and income. The implication is that persons whose productivity is low will earn little, regardless of whether the low productivity is attributable to lack of effort, lack of skill, or low demand for the skill.

Table 6-8 presents income distribution in the United States for a 35-year period. The frame of reference is personal income, which includes that part of national income actually received by persons or households as well as transfer payments from government and business. Wages and

9. Thurow, *Zero-Sum Society*, p. 24.

TABLE 6-8   DISTRIBUTION OF FAMILY INCOME
IN THE UNITED STATES: 1947–1982

| | Share of Total National Income Received | | | | |
	1947	1960	1971	1979	1982
Lowest Quintile	5.0%	4.9%	5.5%	5.3%	4.7%
2nd Quintile	11.9	12.0	11.9	11.7	11.2
3rd Quintile	17.0	17.5	17.3	17.2	17.1
4th Quintile	23.1	23.6	23.7	24.4	24.3
Highest Quintile	43.0	42.0	41.6	41.4	42.7
Top 5 Percent	17.5	15.9	15.7	15.8	16.0
Gini Coefficient	.376	.364	.356	.365	.381

Source: Bureau of the Census, *Current Population Reports, Consumer Income, 1984* (Washington: USGPO, March, 1984), p. 47.

salaries, rent, interest, and dividends are parts of personal income. The table indicates that there has been little change in the distribution of family income based on quintiles. The lowest fifth of the family income recipients received around 5 percent of total income during the period while the highest fifth received around 42 percent.

Whether or not this income inequality is desirable is a matter of opinion. Is income inequality necessary for economic growth? It is generally argued that growth is tied to performance. Economic growth and income distribution are correlated: In order to have growth, it is necessary to have increased financial resources, which are obtained only through higher profits. Moreover, any economy based primarily upon the ownership of private property is bound to create some inequality in the distribution of income.

DEMOGRAPHIC CHARACTERISTICS
OF U.S. INCOME DISTRIBUTION

Political and economic traditions in the United States have focused attention on the rights of the individual—equality of opportunity, voting rights, and support for those individuals who in some sense have fallen below society's norm of acceptability. However, a group consciousness has developed, and the United States has become a society of groups, each demanding a larger scale of the national economic pie, which has not grown much in recent years. Minorities argue that group parity is a fundamental component of economic justice and that incomes should be distributed on the basis of group parity, not individual parity. Therefore, it is necessary to present a more complete analysis of income distribution based on demographic characteristics—sex, race, and age. There are disparities in income distribution related to these characteristics. Affirmative action policies represent a demand for government economic policies to focus on eliminating differences based on demographic characteristics.

SEX   In 1983 the median income of households headed by a male was $23,104 while the median income of households headed by a female was $8,510. The median income of single men was $15,510; the median income of single women was $10,000.[10] There were several reasons for these differences in income. A greater percentage of males were in the labor force in 1983, and a greater percentage of males worked full time. A third factor was a greater concentration of males in the higher-paying occupations. For example, well over one-half of all women in the labor force were concentrated in relatively low-paying clerical and service occupations. On the other hand, men outnumbered women by a ratio of 3 to 1 in management, professional, and technical jobs. Finally, long-term comparisons of median income of full-time workers based on the sex classification reveal that the differences are longstanding. In 1947 the median income of women employed outside the home was 59 percent of the median income of men; the 1983 figure was 58 percent.

RACE   In 1983 white household mean income was $29,875 while black mean household income was $18,317, or around 60 percent of white mean income.[11] Hispanic mean household income was $21,020, or around 73 percent of that of white households. The much lower black household income can be explained in part by the high concentration of households headed by women. About 47 percent of black households were headed by women, compared to 25 percent for white and Hispanic households. There is also a difference in income between white and black workers who are single. Single blacks had a mean income of $9,729 in 1983 compared to a mean income of $14,282 for single whites. The differences in income can be explained in part by a greater percentage of blacks in part-time employment and in part by their concentration in low-paying service jobs.

AGE   For both men and women, income increases from the early work years and peaks in the age bracket 45–54.[12] For example, the highest aver-

---

10. Bureau of the Census, *Monthly Income of Households in the United States, 1984* (Washington: USGPO, March, 1984), pp. 121-124.

11. Ibid., p. 122.

12. Ibid., pp. 154, 155.

age annual income for males with a college education is reached at age 49. After this point, average annual income declines for college-educated males. This pattern is also true for college-educated females and for both males and females with high school educations. The pattern holds true for all occupational categories, with the exception of unskilled workers. This in itself does not prove age discrimination, for there are a number of factors at work. As family income needs decrease, many men wish to increase their leisure time and are less willing to work overtime. In the case of women over 40, a majority have not participated in the labor force for an extended period of time. Many women break the continuity of their employment to bear and rear children. When they return to the labor market it is at a later age, and their lack of work experience results in a lower wage.

DISCRIMINATION

Differences in the distribution of personal income do not in themselves prove discrimination. There must be an allowance for differences in ability and motivation among people. Neither Congress nor the Supreme Court can repeal the human condition that some people can run faster and jump farther than others. Nevertheless, discrimination has to be accepted as one factor responsible for income differences.

In the case of blacks and members of other racial and ethnic minority groups, there has been overt discrimination. Blacks have systematically been denied the same educational opportunities as whites over an extended period of time. This fact is reflected in the occupational mix of blacks, the majority of whom are concentrated in the low-skill, low-pay jobs. There has been discrimination in hiring and promotion policies involving minority workers. Many of the differences in the employment status of blacks and other minorities have been due to their inability to obtain jobs commensurate with their training. This inability has been attributed to some degree to the restrictive practices of trade unions, including union referral arrangements, complex seniority systems, and union shops.

EQUITY AND INCOME DISTRIBUTION

Decisions concerning income distribution compose one of the most fundamental starting points for any market economy. The question of what constitutes an equitable distribution of income is difficult to answer. On purely ethical grounds, it is hard to justify the market economy position that those persons who contribute most to output should receive the most income. Problems arise because individuals and families differ with respect to age distribution, health problems, and in many other ways and therefore have different needs in an objective sense. Unfortunately, there are no accepted ethical standards for determining the degree to which contributions to output should be rewarded, nor are there any accepted economic standards for determining how much effort any individual is capable of making. The result is that the Western market-oriented countries have accepted the idea that income distribution is much too important to be left solely to market-determined forces. In subsequent chapters, income distribution in other countries will be examined. Comparisons with the United States are made difficult by differences in statistical observation and classification as well as the social dimensions inherent in the concept of income distribution.

POVERTY

Poverty exists in a society when the real income or standard of living of some of its members is lower than is considered acceptable for that society. (In some countries, a majority of people would be living in poverty according to U.S. acceptable standards.) In the United States, an income level is established below which poverty is said to exist. This income level is based on family size and ages of its members. A food budget that provides nutritive diets for families of different sizes and ages is determined. This budget is multiplied by three to set the poverty income level.

In 1984, 11.6 percent of all American families were below the poverty line, down from a high of 18.1 percent in 1960, when poverty measurements began, but up from a low of 8.8 percent in 1974. Poverty possesses many demographic characteristics. Black families are more likely to be poor than white families. In 1984, 9.1 percent of white families were below the poverty level compared to 30.9 percent of black families. Twenty-seven percent of all white households headed by a female were below the poverty level; and 51.7 percent of all black households headed by a female were below the poverty level.[13] People living in rural areas and urban ghettos are more likely to be poor, as are young people without skills and the elderly.

13. *Economic Report of the President, 1986* (Washington: USGPO, February, 1986), p. 286.

■ THE U.S. ECONOMY ■
IN THE MIDDLE 1980s

The U.S. economy at the beginning of this decade appeared to be in a state of economic and political paralysis that many persons thought could be permanent. In fact, the title of the opening chapter of Lester Thurow's book *The Zero-Sum Society* probably summed up the conditions of the U.S. economy quite well: "An Economy That No Longer Performs."[14] The economy was stagnant, productivity was low, and inflation was high. Many opinions were advanced to explain the condition of the U.S. economy. One explanation placed the poor performance of the American economy on a decline in the Protestant work ethic, and another explanation put the blame on a low rate of saving in the United States relative to other countries. The success of Japan was attributed, among other things, to a high rate of saving that provided the Japanese with the resources necessary for capital formation. A third explanation was that the U.S. political system seemed to lack the capacity to get things done.

GOVERNMENT ECONOMIC POLICY: SUPPLY-SIDE ECONOMICS

Supply-side economics received considerable attention in the early 1980s. The term supply-side economics is really a reaction against the demand-side economics of John Maynard Keynes, which had guided government stabilization policies in most Western countries since the end of World War II. There is nothing new about supply-side economics. Supply was an important component of nineteenth-century classical economics, with emphasis on increasing total output by concentrating on the quantity and quality of such productive elements as labor, natural resources, physical plant and equipment, and financial capital. This emphasis was updated to place attention on the supply side of the American economy, where certain impediments to economic growth had developed. The foremost impediment was a low rate of saving that retarded capital formation and reduced the growth rate of productivity. The solution, according to the supply-side economists, was to cut taxes, particularly those taxes that impinge upon saving and investment.

14. Thurow, *Zero-Sum Society*, p. 3.

REAGANOMICS

Reaganomics has had five components—a large across-the-board tax cut, a cut in social welfare spending, an increase in defense spending, less government regulation, and restricted growth in the money supply. The tax cut reflected a belief in the efficacy of supply-side economics. The cuts were designed to favor those persons who made $50,000 or more, for they provide the bulk of savings in the United States. Savings were supposed to increase and to be channeled into investment. The flow in tax cut creates savings creates investment creates increased productivity. Cuts in social welfare expenditures were designed to limit increases in entitlement programs. Increases in defense spending were not designed for economic reasons, but had the effect of increasing the deficit in the federal budget because they were larger than cuts in civilian spending. Antitrust and other forms of government regulation were relaxed because they discouraged investment and were too costly to business. The slow rate of growth in the money supply was designed to reduce inflation.

THE ECONOMIC RECOVERY TAX ACT   The cornerstone of Reagan's tax policy was the Economic Recovery Tax Act, ERTA, which was signed into law in August 1981. The act legislated sweeping changes in both the individual and corporate income taxes. It provides for an across-the-board reduction in individual income tax rates amounting to 23 percent over three years, and an immediate cut in the top bracket from 70 to 50 percent. These reduced marginal rates were designed to increase the incentive to invest. There was a shift in emphasis away from using the tax system to redistribute income and toward the creation of national income through economic growth. The corporate income tax was also reduced from 48 percent to 46 percent, and ERTA allowed accelerated depreciation of new capital assets and a system of tax credits for investment. Both of these provisions decreased the effective tax burden on new investment.

CHANGES IN FEDERAL EXPENDITURES   The composition of federal expenditures by the Reagan administration reflected its objectives. As a share of GNP, defense expenditures grew from 4.9 percent in 1980 to 6.3 percent in 1985, as total federal expenditures increased from 21.6 percent of GNP in 1980 to 23.7 percent in 1985. The federal deficit rose from 2.7 percent of GNP in 1980 to 5.3 percent in 1985. Changes in tax laws reduced receipts as a share of GNP to the range that had existed over most of the 1970s— from 21.1 percent in 1981 to an estimated 19.1 percent in 1985.[15] Given

15. Office of Management and Budget, *Budget of the United States Government, Fiscal Year 1986* (Washington: USGPO, 1985), pp. 48-57.

the increase in expenditures and the decrease in tax revenues, it is obvious why the federal budget deficit increased. However, without tax law changes, GNP growth during the 1983–1985 recovery would probably have been lower.

MONETARY POLICY There were four changes in monetary policy over the 1981–1985 period. The first change, which extended to mid-1982, saw the Federal Reserve pursue a restrictive monetary policy designed to reduce inflation. The second change began in the late summer of 1982. Prompted by accumulating evidence that the recession would be deeper and longer than had been expected, the Federal Reserve began to ease credit and the money supply. Interest rates fell sharply as the growth in the money supply accelerated in 1982 and early 1983. The third change began in the spring of 1983 and ran to the latter part of 1984. The concern was that too rapid a recovery of the economy would lead to inflation. Interest rates were permitted to rise and money supply growth was substantially reduced. The fourth change began in late 1984 and has continued through mid-1986. Fear that the economic recovery was running out of steam led the Federal Reserve to increase the money supply, and interest rates fell to one of their lowest points in the decade.

REGULATORY POLICIES A number of federal regulatory agencies were created during the 1970s and regulation increased in such areas as consumer protection and the environment. By the end of the decade, there was a feeling that there was too much regulation of the American economy. During the election campaign of 1980, Reagan promised to get the government off the people's backs. Regulatory approaches to environmental and health and safety problems raised production costs and created considerable uncertainty as rules and regulations continually changed. It was also felt that antitrust regulation was out of step with the times and that concentration of output in the hands of a few large firms in a given industry could not automatically be considered bad. The Reagan administration did not eliminate any of the major regulatory agencies, but it did attempt to cut back on the extent of their enforcement. In the area of antitrust policy, a number of major mergers were permitted, including mergers involving Standard Oil of California, Gulf, Texaco, and Getty, four of the largest oil companies in the U.S.[16]

16. An antitrust case against IBM was dropped by the Reagan administration. On the other hand, in probably the most important antitrust case of all time, AT&T was broken up into different entities— AT&T, which provides long-distance telephone service, and seven regional companies, which provide local operating service.

■ CURRENT ECONOMIC PROBLEMS ■
IN THE UNITED STATES

As mentioned at the beginning of the chapter, the performance of the U.S. economy in the middle 1980s has been solid. The rate of inflation is down to 4 percent or less, compared to the double-digit inflation of the last part of the 1970s. The rate of economic growth has improved and unemployment has remained around 7.3 percent of the labor force—a rate much lower than the unemployment rate in France, West Germany, and other European countries. Moreover, the U.S. economy has created new jobs at the rate of 1.5 million a year. Nevertheless, there are serious problems confronting the U.S. economy that need to be addressed because of their potential impact upon the future of the country. One problem is the deficit in the federal budget, a second is the deficit in the U.S. balance of payments, and a third is the transformation of the United States into a debtor nation. All three problems are related.

THE DEFICIT IN THE FEDERAL BUDGET

The U.S. government has two main ways in which it can finance its expenditures—through taxation and through borrowing.[17] The latter is far less painful to politicians and taxpayers because it involves no immediate sacrifice on their parts. Since 1966 the U.S. government has run a surplus in the budget only once, and in 1985 the budget deficit amounted to around $220 billion. Budgetary receipts came from three primary sources —personal income taxes accounted for 37 percent of total receipts; social security contributions, for 30 percent; and borrowing for 18 percent. There are three main types of expenditures—entitlement expenditures, which accounted for 41 percent of total budget expenditures in 1985; national defense expenditures, which accounted for 29 percent; and interest payments on the federal debt, which amounted to 15 percent.[18] Interest payments have been the fastest growing expenditure in the federal budget over the last 10 years, as interest rates and the federal deficit have increased.

Table 6-9 presents expenditures and receipts in the federal budget for the period 1970–1985. At no time during this period was the budget balanced; outlays were always in excess of receipts. In only two years, 1970 and 1974, was the budget even close to being balanced. The deficit increased considerably during the first term of the Reagan administration as

17. The government can also print more money.
18. OMB, *United States Budget, 1986*, p. 112.

TABLE 6-9   FEDERAL GOVERNMENTAL TOTAL RECEIPTS
            AND EXPENDITURES: 1970–1985
            (billions of dollars)

	Receipts	Outlays	Deficits
1970	$192.8	$195.6	$— 2.8
1971	187.1	210.2	— 23.0
1972	207.3	230.7	— 23.4
1973	230.8	245.7	— 14.9
1974	263.2	269.4	— 6.1
1975	279.1	332.3	— 53.2
1976	298.1	371.8	— 73.7
1977	355.6	409.2	— 53.6
1978	399.7	458.7	— 59.0
1979	463.3	503.5	— 40.2
1980	517.1	590.9	— 73.8
1981	599.3	678.2	— 78.9
1982	617.8	745.7	—127.9
1983	600.6	808.3	—207.8
1984	666.5	851.8	—185.3
1985	734.1	946.3	—212.3

Source: Office of Management and Budget, *Budget of the United States Government, Fiscal Year
1986* (Washington: USGPO, 1985), p. 60; and *Economic Report of the President, 1986*
(Washington: USGPO, 1986), p. 241.

taxes were cut at the same time national defense spending was increased.
The deficit in the budget reached a projected high of $220 billion in 1985.

THE LAFFER CURVE   The centerpiece of supply-side economics was the
Laffer curve and its concept of incentive effects. Figure 6-1 illustrates the
Laffer curve, which is backward bending. Its shape is based on the concept that if government levies no taxes, it collects no revenues; if it levies
100 percent taxes, it collects no revenues—because no one would work.
Tax rates are plotted on the vertical axis, and tax revenues are on the horizontal axis. As tax rates first rise, so do government revenues. However,
the curve eventually bends backward as increased taxes cause a decline in
work and investment large enough to reduce tax revenues. The assumption was made that U.S. economy was at an upper point on the curve. The
increase in national income that a tax cut was supposed to generate would
raise government tax revenues so much that the loss of revenues from the
tax cut would be more than offset. However, this plan did not work; instead, the budget deficit increased.

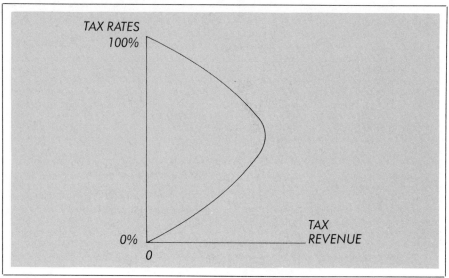

FIGURE 6-1   THE LAFFER CURVE

THE EFFECT OF THE DEFICIT ON THE U.S. ECONOMY   The deficit has two main effects on the U.S. economy: on interest rates and on the U.S. balance of payments with other countries. Interest rates are increased because the U.S. Treasury must compete with private borrowers for loanable funds, thus increasing the amount of interest that the federal government has to pay each year to service the national debt. Interest on the national debt has increased from $26 billion in 1976 to $130 billion in 1985, or from 8 percent of budget outlays to 15 percent.[19] High real rates of interest (that is, the difference between money interest rates and the rate of inflation) attract foreign investment into the United States. This has the effect of driving the value of the dollar up relative to foreign currencies and leads to another major problem confronting the U.S. economy—the deficit in the balance of payments.

BALANCE OF PAYMENTS DEFICIT

In July 1985, the U.S. merchandise trade deficit was $15.6 billion, the highest monthly trade deficit in U.S. history.[20] The high value of the U.S.

---

19. Ibid., pp. 9-59.

20. The U.S. merchandise trade account is a part of the U.S. balance of payments. It consists of exports of U.S. goods abroad and imports of foreign goods into the U.S.

dollar relative to other currencies has made U.S. exports more expensive and foreign imports cheaper. The U.S. has an enormous trade deficit with Japan, projected to be $50 billion by the end of 1985. The high value of the dollar has resulted in the movement of U.S. manufacturing jobs to other countries and has caused increased demand for protection for domestic industries. This protectionist sentiment is primarily focused against Japan and other East Asian countries with whom the U.S. has major trade deficits. Increased protectionism against countries that are in the process of economic development reduces their export earnings, which is detrimental to their capacity to import and is a threat to U.S. export firms.

THE U.S. AS A DEBTOR NATION

At the end of 1985 the United States was a debtor nation for the first time since 1914. At the end of 1984, U.S. foreign investment, including direct ownership of overseas factories, stock and bond holdings by U.S. investors, and bank loans, totaled $914.7 billion.[21] Foreign ownership of assets of the same type in the United States at the same time totaled $886.5 billion, leaving the United States with an investment surplus of only $28.2 billion. The surplus became a deficit in 1985. This is neither all good nor all bad as far as the United States is concerned. Foreign investment in the United States does not create jobs for Americans.[22] Moreover, foreign investment in U.S. government securities is one way of financing the federal budget deficit. However, the United States may become more vulnerable in international capital markets because it must borrow more money from foreigners to pay its debts.

Coupled with the change in the United States to being a debtor nation is the decline of the United States as a manufacturing economy. The United States is in the process of transforming into a service economy, with 70 percent of the labor force employed in a variety of service jobs ranging from banking to fast foods. American manufacturing firms are finding it more difficult to compete at home and abroad in part because of the strong dollar and in part because of higher costs, including higher labor costs. There are those who feel that the United States is headed for long-run trouble: National income will fall, the economy will generate less wealth, businesses will lose important markets, and the standard of living will decline. However, it should be noted that service industries cover a wide variety of jobs—doctors, lawyers, teachers, and engineers are ex-

21. U.S. Department of Commerce, *Business America*, July 15, 1985, p. 3.

22. An example is the Nissan Motors truck assembly plant in Smyrna, Tennessee, which employs around 5,000 people.

amples. Those jobs are powerful producers of income; some 17 million service jobs outside of government paid the median ($326 a week) or more for full-time workers in 1984. The United States also gains from an inflow of income from the provision of various services to foreign countries.[23]

INTEREST GROUP PLURALISM

The foundation of any liberal society, as Daniel Bell points out, is a willingness on the part of individuals to compromise private ends for the public interest.[24] There has to be a set of reciprocal obligations between individuals in a group to hold the institutions of a society together. In the United States there has been a loss of cohesiveness, resulting from the fragmentation of society into a collection of special interest groups. Everybody organizes and goes out to fight. The result is an increase in conflict and in the politics of confrontation. Each group goes its own way and pursues its own goals; the interests of society count for little.

The result is often paralysis on the part of the national leadership. Congress's handling of the federal deficit provides an excellent example. After delaying through most of 1985, it finally undertook half-hearted measures to reduce the deficit. The criterion for cutting government expenditures was: "What special interest groups will the cuts affect the least?" Any attempt to increase taxes was shot down by special interest groups, and attempts at tax reform suffered the same fate. Social security expenditures were not touched for fear of offending the elderly, who represent a large voting block. When it becomes necessary to make a sacrifice, each special interest group expects someone else to make it.[25] It is becoming more difficult to govern by consensus. Politicians are now measured by immediate performance, reflecting the self-gratification syndrome that pervades U.S. society.

23. Services provide a surplus in the U.S. current account.

24. Daniel Bell, *The Cultural Contradictions of Capitalism* (New York: Basic Books Inc., Publishers, 1978), p. 245.

25. Or, as Senator Russell Long once put it: "Don't tax you, don't tax me; tax that man behind the tree."

S U M M A R Y

The deficit in the budget and the strength of the U.S. dollar relative to other currencies were the main problems confronting the U.S. economy in 1985. Whether they continue to remain problems in the future will depend on actions taken to balance the federal budget. Although growth rates are projected to increase through 1986, the deficit does have an inhibiting effect on the future growth of the economy because it reduces the potential supply of savings available for capital formation, contributes to high interest rates, and is responsible for the strength of the dollar. Whether the deficit will be reduced depends upon the political will of Congress and the political will of the president. The dominance of special interest groups makes any possibility of rational compromise on either raising taxes or cutting government expenditures remote.

In the international sphere, the Soviet Union is still the military and geopolitical equal of the United States despite a much lower gross national product. There is a deficit in the U.S. merchandise trade accounts with other countries, particularly Japan and other East Asian countries. Protectionism is now in vogue with many U.S. politicians, who hold the Japanese responsible for American problems instead of themselves and their policies. Japan will be the likely recipient of U.S. trade sanctions. Although the United States remains the dominant economic power in the world, competition has increased, with Japan the main challenge. The paramount issue is global economic growth that opens markets and makes change easier. Unfortunately, in an interdependent world, growth is hostage to rigid domestic interests and policies.

REVIEW QUESTIONS

1. What is supply-side economics?
2. Discuss Reaganomics.
3. Discuss the performance of the American economy from 1980 to 1985.
4. Compare the economic performance of the United States to the performance of other major industrial countries for the period 1980 to 1985.
5. Reduction of inflation has been a major accomplishment of the Reagan administration. Discuss.
6. Discuss some of the demographic characteristics of U.S. income distribution.
7. What is the Laffer curve?
8. What impact does the federal deficit have on the U.S. economy?
9. The United States is in the process of becoming a debtor nation. Is this good or bad?

10. Is the United States in the process of losing its position as the world's leading economic power?

RECOMMENDED READINGS

Lodge, George C. *The American Disease*. New York: Alfred E. Knopf Inc., 1984.

North, Douglas C. *Structure and Change in Economic History*. New York: W.W. Norton & Co. Inc., 1982.

Olson, Mancur. *The Rise and Fall of Nations*. New Haven: Yale University Press, 1983.

Phillips, Kevin E. *Staying on Top*. New York: Random House Inc., 1984.

Rohatyn, Felix G. *The Twentieth Century*. New York: Random House Inc., 1983.

Thurow, Lester C. *Dangerous Currents*. New York: Random House Inc., 1983.

Vogel, Ezra F. *Comeback*. New York: Simon & Schuster Inc., 1985.

Williamson, Jeffrey, and Peter Lindert. *American Inequality*. New York: Academic Press Inc., 1982.

PART 3

MIXED ECONOMIC SYSTEMS

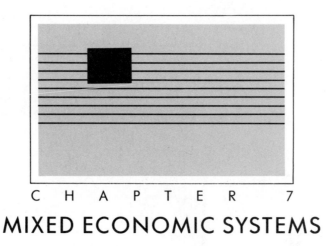

MIXED ECONOMIC SYSTEMS

Many books on comparative economic systems classify countries on the basis of "isms"—capitalism, communism, and socialism. A set of institutions is defined for each system and various countries are classified as belonging to one system or another. At one time there was certainly a clear-cut line of demarcation between the various systems, but recent developments have tended to obfuscate many differences that once existed. Countries can no longer be dumped into a box neatly labeled capitalism, communism, or socialism. Pure capitalism and pure communism do not exist; institutional arrangements of each do. Current economic reforms in China have incorporated many of the arrangements of a capitalist market economy, but the country still considers itself a socialist country in the Marxist sense. Moreover, some of the goals of such disparate societies as the United States and the Soviet Union are similar, but the methods designed to achieve them are different. One example is high growth rates.

The idea, once prevalent in capitalist societies, that acting in one's self-interest benefits other members of society is no longer accepted as an article of faith. With large corporations, labor unions, and big government in all noncommunist industrialized countries, the capitalist system of the early part of this century no longer exists. There is less willingness to let all economic decisions be resolved by the impersonal forces of the market.

One of the most distinctive changes has been a demand for equality in the distribution of income. The issue of equality includes the role of government in reducing or containing income disparities between persons. This has meant an enormous expansion in government transfer payments and services in all Western countries.

■ MIXED ECONOMIC SYSTEMS ■

The term *mixed economic system* can be applied to the western European countries, Japan, and also the United States.[1] A mixed economic system combines some of the basic features of capitalism (private enterprise, the price mechanism, and profit) along with considerable government intervention in the economy. Three countries can be used as prototypes of mixed economic systems—France, Japan, and the United Kingdom. Among these three countries, however, there is considerable variation in the extent and type of government intervention in the economy. In France some industries are state-owned and there is a well-developed social welfare state. The United Kingdom, under the Thatcher government, has attempted some rollback in state participation in the economy. Conversely, Japan does not have a comprehensive social welfare system, most industries are privately owned, and planning is a cooperative arrangement between business and government. Nevertheless, it is possible to identify certain characteristics that are applicable to the economies of these and other Western industrial countries.

1. The role of government in economic policy is pervasive. A commitment to full employment dominated economic policy in most Western countries until the early 1970s. Memories of mass unemployment during the Depression remained fresh in the minds of Western government policymakers. Fiscal and monetary policies were subverted to the objective of full employment; price stability, as an economic goal, was secondary in importance. During the 1970s, serious problems occurred to force at least a partial reevaluation of economic policy. Double-digit inflation and faltering growth rates, caused in part by OPEC oil price increases, focused attention on inflation and growth policies.

---

1. Japan is not a Western country, but it is a capitalist country, with the government playing a strong role in the economy. The Western European countries would be included as Western countries; for that matter, so would Australia, even though geographically it is not Western.

2. The creation of elaborate social welfare programs has caused the name *welfare state* to be used in describing the economic and social systems of these countries, particularly the United Kingdom. These programs provide a wide variety of social welfare transfer payments and constitute a sizable part of total government expenditures. Western governments have become heavily involved in altering the distribution of income through the use of transfer payments. Advanced industrial countries, with their delicate social and physical interactions, cannot tolerate extreme deprivation. It would be too easy for those with nothing to lose to disrupt the rest of society.

3. There is a basic reliance on free enterprise and the market system in all three countries. Facilities for production and distribution remain primarily in the hands of private enterprise.[2] Nevertheless, the government plays an important role. Control over the budget and credit gives the government enormous leverage over the decisions of business firms. Tax policies are used to influence resource allocation and tax incentives are used to stimulate industrial development. In Japan there is a close working relationship between business and government. However, government makes no effort to subsidize or bail out inefficient firms or industries.[3]

4. There is some reliance on economic planning of the indicative type, particularly in France. Planning, as used in France, is a system for centrally guiding the whole economy in the direction the planners would like it to go. Supporters of the French indicative economic planning contend that it is free from the elements of political authoritarianism and economic regimentation associated with Soviet-type command plans and from the defects of the unplanned, free market economies that existed in the United States and Western Europe prior to World War II.

5. There is some state ownership of industry. In France, the private part of the French banking system was nationalized by the Mitterand government in the fall of 1981. However, the major part of the banking system had been state-owned since 1945, when de Gaulle nationalized it. Much nationalization that occurred in both France and the United Kingdom took place in

2. Even in France, which has gone through recent nationalization of banking and other industries, 82 percent of all industry is still privately owned.

3. Yoshi Tsurumi, "How to Handle the Next Chrysler," *Fortune*, June 16, 1980, pp. 87-89.

the period immediately after World War II, for reasons that had little to do with political or economic ideology. For example, the French automotive firm Renault was nationalized by the de Gaulle government because its owners had collaborated with the Nazis.

Before examining the economic systems of France, Japan, and the United Kingdom, it is desirable to explore the characteristics mentioned above in some detail to provide a frame of reference. Perhaps the key point that should be remembered is that, although the free market is recognized as the normal mechanism of resource allocation, government plays a very important role in developing economic policy and redistribution incomes. Few subjects are as emotionally charged as how public policy should be used to influence the distribution of income. At issue is the question of how the total income of society is to be divided among its citizens.

■ ECONOMIC PLANNING ■

The objectives of economic planning are certain general aims of economic policy expressed in qualitative terms: achieving a high rate of economic growth with full employment, achieving price stability and balance of payments equilibrium, lessening the relative income difference between rich and poor, industrializing poorer regions, and so on. Economic planning is an attempt to coordinate the economic activities of different sectors of society in the interest of optimal economic growth and structural balance.

United States history includes examples of economic plans. In the late eighteenth century, both Alexander Hamilton and Albert Gallatin (secretary of the treasury under President Jefferson) prepared comprehensive plans for the development of the country. In fact, the rapid economic growth of the United States in the early nineteenth century may be ascribed largely to Hamilton's foresight and genius for planning. President Kennedy supplied another example of planning in the early 1960s when he established the goal of landing a man on the moon within that same decade. The government aided businesses in developing new technology, a plan was proposed, and the cost was estimated in advance.

Economic planning can be classified as imperative or indicative, with gradations between these two extremes. *Imperative planning* would apply to a centralized macroeconomic plan in an economy dominated by its public sector. The government assumes control and regulation of output, prices, and wages. There is no reliance on the free market to allocate resources. *Indicative planning* would apply in an economy in which the government indicates a series of goals and either directly or indirectly stimulates certain desired economic activities through the budget, tax and transfer payment policies, and control over the supply of credit and interest rates. The free market, subject to some alterations, is recognized as the normal mechanism of resource allocation.

THE SOVIET UNION AND IMPERATIVE PLANNING

The Russian economic plan is an example of imperative economic planning. The planners, as would be true in any country, start with limited resources and must allocate them to each economic sector to maintain some kind of balance for the normal production of goods and services needed for the country. Russian economic planning consists of selected physical targets for output, employment, and consumption by sectors and regions. A plan is built around output goals and capacity growth needed for leading industries and their supportive branches and for other sectors of secondary importance. A system of input-output balances is used to derive the various output and employment targets. Plans are drawn up on the basis of directives from the leadership of the Communist party, which also controls the government. Consumer sovereignty is pretty much disregarded in the Soviet Union, and failure to fulfill the goals defined by the planners redounds to the serious disadvantage of those who are responsible.[4] Needless to say, this leads to state enterprises playing it safe and avoiding innovation.

FRANCE AND INDICATIVE PLANNING

French economic planning is an example of indicative planning.[5] It is much less extreme or coercive than Russian planning and is essentially a set of directives or guidelines to help guide the planning of private industry as well as the public sector of the economy. Nevertheless, there is a certain amount of government intervention in the implementation of planning,

---

4. It has been said that a Russian plan is reducible to an input-output table plus a monopoly on propaganda.

5. The term *indicative* may be a misnomer. Although French planning is not imperative or mandatory, it does attempt to guide the economy in a certain direction, and it does have the machinery to make its preferences effective. The nationalization of private French banks in 1981 gives the state even more control over credit.

which has taken the form of indirect control over credit and taxation to encourage desirable objectives. There exists in France a whole range of measures that enable industries that conform to the plan to be rewarded. These include access to bank credit, tax concessions, and, within the policy for regional development, subsidies for factories and equipment.

DEFECTS IN ECONOMIC PLANNING

Indicative economic planning has been held up by its advocates as a cure-all for economic problems. However, planning has its defects as well as its virtues. Countries with some form of economic planning have not fared any better than the United States in the areas of employment and inflation, particularly in the late 1970s and the early 1980s.[6] Forecasting, which is supposed to be easier when economic planning is involved, has not been that successful. Even in Japan's carefully monitored economy, it has proven to be quite difficult to predict variables in the Japanese private sector for a protracted time span, say, more than six months to a year. Random shocks in the world economy can throw off even the best of forecasts.

■ FISCAL AND MONETARY ■ POLICIES

Government fiscal and monetary policies play important roles in mixed economic systems. The primary purpose of each is economic stabilization, which has the dual goals of controlling tendencies toward inflation or large-scale unemployment. A third objective, which is related, is a desirable rate of economic growth. This refers to real per capita increases in goods and services produced over a time. A high rate of economic growth is reflected in higher living standards. Full employment without economic growth is meaningless. In comparing the efficiency and effectiveness of various economic systems, economic growth is certainly a valid criterion. The process of influencing price level stability and full employment through fiscal and monetary policies can also be used to influence the rate of economic growth.

---

6. The French unemployment rate reached 9 percent in the summer of 1985 and the rate of inflation was around 8 percent. Both rates were higher than the U.S. rates.

FISCAL POLICY

On the whole, policy means the government carries the major responsibility for providing the conditions necessary for economic growth in the Western European countries and Japan. This substantial level of government participation in economic activity is regarded in the United States as properly the sphere for private action. The term *public investment* would embrace a much wide range of economic activities in France or the United Kingdom than it would in the United States. The relatively large government ownership of public utilities, transportation and communication facilities, and many basic industries means expenditure policies in these countries are much more directly involved in the expansion of total productive capacity than is true in the United States. Public investment in these industries has been pursued vigorously to stimulate employment and economic growth.

MONETARY POLICY

Monetary policy refers to central bank actions to lessen fluctuations in investment and consumer spending through the regulation and use of the supply of money. The central banks of France, the United Kingdom, and Japan are state-owned and thus have less autonomy than the Federal Reserve of the United States. The Bank of England enjoys autonomy in determining and guiding monetary policy, but its policies are closely coordinated with those of the government. In Japan the central bank serves as the fiscal agent of the government and is a major source of financial capital.

When inflation became the main economic problem in the Western European countries and Japan, central bank monetary policies became more important than government fiscal policies. The latter, which are easier to expedite during a period of unemployment, become a political liability during inflation, as both Ronald Reagan and Margaret Thatcher have found out. It is easier to cut taxes than to raise them, and it is harder to cut government expenditures than to increase them.

■ STATE OWNERSHIP OF INDUSTRY ■

State ownership of industry is a distinct manifestation of socialism. The reasons for state ownership are perhaps obvious. It is alleged by the socialists that production for profit under a capitalist system leads to social waste and unemployment. In addition, certain wants, such as public health and education, are difficult to express in the marketplace; as a result, they are not adequately fulfilled under capitalism. Since profit is the basic entrepreneurial motive in a free enterprise system, social costs—polluted streams, polluted air, and wasted natural resources—are not considered. There are also certain industries affecting the public interest that are considered by socialists to be too important to be left in private hands. Banks and railroads are examples. Finally, state ownership of key industries gives the government greater control over the enforcement of fiscal and monetary policies.

For the most part, state ownership of industry in Western Europe had no relationship to political ideology until the 1981 election of Francois Mitterand, a Socialist leader, as president of France. In most countries, certain industries have always been operated by government. In France, for example, there was a mixed system of public and private ownership and control before the Franco-Prussian War. The government of the United Kingdom, wishing to coordinate telegraph services with the post office, had the postmaster general take over all telegraph companies in 1869. In 1896 the post office bought all the long-distance telephone lines from private telephone companies, and in 1911 it bought all privately owned telephone properties. In Japan government control and operation of certain industries dates back to the Meiji Restoration of 1868.

STATE OWNERSHIP OF INDUSTRY IN FRANCE

A wave of nationalization developed in the United Kingdom and France in the period immediately following World War II. However, socialism was only one of several factors responsible for it. France emerged from the German occupation a stripped and debilitated economy, desperately short of raw materials, consumer goods, and food supplies. Transportation was paralyzed, industrial production had fallen to 40 percent of the 1938 level, a generalized black market had replaced the usual channels of trade, and an inflated currency threatened to bring the whole economy down in chaos. In order to achieve economic recovery, the French government had to play an important role. The immediate postwar years were consequently characterized by a policy of economic *dirigisme* (direction), as opposed to a quick return to a market economy, which was the way West Germany chose. The *dirigisme* policy brought with it some important nationalizations, affecting the gas and electric power industries, almost the whole of coal mining, the Renault motor works, the Bank of France, the four largest deposit banks, and the larger insurance companies.

RENAULT: A CASE STUDY OF STATE OWNERSHIP   Renault is one of the oldest manufacturers of automobiles. The first Renault car was produced in 1898. In 1914 taxis built by Renault carried French soldiers to the First Battle of the Marne. From 1918 to 1939 the company was the largest producer of automobiles in Western Europe. However, Louis Renault, the company's owner, was accused of collaborating with the Nazis during World War II, and as punishment the company was nationalized by the de Gaulle government in 1945. Since that time the company has been owned by the government and run by government appointees.[7] Renault has been run on strictly commercial lines and is expected to pay its own way. It pays taxes and uses the same accounting system as any private company in France. It is one of France's leading exporters, a factor that has led the government to avoid general interference with managerial decisions.

STATE OWNERSHIP OF INDUSTRY IN THE UNITED KINGDOM

When the Labour party came into office in the United Kingdom in 1946, a limited number of industries were brought under state ownership. Coal was one industry that was nationalized. It is probable that the Conservative party, had it remained in office, would have also nationalized the coal industry. The Bank of England was already in effect a public institution. Its change to nationalized status was hardly more than a change of title. The railroads, nationalized by the Transportation Act, were pretty much subject to government control from the outset.

The nationalization of the British steel industry by the Labour party, however, was a much more specific socialist measure, and it aroused considerable controversy. The industry was nationalized because it was considered desirable for the government to assume control over an industry upon which the British economy was dependent. Government also believed that there was too much concentration of economic power in the few companies in the industry. Through trade associations, these companies had adopted price fixing and other cartel practices.

BRITISH STEEL CORPORATION: A CASE STUDY OF STATE OWNERSHIP
The British steel industry was nationalized by the Labour government in 1951 and denationalized by the Conservative government when it came

---

7. Representatives of the ministries of industries, economy, defense, and transportation are on the supervisory board.

into office in the same year. The industry was renationalized in 1967 by the Labour government, which was once more in office; the 14 largest companies, accounting for 92 percent of total raw steel output, were merged into the state-owned British Steel Corporation. The government saw the nationalization as the only way to inject large amounts of capital into the industry and to eliminate obsolete facilities. Unions regarded nationalization as a means to insure job security and high pay for their members.

The result of nationalization has been poor performance by the British Steel Corporation. It has lost money in each year from 1976 to 1984. In 1984 it lost $382,000, which was covered by the British Treasury. The company cannot compete successfully in the international steel market against Japanese and South Korean steel producers. The number of employees fell from 250,000 in 1971 to 78,750 in 1984, with most pared from the labor force because of increasing company losses.[8] Management of British Steel has been at the mercy of politics and the unions. However, inefficient plants have been shut down and labor productivity has improved, and British Steel cut its losses from $3.8 million in 1980 to the $382,000 in 1984.

■ INCOME DISTRIBUTION ■ AND SOCIAL WELFARE

Despite Marxist predictions of inevitable collapse, capitalism has shown a surprising ability not only to survive but also to expand and adapt to the democratic conditions of modern industrialized society that, it must not be forgotten, it has strongly helped to create. One manifestation of this adaption has been the development of what can be called *welfare statism*. Actually, a precursor of the welfare state was the social welfare program developed in Germany in 1883, when Bismark's opposition to socialism and his jealousy of the trade union movement led him to sponsor health insurance and old-age insurance. Bismark, a political pragmatist of the first order, realized that social legislation was necessary to remove the causes around which socialism was developing. Another precursor of the modern welfare state was the social welfare program of the Liberal government in

8. *Fortune*, August 19, 1985, p. 185.

the United Kingdom. Developed in 1908, the program included social insurance for health and unemployment, old-age pensions, and assistance to low-income workers through the statutory fixing of minimum wages.

The fundamental premise of the welfare state as it has developed in the capitalistic countries is that governments must intervene to achieve certain economic and social objectives. Two goals are emphasized: an equitable distribution of income and wealth and security of living standards against such vagaries of life as unemployment, ill health, and old age. The development of the welfare state stemmed from dissatisfaction with the distribution of income and wealth. Under a purely competitive market economy, market forces would compensate people on the basis of their contributions to total output. However, this idea was modified when extreme income and wealth disparities between the rich and poor developed. Often these disparities had nothing to do with a person's contribution to total output, but were based on inherited wealth or other special privileges.

GOVERNMENT DISTRIBUTION POLICIES

The public sector of an economy is engaged in two major types of activities, each of which can be measured by the expenditures incurred in carrying it out. One activity involves the provision of a broad array of goods and services including roads, education, and police protection. These purchases represent a transfer of resources from the private sector of an economy to the public sector, and they also represent the contribution of the government sector to total gross national product. A measure that can be used to indicate the extent to which Western governments contribute to the national output of goods and services is the ratio of government spending on goods and services to gross national product.

The other activity involves the use of transfer payments as an instrument for the redistribution of income, generally with the dual objectives of greater income equality and the provision of some minimum standard of living for everyone. Transfer payments, as distinguished from government purchases of goods and services, involve only the transfer of income from one group to another and provide no equivalent value in terms of goods and services. Transfer payments in most Western countries have come to include family allowances, old age pensions, accident benefits, and unemployment compensation. Some services, such as free medical care, are normally considered direct government purchases of services that absorb resources the same way as does spending for other goods and services.

THE IMPORTANCE OF GOVERNMENT

The economic influence of government is of paramount importance in the analysis of mixed economic systems. This influence can be measured using several criteria.

1. The relationship of government expenditures to gross national product indicates the extent to which resources have been diverted from private to public use.
2. The relationship of transfer payments to total government expenditures indicates the extent to which government expenditures are used to redistribute income.
3. The relationship of taxes to gross national product indicates the extent to which governments have control over economic resources.

Table 7-1 presents government expenditures expressed as percentages of gross national product for selected industrial countries for 1983. Japan and the United States had the lowest ratio of government outlays to gross national product, while Belgium and the Netherlands had the highest. Expenditures include both government spending for goods and services and transfer payments. Government expenditures as percentage of gross national product increased during the 1970s but leveled off during the 1980s and even showed a decline in some countries as an economic recession created a decline in tax revenues.

Table 7-2 presents transfer payments expressed as a percentage of total government expenditures for the same countries. The United States,

T A B L E 7 - 1   GOVERNMENT EXPENDITURES EXPRESSED AS A PERCENTAGE OF GNP FOR SELECTED COUNTRIES

Italy	49.8%	Denmark	45.6%
Belgium	57.9	Canada	26.0
United Kingdom	42.4	Netherlands	58.9
Japan	18.9	Sweden	44.9
France	42.1	Norway	39.7
West Germany	31.5	United States	25.0

Source: The World Bank, *World Development Report 1985*, p. 225.

TABLE 7-2   TRANSFER PAYMENTS EXPRESSED AS A PERCENTAGE OF CENTRAL GOVERNMENT EXPENDITURES FOR SELECTED COUNTRIES, 1983

Italy	33.6%	Denmark	48.8%
Belgium	45.8	Canada	37.2
United Kingdom	45.2	Netherlands	40.9
Japan	24.9	Sweden	50.4
France	47.1	Norway	35.7
West Germany	50.0	United States	36.1

Source: The World Bank, *World Development Report 1985,* p. 225.

Japan, Norway, and Italy ranked at the bottom, while West Germany and Sweden ranked at the top. It is necessary to point out that only central government expenditures are used. Some countries are much more centralized than others. France is an example. Most government expenditures in France are made by the French government. The United States and West Germany are federal republics, with state and local government expenditures constituting an important component of total government expenditures.

The allocation of resources from the private sector to the public sector is accomplished through taxation. Thus the costs of public activities are borne by the taxpayers of a nation. Taxation can also result in income redistribution if various income groups have different proportions of total national income after taxes than before. Income redistribution will occur particularly if the tax system is progressive. However, there are limits to the extent to which progressive taxation can be used. In France, for example, the bulk of social welfare expenditures is financed by indirect taxation, in particular the value-added tax. In countries with mixed economic systems the growth of social welfare expenditures has brought with it an increase in the use of indirect taxation.

Table 7-3 presents the relationship of taxes to gross national product and a comparison of various sources of tax revenues for the twelve countries. Taxes expressed as a percentage of GNP ranged from a high of 51.7 percent in the Netherlands to a low of 18.5 percent in Japan. Income taxes represented 52.7 percent of total revenue for the United States compared to a low of 17.1 percent for West Germany. Social security contributions expressed as a percentage of total national government revenue ranged from a high of 55.4 percent for West Germany to a low of 3.6 percent for Denmark. Indirect taxes expressed as a percentage of total national gov-

TABLE 7-3 SOURCES OF TAX REVENUES EXPRESSED
AS A PERCENTAGE OF
TOTAL CURRENT GOVERNMENT REVENUE;
TAXES EXPRESSED AS A PERCENTAGE
OF GNP FOR SELECTED COUNTRIES, 1983

	Percentage of Total Government Revenue			Taxes as Percentage of GNP
	Income Taxes	Social Security	Indirect Taxes	
Italy	34.6%	34.4%	23.1%	39.4%
Belgium	39.5	30.0	23.9	45.7
United Kingdom	38.7	16.6	28.0	38.4
Netherlands	27.5	38.9	18.4	51.7
Japan	32.4	19.4	27.6	18.8
France	17.9	42.9	30.0	41.1
West Germany	17.1	55.4	21.4	29.7
Denmark	35.4	3.6	45.7	35.9
Canada	48.4	11.3	21.9	20.6
Sweden	15.6	33.9	29.6	38.4
Norway	27.4	22.0	38.1	43.8
United States	52.7	29.9	5.5	21.2

Source: The World Bank, *World Development Report 1985*, p. 227.

ernment revenue ranged from a high of 45.7 percent in Denmark to a low
of 5.5 percent in the United States. It should be remembered that indirect
taxes, such as sales taxes, are much more widely used by state and local
governments in the United States than by the national government.

INCOME DISTRIBUTION AND EQUALITY

Alexis de Tocqueville argued in the late 1830s that what was distinctive
about modern society was a demand for equality. That thrust has continued today, long after it first emerged as a powerful political force. Income redistribution in favor of lower-income groups has long been a cardinal objective of socialism. While very few socialists would favor complete income equality, recognizing that there are differences in ability and
talent, most would favor the elimination of wide income disparities between rich and poor. Socialists object to the concentration of wealth in the
hands of a few persons, which leads to considerable income inequality.
The *rentier* class, or "coupon clippers," are looked upon with disdain. The

socialists would attempt to correct this unequal distribution of income through the use of progressive income taxes, gift and inheritance taxes, and a wide variety of transfer payments designed to raise the incomes of the poor. In Western society, much of this has already occurred, but not to the extent that many socialists would like. The state has inevitably become the arena for the fulfillment of both private and group wants, but there comes a point where demands cannot be easily matched by state revenues.[9]

It is difficult to reach agreement on what can be considered an optimum distribution of income. Individuals and groups view an economic system from their own positions in society. Unanimity of opinion is therefore impossible, and it is highly doubtful if a concept of optimum income distribution can be agreed upon.[10] If such is the case, the actual effect of taxes and government expenditures on the distribution of income will not be determined on the basis of a particular theory of optimum distribution, but rather as a result of a struggle between the dominant political forces in a society at a particular moment in time. The results will be strongly modified, of course, by political decisions made in the past. This does not mean that theories will play no role whatever, for each social group must have a rationale for its position.

Some industrial countries display more income inequality than others. Comparisons are made difficult because of all the different aspects of the concept of income distribution. Probably the main bone of contention between capitalism and communism concerns how each system distributes its income. But even among countries considered capitalist and countries considered communist, there are wide variations in patterns of income distribution. It is also apparent that no one country has a lock on what can be considered a "just" society. Discrimination of one form or another is likely to exist, regardless of the country.[11]

---

9. Joseph Schumpeter wrote: "The fiscal capacity of the state has its limits not only in the sense in which this is self-evident and which would be valid also for a socialist community, but in a much narrower and, for the tax state, more painful sense. If the will of the people demands higher and higher public expenditures, if more and more means are used for purposes for which private individuals have not produced them, if more and more power stands behind this will, and if finally all parts of the people are gripped by entirely new ideas about public property—then the tax state will have run its course and society will have to depend on other motive forces for its economy than self-interest." "The Crisis of the Tax State," *International Economic Papers,* No. 4 (New York: Macmillan Publishing Co., 1954), pp. 5-38.

10. Even when arbitrary differences such as class or sexual privileges are eliminated, there will be differences in income, status, and authority between persons, differences arising out of talent, motivation, effort, and achievement. And individuals will want to exercise the reward and powers of those achievements. The question of justice arises, as Daniel Bell wrote in *The Coming of Post-Industrial Society* (New York: Basic Books Inc., Publishers, 1976, pp. 9-12), when those on top can convert their authority positions into large discrepant material and social advantages over others.

11. During the 1970s various groups in the United States accused the country of various forms of discrimination—racial, sexual, and so forth. It was inferred that somehow these and other forms of discrimination did not exist elsewhere. That is not true; the Soviet Union probably has more sexism than the United States.

Comparisons between countries are also difficult because of differences in statistical observation and classification. Typically, the data used would have to involve the distribution of income before taxes and transfers because government taxes, expenditures on goods and services, and transfer payments alter the distribution of income.

SUMMARY

The three countries that have been discussed in this chapter—France, Japan, and the United Kingdom—have mixed economic systems, meaning that they have elements of both capitalism and socialism. The governments of these countries pursue economic and social policies of participation and intervention to a greater degree than in the United States. Although private enterprise is dominant and a market system prevails in all three countries, government participation in economic activity cannot be minimized as an influence. It covers several specific areas, which can be summarized as follows.

1. Economic planning, which involves a certain amount of state intervention, is used in varying degrees, ranging from the formal French indicative plan, which is usually set for a four-year period, to more informal forecasting and general direction plans.
2. Fiscal and monetary policy measures are an important part of economic policy. These measures have been generally used to maintain a high level of aggregate demand during most of the postwar period; in the 1970s, however, inflation became the dominant economic problem.
3. State ownership of key industries that can influence the volume of public expenditures is a fact of life. These industries are indeed very large businesses and are often the largest employers in the country.
4. Transfer payments, through the medium of social welfare expenditures, have served to create what can be considered the welfare state. These payments, which are broad and comprehensive in coverage, have an important impact on income redistribution between and within income groups.

It is assumed that a mixed economic system, through government direction and participation, can ameliorate or eliminate some of the major flaws of a purely capitalistic system, namely, unemployment and economic insecurity, as well as accomplish a high rate of economic growth. Whether this is actually the case is highly problematical. The performance of the British economy over the last three decades has generally been poor, particularly in terms of economic growth. Inflation became a problem in the Western European countries in the late 1970s and early 1980s. Economic policy measures that worked when unemployment was the only problem are no longer relevant for the times.

REVIEW QUESTIONS

1. How are supplies of productive agents allocated or distributed among industries in mixed economic systems?
2. Discuss the effects of great income inequality on the distribution of goods and services in a capitalistic system.
3. Discuss some of the reasons for the nationalization of industry in the United Kingdom and France.
4. The term "mixed economy" is probably more applicable to the economic systems of the Western European countries than the terms "capitalism" and "socialism." Why?
5. Discuss the role of government with reference to monetary and fiscal policies in a mixed economy.
6. Discuss the importance of economic planning in a mixed economic system.
7. The major flaws of a capitalistic system—unemployment, income inequality, and social waste—have been eliminated in such countries as France and the United Kingdom. Do you agree?
8. Discuss the importance of social welfare expenditures in a mixed economic system.

RECOMMENDED READINGS

Beveridge, William. *Full Employment in a Free Society*. 2d ed. Atlantic Highlands, N.J.: Humanities Press Inc., 1960.

Dobb, Maurice H. *On Economic Theory and Socialism*. Boston: Routledge & Kegan Paul Inc., 1965.

Friedman, Milton. *Capitalism and Freedom*. Chicago: University of Chicago Press, 1962.

Myrdal, Gunnar. *Beyond the Welfare State*. New Haven, Conn.: Yale University Press, 1960.

Sweezy, Paul W. *Socialism*. New York: McGraw-Hill Book Co., 1949.

Tinbergen, Jan. *Production, Income & Welfare*. Lincoln: University of Nebraska Press, 1985.

Wright, David M. *Capitalism*. Chicago: Henry Regnery Co., 1962.

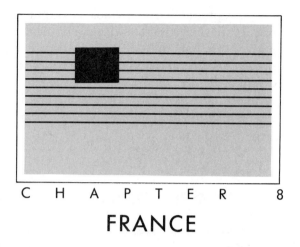

C H A P T E R   8

FRANCE

In May 1981, François Mitterand, a socialist, was elected President of France and the Socialist Party gained control of the French National Assembly, thus creating a mandate for more government control of the French economy. The election of Mitterand was a landmark: It was the first major victory for a democratic socialist party in any major country in this century. Although it is true that France had a socialist government in 1936, called the Popular Front, that was a coalition government that lasted only for a year. Other countries, England and Germany for example, have political parties that embrace many of the principles of demoncratic socialism, but they are not called socialist parties. France, and more recently Greece, is governed by a Socialist Party that believes in specific economic and social principles. Although Mitterand was supported by the French Communist Party, the goals of the two parties are *not* one and the same.

The French economy has had some economic planning since the end of World War II, and some state ownership of industry that dates back to the last century, but the Mitterand government further shifted the public–private resource mix toward the public share. Major changes included nationalization of all but a few of the privately owned banks and creation of a dominant position in practically the whole steel industry, all aluminum production, half of glass production, the whole electronics sector, and an important part of the pharmaceutical and metallurgical sectors, among others. Furthermore, the nationalized sectors became the principal customer and supplier of many other industrial sectors. Thus, even though private enterprise still accounts for around 80 percent of total output of goods and services and the market mechanism is the main allocator of resources, the government directly or indirectly controls many important sectors of the French economy.

■ THE ECONOMIC SYSTEM ■

Government participation in business and industry is far greater in France than in the United States or West Germany. In addition to those industries nationalized by Mitterand, the French government controls all the railroads, coal mines, and virtually all electrical power production and has controlling interest in the airlines. The Bank of France and the four largest deposit banks were controlled by the government before the Mitterand government came to power. A segment of the insurance industry is nationalized. The government has a large interest in the petroleum and natural gas industries and is involved in the production of motor vehicles and planes. Direct regulation and selective intervention in other industries is also common. Investment plans of major companies are often discussed with government agencies able to help provide financing; the government controls mergers and other changes in the organization of private firms.

State intervention in the French economy is not new; it dates back to the time of Jean Baptiste Colbert (1619–1683), who was finance minister under King Louis XIV. Colbert believed that France could and should be the greatest industrial country of Europe. He developed a state policy of supporting national commercial and industrial interests. To promote foreign trade, industries were created using state funds. He also fostered mercantilism, the theory of national economy that held that commerce should be regulated so as to secure a favorable balance of trade, in order to increase the store of precious metals within a country. A canal was dug from the Bay of Biscay to the Mediterranean to improve the flow of trade between the different areas of France, while the highway system was made into the best in Europe.

The Industrial Revolution, for the most part, largely bypassed France. Through the end of the last century, France was primarily an agricultural country, with the *petit bourgeoisie* (small business owners) concentrated in the cities. There was an industrial base in northern France, concentrated in the steel, textile, and coal-mining industries, but by no means was France the industrial equal of England or Germany. The state continued to play an important role in the French economy. In industry, the French railway system was developed by the government, and the telephone system was made a government monopoly in 1889.

WORLD WAR II AND NATIONALIZATION OF INDUSTRY

An increase in government ownership of industry resulted from a series of nationalizations immediately after World War II. The Bank of France, the four largest deposit banks, 34 insurance companies, the electric and gas industries, the coal mines, Air France, and one automobile company were nationalized.[1]

One reason for nationalization was a desire to continue the Popular Front program of 1936, which was an assault on economic institutions that had for decades preserved a hopelessly outmoded capitalism.[2] Manufacturing and agriculture were both protected by high tariffs and import quotas and, in many cases, by subsidies and producers' agreements allocating production and markets. This had led to a static economy with restrictive competition and little incentive to improve production methods or to experiment with new products. The Depression had created mass unemployment and social unrest in France. The Popular Front sponsored social programs similar to those developed by Franklin D. Roosevelt during the New Deal.

A second reason for nationalization was the desire to develop a blueprint to rehabilitate the war-torn economy and stimulate economic growth. Discussions in France concerning the way in which economic recovery could most quickly be accomplished led to the view that the French government would need to play an active role. The result was a call for formal and systematic economic planning. France adopted a policy of economic *dirigisme* (direction), as opposed to a quick return to a liberal or market economy, which was the way West Germany chose. The first economic plan, begun in 1946 and often called the *Monnet Plan*, advocated direct government control over economic activity. The Marshall Plan, which funneled U.S. postwar aid through central governments, strengthened acceptance of the government's role in rebuilding the French economy. It was felt that government control over investment in industries

---

1. The automobile and aircraft companies were nationalized for cooperating with the Germans.

2. The Popular Front was an amalgam of a number of political groups and was headed by socialist Leon Blum, who became the first socialist president of France.

damaged by the war could be carried out best through nationalization of a number of basic industries, such as coal.

NATIONALIZATION UNDER MITTERAND

Socialism, as mentioned previously, represents a departure from the institutions of capitalism. Socialists contend that there are several major flaws in a capitalist system—unemployment, income inequality, and social waste. They would amend these flaws by altering some of the capitalist institutions that presumably are responsible for them. There would be more public ownership of industries considered vital to the national interest. Income distribution would become more of a public function, and income disparities would be reduced through progressive income taxation and transfer payments. Great emphasis would be placed on medical care, family allowances, and retirement benefits. Decisions concerning the kinds and quantities of goods to produce, the allocation of available resources to various uses, and the distribution of resources between consumption and capital goods would be made by the government through some form of planning and greater control over the allocation of credit. There also would be at least a major modification of private profit making.

INDUSTRY   With this blueprint, it is easier to follow the objectives of the new socialist government of President Mitterand. On October 26, 1981, the French General Assembly approved measures designed to restructure industry and banking. Five industrial groups came under full state control. They are the Companie Générale d'Electricité, Saint Gobain (glass and chemicals), Pechiney-Ugine-Kuhlmann (aluminum and chemicals), Rhone-Poulenc (pharmaceuticals), and Thomson-Brandt (electronics and arms). Two other companies were partially nationalized; the Dassault aviation firm has 51 percent state ownership, as does the arms division of Matra. The USINOR and SACILOR steel firms were nationalized by a simple conversion of large state credits into shares. The French government took over the holdings of two U.S.-based companies, ITT and Honeywell.

Table 8-1 presents the financial size of major French companies that were nationalized by the French government. Also included are firms that were nationalized in the past—the French auto firm Renault and the petroleum firm Elf-Aquitaine. It is interesting to note that one-half of the auto industry, as represented by Peugeot, is not nationalized. The large French tire firm Michelin is also privately owned. Nationalization has raised

T A B L E   8 - 1   MAJOR COMPANIES OWNED
BY THE FRENCH GOVERNMENT IN 1984
(millions of dollars)

	Sales	Assets	Industry
Elf-Aquitaine	$20,662	$16,895	Energy
Francais des Petroles	18,159	11,011	Energy
Renault	12,227	10,727	Automotive
Générale d'Electricité	8,480	9,372	Electrical equipment
Saint-Gobain	7,015	5,903	Glass, chemicals
Thomson	6,620	7,285	Electronics
Rhone-Poulenc	5,856	4,487	Chemicals
SACILOR	4,334	4,433	Steel
Pechiney	4,064	3,884	Aluminum
Aerospatiale	2,875	4,627	Aerospace

Source: Fortune, August 19, 1985, pp. 183-189.

problems for holdings of French firms in the United States. At issue is whether investments in the United States should be maintained or managed differently after their parent French companies have been nationalized. There has also been a question about French government compensation for the nationalization of various U.S. business holdings in France, including the properties of ITT and Honeywell.

The French government now owns 14 of the 20 largest industrial firms in France, including the three largest—Elf-Aquitaine, Francais des Petroles, and Renault. The percentage of French industrial sales produced by state-controlled companies increased from 18 to 32 percent after the nationalization. The government's share increased from nothing to 36 percent in computers and office equipment, from 1 percent to 80 percent in steelmaking, from 1 percent to 44 percent in electronics, and from 50 to 84 percent in plane making. As mentioned earlier, the French government also controls all of the major banks. In no other major Western national does the state play such a commanding role in the economy.

BANKING   The Mitterand government has nationalized most of the privately owned banks, leaving only a small percentage of the nation's bank deposits in the hands of privately owned institutions. The action made France the only noncommunist country in the world to have credit almost totally under government control. The rationale for state control of credit was the desire on the part of the Mitterand government to restimulate an economy beset by low growth, double-digit inflation, and unemployment. The government, then, is in the position of deciding how credit is to be allocated, a decision which is made in a pure market system by the forces of supply and demand.

PUBLIC FINANCE

French public finance is highly centralized. The national goverment accounts for about 86 percent of total tax receipts and local governments for the remaining 14 percent. Both national and local governments rely extensively on indirect taxes as revenue sources; in 1984 approximately 72 percent of all tax receipts came from indirect taxes. The most important national tax, the value-added tax, and the most important local tax, the retail sales tax, are both indirect taxes. The most important direct taxes, the personal and corporate income taxes, are both national taxes and have no counterpart at the local level. The property tax, which is the major source of tax revenue to local governments in the United States, is not an important source of revenue at the local level in France.

THE FRENCH TAX SYSTEM   The tax system in France has several characteristics that differ from the tax systems of other countries. Greater emphasis is placed on sales taxation in France than in other advanced industrial countries. Also, tax incentives are widely used—to stimulate scientific research and development, to encourage the modernization of plants and equipment, and to facilitate regional economic development. Another characteristic of the French tax system is innovation. In the value-added tax, France developed a tax that has been adopted by many countries and that has been proposed from time to time in the United States.

THE VALUE-ADDED TAX   The value-added tax is one of the world's most widely used taxes. First introduced in France in 1954, the tax applies to all firms engaged in manufacturing, wholesaling, and services. Value added is gross receipts during the period less amounts paid for commodities. Thus the tax does not discriminate against particular distribution channels because it is reduced for each transaction. At the same time, it permits the impact of the tax to be spread over a wide range of activities. An example of the value-added tax is presented below. Assume three business firms: a manufacturer selling a product to a wholesaler for $100, who sells it to a retailer for $125, who finally sells it to the ultimate consumer for $200. Assume a tax rate of 10 percent on each transaction.

	Value of Product	Value Added	Value-Added Tax
Manufacturing stage	$100	$100	$10.00
Wholesale stage	125	25	2.50
Retail stage	200	75	7.50
Final value	$200	$200	
Value-added tax			$20.00

The French value-added tax applies to all domestic transactions in goods and services at all levels of the industrial and commercial cycle. It is levied on imports at the time of their entry into the French customs territory. The typical rate of the French value-added tax is 18.6 percent.[3] A reduced rate of 5.5 percent applies to the production and sale of food and other necessities; luxury products, including automobiles, are subject to a higher rate of 33.3 percent. Certain basic raw materials, such as cotton and copper, are exempt from the tax.

The value-added tax is used as an economic policy instrument in France. Export transactions are exempted from the tax. It is also used to encourage expansion and modernization of industry because capital goods are, in general, accorded favorable treatment under the tax.

INCOME AND WEALTH TAXES   French taxes also include the personal income tax, which is progressive and is levied on income from wages and salaries, dividends and interest, capital gains, and profits from commercial activities. The personal income tax was made more progressive by the Mitterand government. However, the progressivity of the tax is decreased by the family quotient system, which allows income to be divided into a certain number of shares based on the number of dependents in a family. There is also a wealth tax of 2 percent on assets in excess of 3.5 million francs ($400,000), and there is a social security tax of 15 percent on employee income.[4]

The corporate income tax rate is 50 percent on net profit earned in France. Generally income earned outside of France is not taxed, which

---

3. Harvard Law School, *Taxation in France*, World Tax Series (Chicago: Commerce Clearing House, Inc., 1985), p. 72.

4. *Individual Taxes: A Worldwide Summary* (New York: Price Waterhouse and Co., 1985), pp. 78-83.

provides an incentive for exports. Capital gains are taxed at a rate of 15 percent, and interest income is taxed at rates ranging from 15 to 50 percent.

GOVERNMENT EXPENDITURES   Total French government expenditures amounted to 46 percent of gross national product in 1984. France has two budgets—the national budget and the social budget. The national budget contains the receipts from basic revenue sources, such as the value-added tax and the personal income tax, and the national expenditures, including spending on goods and services, spending for capital formation, and interest on the public debt.

The social budget covers both social security expenditures—old age and disability insurance, medical care, family allowances, and worker's compensation—and outlays for veterans' pensions and miscellaneous welfare payments. The social budget is used because the bulk of French social welfare expenditures is financed not out of national tax revenues, but by special taxes paid by employers and employees. These taxes are not paid to the national treasury, but to special social security funds from which the benefits are paid.

There are two separate social welfare systems—a family allowance system and a general social security system. Both systems are comprehensive in coverage. The family allowance system, which is financed by a tax on employers, provides tax-exempt monthly payments for the second, third, and subsequent children in a family; a special allowance for families with only one wage earner; prenatal and maternity allowances; and, in certain circumstances, a housing allowance. The general social security system provides health insurance, maternity benefits, pension benefits, and old age and survivors' benefits. Health insurance benefits compensate for the loss of earnings, as well as the medical costs of being sick. In addition, there are special systems for farmworkers, coal miners, railroad workers, public utility employees, seamen, and public employees. There is some intermingling of the general and special systems, with workers receiving benefits from both systems. Total transfer payments from the social welfare system—family allowances and social security—accounted for 22.5 percent of French national income in 1984.[5]

Until the election of François Mitterand, redistribution of income was not a major goal of taxation in France. The value-added tax, rather than the personal income tax, was the single most important revenue source.

---

5. "France," *Economic Surveys* (Paris: Organization for Economic Cooperation and Development, June 1984), p. 49.

The progressivity of the income tax was reduced through the family quotient system and income splitting; tax evasion among the French of all social classes was a fact of life. A result was that France had the most unequal distribution of income of all the major Western industrial countries.[6] The Mitterand government raised income, wealth, and inheritance taxes, and doubled tax levels on yachts, speedboats, and luxury cars.[7] The "soak the rich" tax policies of the Mitterand government resulted in the flight of French capital to other countries.

THE BANKING SYSTEM

France has a comprehensive banking system headed by the Bank of France. The system includes two types of banks—commercial banks and specialized credit institutions. Unlike the banking systems of the United States and United Kingdom, the French banking system is, with few exceptions, publicly owned. This gives the government control over the allocation of credit to all sectors of the French economy. Ownership provides the government with direct leverage for the implementation of credit policies that agree with the French economic plan.

THE CENTRAL BANK   The Bank of France was organized by Napoleon Bonaparte in 1800 as a privately owned company. In 1803 it was given a monopoly for note issuance in the Paris area, and in 1848 that monopoly was extended to all of France. In 1946 the Bank of France was nationalized; the shareholders received negotiable government securities in exchange for their stock. The French government was then able to assume ultimate control over monetary policy.

A National Credit Council was created and given the power to regulate the operations of all types of banks in France; this power is exercised through the Bank of France. Members of the council represent government departments concerned with economic problems and various economic and financial special interest groups. Within the policy framework set by the council, the Bank of France has the responsibility for implementing monetary policy. It uses many credit control measures—changes in the discount rate, imposition of rediscount ceilings, control of minimum reserves to be held by the banks in the form of Treasury paper, open market operations, and certain measures of qualitative control. However,

6. Malcolm Sawyer and Frank Wasserman, "Income Distribution in OECD Countries," *OECD Economic Outlook*, July 1976, p. 14.

7. "Bad Times for the Good Life," *Newsweek*, November 30, 1981, pp. 46-47.

the power of the Bank of France to implement monetary policy is circumscribed, to a certain extent, by the existence of specialized credit institutions, which have considerable influence on both the demand for money and the character of investments for which financing is sought.

THE COMMERCIAL BANKS   The three largest commercial banks—Banque Nationale de Paris, Crédit Lyonnais, and Société Générale—were nationalized in 1945. These three banks are among the 10 largest commercial banks in the world.[8] They operate branch banks throughout France and make consumer and business loans, actively competing against each other for the demand and time deposits of the French public. The size of these banks makes it easier to implement the state economic plans and to carry out monetary policy. Nationalization of private banks such as the Crédit Commercial de France by the Mitterand government has increased the extent of state control over commercial banking.[9]

SPECIALIZED CREDIT INSTITUTIONS   There are in France a number of public and semipublic credit institutions. Through these institutions the French government exercises its considerable financial powers to determine the allocation of savings into particular investment channels. They are diverse in that some are banks while others are not, but as a common feature they tend to specialize in one or a few lines of activity. Their loanable funds come from savings deposits, bond issues, and the French Treasury. The French Treasury plays a central and dominant role in the French capital market, and it accounts for around 50 percent of savings in France. The Treasury controls the capital market to the extent that no important borrower can have access to funds without its consent. Moreover, control over the financial circuits of the country means that the Treasury has a priority claim on resources.

THE CAISSE NATIONAL DE CRÉDIT AGRICOLE   The Crédit Agricole, with assets of over $100 billion, is exceeded in size only by two U.S. banks—Bank America and Citicorp.[10] It is the umbrella organization for 94 regional agricultural banks, in which capacity it receives all of their long-term deposits and assumes the risk on their long-term loans. It is a public institution controlled by the Ministry of Agriculture. It receives funds from the Treasury and private depositors and through the issue of bonds in the capital market.

---

8. *Fortune*, August 19, 1985, pp. 214-215.

9. French banks in which foreign investors have a joint interest have not yet been nationalized.

10. *Fortune*, August 19, 1985, p. 215.

THE CRÉDIT NATIONAL   The main function of this government-owned institution is to allocate a part of the funds from the national budget to private industry for investment purposes. (The Treasury retains the right to restrain the borrowing and lending activity of the Crédit National directly.) It makes several types of loans, all of which are made at subsidized rates of interest. These loans go to specially favored economic sectors, particularly exports and energy, at an interest subsidy of 2 to 3 percent.[11] Loans are also made to small business firms.

THE CAISSE DE DÉPOTS   This state-owned institution manages the funds of the social security and postal savings systems. It is a type of intermediary virtually unique to the French banking system, under which the nationwide network of savings banks do no lending of their own. Instead, the Caisse de Dépots receives most of the savings banks' deposits and is responsible for their distribution. It lends a part to local governments and a part to the Treasury itself to finance the federal deficit. It controls the levers on a wide range of credit policy instruments. With the Bank of France, it controls the marginal cost of money to the banking sector and thus influences interest rates.

CREDIT POLICY   The French financial system is characterized by a small number of very large financial institutions ranging from commercial banks to the French Treasury. Since virtually all credit is channeled through these institutions, monetary and credit policies are relatively easy to expedite. The government influences most aspects of this centralized system. It sets lending priorities for banks, limits their total credit extension, and controls their interest rates. This control is the key enabling influence for the implementation of French industrial policy. The existence of a small number of lending institutions makes it easier to allocate credit to those industries given the highest priority in the French economic plan.[12]

LABOR–MANAGEMENT RELATIONS

The French trade union movement is dominated by several large labor confederations that, although ideologically different, are united in a general unwillingness to accept the basic institutions of capitalism. The largest

11. Jacques Melitz, "The French Financial System: Mechanisms and Propositions of Reform" (Paper presented to the Conference on the Political Economy of France, American Enterprise Institute, Washington, D.C.., May 29-31, 1980).

12. U.S. Congress, Joint Economic Committee, *Monetary Policy, Selective Credit Policy, and Industrial Policy in France, Britain, West Germany, and Sweden*, 97th Cong., 1st sess., 1981, p. 35.

trade union confederation is the Confederation Generale du Travail (CGT), which is Communist-led and has a membership of 1.5 million workers. It is militant in philosophy and activity and supports the French Communist Party. The CGT is divided into departmental unions and industrial federations. To be affiliated with the CGT, each union must first join a departmental union, which brings together all unions in a region, regardless of their trade. Other important unions are the Confederation Française Democratique du Travail and the Force Ouvriere, both of which support the Socialist Party.

Employers are also organized into associations. The most important employers' federation is the Conseil National du Patronat Française (National Council of French Employers). It consists of some 170 trade associations and three major federations. The trade associations represent their members in the negotiation of collective bargaining agreements. Another employers' association is the Center des Jeunes Patrons. This association supports government economic planning, maintenance of full-employment policies, and participative labor-management relations.

Given the rather diverse political views of labor and management, relations between the two groups have not been harmonious. Labor-management agreements have tended to transcend the normal areas of wage demands and working conditions. Profit sharing and works councils have also entered into the bargaining process. It is in the works council that plant managers and the elected officials of all the employees sit together and express their views. Several unions may represent the workers in a particular plant. This means that management must face different unions, acting through different channels. The situation is much more complex and ambiguous than in other countries, where management usually faces only one union and handles problems with that union through collective bargaining.

Since most labor unions supported the election of François Mitterand, it was expected that unions would gain in terms of political influence. Mitterand had proposed a 35-hour work week, an increase in the minimum wage, increases in social welfare benefits, and changes in the profit-sharing plans of employers. When Mitterand took office, some benefits to labor were forthcoming. The work week was reduced from 40 hours to 39 without an offsetting pay cut, and a fifth week of paid vacation was added. Government social welfare expenditures also were increased.

However, trade deficits and high inflation rates put pressure on the economy. In 1983, the Mitterand government cut spending on social welfare programs and reduced employment in unprofitable steel mills and coal mines. This brought the government into direct confrontation with the French unions. Mitterand also lost communist support, as he swung more toward the center in his approach to France's economic problems.

GOVERNMENT AND BUSINESS

State intervention in the economy dates back many centuries and has come to be accepted as permanent. Public policies in France have included both protection and promotion of key industrial sectors through financial subsidies of many types, price controls, encouragement of mergers to increase the size and market power of French-owned corporations, export promotion, and support for new technology in industries such as computers, semiconductors, and aerospace.[13] In addition, there is considerable government ownership in the French economy, which has been increased by the Mitterand government. In fact, the sharp distinction between public and private sectors of countries such as the United States and Japan has never existed in France. The French government is highly centralized with an elite bureaucracy that has considerable autonomy in shaping industrial policy that affects both nationalized and private industries. Although a variety of government agencies influence policy making, much of the power resides in the state-owned financial institutions. Thus, government is very much a part of business.

Some specific government control devices are discussed below. They include public investment both in the nationalized sector of the economy and officially approved private channels, compulsory profit sharing, taxes and subsidies, and price controls.

THE NATIONALIZED INDUSTRIES   Nationalization of important sectors of the economy has given the government control over the prices and products of key industries. It has also given the government considerable control over the allocation of credit through the public lending institutions that channel savings into favored sectors of the economy. A shortage of capital after World War II gave the government considerable leverage in the manipulation of credit to influence business decisions.

The nationalized industries function for the most part under the nominal control of public boards on which representatives of labor, management, and the customers of the enterprise in question are represented. In practice, however, the government has retained a strong hand through its authority to appoint the general managers, whose powers have increased at the expense of the public boards. More and more basic policy is determined by the ministries under whose jurisdiction the nationalized industries fall. Decisions with respect to prices, costs, and investment have become the responsibility of various government agencies.

---

13. Joseph Zysman, *Political Strategies for Industrial Order: State, Market, and Industry in France* (Berkeley: University of California Press, 1977), pp. 59-67.

The nationalized industries are operated within a framework of objectives. These objectives include increasing production to meet certain economic goals, implementing a large-scale modernization program to expand capacity and raise productivity, lowering industrial costs, subsidizing various economic and social groups, improving working conditions and labor relations, and achieving the breakeven point in production.

COMPULSORY PROFIT SHARING Aside from the nationalized industries, the interference of the French government in business is considerable. For example, in January 1968, the government established an obligatory profit-sharing plan affecting the employees of all private enterprises in France employing more than 100 people. The workers' share of profits is calculated on the percentage contributed by labor to the total value added by the enterprise. Prior to calculating the amount of profits that are to be distributed to the workers, however, enterprises are permitted to deduct from taxable profits the corporate income tax as well as a 5 percent return on invested capital, including legal reserves. Employers and employees are supposed to form company works committees to select the method by which profits are distributed.

MONETARY AND FISCAL DEVICES   The French government has been very active in the use of monetary and fiscal devices designed to foster investment and influence regional development. Regional development is a fundamental goal of French economic policy, and many tax incentives are provided to industry to encourage industrial decentralization. Special grants are provided to firms that locate in regions that have below-average incomes. Exemptions from local business taxes and special depreciation provisions are also provided. The government has also used tax incentives to encourage corporate mergers.

PRICE CONTROLS Direct price controls have been used extensively since the end of the war. Three separate systems of controls were established in 1945 and form the basis of current controls: *liberté totale,* in which industries are subject to no price controls or in which the price of a product is free of control through several stages of production; *liberté surveillée,* in which industries are subject to direct price controls fixed by the government; and *liberté controllée,* in which producers or distributors may set or change prices but are required to explain to the government the reasons for their decisions. The price control authorities may accept or reject their reasons, and in either case firms must delay price changes for a 15-day examination period.

Recourse to price controls has varied considerably in recent years. The trend, however, is toward the relaxation of controls. Price controls were dropped in 1976. But both wage guidelines and price controls were imposed again for many industrial and consumer products in late 1981 by the Mitterand government in an attempt to slow inflation.

ECONOMIC PLANNING

There was a time when French economic planning received considerable attention in Western countries. It was regarded as a middle-ground approach between an unplanned, free market capitalist system and an imperative, or directive, planned economic system.[14] The worst evils of each system were presumably eliminated by French planning, which provided a series of blueprints for the economy to follow over a specific period of time. There would be less wasteful use of resources than in an unplanned market economy, but there would be more reliance on the price mechanism to allocate resources than in a centrally planned economy. There was no element of overt coercion, but the government could influence the allocation of resources into areas that conformed with the plan objectives. Priorities set in the plan provided business firms with a frame of reference in terms of investment decisions. Many people believed that economic planning was responsible for the above-average postwar rate of economic growth in France.

However, in decades following the end of World War II, French economic planning became less important. By the 1970s indicative planning as originally conceived had been largely abandoned—in part a victim of the increasing complexity of the expanding French economy and in part because of the impact of world prices, particularly of oil, on the French economy. Planning has survived, however, and has regained influence as the focal point of the decision-making process of the socialist government. For one thing, the institutions that already existed to facilitate economic planning have equipped the government with the tools for regulating the economy and promoting economic growth. The gamut of French industry, ranging from aerospace to steel, has all benefitted from state support and a state-created environment of steadily increasing demand.[15] The French planners also established a series of specialized credit institutions to ensure priority industries access to credit and to direct subsidies from the French Treasury. The socialists, who believe in a strong government role

14. Stephen Cohen, *Modern Capitalist Planning: The French Model* (Berkeley: University of California Press, 1977),, pp. 7-27.

15. U.S. Congress, Office of Technology Assessment, *U.S. Industrial Competitiveness: A Comparison of Steel, Electronics, and Automobiles*, 99th Cong., 1st sess., 1985, p. 195.

in the French economy, inherited a planning mechanism and institutions that expedited state control of the economy.

The instruments through which planning has been expedited since its inception are simple and direct. The state spends money, the state lends money, and the state owns and operates major enterprises in both the infrastructure and the final-goods manufacturing sectors. Let us review the development of French economic planning from its inception after World War II, keeping in mind that planning was a part of the policy of economic *dirigisme* that began with the Monnet Plan.

DEVELOPMENT OF FRENCH PLANNING   The formation of the Popular Front government in 1936 under Socialist Premier Leon Blum marked the first phase of economic planning in France in that it extended the responsibility of the government more deeply than ever before into the economy. The Popular Front nationalized the armament industry, introduced a graduated income tax, and institutionalized a government-protected system of collective bargaining.

In 1944 the National Council of the Resistance, a coalition group, produced a plan for France's future that called for the nationalization of primary resources and energy, state control of banks and insurance, and the participation of labor in industrial management. Formal planning began with the Monnet Plan, or "First French Plan," which had the objective of restructuring six basic areas of the French economy—coal, electricity, steel, cement, transportation, and agricultural equipment. Its primary objectives were set out in terms of the growth in capacity and output needed in those sectors. The corresponding investments were, in large part, financed out of funds provided by the Treasury. Controls were placed over new capital issues and over the distribution of medium- and long-term credit. Priority allocations of raw materials, building permits, and permits to install new equipment were also used to channel production and investment in the desired direction.

Altogether, eight plans have been completed, with a ninth in process. The typical plan has lasted for four years. The plans have varied in their objectives.[16] The First Plan was designed to develop basic sectors of the economy that would exert a motivating force on all economic sectors. The Second French Plan (1954–1957) differed from the First Plan in that it applied to the entire economy rather than to a few basic sectors. Other plans have aimed at developing various social and economic sectors of the country. The Fourth Plan (1962–1965) involved social action in support of the

---

16. For a more complete discussion of each plan, see the third edition of this text, pages 166 and 167.

less favored sectors of society—farmers, the aged, low-income workers, and students. This was done through increasing subsidies and welfare benefits. The Sixth Plan (1971–1975) placed emphasis on the development of a computer industry. The plan also gave priority to the aerospace industry.

PLANNING UNDER MITTERAND   Economic planning has become important under the Mitterand government. The Eighth Plan, which had been initiated by Mitterand's predecessor, Giscard d'Estaing, was discarded, and an interim plan, covering the period from 1982 through 1983, was added. The plan had several objectives, one of which was the nationalization of five major industrial groups as well as banks and financial institutions.[17] A second objective was the decentralization of economic and political power to the regions, departments, and communes of France. Another objective was to reduce the work week to 39 hours and to increase social welfare expenditures. An objective which was not achieved was to increase the real economic growth rate of the French economy to 3 percent per year over the interim two-year period.

The Ninth Plan, which is to last from 1984 to 1988, was then developed. Inflation was a major problem, economic growth rates had declined, and there was a need to improve France's industrial competitiveness in world markets. The state of the French economy forced a general retrenchment on social spending, much to the displeasure of doctrinaire socialists and communists. The Ninth Plan has several major goals, the first of which is an industrial strategy. The objective is to increase investment from 11.1 percent of French gross domestic product in 1982 to 12.3 percent in 1988, and from 3.0 percent to 4.4 percent over the same period for the nationalized industries.[18] Emphasis is placed on internal financing for the nationalized industries to make them more competitive in world markets. A second goal of the plan is to achieve an annual real economic growth rate of 1.5 to 2.5 percent during the plan period. This was not achieved in 1984 or 1985. Other objectives of the plan include the development of small-and medium-sized firms in the private sector of the economy and the introduction of new technology in the consumer goods industries.

THE MECHANICS OF FRENCH PLANNING   French planning is essentially a statement of the direction the economy should take over a period of time.

17. "France," *Economic Surveys*, p. 40.

18. *Quarterly Economic Review of France*, Second Quarter, 1984 (London: The Economist Intelligence Unit, 1984), p. 4.

The government, in concert with the representatives of agriculture, business, and labor, draws up a plan for the future development of the economy. The Commissariat au Plan (Planning Commission) is the administrative agency responsible for the development of the plan. The commission has no power of its own, but prepares the plan, submits it for approval to government authorities, and sees to its implementation once it is approved. It is responsible to the premier for its actions. It is headed by a commissaire general (director) and has a staff of planning specialists. A large contribution toward the work of preparing the plan comes from other government offices.

INSTRUMENTS OF FRENCH PLANNING   French economic planning relies on allocation of investment funds and on tax incentives to accomplish its implementation, rather than on authoritarian directives or exhortations. Physical restraints are few and are limited to permits required for opening new petroleum refineries or expanding old ones. For environmental reasons, special installation permits are required for new plants and plant extensions of more than a certain size in the Paris area.

CREDIT ALLOCATION   Allocation of credit is an important instrument of French planning. The Treasury is the major source of funds that finance investment in the public and private sectors of the economy. Most of these funds are channeled through a special Treasury account called the *Fund for Economic and Social Development.* Because interest rates on the loans are below what the borrower would have to pay in the market, there is great demand for them. The Fund can see that there is conformity with the objectives of the Plan, both in the nature and priority of investments.

There are other ways in which investment can be influenced to favor the objectives of the Plan. One is selective control by the Ministry of Finance over all issues of stocks and bonds; another is control by the Planning Commissariat over long-term borrowing from the major semipublic credit institutions—Crédit National, Crédit Foncier, and Crédit Agricole. These public institutions can make long-term loans out of advances from the Fund for Economic and Social Development, from their own resources, and from funds raised in the capital market.

Selectivity in the granting of short-term credit was used for the first time in 1963 to reduce the inflationary pressures prevalent in the economy. However, the commercial banks favored borrowers who intended to follow the objectives of the Fourth Plan, particularly with respect to investment in areas with high unemployment. This favoritism represented an attempt by the government to influence investment decisions through the short- and medium-term lending policies of the commercial banks.[19] Favorable consideration was also to be shown to borrowers who intended to finance investments that would reduce costs and prices of exports.

TAX INCENTIVES   Tax incentives are selective between one activity that conforms to the aim of the Plan and another that does not.[20] There are several examples of selective tax measures.

1. As mentioned previously, incentives are provided under the value-added tax. Special credits under the value-added tax are also provided for housing construction.

2. Although dividends are not generally deductible from taxable income in computing the corporate income tax, corporations can make this deduction provided that the proceeds received for the stock were used in connection with regional development or plant and equipment modernization plans. Application for deduction must be filed with the Planning Commissariat, and approval or disapproval is given by the Ministry of Finance.

3. A reduction is also given on the transfer tax on land and buildings if the transfer is connected with the program for regional development and industrial decentralization.

4. There is partial relief or total exemption from the business license tax for firms that help promote the Plan's regional development programs.

The use of tax incentive devices to hasten the modernization and decentralization of French industry is an essential feature of the French tax system. Tax incentives are used by many European countries to accomplish the same objectives, plan or no plan. Since modernization and decentralization of industry are objectives of the French Plans, tax incentives can be considered a legitimate instrument of French planning.

---

19. The commercial banks were asked, not ordered, by the government to pursue a selective lending policy.

20. The use of tax incentives is not new in France. Its use dates back to the time of Colbert and French mercantilism. It reflects a view that taxation should not be neutral but should be used to achieve certain economic objectives. However, the neutrality aspects of the French tax system considerably outweigh the incentive aspects. Tax incentives are basically confined to regional development, housing construction, exports, and scientific research, and to a considerable degree are automatic in that no government approval is needed.

PUBLIC INVESTMENT Public investment is also an important instrument of French economic planning. It has increased under the Mitterand government, with much of the increase going to the industries that were nationalized. Part of the increase has gone to industries to finance research and development in order to make them more competitive in world markets, and another part has been used to fund job-creating projects.

In 1984, investment financed by the French government amounted to about $88 billion, or about 53 percent of all industrial investment in France. Public investment is financed from two main sources—general tax revenues and deficits in the French national budget. The investments of the nationalized industries, from their retained earnings, also represent a part of total public investment.

■ AN APPRAISAL ■
OF THE FRENCH ECONOMY

The performance of the French economy relative to the economies of other major industrial countries has been quite good, particularly during the period 1950–1970. However, it is hard to attribute this performance to the economic plans because numerous factors in addition to economic planning had an impact on the post-World War II development of France. The French economy had to be rebuilt after the war, and institutional arrangements were altered by the war and by the postwar nationalization of certain industries. The new institutional arrangements provided the state with the tools for a comprehensive strategy of promoting growth. Economic policy as embodied in the economic plans was designed to facilitate this growth. France had the second highest average growth rate over the postwar period and the second highest standard of living among major European countries by 1970. The growth of France's real gross national product averaged 5.6 percent from 1957 to 1970, compared to 5.7 percent for West Germany and 2.8 percent for the United Kingdom.[21]

During the more recent period 1970–1980, the performance of the French economy, as measured by average annual increases in real gross domestic product and industrial production, was the best in Western Europe. For example, growth in industrial production increased at an annual average rate of 3.4 percent in France compared to 2.5 percent in West Germany and 1.8 percent in the United Kingdom.[22] Real gross na-

---

21. *Annual Supplement 1981* (London: Economist Intelligence Unit, December 1981), pp. 1-3.
22. *Economic Report of the President 1986* (Washington: USGPO, 1986), p. 376.

tional product in France increased at an average annual rate of 3.6 percent for the decade, which was the highest for any major industrial country except Japan.[23] The average annual increase in real per capita gross national product was 3.8 percent for France, which was exceeded only by a rate of 6.3 percent for Japan.[24] However, the Arab oil embargo of 1973 had a particularly deleterious impact on the French economy. Not only did the price of oil rise, but to mitigate this increase the French undertook a massive investment in alternative energy sources, particularly nuclear power. Deficit financing was necessary to finance state expenditures on nuclear power.

PERFORMANCE IN THE 1980s

A recession hit Western Europe in the late 1970s and continued into the 1980s. The French economy was adversely affected by the recession, and its performance in the 1980s has been well below that of preceding time periods. The unemployment rate, which averaged around 4 percent a year during the late 1970s, increased to 6.4 percent in 1980 and reached a high of 10.1 percent in 1984.[25] The rate remained high through 1985 because of the Mitterand government's efforts to modernize production in the basic manufacturing industries. Increased automation and the closure of inefficient facilities will result in the displacement of workers.

The inflation rate, which averaged around 8 percent a year during the 1970s, showed a marked increase during the early 1980s. The consumer price index increased at an annual average rate of 12 percent between 1978 and 1982.[26] This has had a negative effect on French exports and the balance of payments. The index of industrial production showed a decline in 1982 and 1983 and minor increases for 1984 and 1985, and the rate of gross capital formation has declined at an average annual rate of −0.4 percent since 1980.[27]

Table 8-2 compares average annual growth rates in real GNP for France and other major Western European countries for several time periods. The United States is included to provide a frame of reference. As the table indicates, the overall performance of the French economy has been generally quite good. Some people have credited the performance of the economy to the use of economic planning, but others feel that this is

---

23. Ibid., p. 378.
24. The World Bank, *World Development Report 1983*, p. 149.
25. *Economic Report of the President 1986*, p. 377.
26. Ibid., p. 376.
27. Data furnished by the U.S. Embassy in Paris.

TABLE 8-2 GROWTH RATES IN REAL GROSS NATIONAL PRODUCT

	1961–1965	1966–1970	1971–1976	1976–1980	1981	1982	1983	1984	1985
France	5.8%	5.4%	4.0%	3.3%	0.5%	1.8%	0.7%	1.3%	1.0%
West Germany	5.0	4.2	2.1	3.4	0.2	−0.6	1.2	2.6	2.2
Italy	5.2	6.2	2.4	3.8	0.2	−0.5	−0.4	2.6	2.2
United Kingdom	3.2	2.5	2.1	1.6	−1.4	1.5	3.4	1.8	3.2
Developed Countries	5.2	4.8	3.7	3.2	0.4	−0.1	0.5	0.9	2.8
United States	4.6	3.0	2.2	3.4	1.9	−2.5	3.5	6.5	2.3

Sources: Economic Report of the President 1986 (February 1986), p. 378; Quarterly Economic Review of France, Fourth Quarter (London: Economic Intelligence Unit, 1985), pp. 7-10.

not necessarily the case.[28] Numerous factors in addition to economic planning have also had an effect on the development of the French economy. Moreover, economic planning declined in importance during the 1970s, as successive conservative governments placed emphasis on less state direction in the economy and gave more reliance to free market forces. The performance of the economy during this period was among the best of the Western industrial countries.

ECONOMIC POLICY

French macroeconomic policies in 1984 and 1985 emphasized reduction of the foreign trade deficit and the rate of inflation. These policies followed an abortive attempt to inflate the economy in 1981 and 1982 that was out of step with the economic policies of France's major trading partners, including the United States. Exports declined and the balance of payments deficit increased. Austerity measures were introduced to reduce inflation. Price controls were increased on both industrial and consumer goods and an incomes policy was adopted.

Contrary to the expectations of many of his followers, in 1984 and 1985 President Mitterand moved toward a more centrist position in response to the failure in economic policy. Government intervention in the economy has decreased in favor of free market forces. Government subsidies were denied to one of France's most prestigious firms, Creusot Loire, thereby allowing it to go into bankruptcy and subsequent dismantling. Some 200,000 jobs have been eliminated in the nationalized industries and cuts in social welfare spending have been made in the French budget.

POSSIBLE CHANGES FOR THE FUTURE

In the French parliamentary elections held March 16, 1986, the Socialists lost their parliamentary majority to a coalition of conservative political parties. The conservatives won only a very small majority of the seats, so it does not appear that there will be any great changes in the operations of the French economy as described earlier in this chapter. President Mitterand appointed conservative leader Jacques Chirac as prime minister and

28. John Hackett and Anne Marie Hackett, *Economic Planning in France* (Cambridge: Harvard University Press, 1963); Pierre Bauchet, *Economic Planning, the French Experience* (New York: Praeger Publishers, 1964); Vera Lutz, *Central Planning for the Market Economy: An Analysis of the French Theory and Experience* (London: Longmans Green, 1969); J.J. Carre et al., *French Economic Growth* (Stanford: Stanford University Press, 1975).

has agreed to the appointment of several other conservatives to the cabinet. The conservatives are expected to push for an end to all price controls, less government regulation of business, and denationalization of one or more state-owned companies.

S U M M A R Y

More state control of the French economy occurred after the election of a socialist government in 1981. However, state control is not new in France; it dates back to the time of Louis XIV and his finance miniter Jean Baptiste Colbert. In late 1981 the Mitterand government implemented plans to nationalize most private banks and a number of large French business firms. Taxes were levied on the rich, and transfer payments were increased for lower-income groups. The mix of public–private ownership of business was tilted more toward public ownership, but France remains basically a mixed economic system. The French economy depends upon both public and private enterprise, and there is reliance on economic planning. The French Plans indicate directions that the general development of the economy should take but no longer indicate special targets for each industry or firm. Special incentives, including special credit policies, tax incentives, and favorable treatment of exports, are used to stimulate industrial growth according to the plan.

R E V I E W   Q U E S T I O N S

1. French economic planning is called indicative rather than imperative. Explain.
2. Discuss the reasons for the postwar nationalization of certain of the French industries.
3. The French government plays an important role in the banking system. Explain.
4. The French government influences the investment decisions of business firms in several ways. What are these ways?
5. Discuss the policy instruments used to implement the French Plans.
6. What is the function of the Bank of France?
7. What are some of the changes the Mitterand socialist government has made in the French economy?

RECOMMENDED READINGS

Ardagh, John. *France in the 1980s*. New York: Penguin Books, 1983.

Bell, Davis S. *The French Socialist Party: Resurgence and Victory*. Oxford: Oxford University Press, Inc., 1984.

Cerny, Philip, and Martin Schain, eds. *Socialism, the State, and Public Policy in France*. New York: Methuen Inc., 1985.

Cohen, Stephen and Peter Gourevetch. *France in the Troubled World Economy*. Boston: Butterworth Publishers, 1982.

Jacobs, Dan, ed. *Comparative Politics: An Introduction to the Politics of the United Kingdom, France, Germany, and the Soviet Union*. Chatham, N.J.: Chatham House Publishers, Inc., 1983.

Kuisel, Richard. *Capitalism and the State in Modern France*. New York: Cambridge University Press, 1982.

Mitterand, Francois. *The Wheat and the Chaff*. New York: Seaver Books, 1982.

Peyrefitte, Alain. *The Trouble With France*. New York: Alfred A. Knopf Inc., 1982.

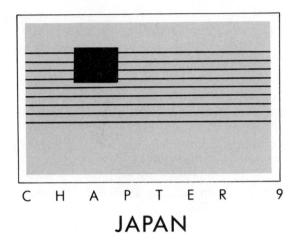

C H A P T E R 9

JAPAN

World War II formally ended in August 1945, when Japan capitulated to the United States. Although the United States won the war, it may lose the current one—namely, a fight for supremacy as the world's economic power. The evidence is that Japan is gaining fast and could conceivably overtake the United States. The United States was the leading producer of motor vehicles from 1908 to 1979, but in 1980 Japan assumed world leadership and has retained it ever since. The U.S. was the world leader in television production during the 1960s, but this field is now dominated by Japan. Japan now produces 60 percent of all robots despite the fact that the United States initiated their development.[1] Robots have helped Japan gain a competitive advantage over the United States in the production of autos and steel. In computers, telecommunications, fiber optics, and pharmaceuticals, Japan has increased its world market share during the 1980s, including its market share in the United States.[2]

In 1985 the United States had a $40 billion deficit in its merchandise trade account with Japan.[3] This deficit has led to acrimonious debates in

1. U.S. Congress, Joint Economic Committee, *The Impact of Robotics on Employment*, 98th Cong., 1st Sess., 1983.

2. Ezra Vogel, *Comeback* (New York: Simon and Schuster Inc., 1985), p. 18.

3. U.S. Department of Commerce, *Business America*, September 16, 1985.

the United States concerning U.S.–Japan economic relations. Political solutions are now being sought for economic problems. Protectionist bills flourish; foreigners, and the Japanese in particular, are blamed for U.S. problems; and the ghost of Smoot-Hawley rides high in the land.[4]

There has always been a tendency in the United States to underestimate the Japanese. After all, John Wayne and Errol Flynn destroyed whole Japanese armies singlehandedly in World War II war movies, and the Japanese used to make junk goods that were sold in dimestores. A later phase had many people in the U.S. saying that the Japanese were good at imitating others, but that they were not creative enough to be good in the sophisticated area of computers and telecommunications. Myths die hard, but the Japanese are for real.

The phenomenal performance of the Japanese economy is even more remarkable when one considers the economic base from which the country operates. The land area of Japan is small, the natural resources are limited, and the population is large. Japan is vulnerable to world upheavals because it imports such a high percentage of resources. Dependence on exports and imports is a way of life for the Japanese economy. There has been considerable pressure to gain reserves of foreign currency and gold to cover a balance-of-payments deficit incurred to pay for the imports necessary to sustain industrial development. Thus, it is imperative for the Japanese to be successful in world competition so that they can earn the foreign reserves necessary to cover their import needs. Government tax and foreign trade policies encourage industries that can be competitive in international markets.

During the 1970s and early 1980s, the Japanese economy has been the most successful in the world. It is important to examine the factors responsible for this success. How could a country come back from the zero point in August, 1945, when the war ended and the economy was in ruins? Forty percent of the urban area had been destroyed and urban population had dropped to less than half of prewar levels. Industry was at a standstill and agriculture, short of equipment and personnel, had declined. The per capita annual income was $20; 50 percent of the working population was unemployed. The economy, with American aid, could go no place but up, and it has gone up at a rate unprecedented in the Western world. Success can be attributed to a combination of factors the Japanese have melded together. Japan stands as a model to the world, especially the Third World, for its success transcends its culture and history.

---

4. The Smoot-Hawley Tariff Act was passed in 1932. It raised tariffs on a wide range of agricultural and industrial products to their highest levels in U.S. history. The purpose was to protect domestic jobs and industries against foreign competition. In fact, it had the opposite effect.

■ THE ECONOMIC SYSTEM ■

Japan has an economic philosophy that embraces the basic concepts of a modern capitalist economy. This philosophy was grafted onto a country that had virtually no outside contact with the Western world before 1853, when Commodore Matthew C. Perry and his American naval squadron forced Japan to open itself to the West against its own will.[5] With the shock of exposure to the outside world, it became apparent to the Japanese that they had to make a choice: either create a modern industrial state or become another market for Western goods. They chose the former, and in a relatively short period, Japan was transformed from an underdeveloped country into a world economic power. It did this by emulating the industrial powers of the West in every possible way; it cast aside behavioral patterns of centuries in favor of anything Western. By the beginning of this century, Japan had achieved sufficient industrial and military might to inflict a military defeat upon the forces of the Russian empire.

The economic development of Japan can be divided into two major time periods: the Meiji Period from 1868 to 1913 and the period following the end of World War II from 1948 to 1960. Each period is signficant in understanding how Japan has transformed itself into a major world power. A common denominator of each period was the role the Japanese government played in stimulating economic development. Human capital was also important in aiding economic growth, for Japan has had few natural resources and land was far from abundant relative to the size of the population.

THE MEIJI PERIOD, 1868–1913

The Meiji Restoration of 1868 marks the beginning of the development of Japan as a modern industrial nation.[6] In the first years after the Restoration, the most important development in Japan was the creation of an environment conducive to economic growth. In order to survive the economic encroachments of the Western powers, Japan, by national policy, had to master the secret of industry. To gain the necessary knowledge,

5. Actually Christian missionaries had reached Japan by the middle of the fifteenth century. The Dutch established a trading post at Nagasaki in 1638 and maintained it for several centuries. Dutch became the language of Western learning in Japan, and through books brought in from Holland, Japanese scholars managed to keep at least partially abreast of intellectual and scientific progress in the West.

6. The Meiji Restoration was called a "restoration" because the powers of the government that the Tokugawa Shogunate had usurped were restored to the emperor of Japan, who came to be known posthumously as the Emperor Meiji.

Japanese students were sent to study the technology of Western nations. Also, Western engineers and technicians were temporarily employed in Japan to teach the Japanese the techniques of production. The Japanese learned to adapt the technology of the West for their own purposes.

THE ROLE OF GOVERNMENT   The government became a major operator of key industries. The modernization of Japan during the later part of the last century included the nationalization of key sectors of the economy—the postal service, telephone and telegraph communications, and railways. The government also built and operated iron foundaries, shipyards, machine shops, and factories. Tobacco, salt, and camphor became government monopolies.[7] The government provided technical and financial assistance to private interests in other industries.

The financial and monetary base for the economy was provided in 1882 when the Bank of Japan was formed. Tax policies were designed to stimulate capital formation. Taxes were levied on agricultural land and the sale of farm products. The proceeds provided for public capital formation, which went into the development of roads and education facilities. Expenditures on arsenals, navy yards, warships, and the like provided a military underpinning to the process of economic development.

THE ROLE OF PRIVATE ENTERPRISE   While the government was involved in providing the conditions requisite to economic growth and industrial development, private enterprise also flourished and developed during the Meiji Period. An important development during the Meiji Period was the displacement of the *samurai*, or warrior caste, which had dominated Japan for centuries. The samurai were integrated into Japanese society, and some went into business. Therefore, in Japan, business people were drawn from the upper classes of society and enjoyed immediate respect and prestige. In this respect, Japan started at an advantage, for in most developing countries, the business class is largely composed of people in lower social classes or racial and religious minorities not respected by the population. By building up export industries based on low-cost labor, Japan was able to increase exports to provide foreign exchange to purchase food and raw materials needed by the economy.

Japanese capitalism was characterized by the development of concentrated economic power in the form of business combines called *zaibatsus*. Each combine consisted of 20 to 30 major firms, all concentrated around a

---

7. The government also financed the development of experimental or pilot plants to train Japanese workers and to adopt Western production techniques to Japanese conditions. These plants became models for private industry to follow.

large bank. These major firms represented each of the important industrial sectors in the economy, so that a group would typically include a shipping company, a steel company, an insurance company, and so forth. Zaibatsu combines were larger than any American corporation and were under the control and management of a few family dynasties. The Mitsui combine, for example, employed 1,800,000 workers prior to World War II, and Mitsubishi employed 1,000,000 workers.[8] There was a working relationship between the zaibatsus and the Japanese government in that the latter, through military force or otherwise, provided penetration of new markets.

POST-WORLD WAR II DEVELOPMENT OF JAPAN

With Japan's defeat in World War II and the subsequent occupation by the United States came problems of reform and reorganization for the economy. A new constitution, which incorporated Western principles of democratic parliamentary government, was promulgated in November 1946.[9] The dissolution of the zaibatsu into a number of independent business enterprises was another part of U.S. occupation policy. Antitrust laws molded after the U.S. Sherman and Clayton Acts were imposed on the Japanese. Later, however, the Japanese government enacted various laws to exempt certain industries from antitrust laws. These exemptions were designed to improve Japan's position as a world exporter by allowing certain types of export cartels.[10] The U.S. occupation of Japan also resulted in the introduction of consumer technology, which the Japanese readily assimilated. The Japanese became wards of the United States and received gifts, low-interest loans, and machinery that restored productive capacity in a number of industries, especially textiles.[11]

However, Japanese economic development policy could not depend on American largesse alone. Local needs had to be satisfied first. The shipbuilding industry was destroyed during the war and, as a small island country, Japan needed ships of every type for survival. With government aid, the shipbuilding industry developed rapidly; by 1956 the Japanese had become the world's largest producer of ships.

8. Corwin Edwards, "The Dissolution of Zaibatsu Continues," *Pacific Affairs*, September, 1946, pp. 8-24.

9. The U.S. military occupation of Japan ended in 1952.

10. Japanese antimonopoly laws permit the development of cartels and other forms of business combinations to a far greater extent than is permitted by U.S. antitrust laws.

11. Jean-Jacques Servan-Schreiber, *The World Challenge* (New York: Simon and Schuster Inc., 1981), pp. 178-184.

Japan also developed an export strategy to achieve industrial development. For exports, the country's leaders recognized that they would have to depend on handicrafts, textiles, and other small-scale industries in which Japan enjoyed the advantage of low-cost labor. Human capital was an important factor in the early post-war period. Veterans were absorbed in the labor-intensive industries. Earnings from exports were used to finance the acquisition of machine tools that would help Japan produce modern machinery. This led to the development of other industries, notably Honda, which developed from a one-man operation in 1951 to the largest motorcycle company in the world.

THE ROLE OF THE JAPANESE GOVERNMENT   The Japanese government has played and continues to play an important role in the development of the Japanese economy. The postwar development of Japanese industry was facilitated through government grants and low-interest loans. There has also been extensive use of fiscal and monetary policies to stimulate economic growth. Tax policy is used to achieve specific policy objectives. Special tax incentives are used to promote a high rate of saving, investment, and capital formation. There are also special tax incentives to promote the introduction of new products and technology. Probably most important of all has been the development of a close working relationship between government and business. This relationship is based to some extent on the realization that Japan has few natural resources and that it is necessary to reach some concensus over resource allocation. Government and business leaders attempt to decide on policy objectives that will promote the national interest rather than that of a special interest group.[12]

THE ROLE OF PRIVATE ENTERPRISE   Japan is characterized as having a *dual economy*. Japanese corporations are among the world's largest, and many engage in a wide variety of business activities. Around each major corporation are several satellite companies. These satellite companies, which are often small, family-owned operations employing up to 100 workers, are important to the Japanese economy. They typically manufacture a subassembly or provide a service sold only to their major customer.[13] The relationship between a satellite company and its major customer constitutes a bilateral monopoly, in which the satellite has only one customer for its product, and the major firm has only one supplier for each of its in-

---

12. Peter F. Drucker, "Behind Japan's Success," *Harvard Business Review*, January–February 1981, pp. 83-90.

13. William Ouchi, *Theory Z* (Reading, Mass.: Addison-Wesley Publishing Co. Inc., 1981), p. 18.

puts. This bilateral monopoly relationship makes it difficult for foreign firms to do business in Japan.

The zaibatsu combines, although outlawed after World War II, have regrouped and form a considerable part of the economic base of Japan today. The combines take the form of large trading companies that are among the world's largest corporations. These trading corporations have control over other companies. Business firms within an industry in Japan are linked through personal friendships, and there are regular meetings among leaders. Interlocking directorates, information sharing, mutual stockholding, and in case of trouble, mutual assistance all come into play. Within the group, trading companies play the coordinating role, for they have maximum contact with other group companies. Banks are also an integral part of a group and provide loans for capital investment. In new fields like computers and telecommunications, other group-affiliated companies may help finance a new company, thereby tying it closely to the group.

PUBLIC FINANCE

One factor that complicates the subject of public finance in Japan is the role industrial enterprise plays in the life of the average Japanese worker. It can be said that enterprise has usurped many of the functions of the welfare state. One important characteristic of many Japanese companies is lifetime employment, which is the rubric under which various facets of Japanese life are integrated.[14] Once hired, a new employee is retained until mandatory retirement at age 55.[15] A number of functions that are normally provided, at least in part, by the government are produced by the Japanese enterprise. Such things as medical care, low-cost housing, and subsidized meals are provided, all of which would count in the income redistribution process. Upon retirement, a company pays each retiree a lump sum separation amounting typically to five or six years' salary. This means that social welfare expenditures in Japan are low in comparison with other countries.

Government spending and transfers are handled in the national budget, which consists of general accounts, special accounts, and government agency accounts. General accounts include expenditures for education, science and technology, social security, land conservation and develop-

14. Not all Japanese workers are guaranteed lifetime employment; about 35 percent of the work force has lifetime employment.

15. Ouchi, *Theory Z*, pp. 17-18.

ment, allocations to local governments, and national defense. The main revenue sources are taxes, monopoly profits, and bond revenues. Special accounts are used for purposes where the government either undertakes specific projects or finances a specific expenditure with a specific revenue. The government agency accounts are for those public corporations financed by the government whose budgets are subject to the approval of the Diet.[16] These include three public corporations, the Japan Telephone and Telegraph Company, the Japan National Railways, and the Japan Monopoly Corporation; two banks, the Japan Development Bank and the Japan Export-Import Bank; and several other credit institutions, including the Small Business Finance Corporation and the Housing Loan Corporation.

TAXATION IN JAPAN   The two most important taxes in the Japanese tax system are the personal and corporate income taxes. In 1985 these taxes accounted for 68 percent of national government revenue obtained from tax sources.[17] The tax rates are altered frequently, for the national government has the authority to alter the rates and base annually and usually does. Annual changes in the tax laws constitute an important part of the government's budgetary policy and are called the "tax cut" policy. Because of a high rate of economic growth, the national government has reduced the rates of personal and corporate income taxes almost every year since 1950. Since the income elasticity of both taxes is greater than 1, if tax rates had not been cut, tax revenues would have increased at a much faster rate than national income.

   An important characteristic of the Japanese tax system is an enormous number of special tax provisions under which taxes are reduced selectively to accomplish specific national policy objectives. Examples of these objectives and provisions are considered below.

   SAVINGS   To stimulate savings, interest income from small deposits is exempted from personal income tax. For example, the annual interest on the first 3 million yen ($13,700) deposited in a Postal Savings account is tax exempt.[18] In addition, an individual can set up several Postal Savings accounts in the names of family members so that each can get the maximum tax-free interest.[19] Income from dividends and capital gains is subject to a

---

16. The Diet is Japan's legislative body to which representatives of the political parties are elected.

17. *An Outline of Japanese Taxes 1985* (Tokyo: Ministry of Finance, 1985), pp. 294-295.

18. U.S. Congress, Joint Economic Committee, *Japanese Taxation Policy*, 98th Cong., 2d Sess., September 1984, p. 21.

19. *Individual Taxes: A Worldwide Summary, 1985 Edition* (New York: Price Waterhouse and Co., 1985), p. 119.

flat tax rate, which is less than half the rate of the income tax on ordinary income. These inducements contribute to a savings rate that is the highest in the world.

INVESTMENTS   Considerable use is made of accelerated depreciation tax provisions to stimulate investment. These provisions are selective in their application and apply only to industries designated as contributing to exports or to the modernization of the economy. For example, to encourage the use of robots, special tax provisions permit companies to write off 53 percent of the cost of a robot during the first year of its use.[20] The government also sponsors a number of programs to provide low-cost loans to small- and medium-sized companies that want to install robots. As a result, industrial robots are more widely used in Japan than in any other country in the world.

NEW PRODUCTS AND TECHNOLOGY   There are tax provisions to promote the introduction of new products and technology. These include exemptions from personal or corporate income taxes on revenues from the sale of new products approved by the Ministry of Finance, duty-free importation of certain types of machinery and equipment, and favorable tax treatment of patent royalties.

EXPORTS   There are tax provisions to stimulate exports. A portion of income from exports is exempt from the personal and corporate income taxes. Accelerated depreciation privileges are also granted to export industries, provided that income from exports in one year shows a gain over the preceding year.

GOVERNMENT EXPENDITURES   In 1984 total government expenditures of all types amounted to 24 percent of Japan's gross national product, a lower percentage than any other major industrial nation.[21] Government spending is broken down into two categories—general government consumption and spending on capital formation. General consumption spending is evenly divided between the national government and local governments. Japan has had a long tradition of local autonomy, and the importance of local finance in relation to national finance is greater in Japan than it is in the United Kingdom or France.

Spending on capital formation is made by the national government and equals about 10 percent of gross national product. This spending is

20. Ibid., p. 183.

21. "Japan," *Economic Surveys* (Paris: Organization for Economic Cooperation and Development, July 1985), p. 18.

made through the *Financial Loan and Investment Program,* which is a separate budget entity. Included in this program is spending for housing; water and sewage facilities; agriculture and small industries; roads, transportation, and regional development; and key industries and export promotion.

Government expenditures and tax policies place more emphasis on a high rate of economic growth than on income redistribution. Priority within the budget is given to spending that increases capital formation and thus allows the nation to increase its output of goods. A lower priority has been assigned to social welfare expenditures, in part because of the policy of lifetime employment provided by large industrial enterprises. The industrial enterprise is regarded as a family where employees, rather than being hired, are adopted as members of the family. Their participation in the enterprise family is based on more than their actual contribution in terms of skill. The wage system is not simply compensation for work but is rather a kind of "life income" determined by an employee's age and family situation. The basic wage often comprises only 50 percent of annual income; the remainder is paid in the form of various allowances and benefits.[22]

FISCAL POLICY   Fiscal policy plays an important role in the development of the Japanese economy. Changes in the level of taxation, in spending in the government general accounts budget, and in the government financial loan and investment program are the three devices used to affect the level of aggregate demand. Maintenance of a high rate of economic growth, as opposed to income redistribution or the provision of socially desirable goods and services, has been the dominant objective of fiscal policy. However, the emphasis on sustained economic growth works to the advantage of the Japanese people in the form of continued increases in the per capita output of goods and services. Government fiscal policy, by supporting a continuous increase in private and public investment, has been conducive to a high rate of economic growth in Japan.

THE BANKING SYSTEM

The banking system of Japan can be divided into a number of institutions, with the Bank of Japan providing the connecting link in the system. Japanese banks are classified as commercial banks, long-term credit banks, and foreign exchange banks. There are private financial institutions that

22. Robert Christopher, *The Japanese Mind* (New York: Simon and Schuster Inc., 1983), p. 248.

specialize in financing small- and medium-sized enterprises and investment in agricultural equipment. In addition, there are also government-owned financial institutions that supplement the functions of the private financial institutions. Included among the government financial institutions are the Japan Development Bank, Postal Savings, Export-Import Bank of Japan, Housing Loan Corporation, and Small Business Finance Corporation. Most of these government financial institutions were created after the end of World War II and currently play an important role in the financial operations of the nation.

The largest borrowers of funds in Japan are corporate business concerns, which dominate investment activities in the country. The biggest source of savings is private individuals who invest their money in Postal Saving accounts. This money, along with government trust and pension funds, is funneled into the government-owned lending institutions mentioned above. Large- and medium-sized Japanese corporations borrow from private Japanese banks or issue stocks and bonds to raise money; small companies (that are usually the subcontractors to the larger ones) get most of their loans from the government through the Small Business Finance Corporation.

THE CENTRAL BANK   The Bank of Japan was established in 1882. Since its establishment, the Bank has always served as the fiscal agent for the government. It provides the government with borrowing facilities and over the years has also assumed a wide range of activities, including handling the public receipts and payments, Treasury accounts, and government debt, and buying and selling foreign exchange.

The Bank of Japan also carries out a wide variety of activity with commercial banks and other institutions. These include receiving deposits, making loans, discounting bills and notes, and buying and selling Treasury bills. Commercial banks turn to the Bank of Japan as a source of funds similar to the way U.S. banks borrow from the Federal Reserve. Since the commercial banks depend upon the central bank for credit, discount policy has played an important and effective role in maintaining general economic stability. A restriction of central bank credit has an immediate and significant impact on commercial bank policy.

COMMERCIAL BANKS   The commercial banks are privately owned and are divided into two types—city banks and local banks. City banks are located in large cities and operate on a nationwide scale with a network of branch offices distributed throughout the country. Since the Meiji period, these banks have played a principal role in supplying the funds necessary for the rapid expansion of the economy. City bank loans, for the most part, are granted to large-scale enterprises; however, in recent years they have become more oriented toward the consumer market and have gone into the area of consumer credit. The city banks account for one-third of the total fund resources of all financial institutions, public and private, in Japan and account for 60 percent of the deposits of all banks.[23] There are 15 city banks in Japan.

Local banks are commercial banks conducting business principally in regional areas. There are 63 local banks, and each is based in a prefecture and extends its operations to neighboring prefectures.[24] Loans to small- and medium-sized enterprises make up the greatest part of local bank loans, and individuals' time deposits make up the greatest part of local deposits. Local banks also lend to public entities and are an important supplier of call loans.

In addition to the commercial banks, there are also long-term credit banks and trust banks. To raise funds for loans, they are allowed to issue debenture bonds in an amount up to 20 times their total capital and reserves. Trust banks and long-term credit banks provide long-term funds for investment in plant and equipment. Both the long-term credit banks and the trust banks are privately owned.

GOVERNMENT FINANCIAL INSTITUTIONS The government itself is engaged in substantial financial activities through the ownership of a number of specialized credit institutions. Loans are provided for long-term industrial development, export financing, and agriculture as a part of government policy for stimulating economic growth in an economy where capital is scarce. These institutions obtain loanable funds from the special counterpart fund in the national budget and from individual savings in the form of postal savings, postal annuities, and postal life insurance. These savings and the surplus funds from special budgetary accounts are deposited in a Trust Fund Bureau, which can use the funds for loans to public enterprises and financial institutions. Loans are also made to the private sector of the economy, particularly to industries that are export-related. However, as a rule, private sector financing is undertaken in cooperation with private lending institutions.

THE EXPORT-IMPORT BANK   The Japan Export-Import Bank provides long-term loans at subsidized interest rates to exporters of Japanese products. For example, loans have been provided for the construction of

---

23. *The Financial System of Japan* (Tokyo: The Bank of Japan, 1984), p. 32.

24. A *prefecture* is an administrative unit that corresponds to a metropolitan area or a province.

tankers, textile machinery, and railroad cars. Loans have also been provided for the financing of projects, such as the development of iron ore mines in India and the construction of textile mills in South America. The Bank also provides financing and debt guarantees to attract foreign capital into Japan. To stimulate economic development in Southeast Asia, the government set up a special account with the Bank and called it the Southeast Asia Development Corporation Fund. Funds were provided out of the national budget. The fund was eventually transformed into an independent corporation and currently finances long-term investment in Southeast Asia.[25]

JAPAN DEVELOPMENT BANK   Another important government-owned financial institution is the Japan Development Bank. The bank was created in 1951 to aid in the postwar reconstruction of the economy. Most of its loans were originally concentrated in the electric power, shipbuilding, and coal industries. However, in recent years its loans have been channeled into the petrochemical and rubber industries and also into the promotion of regional development, city transportation, and international tourism. The bank provides long-term loans at low interest rates to basic domestic industries. Through its control over loanable funds that are in the hands of official financial agencies like the Japanese Development Bank, the government is able to exercise some control over national investment and thereby exert some influence with respect to its national economic plans.

Another financial institution directly owned and operated by the government is the Small Business Finance Corporation, which provides long-term loans to small businesses when financing by ordinary financial institutions proves difficult. The government-owned Agriculture, Forestry, and Fisheries Finance Corporation provides long-term, low-interest loans for investment in agricultural equipment by agricultural cooperatives and individual farming enterprises. Loanable funds for both corporations are obtained from the national budget and from earnings on investments in securities and call loans.[26]

MONETARY POLICY   The Bank of Japan has three instruments used to control the volume of credit and money—bank rate policy, open market operations, and reserve requirements. Bank rate policy involves the lowering or raising of discount rates and interest rates. The alteration of these

---

25. *Banking in Modern Japan* (Tokyo: The Bank of Tokyo, 1980), p. 35.

26. Ibid., pp. 37-38.

rates is the most important monetary policy instrument in Japan because city banks rely heavily on loans from the Bank of Japan, and industries, in turn, rely heavily on bank loans. Costs in general and the availability of bank funds are highly responsive to changes in the discount and interest rates on commercial and export trade bills, overdrafts, and general secured loans. In addition, the Bank of Japan also can place a ceiling on borrowing for each bank, above which it can impose a penalty rate or refuse to make loans. Open market operations are inhibited by the lack of a well-developed capital market and are not important as an instrument of monetary policy. Legal reserve requirements are far below the standard of reserve requirements in other major countries, and manipulation of these requirements by the Bank of Japan is a supplementary instrument of monetary control.

In Japan the function of monetary policy is more circumscribed than that of fiscal policy. In general, monetary policy has been expansionary to encourage a high rate of economic growth. Successive cuts in the offical discount rate brought it down to an all-time low level of 4.25 percent in June 1972. However, in 1974 and 1975 the discount rate was raised to 9 percent because of inflation caused by the oil embargo. After 1975, the discount rate was lowered as inflation subsided. In 1984, the average Japanese discount rate was 6.5 percent. The Japanese have relied more on monetary policy in recent years as an anti-inflationary device.

LABOR–MANAGEMENT RELATIONS

The distinctive feature of Japanese trade unions is that they are usually company unions. The typical Japanese labor union is made up of the employees of a single company or of a single operational unit within a company, regardless of their occupation. The result is that there are many trade unions in Japan—more than 70,000 in 1984.[27] Approximately one-fourth of the Japanese labor force belongs to trade unions, with each union loosely tied to one of four central labor organizations. However, the central organizations have little authority over the company unions, which carry on the bargaining with employers. Negotiations between labor and management are conducted within each enterprise; however, there are several points of difference between Japanese labor practices and those of other countries.

Many Japanese firms, in particular the larger ones, provide lifetime employment for their employees. This makes for a very different balance

---

27. *Japan Statistical Yearbook, 1984* (Tokyo: Office of the Prime Minister, 1984), p. 130.

of power between union and management in Japanese firms. The employees know that their future depends on their company's future and that labor work stoppages could hurt their company's competitive position.[28] Since it is difficult to obtain employment by leaving one company for another, the union will rarely press its demands so far as to seriously damage the company. Forcing a company into bankruptcy, for example, would put workers at the mercy of the labor market.

Positions within a company are determined largely on the basis of age and length of service. Japanese companies routinely provide a number of fringe benefits for their employees. Thus, negotiations between labor and management in Japan are limited primarily to wages. During February through April each year, unions begin what is called the *shunto*, "spring wage struggle," with their respective companies. If agreement is not reached, the union may go out on strike. But since there is one union for each company, industry-wide strike efforts are rare. Unions may also resort to public demonstrations to make the community aware of their demands.

This is not to say that Japanese labor-management relations are perfect. There is industrial conflict, as evidenced by the frequent wildcat strikes on the government-owned national railways. Worker-days lost through strikes, though much lower than in the United States, are higher than in Sweden or West Germany.[29] The number of work stoppages is also high in comparison to West Germany and France. With the current emphasis on automation, the potential for labor conflict may well increase in Japan during the next few years. The failure of successive conservative governments to develop labor-oriented social welfare programs also provides a potential for labor unrest.

Japanese employers are also organized into several confederations, the largest of which is the Federation of Economic Organizations (*Keidanran*). It is made up of financial, industrial, and trading associations that include almost all of Japan's largest business firms. Membership in the federation is institutional, and its work is carried out by standing committees. Keidanran wields considerable influence in government economic policies because many business and political leaders are bound together by a common educational background and family ties. The Federation provides the Japanese with a mechanism for reconciling industrial policy objectives with political and social goals.

---

28. Christopher, *Japanese Mind*, pp. 248-249.

29. In 1984, the U.S. lost 50 times as many days in labor disputes as Japan lost.

GOVERNMENT AND BUSINESS RELATIONS

The combination of free enterprise and government control in Japan dates back to the Meiji Restoration in 1868. The government was active during the Meiji era in introducing Western industrial methods into Japan and also took the lead in promoting the development of industries of strategic importance. Fundamental shifts took place in government policy during the 1930s. To counteract the effects of the worldwide depression, state intervention in the economy increased. The electric power industry was nationalized in 1938, and other strategic industries were brought under government control.

After World War II was over, the government continued its role in the economy as an expediter of business development. Policies to increase exports encouraged mergers that resulted in large-scale business operations and the revival of the zaibatsu combines. Special tax privileges, subsidies, and low interest loans were used to strengthen certain industries and certain types of economic activity. The Japanese government continues to exercise an important role in the nurturing of Japanese industry.

THE MINISTRY OF INTERNATIONAL TRADE AND INDUSTRY—MITI MITI is probably the most important and powerful government agency in Japan, at least as far as Japanese business is concerned. It was created in the late 1940s to guide industrial modernization and promote exports. Its mandate was to determine a basic course of action to improve Japan's future comparative advantage and to mobilize each sector to make its contribution to the whole. Building a steel industry was one of Japan's most important postwar priorities. MITI encouraged Japanese banks to supply the capital that purchased steel-producing equipment and technology from the West, mostly from the United States. Tax incentives, low interest loans, and other financial incentives were also given to the steel industry. MITI has continued to restructure industry by concentrating resources in areas where it thinks Japan needs to be competitive in the future.

The primary function of MITI is to offer guidance to Japanese industry. It provides the "big picture," so to speak, of where it thinks Japan as a country should be heading. It formulates and guides the implementation of an industrial strategy consistent with Japan's national interest. In March 1980, MITI published a document setting forth priorities for the 1980s.[30] Recognizing that Japan is dependent on outside energy sources, the MITI

---

30. *Vision of Industry in the 1980s* (Tokyo: Minstry of International Trade and Industry, March, 1980).

plan was to base much of Japan's economic future on high technology industries, which require far less energy that traditional industries.[31]

MITI does not have the power to coerce Japanese industry into following a strategy, and industry may choose to ignore it. It does not have the authority to make direct loans and grants to industry, but must persuade the Export-Import Bank, the Development Bank, and other public and private lending insitutitons to make the loans it recommends. It does have the power to grant licenses and patents and to determine which firms will participate in development projects, but its real power is consultative.[32]

AGENCY OF INDUSTRIAL SCIENCE AND TECHNOLOGY—AIST   AIST is another government agency involved with economic development. It is a semi-independent agency under the jurisdiction of MITI and is responsible for the promotion of technology.[33] It monitors scientific and technical developments abroad and identifies new technology that will be important to Japanese industries. One of the strengths of Japanese industry is that it is well informed about worldwide scientific and technological developments. AIST consults with Japanese industry to encourage the use of new technologies that will further the national interest; its sponsors research that will make the needed technology available. It is also responsible for the development of patents.

GOVERNMENT SAVINGS AND INVESTMENT   To facilitate the development of high-technology industries, government agencies will provide financial aid. As mentioned previously, funds from the national budget are channeled through various lending institutions also to help provide industries with the funds necessary for expansion and development. The government and its agencies account for as much as one-fourth of all investment spending in Japan—a high percentage for an economy largely based on private enterprise. In 1981 MITI persuaded the Agency of Industrial Science and Technology to provide high-technology industries $500 million in no-interest loans.[34] The Development Bank of Japan lent the computer and electronics industry an additional $210 million for projects related to some aspect of government policy.[35] Preferred interest rates were given to the high-technology industries.

31. The main areas are telecommunications, semiconductors, and information processing.

32. Chalmers Johnson, *MITI and the Japanese Miracle* (Stanford: Stanford University Press, 1982).

33. Vogel, *Comeback*, p. 65.

34. "Japan's Strategies for the 1980s," *Business Week*, December 14, 1981, pp. 39-40.

35. Ibid., p. 41.

Figure 9-1 illustrates the financial relationship between government and industry in Japan. Funds flow from the national budget into many lending accounts. The Japan Development Bank derives most of its loanable funds from the government-owned Postal Savings system and lends only for private industry projects that are a part of government policy. It has financed such projects as the commercial development of Sony's Trinitron tube for color television.

ECONOMIC PLANNING

Japanese economic planning is indicative rather than imperative and is similar to French planning in that it develops goals for industrial development, social welfare, labor relations, and related major economic and social sectors. Plans represent goals the Japanese government would like to see achieved. Plans, as announced, represent the consensus of not only government, but also of private groups, including business, labor, and the academic community. Each group is expected to fit its self-interest into a framework of national needs, national goals, and national aspirations.[36] This forces Japanese leadership groups to take responsibility for developing policies in the national interest. The private sector, therefore, has full knowledge, through its government input, of any government planning.

HISTORY OF JAPANESE PLANNING

Since the end of World War II, there have been several sets of economic plans. The first set of plans were aimed at reconstruction of the postwar economy. When this was accomplished, a second set of plans was adopted to develop a viable economy without economic assistance from the United States. A more recent plan covered the period from 1979 to 1985. It concentrated on correcting an imbalance among various sectors of the economy and on restructuring older industries. Emphasis was placed on shifting from an economy based primarily on heavy industry to one based on high technology, knowledge, service, and information industries. Priority industries were identifed: industrial robots, semiconductors, microprocessors, computers, optic fibers, and bioengineering.[37] Energy independence,

36. Drucker, "Behind Japan's Success," pp. 86-87.

37. "Economic and Social Development Plan, 1979–1985," *Japan Times* (Tokyo: Economic Planning Agency, 1980).

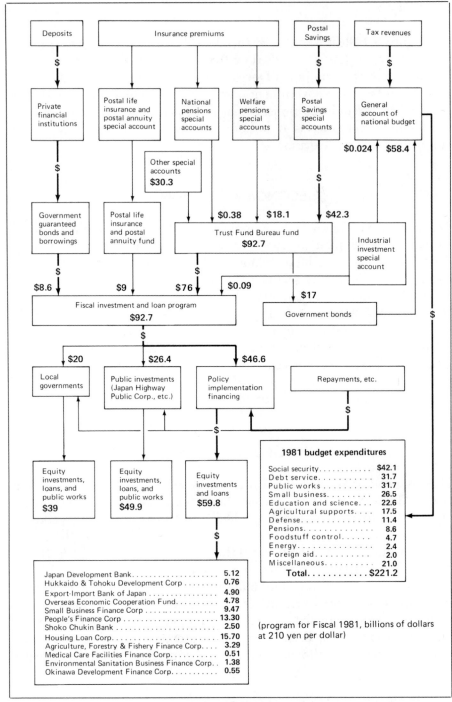

FIGURE 9-1   HOW GOVERNMENT CHANNELS ASSETS
INTO JAPANESE INDUSTRY

Source: Reprinted from the December 14, 1981, issue of *Business Week* by special permission,
© 1981 by McGraw-Hill, Inc., New York, NY 10020. All rights reserved.

at least as far as oil is concerned, was to be achieved by 1985. This goal has not yet been met. Government expenditures on social overhead capital were to increase by 100 percent over the amount in the 1979 national budget.

THE ECONOMIC PLANNING AGENCY   The Economic Planning Agency, established in 1955 when economic priorities shifted from postwar recovery to economic growth, provides indicative planning for the whole economy. It provides targets for long-term trends and specifies what is necessary for national economic and social development. It is responsible for coordinating the plans of other executive agencies of the Japanese government, analyzing and measuring national economic resources, and identifying future needs. Planning policies that involve foreign trade, agriculture, transportation, and labor are put into effect through cooperation with the ministries responsible for these activities. The Economic Planning Agency itself does not have the power of a ministry and can exercise little independent initiative or coordination.

The *Economic Council* is responsible for the development of the actual plan. It is composed of key members of the financial community, industry, and government, who are appointed by the prime minister to a two-year term. In addition, a number of experts on technical matters are used in formulating the plan. There is a General Policy Committee and a number of specialized committees, each of which is concerned with certain areas of the Japanese economy, such as agriculture, mining, and forestry. Their reports are integrated into a draft of the plan, which is sent by the Council to the prime minister for approval. Then the plan is returned to the Council for implementation.

To carry out its functions, which are not limited exclusively to long-term economic planning, the Economic Planning Agency must work with various executive departments and agencies. The Agency works with the Bank of Japan, whose support is crucial because it is the center of Japanese monetary policy formulation. It must also work with the Ministry of Finance, because of its control over expenditures and the national budget, which affect the successful operation of any plan. Planning policies that involve foreign trade, agriculture, transportation, and labor are put into effect through cooperation with the ministries responsible for these activities. The plan itself is more than just an estimate of the future, for the government is able through fiscal policies and control over financial institutions such as the Japan Development Bank to encourage or compel plan objectives.

■ AN APPRAISAL ■
OF THE JAPANESE ECONOMY

For all practical purposes, the economic development of Japan began with the Meiji Restoration of 1868. At that time, Japan was at about the same stage of economic development that the United States was at in 1776. The Japanese had to start from scratch to catch up with the industrial West, and they have done exactly that. In 1880, the real per capita GNP was one-twentieth of that for the United States and the United Kingdom and one-fourth of that for the Soviet Union.[38] By 1920 Japanese real per capita GNP had passed that of the Soviet Union and was one-fourth of that for the United States. After the end of World War II, real per capita GNP in Japan declined to one-twelfth of the real per capita GNP for the United States and was lower than that for the Soviet Union. By 1955 Japan had again passed the Soviet Union; by 1970 it had passed the United Kingdom. In 1984 Japanese real per capita GNP was about 65 percent of that of the United States, and 75 percent of that of West Germany.

Table 9-1 compares real growth rates for Japan and the major Western industrial countries for the period 1971–1983. As the table indicates, the Japanese economy performed the best, and the United Kingdom the worst, during this time period. The oil crisis in 1974 accelerated plans to push Japan into service and knowledge-intensive industries rather than energy-intensive ones. This is the strategy it is pursuing in the 1980s. The Japanese economy rebounded from the oil crisis and maintained an average annual rate of real growth of 4.6 percent during the remainder of the 1970s. All countries were affected by a world recession that began in 1979, but Japan was affected the least.

Table 9-2 compares real growth rates, inflation, and unemployment rates for the same countries for several time periods. As the table indicates, the performance of the Japanese economy was the best with respect to the real rate of growth in per capita GNP for the period 1965–1983. The rate of inflation in Japan was higher for the period 1965–1973 than it was for the other industrial countries with the exception of the United Kingdom. For the period 1973–1983, the rate of inflation was lower than the other countries, with the exception of West Germany. The unemployment rate in Japan for the period 1965–1973 was lower than the other countries, with the exception of West Germany. For the period 1973–1983, the unemployment rate in Japan was the lowest of the six major industrial countries.

---

38. *Comparative Economic Statistics* (Tokyo: Bank of Japan, 1984), p. 4.

TABLE 9-1 REAL GROWTH RATES IN GNP FOR MAJOR INDUSTRIAL COUNTRIES, 1971–1983

	Japan	U.S.	West Germany	France	U.K.	Italy
1971	4.6%	3.3%	3.1%	5.4%	2.6%	1.6%
1972	8.8	5.6	4.1	5.9	2.2	3.2
1973	8.8	5.5	4.6	5.4	7.6	7.0
1974	−1.0	−0.8	0.5	3.2	−0.9	4.1
1975	2.3	−0.9	−1.7	0.2	−0.8	−3.6
1976	5.3	5.3	5.5	5.2	3.7	5.9
1977	5.3	5.5	3.1	3.1	1.2	1.9
1978	5.0	4.9	3.1	3.8	3.5	2.7
1979	5.1	2.4	4.2	3.3	2.0	4.9
1980	4.9	−0.3	1.8	1.1	−2.3	3.9
1981	4.2	2.7	−0.0	0.2	−1.0	0.1
1982	3.0	−1.7	−1.0	2.0	2.2	−0.3
1983	3.2	3.5	0.9	1.0	3.5	1.0

Source: Japan 1984: An International Comparison (Tokyo: Mitsubishi Research Institute, 1984), p. 13.

T A B L E 9 - 2 REAL GROWTH RATES, INFLATION, AND UNEMPLOYMENT FOR MAJOR INDUSTRIAL COUNTRIES

| | Average Annual Growth Rate | Average Rate of Inflation | | Average Rate of Unemployment | |
	1965–1983	1965–1973	1973–1983	1965–1973	1973–1983
Japan	4.8%	6.0%	4.7%	1.2%	2.2%
U.S.	1.7	4.7	7.5	4.5	7.3
West Germany	2.8	4.7	4.3	0.7	3.9
France	3.1	5.3	10.8	2.5	6.3
U.K.	1.7	6.2	14.3	2.8	9.3
Italy	2.8	5.1	17.4	3.4	4.4

Sources: The World Bank, *World Development Report 1985*, p. 175; *Economic Report of the President, 1986*, p. 377

Table 9-3 compares the Japanese economy with other economies both in the past and projected into the future. In 1960 Japan had 3 percent of the world's gross national product; it is projected to have a 12 percent share by the year 2000. Conversely, the U.S. share of the world's gross national product declined from 33 percent in 1960 to 22 percent in 1980. This decline was to be expected, for Japan and other countries were still in the process of recovering from the devastation of World War II. The developing countries, including Taiwan, Singapore, and other East Asian countries, have increased their share of world GNP. In fact, the Japanese share of world GNP combined with the shares held by China and the developing countries of East Asia will exceed the share held by the Western European countries by 2000; it already exceeds the share held by the Soviet Union and the Eastern European countries. The highest real growth rates during the period 1986–2000 are projected for Japan and other East Asian countries, including China, which is in the process of initiating economic reforms.

TABLE 9-3   WORLD GNP SHARES OF SELECTED COUNTRIES AND REGIONS

	Share of World GNP			Real Growth Rate Per Annum	
	1960	1980	2000	1970–1979	1980–2000
Japan	3%	10%	12%	5.2%	4.0%
U.S.	33	22	20	3.1	2.5
Industrial Countries	62	63	58	3.3	2.8
LDC's[1]	11	11	13	5.7	4.0
Developing Countries	14	15	20	6.3	4.6
U.S.S.R.	15	13	12	5.1	3.0
Eastern Europe	4	5	5	5.9	3.0
China	5	4	5	5.8	4.0
Communist Bloc	24	22	22	5.4	3.2

[1]Less developed countries

Source: *Japan 1984: An International Comparison* (Tokyo: Mitsubishi Research Institute, 1984), p. 16.

STRENGTHS OF THE JAPANESE ECONOMY

Japan has emerged as the world's most viable industrial economy. Its rate of economic growth over the last 25 years has been the best of all industrial economies, its unemployment rate the lowest; and inflation has not become a serious problem. Although Japan is not an egalitarian society, it has a more equal distribution of income than other industrial countries. This may appear surprising, for the level of transfer payments is lower in comparison to other countries. There are several factors that explain the more even distribution of income in Japan: less inherited wealth than in other countries, a lower rate of stock and bond ownership, and lower incomes for executives in comparison to workers. Given the success of the Japanese economy, it is important to examine the reasons for it. Many Westerners search for cultural explanations for Japan's success, but that would be only a partial explanation.

A QUEST FOR KNOWLEDGE   One of the most important strengths of Japan is a common drive for knowledge. In virtually every important organization, from the national government to individual private firms, nothing is more important than the information and knowledge that the organization might some day need. Coupled with this desire for knowledge is an educational system that is regarded by many as the best in the world.[39] The accumulation of knowledge is a process that continues through life and involves all segments of the Japanese economy. From the beginning of the Meiji period in the midnineteenth century to the present, the Japanese government has sent missions abroad to study technology. As the spectrum of learning has widened, the process of acquiring information has become more elaborate.

INDUSTRIAL POLICY   An industrial policy, and the cooperation of government and business in carrying it out, is a second reason for Japan's success. Industrial policy gives Japan a sense of national purpose. One result is the emergence of Japan as a world leader in the semiconductor industry—an industry previously dominated by the United States. Resources are allocated by the Japanese government to favor priority industries. Japan is the world leader in the production of industrial robots, and the government has provided industry with $140 million over a seven-year period to develop robots capable of assembling an automobile.[40] It should be em-

---

39. U.S. Congress, Joint Economic Committee, *International Student Achievement Comparisons and Teacher Shortages in Math and Science*, 98th Cong., 1st Sess., 1983.

40. U.S. Congress, Joint Economic Committee, *Foreign Industrial Targeting Practices*, 98th Cong., 1st Sess., 1983.

phasized, however, that what may work well for Japan may not work at all in the United States, for the economies are too different. The U.S. economy is far more diverse.

BUSINESS LEADERSHIP   Superior management techniques, at least in comparison with American management, are regarded by some people as the key reason for the success of Japan in world markets.[41] Management by consensus allows workers to provide input into the decision-making process. In addition to providing employees with economic incentives for long-term loyalty, company officials do their best to reinforce employee identification with the company. Special attention is paid to quality control, with the result that Japanese products enjoy the reputation of being very well made.[42] Japanese managers also appear to be better informed about the world than their counterparts in other countries. No company in the West compares with the Japanese firm in its capacity to introduce rapid change.[43]

SAVINGS   One of the reasons for the success of Japan is a high rate of savings, which makes funds available for capital formation. Japanese tax policy encourages saving and capital formation at the expense of current consumption. The high rate of savings is attributed by some to the culturally derived frugality of the Japanese.[44] Others attribute the high savings to government fiscal policy.[45] Regardless of the cause, savings are there for investment. Gross domestic investment increased at an average annual rate of 14.1 percent from 1965 to 1973 and at a rate of 3.1 percent from 1973 to 1983.[46] The rate was the highest of all industrial countries for both time periods. The comparable rates for the United States were 2.7 percent and 1.0 percent.

WEAKNESSES OF THE JAPANESE ECONOMY

In Japan a complicated set of reciprocal relations between groups has held the institutions of society together. Before World War II, these ties were

---

41. Ouchi, *Theory Z*, p. 45; Drucker, "Behind Japan's Success," p. 90.

42. Quality control was first developed in the United States. After World War II, the Japanese invited W. Edward Deming, the father of quality control, to come to Japan to teach them the techniques. The result was that the Japanese have made better use of the techniques than the United States has.

43. Ezra Vogel, *Japan as Number One* (Cambridge: Harvard University Press, 1979), p. 180.

44. Christopher, *Japanese Mind*, pp. 27-32.

45. Joint Economic Committee, *Japanese Taxation Policy*, 1984, pp. 89-93.

46. *World Development Report 1985* (New York: The World Bank), p. 181.

centered in the nation as represented by the army, the zaibatsu, the state, and the emperor. The relations between groups were transferred after the shattering military defeat of World War II into the mundane tasks of economic reconstruction and growth. New groups developed after the war, and one foundation of Japanese society has been a willingness to compromise private ends for the public interest. The success of Japan up to now has been awesome. Its economy has performed better than those of Europe and the United States. If this success continues, Japan could well be the number one economic power in the world by the end of this century. However, the Japanese economy is not free from problems; it is vulnerable to forces over which it has little or no control.

DEPENDENCE ON WORLD TRADE   Japan is vulnerable to changes in the world economy. It imports a high proportion of resources required to meet its energy needs. High energy costs have made it difficult for certain Japanese industries, in particular aluminum, chemicals, and steel, to compete in world markets. Balance of trade deficits in the United States and Western Europe have created pressures to limit the flow of Japanese imports into these areas. There is also pressure from the United States and other countries on Japan to liberalize its restrictions on imports. For a country like Japan, which cannot survive without trade, these pressures have created serious problems. The very success of Japan has turned other countries against it. The maintenance of a stable world economy and continued foreign trade, particularly with the developed countries, are the basic conditions for the future development of the Japanese economy.[47]

A CHANGE IN WORK ATTITUDES   Although the Protestant work ethic may be associated with the United States and other Western industrial countries, the Japanese have their own legacy of the work ethic. It is in part predicated on Confucianism, which places a high value on education and hard work. Many Japanese believe work is the reason for living and pass up vacations in order to continue work. It appears that this "workaholism" has begun to abate, particularly among younger Japanese, who are opting for a more Western life style with an emphasis on consumption. Some older workers allege that younger Japanese have caught the "British disease," namely, a desire to substitute leisure for work.[48] What this will do to the Japanese work ethic remains to be seen.

47. "Problems Facing the Japanese Economy in the 1980s" (Tokyo: Keizai Koho Center, March 3, 1983).

48. Takayoshi Hamano, "The Japanese Economy in the 1980s" in *Japan in the 1980s*, Rei Shiraton, ed. (Tokyo: Kodansha International, Ltd., 1982), pp. 142-143.

URBAN GROWTH   Japanese economic growth has not been an unmixed blessing. The Japanese now realize that they have paid heavily for their obsession with economic growth. Tokyo, Osaka, Yokohama, and other metropolitan areas have become megapolitan nightmares, hopelessly congested and permeated with fumes. The Japanese have been forced to undertake a vast restructuring of the nation and its economy. To check pollution and urban congestion, factories have had to be dispersed to the countryside. Dozens of new towns have been created and linked together by networks of highways and express railways.

Export trade and a high rate of saving have been given high priority at the expense of investments in infrastructure. The potential demand for new housing is strong, and there is much room for such qualitative improvements as reconstructing old dwellings. Since Japan's infrastructure is inferior to that of the United States and Western Europe, it will need much more public investment.

DEMOGRAPHICS   The median age of the Japanese population has risen rapidly. Under the present national retirement system, the financing of pensions will inevitably face bankruptcy in the future. It will be necessary to refinance the whole public pension system and to raise the age, currently 55, at which a person can retire.[49] The demand for social services is increasing at the same time that a shortage of skilled workers has developed. An increase in transfer payments will result at a time that Japan is running a deficit in the national budget. In recent years, these deficits have amounted to one-third of the budget. The stimulative effects of Japanese tax policy may well have run their course, as more taxes are needed for government programs and services.

---

49. Workers for Japanese industries are required to retire at 55, though they may go on to hold other jobs. Social-security type pensions are paid at the age of 60.

SUMMARY

The Japanese economic system is essentially capitalistic. With the exception of certain public services and monopolies operated by the Japanese government, private enterprise is dominant in the economy. The government leaves the initiative for production and distribution in private hands, and it has for many decades devoted itself to creating an environment favorable to investment by private enterprise. Business firms have flourished under the protection of the government, and leaders in these two fields are often connected by common educational and family ties.

Nevertheless, the government intervenes constantly to turn industry into directions thought to be desirable for the economy as a whole. By controlling the flow of funds from the Bank of Japan to commercial banks and thence to industry, the government has exerted pressure on industry. Through tax benefits, special depreciation allowances, and favorable interest rates, the government has stimulated savings and investment. Pervasive pressures are exercised one way or another on the investment decisions of business firms. The government also has controlled a considerable proportion of the nation's investment during the boom of the last decade. A policy of tax reductions has served to stimulate aggregate demand, which in turn has caused yearly surpluses in the budget. From this source came 25 percent of the nation's savings over the last decade.

The rate of economic growth has been the most rapid of all the major industrial countries. Although the increase can be explained in part by the fact that the economy had nowhere to go but up after the devastation brought about by World War II, other factors are much more important in explaining the growth rate. A stimulus to growth has come both from rising consumption demands at home and market opportunities abroad. Other stimuli include a reverse gap between productivity and wages, an abundant labor supply, a high rate of personal savings, and an undervalued currency.

Economic planning is indicative rather than imperative. A series of plans have been used since the end of World War II to accomplish set economic objectives. Japanese planning points out a series of desirable goals the economy should try to achieve, giving industry a frame of reference within which to operate. No direct coercion (which would be used in imperative planning) is used to make industry operate within the framework of the plan. The government, however, has indirect and more subtle ways to assure compliance with the objectives of planning. Control over the supply of credit gives the government leverage in enforcing compliance. Selective fiscal measures designed to favor exports or certain types of industries, investment, or personal savings can also be used to encourage conformance with the plan. The national budget can also be used to allocate expenditures into desirable areas. Even where no fiscal and monetary controls exist, it is customary for the government to provide personal guidance to industry or, conversely, for industry to consult the government before making major business decisions.

The Japanese economy is not free from socioeconomic problems as it enters the 1980s. There is still a dependence on foreign sources of energy and raw materials. The work force is aging, and there are shortages of workers in the technical areas. The much-heralded consensus between government, business, and other sectors of the economy could break down if prosperity is not maintained. There is also the possibility that more Japanese workers will opt for leisure time at the expense of working, and social welfare expenditures could divert government expenditures away from capital formation into consumption.

REVIEW QUESTIONS

1. Comment on the Japanese system of lifetime employment with one firm. Would this system work in the United States?
2. The Japanese economic system involves management by consensus. Discuss. Would this system work in the United States?
3. Discuss the relationship between government and business in Japan.
4. What factors are responsible for the high rate of economic growth in Japan?
5. Discuss the objectives of Japanese economic planning.
6. Explain some of the factors that have been responsible for a high rate of personal savings in Japan.
7. Discuss the ways in which the Japanese government provides financial support to business.
8. What is the role of the Japan Development Bank in the Japanese banking system?
9. What are some of the problems confronting the Japanese economy?
10. Discuss the role of the Ministry of International Trade and Industry (MITI) in the Japanese economy.

RECOMMENDED READINGS

Christopher, Robert. *The Japanese Mind*. New York: Simon and Schuster Inc., 1983.

Gressner, Julian. *Partners in Prosperity*. New York: McGraw-Hill Book Co., 1984.

Johnson, Chalmers. *MITI and the Japanese Miracle*. Stanford, Calif.: Stanford University Press, 1982.

Kojima, Kiyoski. *Japan's General Trading Companies: Merchants of Economic Development*. Paris: Organization for Economic Cooperation and Development, 1984.

Kosai, Yutaka. *The Contemporary Japanese Economy*. London: Macmillan & Co., 1985.

Sheratori, Rai. *Japan in the 1980's*. Tokyo: Kodansha International Ltd., 1983.

U.S. Congress, Joint Economic Committee. *Japanese Tax Policy*. 98th Cong., 2d Sess., 1984.

Vogel, Ezra. *Comeback*. New York: Simon and Schuster Inc., 1985.

Yoshihara, Kunio. *Japanese Economic Development*. New York: Oxford University Press Inc., 1984.

C H A P T E R   1 0

THE UNITED KINGDOM

One hundred years ago England was at the apogee of its power. The British Empire extended from England to Africa, from India to New Zealand, and British interests owned and operated everything from diamond mines in South Africa to tea plantations in Ceylon and paper mills in Canada. Brittania ruled the waves, and British citizens throughout the world were able to apply the Roman words *civis Romanus sum*[1] to themselves and know that they would enjoy the protection of the British government.

However, the days of Kipling and the British Empire are long since gone, and the society that once produced Charles Dickens and Alfred Tennyson now produces author Barbara Cartland and comedian Benny Hill. The British economy has fallen on hard times. Slow growth, low productivity, inflation, unemployment, and balance-of-payments crises have plagued the British economy over the last two decades. Successive governments have had little success with these problems in anything but the short run. Prime Minister Margaret Thatcher's electoral victories and the policies she has adopted can be explained partly by the inability of previous governments to manage the economy successfully and, in particular,

1. "I am a Roman citizen." Because one British citizen of Greek extraction was killed in a riot in Greece, the British declared war on Greece.

to restrain inflation. It remains to be seen whether her policies are successful.

It may well be that the United Kingdom represents a watershed in Western society. Oswald Spengler, a German philosopher, wrote a book called *Decline of the West* that forecasted the decline of Western civilization.[2] Spengler claimed to be able to discern the outline of a life cycle through which, he believed, all civilizations must pass. Western civilization was compared with Greco-Roman civilization in terms of form, duration, and meaning. His view of Western civilization was a gloomy one. The West, according to Spengler, had already passed through the creative stage of culture into a period of material comfort. The end of the creative impulse begins the process of decline. There is no prospect for reversing the decline, for civilizations blossom and decay like natural organisms and true rejuvenation is impossible. He used a biological metaphor to describe the fateful trajectory of a civilization: "For everything organic the notions of birth, youth, age, lifetime, and death are fundamental."

The Industrial Revolution first began in the United Kingdom, and that may be part of its problem. An aggressive country (Germany and Japan are examples) entering later into the industrialization cycle is able to take advantage of newer technologies in plant layout and design, while countries that industrialized earlier have older and less inefficient plants. The United Kingdom began to lose ground in areas of advanced technology, first to Germany and then to the United States. British economic dominance of the world crested in 1910, and eventually the economy began to live off the foreign earnings of its corporations. Many British industries today are in advanced stages of atrophy and need large amounts of capital to increase productive capacity. In many crucial areas British industry has lost its advantage to the younger and more viable industries of Germany, France, and the United States. But these industries, too, face challenges from the Japanese and South Koreans.

The remainder of the chapter will be devoted to a discussion of the British economy in the 1980s. To most Americans, the problems of the British economy are a familiar litany of woe: high inflation, low investment, low productivity, declining industrial competitiveness, and in recent years, increasing unemployment and declining living standards. The causes of the British problem are controversial, as are the cures. Prime Minister Thatcher has focused on a different approach to the problem from that of her predecessors. This approach will be presented in some detail, but first it is necessary to examine the institutional arrangements of the British economy.

---

2. Oswald Spengler, *Decline of the West* (New York: Alfred A. Knopf Inc., 1939), pp. 1-7.

■ THE ECONOMIC SYSTEM ■

The British economy is mixed. Although private enterprise is dominant, the government plays an important role in economic activity in three ways: through the nationalized sector of the economy, through social welfare measures aimed at achieving income redistribution and economic and social well being, and through fiscal and monetary policy measures used to pursue such macroeconomic goals as full employment.

Nationalization took place in the period immediately following World War II. The nationalization program of the Labour government involved the Bank of England, the railways, the coal mines, the steel industry, trucking, and the public utilities—especially the electrical and gas industries. The owners were compensated at approximately the market price of their holdings. In some cases, nationalization was neither revolutionary nor controversial. The Bank of England was already, in effect, a public institution; its changed status was hardly more than a change in title. The railroads and coal mines had been losing money for years, and their owners were perfectly willing to accept nationalization.

Apart from the nationalized industries, economic activity is organized pretty much in the capitalistic fashion. Business firms are free to organize in any of the traditional forms and may make their decisions on the usual capitalistic bases of price and cost. Through the use of monetary and fiscal policies, however, the government can exert indirect control on the activities of private enterprises. For example, the government has wide powers to encourage the development of industries in geographic areas that are depressed because of the dependence on a single industry, usually coal mining or ship building. The government can also influence and control industrial, residential, and public construction.

PUBLIC FINANCE

The British budget is a powerful weapon for influencing the general level of activity in the economy. Its purpose is not only to raise revenue to meet government expenditures, but also to regulate the national economy. An important goal in determining the budget is to bring about a balance between the total goods and services that are likely to be available to the nation and the total claims that will be made upon them.

The budget does not include all public sector expenditures. It does not include either local governmental expenditures or nationalized industry investment, though it does cover grants to local authorities and loans and deficit grants to the nationalized industries, as well as the British government's contributions to the National Insurance Funds. The budget does include all national government expenditures other than payments out of the National Insurance Funds. The expenditure figures in the budget are one measure of the national government's share of the total demand for goods and services.

The nationalized industries, local authorities, and other public bodies often need to borrow to finance expenditures on capital projects. Most of this borrowing is done from the National Loans Fund, which is responsible for the bulk of domestic lending by the government. The National Loans Fund and the Consolidated Fund, which balances current revenue against current expenditures, are the two basic components of the budget.

THE BRITISH TAX SYSTEM   Taxation in the United Kingdom is fairly evenly balanced between direct and indirect taxes. The most important direct tax is the personal income tax. No other European country, except Sweden, imposes personal income taxes to a greater degree than does the United Kingdom, nor do personal taxes account for nearly so high a percentage of gross national product in France, Germany, or the United States as they do in the United Kingdom and Sweden. There is also a heavy reliance on indirect excise taxes on tobacco, alcohol, and gasoline. The tax yield on these three commodities amounts to nearly 7 percent of the British gross national product, over half again as much as Sweden, twice as much as Germany and France, and three times the U.S. proportion.

PERSONAL INCOME TAXES   For many years the British income tax structure included an income tax and a surtax. However, in 1973 this system was replaced by a single graduated income tax. British income tax rates were among the highest in the world, exceeded only by the tax rates of the Scandinavian countries. A distinction was made between earned and unearned income, with rates as high as 98 percent on the latter. In 1980 minimum and maximum rates were lowered on both earned and unearned incomes. The minimum rate on earned income was reduced to 30 percent on income up to £15,400 (approximately $21,000), and the maximum rate was reduced to 60 percent on income in excess of £38,100 (approximately $53,000). The top rate on unearned income was reduced from 98 percent to 75 percent.[3] There are exemptions for children that vary with ages, and flat exemptions for single and married taxpayers. In 1984 the personal income tax accounted for 10.8 percent of gross domestic product.[4]

---

3. *Individual Taxes: A Worldwide Summary* (New York: Price Waterhouse and Co., 1983), p. 255.

4. "The British Economy in Figures" (London: Lloyds Bank, 1985), p. 1.

OTHER TAXES   In addition to the personal income tax, there is also a corporate income tax. In 1985 a 45 percent tax rate was applied to corporate incomes.[5] Capital gains are taxed at a flat 30 percent rate. However, there are generous allowances for capital investment. Britain has experimented with a wide variety of subsidies to promote investment or regional development or both. It has used, at one time or another, accelerated depreciation, high initial depreciation allowances, investment tax credits, and investment grants.

There is also a value-added tax calculated at a single flat tax rate of 15 percent of the value of a good or service. Certain commodities, including drugs and medicines, are exempt from the value-added tax. As mentioned earlier, excise taxes are also levied on consumer goods, especially tobacco, alcohol, and gasoline. One feature of these excise taxes is the large proportion they represent of the total sales price. For example, the tax on cigarettes is 90 percent of the purchase price.

Finally, in the United Kingdom as in other countries, the social security system is financed largely from payroll taxes. At one time, contributions from both employees and employers were paid at a flat amount per employee per week. Since 1975 the social security tax has been levied as a percentage of the employee's earnings. In 1985 the rate was 9.0 percent for fully covered employees. Employers paid at a rate of 10 percent on the first £120 of earnings a week.

GOVERNMENT EXPENDITURES   Total central government expenditures for the fiscal year 1984–1985 amounted to $127 billion. These expenditures can be divided into two categories—current and capital. Current expenditures can be further divided into four categories: expenditures for goods and services, subsidies, current grants to the personal and public sectors, and interest on the public debt.[6] Capital expenditures include gross domestic fixed capital formation, capital grants, and loans.

When local government and central government spending are added together, total public expenditures of all types are around 44 percent of the gross national product. One reason that the public sector contribution to investment is much higher in Great Britain than in the United States is the importance of public enterprises. This continues to be true despite the fact that the Thatcher government has privatized (denationalized) a number of enterprises that had been owned by the government.

---

5. *Corporate Taxes: A Worldwide Summary* (New York: Price Waterhouse and Co., 1985), p. 371.
6. "Monthly Quarterly Bulletin," December, 1984 (London: Bank of England).

THE WELFARE STATE The United Kingdom has a comprehensive social welfare system. It can be divided into two categories: the medical care and social security program, which includes family allowances; and the national health insurance program, which provides unemployment and sickness benefits, old age pensions, maternity benefits, and death grants. Both programs were developed partly as a result of deprivations sustained during World War II and partly as a remembrance of prewar British capitalism, which was characterized by high rates of unemployment as well as excessive and widespread inequalities in the distribution of wealth and income. In 1924, for example, two-thirds of the total wealth in the United Kingdom was held by 1.6 percent of all wealth owners (property owners—real estate, stocks, bonds).[7]

MEDICAL CARE AND FAMILY ALLOWANCES The best-known social welfare program is medical care, which is provided in the United Kingdom under the National Health Service as a free public service and is not a part of the regular social insurance program. All residents are eligible for health services. General practitioner care, specialist services, hospitalization, maternity care, and treatment in the event of industrial injuries are provided by the National Health Service. There are charges for some medical prescriptions and cost sharing by the patient for such devices as dentures and hearing aids. Most of the cost of the National Health Service program is financed by the British government out of general revenues from the budget. The employer and employee pay flat-rate weekly contributions that meet about one-fifth of the total cost of medical care.

In addition to medical care, there are family allowances, cash payments for the benefit of the family as a whole. They are financed out of general revenues rather than from taxes on employers and employees and are paid to families with two or more children under certain age limits.

NATIONAL INSURANCE Separate and apart from the National Health Service, a comprehensive program of social security comes under the category of national insurance. This program provides fixed-rate sickness benefits for up to one year to working men and women and widows. Dissatisfaction with this program has led to a rapid increase in the number of individuals who purchase private medical insurance. Old-age pensions and unemployment benefits are similar in make-up to sickness benefits. As a corollary to regular old-age pensions, a graduated pension scheme pro-

7. James Wedgwood, *The Economics of Inheritance* (London: Routledge & Kegan Paul, Ltd., 1929), p. 42.

vides higher rates to higher-paid contributors. A maternity allowance is paid to women who give up paid employment to have a baby, and there is also a lump-sum maternity grant paid to most mothers. A death grant is payable on the death of the insured person or the spouse or child of an insured person. Finally, there are widows' and widowed mothers' allowances, the latter based on the number of dependent children.

THE BANKING SYSTEM

The British banking system consists of the Bank of England, the central bank of the nation, and a few large commercial banks that have assumed an oligopolistic structure as a result of mergers and integration. Besides the commercial banks, whose primary function is financing the economy in general, there are other institutions whose activities are more specialized but whose aggregate importance is very great. These are the merchant bankers and the acceptance houses, whose primary concern is with the financing of foreign trade. The insurance companies and building societies are the most important suppliers of investment capital in the United Kingdom.

THE BANK OF ENGLAND   The Bank of England was chartered by an act of Parliament in 1694. In 1844 it was given the sole right of note issue. By the second half of the nineteenth century, the public service aspects of the Bank's activities began to eclipse its private banking business. It became the lender of last resort to the commercial banks and the regulator of the great international gold and capital market in London.

In 1946 the Bank was nationalized by an act of Parliament. The government acquired the entire capital stock of the Bank and was empowered to appoint the governor, deputy director, and directors of the Bank for fixed terms. The Treasury has the power to give directions to the Bank, through consultation with the governor.

The Bank has the overall responsibility for the management and control of the British monetary and financial system. It exercises monetary control through a combination of open market operations and discount policy, done on the basis of institutional arrangements peculiar to the British monetary system. Unlike the Federal Reserve system of the United States, the Bank does not lend to commercial banks, but only to discount houses, whose main business is to underwrite the weekly Treasury bill issue with call loans secured mostly from London clearinghouses.

Credit is restricted to selling Treasury bills or government bonds through discount houses and securities dealers, thus absorbing cash from the banking system. The discount market chiefly consists of 12 major houses that are members of the London Discount Market Association, the organization that is responsible for bidding on Treasury bills each week. To restore their cash and liquidity positions, banks can withdraw their call loans from the discount houses; the discount houses, in turn, may be forced to borrow money from the Bank of England at a penalty rate, which is set higher than the average yield from the discount houses' earning assets.

THE COMMERCIAL BANKS The commercial banking system operates under private ownership and management. There are five major commercial banks—Barclays, Lloyds, Midland, National Provincial, and Westminster. Two other large banks are the District Bank and Martins. These banks undertake all normal types of banking business, such as deposits, advances, bill discounting, and foreign exchange. They do not participate directly in industry; their financing of industry is limited to short-term advances and overdrafts that are formally repayable on demand. British banks have a traditional preference for financing working rather than fixed capital expenditures.

DISCOUNT HOUSES Discount houses play a very important role in the British financial system. Their most important function concerns the financing of Treasury bills. The discount houses purchase the Treasury bills on a weekly basis with loans obtained from the commercial banks or with their own funds. The proceeds of these purchases provide the government with day-to-day financing.

The discount houses are also the intermediary through which the Bank of England acts as a lender of last resort to the banking system. As mentioned above, the discount houses obtain a substantial amount of their funds to purchase Treasury bills from the commercial banks on a *call loan* basis. If loan repayment is demanded by the banks, the discount houses can borrow from the Bank of England through rediscounting bills or by advances against collateral. In this way, funds flow into the commercial bank. The minimum rate at which the Bank of England will make funds available to the discount houses is called the *bank rate*, and it is the key rate in the whole structure of interest rates in Great Britain.

OTHER FINANCIAL INSTITUTIONS Funds for investments are also provided through other sources, such as insurance companies, building societies, investment trusts, and pension funds. The insurance companies, pension funds, and building societies are the dominant sources of long-term loans. Insurance companies are privately owned and provide a supply of capital to the long-term market.

Building societies, also privately owned, are second only to the insurance companies as a source of long-term loanable funds. The building societies rely on the savings of the public, and they provide financing for about two-thirds of private home building. The societies offer both shares and deposits to the public. Shares are nonmarketable and pay a higher rate of interest.

Investment trusts are also an important source of long-term capital funds. In the past, trusts played an important part in the development of the Commonwealth countries. During the period from 1870 to 1914, they also contributed much to the economic development of the United States.

In investment banking, there is no doubt about the power of the government to exercise control. Under the Banking Control and Guarantee Act of 1947, the government has the power to regulate new issues of stocks and bonds and establish priorities that are deemed essential to the national interest. The act also empowered the Treasury to guarantee long-term loans made to facilitate industrial development.

MONETARY POLICY   Monetary policy in the United Kingdom is used as a stabilization device and consists of several arrangements.

Hire purchase controls are used to regulate the volume of consumer expenditures. This type of control is selective in that it involves the amount of down payment required to consummate the purchase of consumer goods and also involves the maximum period of repayment. It has proven to be an important monetary policy instrument and has an advantage over other monetary and fiscal policy instruments in that it can be imposed immediately.

The use of the *bank rate* is also an important monetary policy device. The bank rate is the price the Bank of England will pay when rediscounting bills. It is a penalty rate that is usually set above the market rate of discount and has its impact on the discount houses. As mentioned previously, the discount houses occupy a special position in the market for Treasury bills, and from the standpoint of monetary policy the Treasury bill is a major instrument in the money market. The discount houses link the commercial banks to the Bank of England. They purchase Treasury bills with money borrowed at call from the commercial bank; if they have to borrow from the Bank of England, the bank rate, or "penalty rate," can be employed. Changes in the bank rate force changes in other interest rates.

Open market operations constitute another monetary policy instrument. This term refers to the buying and selling of Treasury bills and other short-term obligations in the money market by the Bank of England. These transactions affect the liquidity of the commercial banks by expanding or contracting their balances with the Bank of England.

A direct control, which takes the form of special deposits, can be imposed on commercial banks by the Bank of England. The purpose of this device is to alter the liquidity ratio of commercial banks. The *liquidity ratio*, which is the ratio of liquid bank assets to total assets, is set at 30 percent of total bank assets. Special deposits have the effect of reducing the liquidity ratio.

SUPPLY-SIDE ECONOMICS AND THE THATCHER GOVERNMENT

Margaret Thatcher came to office in 1979 in the wake of the Labour government's unsuccessful attempts to use demand management and incomes policy to deal with the problems of the British government. She espoused an economic program based on monetarist theories and belief in a freely operating market economy. Thatcher came to office committed to a policy of increasing aggregate supply by decreasing the role of the government in the economy and improving incentives for individuals in the private sector. To increase incentive and reward initiative, personal income tax rates were cut. Short-term stabilization polices used by previous governments were rejected in favor of policies considered necessary for reducing inflation and creating the conditions for an increase in total real output and employment in the long run.

The following policies were adopted by the Thatcher government.

1. The role of monetary policy became the linchpin of economic policy. Emphasis changed from the level of interest rates to control over the money supply through progressive deceleration, over the medium term, of the growth rate of one of the money aggregates. This aggregate, called M3, consists of notes and coins in circulation plus all sterling bank deposits held by the private and public sectors.
2. An attempt was made to increase total output by decreasing the interference of the government in the economy and by promoting the free operation of markets. As mentioned previously, the basic income tax was reduced, top rates on both earned and unearned incomes were reduced, and personal tax allowances were increased. The base of the corporate income tax was changed, and subsidies to industries in depressed areas were reduced. Foreign exchange controls were lifted and quantitative credit controls removed.
3. The government also intended to limit its role in the price and income determination process. It was believed that monetary policy would affect wages by influencing expectations in that a

restrictive monetary policy would moderate wage demands. However, the government decided that public sector pay had to be restrained because high public sector wage settlements were contributing to excessive government expenditures.

RESULTS   The results of Thatcher's economic policies, at least at the end of 1985, have been mixed at best. Although the rate of inflation is down to well below 10 percent, the unemployment rate is the highest since the Great Depression. The rate of economic growth of the British economy was negative for 1980 and 1981, but in excess of 2 percent for 1982, 1983, and 1984. The growth rate for those three years was higher than the growth rates for France, Italy, and West Germany. Industrial production increased at an average annual rate of less than 1 percent during the 1980–1985 period, and gross private domestic investment increased at an annual rate of 5 percent. The government's success in decreasing wage and price inflation resulted more from increases in the rate of unemployment and appreciation of the pound sterling than from a decrease in the money supply. Wage settlements, though moderating, still remain well in excess of any increase in productivity.

Toward the end of the 1970s, inflation increasingly became the focus of economic policy not only in Great Britain but also in the United States and other Western countries. However, it was not until Thatcher came to office that inflation became the sole priority of economic policy, and monetary policy totally replaced traditional Keynesian methods of demand management. Since the exponents of monetary policy believe that there is a clear relationship between the growth rate of money supply and the rate of inflation in the medium term, a reduction in the money supply is supposed to reduce the rate of inflation. But the problem with monetary policy is that its curative effects may kill the patient in the process. By the time inflation is ultimately wrung out of the economy, unemployment, high interest rates, and the decline of industries sensitive to high interest rates can cause considerable social unrest.

LABOR–MANAGEMENT RELATIONS

Unions occupy a powerful position in the United Kingdom. During the post-World War II period full employment contributed to the development of union power, and wages increased faster than productivity. In general, British labor-management relations have been rather acrimonious, with some of the worst labor disputes occurring in the public sector. Many labor unions are afflicted with a class struggle mentality, and there is no question that union intransigence on issues involving productivity has been a factor contributing to the general decline of the British economy during the postwar period. British unions are politically active and constitute the main base of support for the Labour party.

Unlike the United States, where union membership expressed as a percentage of the work force has decreased, union membership in the United Kingdom has increased, particularly during the period 1968–1980. In 1984 union membership amounted to about 46 percent of the British labor force of 26 million workers.[8] To some extent this increase in union membership was caused by high inflation, which led workers to seek the protective security of unions. Also, as the importance of the public sector increased, there was a greater incentive to join a union that would represent worker interests in the complex negotiations for benefits conferred by the state.[9]

There are some 500 trade unions in the United Kingdom, and most belong to the British Trades Union Congress (TUC). Unions affiliated with the TUC vary in size and character and in the views they hold regarding organization. There are craft unions, industrial unions, general workers' unions, and nonmanual and professional organizations. Although the unions operate individually, they come together, industry by industry, through federations set up for the purpose of collective bargaining. A single union may have members in several industries and may therefore be affiliated with several federations.

Industrial relations in the United Kingdom are governed by two acts, the Trade Union and Labor Relations Act of 1974 and the Employment Protection Act of 1975. The Employment Protection Act is the more important in that it sets employees' rights. Under the provisions of the act, guaranteed minimum weekly wages and paid maternity leave became legal requirements, along with such things as time off with pay for union duties. Written terms for dismissal and redundancy (the British term for being laid off) have to be provided. Government intervention in all aspects of collective bargaining came to be an increasingly important policy priority. The Advisory, Conciliation, and Arbitration Service (ACAS) was created to adjudicate collective bargaining disputes. Decisions of the ACAS can be appealed to the Employment Appeal Tribunal.

GOVERNMENT AND BUSINESS

The government has control over a number of industries, such as coal, inland transportation, and steel. The nationalized industries produce about

---

8. *Monthly Digest of Statistics* (London: British Central Statistical Office, August 1985), Table 7.

9. Robert Price and George S. Bain, "Union Growth Revisited: 1948–1974 in Perspective," *British Journal of Industrial Relations*, November 1976, pp. 339-355.

6 percent of gross domestic product. The steel industry was nationalized after World War II, denationalized by the Conservative party when it came to power in 1951, and nationalized again by the Labor government in 1966. Two industries were nationalized during the 1970s—ship building and aerospace—and the British National Oil Company (BNOC) was formed chiefly on the basis of the North Sea oil assets previously owned by the National Coal Board.

NATIONALIZATION AND PRICING POLICIES   In 1967 explicit price and investment rules were established for the nationalized industries.[10] On pricing, marginal cost pricing was laid down, though accounting costs were to be covered by revenue. Unit prices proportional to marginal cost were recommended for the apportionment of fixed costs among consumers where necessary to cover total costs. Social cost-benefit analysis was proposed for investment appraisal, and it was stated that the returns on investment should be presented in terms of discounted net present value. A test discount rate of 8 percent was laid down for project appraisal. The government explicitly recognized the noncommercial operations undertaken by nationalized industries and stressed the need to distinguish social obligations from commercial operations. When social obligations were involved, subsidies from the government could be provided to cover costs.

In 1978 the government recognized that in many cases prices are market-determined, and even where this is not so the difficulties of practical application of marginal cost pricing can be severe. The main focus of current policy was shifted from those matters affecting individual services and projects to the opportunity cost of capital in the industry as a whole.[11] A real rate of return on assets was defined and was to be achieved by the nationalized industries on new investment as a whole. The real rate of return is principally related to the real rate of return in the private sector, taking into consideration questions of the cost of finance. It was set initially at 5 percent and is to be reviewed every three to five years. Thus the main ways over which the government has sought to exercise control since 1978 are the real rate of return and the financial target together with the general level of prices.[12] Individual prices and investment priorities are left largely up to the industries themselves.

10. *Nationalized Industries: A Review of Economic and Financial Objectives*, Command Paper 3437 (London: HMSO, November 1967).

11. *The Nationalized Industries*, Command Paper 7131 (London: HMSO, March 1978).

12. Andrew Likierman, "The Financial and Economic Framework for Nationalized Industries," *Lloyds Bank Review*, October 1979, pp. 16-32.

PRIVATIZATION OF BRITISH INDUSTRY One thing Margaret Thatcher and Ronald Reagan have in common is that they both want to get their governments out of business through the privatization of a number of activities that have been done by government. Since there is much more government ownership of industry in the United Kingdom, Thatcher has a much longer way to go. Nevertheless, she has made a significant start. In the six years that she has been in office, she has overseen the sale of more than two dozen major state-owned businesses to private enterprise. Included are the British telephone system, Jaguar Cars, British Aerospace, British Airways, sugar refineries, port facilities, and freight transportation.[13] She plans in 1986 to privatize British Gas, British Airports Authority, National Bus Company, an auto-parts company, and an armament and munitions maker. In 1987, she plans to turn over to private operation Rolls-Royce, the aero-engine company, and the remaining 31 percent state-owned share of British Petroleum.

Privatization has reduced the participation of the British government in the British economy in several ways. It has decreased the state's share of total domestic output from 10 percent to 6 percent. It has reduced the number of government workers by 400,000 and has doubled the number of British stockholders. It has also increased British Treasury funds by $28 billion from the sale of the industries to the private sector.[14] However, coal, steel, railways, and a large part of the auto industry are still in the public sector. These industries are not paying their own way. In 1985, the projected losses of these industries are approximately $3.6 billion despite the fact that they are supposed to pay their own way.[15] These industries are not likely to be privatized, for they are not attractive to private investors.

GOVERNMENT INFLUENCE ON PRIVATE ENTERPRISE The government influences British industry through the use of monetary and fiscal policies and through laws governing mergers, restrictive trade practices, and resale price maintenance. It also has control over credit and investment policies and can establish priorities that it deems to be in the national interest. A case in point is the National Enterprise Board, created by the Industry Act of 1975. Its purpose is to provide financial aid to business firms in exchange for a share in their ownership. Priority was to be given to the manufacturing industry. Shares of British Leyland and Rolls-Royce, two companies

---

13. *U.S. News & World Report,* January 13, 1986, p. 18.

14. Ibid., p. 19.

15. *The Economist,* October 15, 1985, p. 12.

with financial problems, were transferred to the National Enterprise Board when it was set up. To some extent the board was set up to bail out ailing business firms, but in the process state control over these enterprises was increased through equity ownership. The Thatcher government has cut back some of the board's activities in private investment.

■ AN APPRAISAL ■
OF THE BRITISH ECONOMY

By any economic standard, the performance of the British economy has been poor in comparison with other industrial market economies. A good example can be provided by comparing per capita gross national product for the United Kingdom and other major industrial countries over a period of time. In 1967, for example, the per capita nominal gross national product for the United Kingdom was $1,980, compared to $2,190 for France, $2,030 for West Germany, and $1,150 for Japan. By 1983 the per capita nominal gross national product for the United Kingdom was far below those for the other countries: $9,200 for the United Kingdom, $10,500 for France, $11,430 for West Germany, and $10,120 for Japan.[16] In 1983, the United Kingdom ranked thirteenth in per capita GNP out of the 19 developed industrial market economies; in 1951, it ranked second only to the United States.

GROWTH RATES

The United Kingdom was the first country to industrialize and it had export markets in its colonial possessions that were not available to latecomers to industrialization. Thus, though its economic situation in the long run was such that it could not hope to retain its early lead, it did experience a full century of prosperity. During the nineteenth century, every invention could be put to immediate use, either in agriculture or in industry. British industry was in a very strong position, and it was aided and encouraged by the government. There was no shortage of markets for British goods at prices which undercut competitors in the fields in which British industry specialized, primary cotton textiles and machinery. However, by latter part of the 1800s other countries were undercutting the British prices. The Germans, starting late, had newer machinery, and they had a

16. The World Bank, *World Development Report 1985*, p. 175.

spirit of enterprise that was beginning to falter in late-nineteenth century Britain.

Table 10-1 compares average annual real per capita growth of GNP for the United Kingdom and other Western industrial countries for two periods, 1870–1913 and 1913–1950. In the first period, which ended before World War II, the performance of the German economy was best. This performance exacerbated a rivalry between the major world powers and was a contributing factor to World War I. The real annual average rate of growth for the United States during that period was a respectable 2.2 percent. Although the growth rate of the United Kingdom was 1.2 percent, it was still the dominant world power before World War I. The period 1913–1950 encompassed two world wars and the Depression of the 1930s. All were particularly hard on the British economy. It was also during this time period that the United Kingdom lost most of its colonial possessions—a source of markets for British goods. The economies that performed the best were those that were relatively unaffected by the two major wars.

The performance of the British economy during the 1950s and 1960s was the poorest of all of the major industrial market economies. During the period 1950–1960, the average annual rate of increase in real per capita GNP was 2.2 percent for the United Kingdom, 8.8 percent for Japan, 6.5 percent for West Germany, and 3 percent for France.[17] Only the United States, with an average annual real growth rate of 1.6 percent, had a rate lower than the United Kingdom. In the decade of the 1960s, the United Kingdom had the lowest rate of economic growth of the major industrial market economies. The average annual rate of increase in real per capita GNP for the decade was 2.8 percent compared to 10.6 percent for Japan, 4.0 for the United States, 5.6 percent for France, 4.7 percent for West Germany, 5.2 percent for Canada, and 5.6 percent for Italy.[18] As Table 10-2 indicates, there has been no real improvement in the economic growth of the United Kingdom relative to the other countries for the period 1971–1985, except for the years 1983 and 1985.

INFLATION AND UNEMPLOYMENT

Over the last 15 years, Britain has suffered relatively greater increases in both inflation and unemployment than comparable mixed economies such

17. Angus Maddison, *Economic Growth in the West* (London: George Allen & Unwin, Ltd., 1964), p. 21.

18. *Economic Report of the President 1985* (Washington: USGPO, 1986), p. 378.

**TABLE 10-1   AVERAGE ANNUAL REAL
PER CAPITA GROWTH RATES
FOR WESTERN INDUSTRIAL COUNTRIES,
1870–1913, 1913–1950**

	1870–1913	1913–1950
Belgium	1.7%	0.7%
Canada	2.0	1.9
Denmark	2.1	1.1
France	1.4	0.7
Germany	2.8	0.4
Italy	0.7	0.6
Netherlands	0.8	0.7
Norway	1.4	1.9
Sweden	2.3	1.6
United Kingdom	1.2	0.8
United States	2.2	1.7

Source: Angus Maddison, *Economic Growth in the West* (London: George Allen & Unwin, Ltd., 1964), pp. 7-21.

as France, Japan, and West Germany. The problem of *stagflation,* or a combination of increases in inflation and unemployment coupled with low growth rates, has led many people, including conservative politicians in both the United States and Japan, to speak of the "British disease," as if it were something that is contagious and to be avoided at all costs. Some attribute the "disease" to inflexibility of both labor and management, which may be a result of long-standing class consciousness. The British disease has also been attributed to allleged flaws in the British national character, such as an unwillingness to work hard and be productive or a willingness to accept more government largesse.

Table 10-3 compares the combined average annual rates of inflation and unemployment for the United Kingdom and other major industrial market economies for the period 1973–1983 and for 1984–1985. As the table indicates, the performance of the British economy was, in general, the worst of the countries shown for the time periods. Both inflation and unemployment have been high in the United Kingdom, but inflation was reduced to less than 4 percent in 1985. Conversely, in West Germany inflation has declined while unemployment has increased. The rates of inflation and unemployment have been the lowest in Japan. In 1985 the estimated combined rate was around 5.1 percent in Japan, compared to 17.1 percent for the United Kingdom.

TABLE 10-2 AVERAGE ANNUAL GROWTH RATES IN REAL PER CAPITA GNP FOR THE UNITED KINGDOM AND OTHER COUNTRIES, 1971–1985

	1971–1975	1976–1980	1981	1982	1983	1984	1985
United States	2.2%	3.4%	1.9%	−2.5%	3.5%	6.5%	2.3%
Canada	5.0	3.3	4.0	−4.3	2.8	5.4	4.0
Japan	4.6	5.1	4.2	3.1	3.3	5.8	5.0
France	4.0	3.3	0.5	1.8	0.7	1.3	1.0
West Germany	2.1	3.4	0.2	−0.6	1.2	2.6	2.2
Italy	2.4	3.8	0.2	−0.5	−0.4	2.6	2.2
United Kingdom	2.1	1.6	−1.4	1.5	3.4	1.8	3.2

Source: Economic Report of the President 1986 (Washington: USGPO, 1986), p. 378.

TABLE 10-3   COMBINED INFLATION AND UNEMPLOYMENT RATES FOR THE UNITED KINGDOM AND OTHER INDUSTRIAL COUNTRIES, 1977–1985

	Average Rate of Inflation 1973–1983	Average Rate of Unemployment 1973–1983	Combined 1973–1983
Japan	4.7%	2.2%	6.9%
U.S.	7.5	7.3	14.8
W. Germ.	4.3	3.9	8.2
France	10.8	6.3	17.1
Italy	17.4	4.4	21.8
U.K.	14.3	9.3	23.6
	1984–1985	1984–1985	1984–1985
Japan	2.8%	2.3%	5.1%
U.S.	3.6	7.3	10.9
W. Germ.	3.1	8.9	12.0
France	8.6	8.8	17.4
Italy	10.1	4.8	14.9
U.K.	3.7	13.4	17.1

Sources: The World Bank, *World Development Report*, p. 175; *Economic Report of the President 1985* (Washington: USGPO, 1985), p. 355, *Monthly Report of the Deutsches Bundesbank* (September, 1985), p. 3, and *Lloyds Bank Review* Third Quarter, 1985), p. 80.

INCOME REDISTRIBUTION   The British government plays an important role in changing the distribution of income. Taxes and transfer payments are the major means of accomplishing this objective, with taxes reducing the incomes of some persons and transfer payments adding to the incomes of others. Income redistribution is accomplished through the progressivity of the personal income tax. The top bracket rate and rates at higher income levels make the progressivity of the personal income tax one of the highest in the world.[19] Even for the average workers, the marginal tax rate is high in comparison to rates in France, Germany, Japan, and the United States. With marginal rates in excess of 40 percent for the average production worker and higher for professional workers, the incentive to substitute leisure for paid employment is considerable.[20] The basic, or lowest, income

19. Joseph A. Pechman, "Taxation," in Richard E. Caves and Lawrence B. Krause, eds., *Britain's Economic Performance* (Washington: Brookings Institution, Inc., 1980), pp. 207-208.

20. From 1959 to 1975 the average income tax burden of the middle-income groups tripled. See Royal Commission on the Distribution of Income and Wealth, *Third Report on the Standing Reference*, Command Paper 6999 (London: HMSO, 1977), pp. 13-66.

tax rate of 30 percent is much higher than the basic tax rate of 11 percent for the United States. Moreover, personal exemptions are low in comparison to other countries even though numerous special provisions have been adopted. The tax on investment income, which once reached a maximum rate of 98 percent but is now 75 percent, is also high by world standards.

Other taxes, in particular excise taxes on liquor and tobacco, tend to add an element of regressivity into the British tax system, thus counterbalancing to some extent the progressivity of the income tax. In comparison to the United States, the total tax burden in Great Britain is higher at all levels of income.[21] Tax policy may have had a significant impact on the poor performance of the British economy, particularly in the area of saving.

GREATER INCOME EQUALITY   A prime goal of the British welfare state when it was created in 1945 was a more equal distribution of income. This was to be accomplished through a progressive income tax levied on both earned (wages and salaries) and unearned (interest and dividends) income and an inheritance tax. However, the structure of the income and inheritance taxes has changed frequently since 1945 because the tax philosophies of the two major political parties, Conservative and Labour, differ markedly. Each party makes changes in the tax structure when it comes to power. Thatcher's Conservative government emphasizes a reduction in government spending, enforced by stringent limits on expenditures, and a shift from direct to indirect taxation.

Table 10-4 shows the distribution of before- and after-tax income for the upper 1 percent and 5 percent of income earners for selected years. In 1949, for example, the upper 1 percent of all income earners received 11.2 percent of before-tax income and 6.4 percent of after-tax income, while the top 5 percent received 23.8 percent of before-tax income and 17.7 percent of after-tax income. As can be seen from the table, there was little change in income distribution from 1957 to 1967, but a rather sharp change from 1967 to 1983. The fact that there are relatively few people with high incomes makes the redistribution of income difficult because the extra revenue that can be squeezed out of them is small.

INEQUALITY OF WEALTH   Inequality in the distribution of wealth is perhaps more closely identified with the United Kingdom than with any other major industrial country because, after all, the Industrial Revolution really developed in this country. A concomitant of the Industrial Revolu-

---

21. Pechman, "Taxation," p. 211.

TABLE 10-4   DISTRIBUTION OF INCOME
             FOR THE UPPER 1 PERCENT AND 5 PERCENT
             OF BRITISH INCOME EARNERS
             FOR SELECTED YEARS

	Before Taxes		After Taxes	
	Top 1 Percent	Top 5 Percent	Top 1 Percent	Top 5 Percent
1949	11.2%	23.8%	6.4%	17.7%
1953	9.8	21.9	5.8	15.9
1957	8.2	19.1	5.0	14.9
1960	8.5	19.9	5.1	15.6
1961	8.1	19.2	5.5	16.0
1967	7.9	19.2	5.0	15.5
1975	6.2	16.8	4.0	13.7
1977	5.5	16.3	3.8	13.8
1983	5.6	16.5	4.1	14.0

Source: National Income Blue Book (London: British Central Statistical Office, 1984), p. 20.

tion was the concentration of property in the hands of a few persons. Vast fortunes were made, particularly during the development of the British Empire with its markets and resources. These fortunes, for the most part, were not touched by taxation, but were allowed to accumulate and be passed down from generation to generation.

Studies of the distribution of wealth are not often made. One of the first studies of the distribution of wealth in the United Kingdom covered the years 1912 and 1924.[22] In 1912, 43 percent of all wealth of the country was owned by only 0.8 percent of wealth owners.[23] During the intervening 12-year period World War I occurred, causing some dislocations in the British economy. The tax structure was also revised considerably in 1914 and in subsequent war years by the imposition of a surtax on incomes exceeding a particular level—$7,200 in 1914 and $4,800 in 1918. Minor shifts occurred in the distribution of wealth. In 1924 two-thirds of the wealth was owned by 1.6 percent of all wealth owners, compared to 0.9 percent in 1912.[24] Some 93 percent of all of the wealth was owned by 13.3 percent of the owners in 1912 and by 23.0 percent of the owners in 1924.[25]

22. Wedgwood, *Economics of Inheritance*, p. 47.

23. Ibid.

24. Ibid., p. 48.

25. Ibid., p. 49.

Considerable shifting in the distribution of wealth has occurred since 1924, as is indicated in Table 10-5. The share of the highest 1 percent fell from 61 percent in 1924 to 21 percent in 1982. The main influences at work on the distribution of wealth have been an increase in real income, which has allowed many people to buy their own homes and to accumulate other assets, and the impact of the estate tax, which reduced wealth inequality directly and also encouraged wealthy persons to distribute their incomes before death. However, the role of inheritance in the creation of the largest wealth holdings remains large. Notice that the top 20 percent of the wealth holders still own 74 percent of the total personal wealth in Britain.

EXPLANATIONS FOR THE DECLINE OF THE BRITISH ECONOMY

The British invested modern economic growth. However, the United Kingdom began to fall behind other countries, particularly Germany, in the last decades of the nineteenth century, and the decline has accelerated since World War II. A number of explanations have been offered for the decline of the British economy. The "British disease" of low productivity and a malaise of the national spirit is attributed by some to the unusually large role that the British government has played in economic life.[26] However, the government's role in the economy is no larger than in the average developed country; in the proportion of gross national product accounted

TABLE 10-5   PERCENTAGE DISTRIBUTION
             OF PERSONAL WEALTH
             IN THE UNITED KINGDOM

	1924	1976	1982
Top 1 percent	61%	25%	21%
Next 2 to 5 percent	21	21	20
6 to 10 percent	7	14	15
11 to 20 percent	5	17	18
21 to 100 percent	6	23	26

Source: Commission on the Distribution of Income and Wealth (Diamond Commission), *Report No. 7*, Command Paper 7595 (London: HMSO, July 1979); *Income and Wealth* (London: British Central Statistical Office, 1985), Table 22.

26. M.L. Kirby, *The Decline of British Power Since 1870* (London: George Allen & Unwin, Ltd., 1981).

for by government spending, the United Kingdom ranks somewhere in the middle. Other explanations have also been offered.

One well-known ad hoc explanation for the poor performance of the British economy focuses on a class divisiveness that allegedly reduces social mobility, fosters exclusivity based on social position, and maintains prejudice against commercial activities. Whether the British were less class-conscious in the nineteenth century when their rate of economic growth was the highest in the world is a matter of opinion. Rank in the military depended on social status, with the military leaders from the Duke of Wellington to Sir Douglas Haig in World War I drawn from the nobility. However, Napoleon, who was not of the French nobility, contemptuously referred to Britain as a nation of shop keepers. British commercial interests were not restricted to any social class, and interchange between people of various stations in life was freer than in France and other countries.

A second explanation for the decline of the British economy involves the "stop-go" economic stabilization policies used by British governments since the end of World War II.[27] "Stop-go" refers to deliberate government action to alternatively restrain and stimulate economic activity through the use of fiscal and monetary policies.[28] Alternating policies of contraction and expansion of aggregate demand are constantly used to try to manage the economy. Although there is no objection to a sequence of expansionary and restrictive changes in fiscal and monetary policies if these changes secure a sustained performance in the economy, such success has not been achieved. When taxes are constantly being raised or lowered to affect the level of aggregate demand, decisions to save and invest are adversely affected. Constant changes in interest rates and the money supply have the same effect.

Another explanation for the decline of the British economy is that most Western countries started at a lower stage in the level of economic development and are merely in the process of catching up. France, Germany, and Japan were largely destroyed by World War II, and therefore had to start from scratch. They had no choice but to invest in the most modern plants and equipment. Britain, by contrast, had a large inheritance of capital that was not modern. However, World War II has been over for 40 years, and this theory does not explain why these countries have continued to grow more rapidly than the United Kingdom after they had reached their prewar level of income and even after they had surpassed the British level of per capita income.

27. John Hackett and Anne-Marie Hackett, *The British Economy* (London: George Allen & Unwin, Ltd., 1967), pp. 44-54.

28. "Stop-go" is analogous to a constant application of the brakes in a car after speeding up.

Mancur Olson of Yale University presents an interesting explanation for the decline of the British economy. He notes that countries that have democratic freedom of organization without internal revolution or foreign invasion can suffer the most from growth-repressing organizations.[29] These special-interest organizations reduce efficiency and aggregate income in the societies in which they operate and make political life more divisive. They slow down a society's capacity to adopt new technologies and reallocate resources in response to changing economic conditions, and thereby reduce the rate of economic growth. Labor unions resist attempts to improve work efficiency and productivity, and companies demand protection from foreign competition. This may explain why the United Kingdom, which has had immunity in this century from dictatorship, foreign invasion, and revolution, has had a lower rate of growth than other large, developed democracies. British society has acquired so many strong special-interest groups that it suffers from an institutional sclerosis that slows its adaptation to change.

There is obvious validity to Olson's explanation. One has only to look at the United States as a prime example of the dominance of special-interest groups in society. The federal budget cannot be balanced either through tax increases or decreases in government spending because special-interest groups thwart all attempts. Tax reform is difficult because special-interest groups oppose any effort to close out their tax breaks. Special-interest groups are not just limited to the United Kingdom and the United States. France, Germany, and Japan have their share, but for one reason or another, they have not had the same impact on economic growth.[30]

In terms of growth in the amounts and productivity of resources, the United Kingdom has lagged behind most of the major industrial market economies.[31] In a study of nine industrialized countries, Edward Dennison found that the United Kingdom was next to last in labor inputs as a source of economic growth. Included in labor inputs were employment, hours of work, and education. The United Kingdom was also next to last in a second determinant of economic growth, capital inputs, which includes investment in plants and equipment, and inventories.[32] The United King-

29. Mancur Olson, *The Rise and Decline of Nations* (New Haven, Conn.: Yale University Press, 1982), pp. 75-87.

30. Ibid., pp. 76-77.

31. Edward F. Dennison, "Economic Growth" in Richard E. Caves, ed., *Britain's Economic Prospects* (Washington: The Brookings Institution, Inc., 1968), pp. 231-278.

32. Edward F. Dennison, *Why Growth Rates Differ: Post-War Experiences in Nine Western Countries* (Washington: The Brookings Institution, Inc., 1967).

dom was dead last in land inputs. The low growth rate of the British economy cannot be ascribed to built-in handicaps; other countries were more successful in securing growth from sources where the United Kingdom had no apparent disadvantage.

SUMMARY

Prime Minister Margaret Thatcher has made some dramatic changes in the British economy since she was first elected to office in 1979. The most important change was the privatization of industries that were formerly owned and operated by the British government. Since she has been in office, she has sold more than two dozen major state-owned businesses to private enterprise. She has also attempted to stimulate economic growth and productivity by cutting tax rates for both corporations and individuals. Inflation was a major problem when she took office in 1979. By following monetary policies similar to those used by the Federal Reserve in the late 1970s and early 1980s in the United States, the Thatcher government reduced the rate of inflation from 17.9 percent in 1980 to around 4.0 percent in 1985. Conversely, the rate of unemployment increased from 6.8 percent of the labor force in 1980 to 13.4 percent in 1985. The real rate of economic growth ranged from a low of 2.3 percent in 1980 to a high of 3.2 percent in 1985.

REVIEW QUESTIONS

1. What are some of the problems confronting the British economy?
2. Discuss the economic policies of the Thatcher government.
3. Discuss the relationship of the Bank of England to the British banking system.
4. Discuss the role of fiscal and monetary policy as economic stabilization devices in the United Kingdom.
5. What trends have developed over time in the distribution of income and wealth in the United Kingdom?
6. The rate of economic growth in the United Kingdom has lagged behind growth rates of other major countries. What are some of the reasons for this lag?
7. What is the function of the National Enterprise Board?

8. Discuss some of the reasons for the denationalization of industries under the Thatcher government.
9. Discuss pricing policies in the nationalized industries.

■ ─── ■
R E C O M M E N D E D   R E A D I N G S

Black, John. *The Economics of Modern Britain*. Oxford: Martin Robertson, 1983.

Brittan, Samuel. *The Role & Limits of Government*. Minneapolis: University of Minnesota Press, 1983.

Challen, D.W. *Unemployment & Inflation in the U.K.* New York: Longman Inc., 1984.

Friedman, Milton. *Money Talks: Five Views of Britain's Economy*. Alan Horrox and Gillian McCredie, eds. London: Thames Methuen, 1983.

Kirby, M.L. *The Decline of British Power Since 1870*. London: George Allen & Unwin, Ltd., 1981.

Olson, Mancur. *The Rise & Decline of Nations*. New Haven, Conn.: Yale University Press, 1982.

Prest, A.R., and D.J. Coppock, eds. *The United Kingdom Economy: A Manual of Applied Economics*. 9th ed. London: Weidenfeld & Nicholson, 1984.

Sampson, Anthony. *The Changing Anatomy of Britain*. London: Haddis & Stoughton, 1982.

MODERN CENTRALLY PLANNED ECONOMIES

Modern society offers two institutions through which resource allocation decisions are made—the market and government. In reality, of course, no economic society allocates all of its resources through a single institution. Instead, each economy in the world is mixed, to one degree or another, between market-determined and government-determined resource allocation. A continuum can be used to show some of the major alternative techniques that can be used to affect resource allocation. These techniques range from those applied directly and completely by the government to those where the public sector's influence is very indirect. At one end of the continuum, government allocation influence is direct and complete, and at the other end market forces are dominant.

The centrally planned economies of today show considerable variation in terms of their positions on the continuum. Different countries use different allocative techniques. Hungary is a case in point. Its New Economic Mechanism, with its emphasis on the forces of the marketplace and the incentives of the profit motive, has meant the partial dismantling of centralized state planning. In East Germany, as another example, agriculture (with very minor exceptions) has been collectivized, while in Poland most of agriculture remains in private hands. There is private ownership of industry in Yugoslavia and Hungary, but in the Soviet Union private ownership of industry is nil. No two countries can be fit into the same mold.

However, there are various institutional arrangements common to the socialist countries. These arrangements are the subject of this chapter.

The advanced centrally planned economies include the Soviet Union and the Eastern European countries of Bulgaria, Czechoslovakia, East Germany, Hungary, Poland, and Romania. These countries account for approximately 9 percent of the world's population and produce approximately 20 percent of the world's real gross national product. Table 11-1 presents estimated real gross national product for the Soviet Union and the Eastern European countries for 1984.

■ ECONOMIC PLANNING ■

The method of deciding key economic questions in socialist industry— what to produce, how much of each item, for whom, and the allocation of resources necessary to achieve the desired production and distribution—is state economic planning. Although centrally planned economies use a monetary system and prices, the prices of goods and services and those of factors of production are not determined by the interaction of buyers and sellers in the market and hence are not reliable guides for economic decisions. A centrally planned economic system has the ability to make economic plans and to see to it that these plans are carried out. This is because the productive wealth of the system—land and capital—is owned by

TABLE 11-1 ESTIMATED REAL GROSS NATIONAL PRODUCT FOR THE SOVIET UNION AND EASTERN EUROPE FOR 1984
(billions of U.S. dollars)

Soviet Union		$1,956
Eastern Europe		771
Bulgaria	56	
Czechoslovakia	128	
East Germany	164	
Hungary	77	
Poland	228	
Romania	118	
Soviet Union and Eastern Europe		$2,730

Source: Central Intelligence Agency, *Handbook of Economic Statistics 1985* (Washington: USGPO, 1985), p. 35.

society as a whole; society, as reflected through the state, controls most lines of economic activity.

Both production and distribution are implemented through the use of economic plans. Formally approved state plans, buttressed by rules of behavior and various types of incentives, govern production and distribution decisions. The plans represent an attempt to balance the supply of and demand for resources in order to achieve an equilibrium. In a market economy consumer choice influences resource allocation, but this is not true for a centrally planned economy. Planning embraces many aspects of socialist economic life. It is not content with merely making the system operate; it also has such objectives as increasing national wealth or rapidly industrializing the economy. In other words, economic planning can have both short- and long-term goals. Planning relies on directives from the state for its implementation; it is controlled by a central planning agency, by financial organizations, and, above all, by the political authorities.

Economic plans may be divided into several categories. First, general plans may extend for a period of 15 to 20 years. These plans are primarily concerned with long-term problems of structural changes on the national scale, technology, the training of labor, and the like. Second, there are medium-term plans, usually covering a period of five years and concerned mostly with changes in the capacity and rate of production of different industries and enterprises. This type of plan is subject to perpetual revision as it is carried out. Third, there are annual plans within each five-year plan. These plans provide a detailed description of production plans for the year and serve as a control mechanism to ensure compliance by enterprises. Finally, there are quarterly plans within each annual plan, and even monthly plans for plants or groups of plants within specific branches of industries.

It is also necessary to distinguish between physical input–output planning and financial planning. Actually, economic planning consists of both types. Basic planning in the socialist countries is in real terms and involves physical output targets for industrial and agricultural commodities, the allocation of labor and important types of raw materials and equipment at the national level, and total national capital investment. The financial plan is important as a control mechanism. It is used to control the execution of the national physical, or real, input–output plan. Although subordinate to the physical plan in the overall planning system, it is used to maintain a discipline in the physical planning process—a discipline imposed by the banking system. The financial plan is also used to maintain a balance between consumer disposable income and the volume of consumer goods and services available. It consists of three parts—the state budget, the credit plan, and the cash plan of the central bank. The credit and cash plans control the outlay of short-term credit and the currency issued by the central bank. The credit plan plays an important role in financial planning because it exercises several control functions, such as seeing that loans to enterprises are used in conformance with physical planning objectives.

Economic planning must address the need to balance plan targets with available economic resources. There are two ways in which this problem is resolved: through the use of (1) material balances or (2) input–output analysis. Material balances present an intended relationship between supplies and their allocation for specific commodities. The balances, normally expressed in physical units, provide a basis for the financial counterpart of the plan. Input–output analysis involves interbranch balancing, which means that the economy is divided up into a number of branches, each of which has assigned inputs and outputs. These branches are presented on a statistical grid showing how much each economic sector buys and sells from every other major sector. For example, the grid shows how much of the output of the steel industry goes into the auto, construction, or farm machinery industries. At the same time, it shows how much the steel industry itself receives from these other industries.

MECHANICS OF PLANNING

Economic planning is a complicated process in which production and consumption are controlled by the central planning authorities on the basis of predetermined economic and political objectives. Typically priority has been given to the development of industries that will contribute the most to the attainment of national economic and political goals. Economic plans provide for maximum development of certain branches of an economy through priorities in investment, materials, and human and financial resources. It is assumed that the accelerated expansion of certain key industries, such as the chemical, oil, gas, and power industries, makes it possible to increase the overall rate of growth of industrial and agricultural production.

The East German plan can be used to illustrate the intricacies of economic planning. Figure 11-1 presents the framework of the plan. The plan is initiated each April by the State Planning Commission. However, it is based on the policy directives of the Council of Ministers of the German Democratic Republic, which is the highest administrative level in East Germany. The Council is also responsible for the approval of the final plan. Guidelines for developing the plan are provided by the State Planning Commission and sent to districts and municipalities and to all enter-

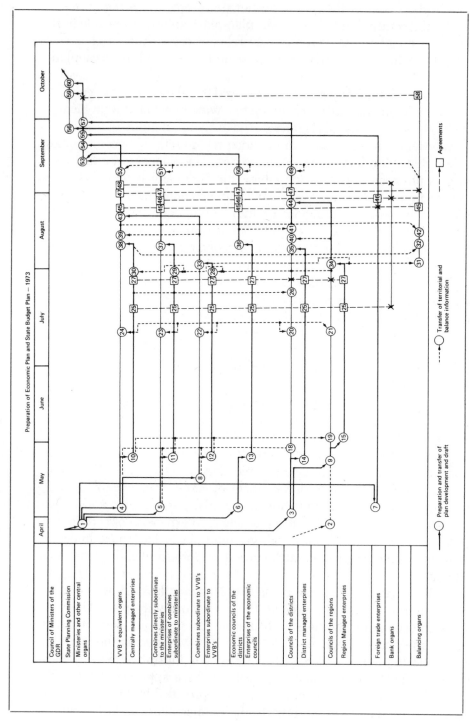

FIGURE 11-1 PREPARATION OF ECONOMIC AND STATE BUDGET PLAN

248

prises. The connecting links between the Planning Commission and the various economic and political units are the industrial, agricultural, and trade ministries.

Each ministry is responsible for the application of control figures to its given area of jurisdiction. These control figures are also sent down to ministry subdepartments at district, county, and local levels. The purpose of this dissemination is to provide information that can be used as a basis for plan formulation by all production and distribution units. After the control figures have been made available to the various economic units and the lower levels of government, there is a plan counterdesign that starts with the formulation of plans by industrial and trade enterprises, state farms, and other local economic units. These plans cover all phases of their operations. The plans, which can be considered as target plans, then travel upward for their integration into the national plan. At each administrative level the plans cumulate into a national whole.

The numbers in Figure 11-1 correspond to the various state administrative units and enterprises involved in planning. For example, number "1" represents the initiation of the planning process when the basic targets of the plan are sent to the ministries for transmission to the various industries under their jurisdiction. The lines emerging from "1" represent the preparation and transfer of the plan. The ministries disaggregate the plan goals and transmit them to the respective executors. In East Germany the next step is number 4, when the plan directives go to the VVBs (*Vereinigung Volkseigener Betriebe*), associations of industrial and trade enterprises. Each VVB represents the most important link between the administration of the industrial system and the basic enterprise units. In recent years VVBs have been dissolved in favor of a two-level system. Although efforts have been made in East Germany and other countries to simplify and decentralize planning procedures, Figure 11-1 still reflects the basic steps in developing the economic plan.

The comprehensiveness of the plan is apparent. As has already been mentioned, the state budget is an integral part. There must be a reconciliation of individual enterprise needs to the availability of bank credit. Consumer needs must be balanced against the supply of producers' goods. Foreign trade also must enter into planning decisions. All of this is done during the period from April to September. By October the final process of reconciliation is done by the State Planning Commission.

After the national economic plan is prepared, it is sent to the Council of Ministers for approval. Once approved, the plan in essence becomes law, and it passes down the administrative ladder until it reaches the enterprises. It should be emphasized that this annual plan is an operating plan that must be followed, within prescribed limits, by all production and distribution units.

The basic method of East German economic planning involves the use of material balances, which are usually recorded in physical terms and which present an intended relationship between supplies and their allocation for specific commodities. Material balances are drawn up for all of the important types of industrial and agricultural products. Targets are reconciled with the constraints of available resources. The balances provide a basis for the financial part of the plan. According to the existing practice in East Germany, the overall balance of the national economy comprises several flows that have to be harmonized. These flows include production, consumption, and accumulation, as well as the distribution of national income. The material balance method is cumbersome to handle; moreover, it obscures the repercussions of economic changes.

DEFECTS OF PLANNING

In a system of central planning directives, a powerful bureaucracy develops that generally identifies economic life with the internal norms of the state apparatus. This bureaucracy generally tries, regardless of its stated intentions, to perpetuate and consolidate its position. Every system of guidance has its internal logic; in the case of central planning, deficiencies often result because individual enterprises are circumscribed in terms of planning directives. It is impossible to guide a complex and interdependent economy on a directive basis without running the risk of serious economic trouble. The hierarchical nature of planning and administration makes a centralized system unwieldy and not easily adaptable to the change demanded by modern developments.

Under centralized planning, not enough attention has been paid to problems at the microeconomic level. Planned economies have tended to neglect the problems of management and use of resources at the operational level. Seen from a purely economic point of view, planning provides practically no incentive to be efficient. A dual system of decision making, which cannot be avoided in the absence of free enterprise, contains a danger of incongruity and divergence. Experience shows that it is not easy in practice to reconcile targets set at the central level, even though they may be optimal, with the interests of the individual enterprise.

■ PUBLIC FINANCE ■

A major difference between the fiscal systems of the socialist countries and the industrialized countries of the West lies in the role and size of the budget. In the United States there are three basic levels of government—federal, state, and local—and each level operates its budget in substantial independence from the other. However, in the Soviet Union as well as in its satellite countries, the budget represents a financial control mechanism for carrying out the state economic plans. The budget is centralized and represents a consolidation of all budgets—national, republic, and local. The result is the consolidated state budget, which assumes the key role in the distribution of the national income in each country.

SIGNIFICANCE OF THE STATE BUDGET

The state budgets of the socialist countries are much larger in terms of the relationship of government expenditures to national income than the budgets of the leading nonsocialist countries. About half of the national income of the Soviet Union flows through its budget. The reason for the size of the state budget is obvious. Under the socialist system many goods and services that would be financed in a capitalistic system by private enterprise or private individuals are financed by the government. For example, investment expenditures, which in the United States would be financed by private enterprise, are financed to a considerable degree by the state budget in a socialist country. Many other expenditures, such as those for health, education, and research, which would be financed at least in part by the private sector in a capitalistic country, are financed out of the state budget.

In such socialist countries as the Soviet Union and Poland, the national economic plan sets forth the level and distribution of economic resources necessary for the fulfillment of national objectives. The state budget of these countries is an integral part of the financial plan. The financial plan involves the cash, credit, and investment financing necessary to implement the attainment of the physical output goals spelled out in the national economic plan. It is through the state budget office that the turnover tax, deductions from profits of enterprises, and the other fiscal resources of the government are collected and redistributed. The state budget is the prime vehicle for the allocation of resources among various ends, whereas in a market economy, the market transmits preferences to producers who, in the process of adjusting output to correspond with these preferences, direct economic resources into alternative uses. The state budget is also a control mechanism because it provides a considerable proportion of the investment funds for enterprises. These funds are provided for certain purposes within the framework of the financial plan. This control restricts the opportunity of enterprises to indulge in investments outside of those specified in the plan.

TAXATION

An outstanding feature of the fiscal systems of Poland, the Soviet Union, and Yugoslavia is the predominance of indirect taxation over direct taxation. This is surprising in view of the fact that Marxist doctrine would hold that the use of indirect taxes discriminates against the working classes because the taxes are regressive and inequitable. However, there are reasons for this reliance on indirect taxation. First, indirect taxes are easier to administer and harder to avoid than direct taxes. They are collected from thousands of enterprises rather than millions of individuals; in the early stages of socialist development this was important because the administrative machinery of government was not well established. Second, the role of the government, as reflected by the size of the national budget, is more important in the socialist countries, so taxation by necessity must also be higher. Direct taxes at an acceptable level would not provide the revenues necessary to support government expenditures. Direct taxes would also have a greater negative impact on work incentive than indirect taxes.

BASIC TYPES OF TAXES   A very important tax in the Soviet Union is the turnover tax. It is applied primarily to consumer goods and is levied at the later stages in the production process. The turnover tax is a highly discriminatory tax in that the rates vary from product to product and also from geographic region to region. In addition to being a leading revenue source, the tax exercises an important control function in that it is used to regulate the level of aggregate demand. The tax is also often levied when, though goods are abundant, consumption is considered undesirable. For example, a high turnover tax is levied on alcohol and tobacco and luxury items such as furs and jewelry. The turnover tax is also used to regulate profits in that the tax rate can determine the amount of profits allowed to producers.

Deductions from profits represent another important source of revenue for the government, particularly in the Soviet Union. Profits, as defined in Soviet terms, represent the difference between the total income received by an enterprise from the sale of its products and its production costs. In many instances, profits are the difference between the government-determined price for a commodity and the cost to an enterprise for producing it. When profits are made by an enterprise, they are used in two ways —one part is remitted to the state and the other part is retained by the enterprise. The part that is returned to the government can be viewed as a transfer of revenue rather than a direct tax. However, since it is a cost over and above costs of production, it is incorporated in the final selling price. In this respect, deductions from profits can be considered to have the same effect as sales taxes since each can be shifted forward to consumers.

The personal income tax is not an important source of revenue in the socialist countries. There are two reasons for this lack of reliance on the personal income tax. First, virtually all wage and salary earners are employed by state enterprises or enterprises closely controlled by the state. Therefore, a personal income tax would only be an administrative device for doing what could be done with less trouble by adjustment of the wages and salaries originally paid. Second, the socialist countries rely on wage differentials to allocate labor. Material incentives play a very important role in stimulating worker productivity. It is felt that a direct tax, such as the personal income tax, would have a more negative impact on work incentive than indirect taxes. An indirect tax, such as the turnover tax, is less visible than an income tax and would not have the effect of reducing the tax-home pay of the worker. In the Soviet Union, the personal income tax on wage and salary earners was supposed to be abolished after October 1, 1965. Although some staged reductions in the income tax have been carried out, the tax is still being used.

FISCAL POLICY   There is little doubt that the three basic economic goals of full employment, price stability, and economic growth are highly desirable in both the market economies and the centrally planned economies. Both fiscal and monetary policy can be used to contribute to the attainment of these goals. Fiscal policy, as defined previously, deals with government receipts and expenditures. The signficance of fiscal policy lies in the fact that it deals directly with matters that immediately influence consumption and investment expenditures, and hence the income, of the economy. Monetary policy, as also defined previously, is concerned with the provision of money, defined to include currency and demand deposits at commercial banks. It seeks to maintain a balance between real aggregate demand and supply through control of the aggregate monetary demand for goods and services.

In the Soviet Union the turnover tax is the basic fiscal policy instrument used to achieve a balance between aggregate supply and demand. Consumer goods are in short supply relative to the demand for them. Soviet economic policy has usually stressed the development of the industrial goods sector of the economy, and resources have been allocated for this purpose. The production plans of the government also provide that a given amount of consumer goods be made available annually. However, to maintain incentive and partly because of errors in planning, consumers may receive more purchasing power than can be absorbed by the goods available to them. This excess purchasing power is siphoned off by the turnover tax applied at the various stages of production of the goods.

■ BANKING ■

Monetary systems vary considerably from country to country. This is particularly true when viewed from the standpoint of the relationship of central banks to governments. This relationship varies from the considerable constitutional independence of the U.S. Federal Reserve Banks to the integral role Gosbank plays as an instrument of state economic policy in the Soviet Union. The United States is a country that always has been devoted to the doctrine of the separation of powers. Economic policy emerges from the interplay of various forces: The Federal Reserve Board certainly is free to hold, or openly advocate, different views of economic policy from those of the government. This is hardly the case in the Soviet Union; Gosbank is an essential part of the Soviet economic control mechanism in that it contains the accounts of all state enterprises and can see that expenditures are made in conformance with basic economic objectives.

CENTRAL BANKING

In some respects there is a similarity among all central banks. For example, Gosbank, the Bank of Japan, the Bank of France, and other central banks issue bank notes, serve as repositories for gold holdings, and make international payments. Gosbank serves as a fiscal agent for the Soviet government in that virtually all governmental receipts and expenditures flow through various deposit accounts. The same holds true of the People's Bank of China. In this respect, both are similar to the Bank of Japan, which has served since its inception in 1882 as the fiscal agent of the Japanese government. The Bank of Japan handles public receipts and payments, government debt, and Treasury accounts.

There is also a similarity from the standpoint of credit control between socialist and capitalist central banks. In France, for example, the central bank exercises tight control over the credit-creating banks. The central banks of the Soviet Union, Poland, and Yugoslavia also control credit, but to a degree that is unheard of in the market economies. In centrally planned economies, the central banks are essentially *monobanks* in that they combine the functions of both central and commercial banking. These monobanks, with the exception of a few specialized banks, are the banking system of each country and purvey most of the total credit. This means that they are provided with a control mechanism in that they can supervise the amount of credit granted and the purposes for which it is used.

MONETARY POLICY

The function and instruments of monetary policy differ between the centrally planned and market economies. Although the central bank is at the apex of the banking system in both types of economies, there are different institutional arrangements. Japan and the Western countries have a well-defined commercial banking system and private capital ownership. Neither exists in the Soviet Union and other socialist countries. In the market economies imbalances between aggregate demand and aggregate supply are adjusted through the use of both monetary and fiscal policies; the centrally planned economies rely on fiscal policy. The Soviet turnover tax, as mentioned previously, is an example of the use of fiscal policy to regulate consumer demand.

In the market economies, monetary policy is a flexible instrument used by the central banks in response to changes in the market economy. The basic tools of monetary policy include control over the minimum liquidity requirements of commercial banks, changes in the rate of rediscounting short-term commercial notes, and open market operations. The importance of each of these instruments varies from country to country. Monetary policy is implemented by the central banks through the commercial banks, with the ultimate objective of influencing changes in both the cost and the availability of credit. These changes are designed to affect the consumption and investment expenditures of both individuals and companies.

In the centrally planned economies, monetary policy is not used as an economic stabilization measure to effect a balance between aggregate demand and supply. The basic monetary policy instruments are irrelevant because the investment decisions are made by the state in the economic plan rather than by private enterprise operating within the framework of a market economy. Instead, monetary policy is a part of the financial plan and is concerned with controlling the amount of money in circulation and providing credit for enterprises. Its role is passive in that it is not used to correct disequilibria between supply and demand through changes in the cost and availability of credit. In other words, in Japan and the Western countries, monetary policy is a flexible instrument used continuously to respond to market changes, while in the socialist countries, monetary policy is inflexible and is used to expedite the implementation of the governments' financial plans.

COMMERCIAL BANKS

A major difference between the banking systems of the socialist and capitalist countries is the virtual absence of commercial banks in most socialist countries.[1] In market economies such as the United States and Sweden, commercial banks are a separate and integral part of the banking system. They are privately owned business firms operating for the purpose of making a profit. They provide facilities for deposits on which depositors receive interest and extend credit to a great variety of borrowers by making loans and purchasing securities. The essence of commercial banking in the market economies is the extension of credit through the creation of money. Their ability to create spendable purchasing power in the form of demand deposits gives commercial banks a unique quality among financial institutions. Commercial banks in most market economies are normally the largest single and the most diversified source of credit.

In the Soviet Union the functions of commercial banks have been assumed by Gosbank. In addition to serving as the central bank of the country, Gosbank has a monopoly over the provision of short-term credit. Each enterprise has an account in Gosbank, originally put there by the government, which is supposed to supply it with working capital. When a sale is made between two industrial enterprises, the bank simply deducts the amount of the sale from the buyer's account and adds it to that of the seller. Under ordinary circumstances purchases and sales tend to offset each other, thus making no inordinate demand on an enterprise's working capital, but in the event that it is temporarily in need, it can obtain short-term credit from Gosbank. This credit is extended to enterprises for the purpose of procuring inventories and also for financing goods in transit.

SAVINGS BANKS

Savings banks exist for the purpose of making the accumulations of small savers available for use in financing the economic system, and savings are encouraged as a means of regulating consumer demand. Savings banks accept deposits from individuals and organizations such as trade unions or cooperatives, and pay interest on these deposits. They also perform other services, such as collecting rent and utility bills and selling government bonds. Most of their funds are invested in government bonds, and it is in this way that personal savings make their way back into the economy. Savings banks may exist as part of a nationwide system, as is that case of the satellite countries, or they may exist as a part of the central bank, as in both the Soviet Union and China.

---

1. The term *commercial banks* is used to describe various types of depository institutions in the United States—banks, savings and loans, mutual savings banks, and credit unions.

SPECIAL-PURPOSE BANKS

Special-purpose banks are included in the structure of the socialist banking systems. For example, foreign trade banks operate to finance foreign trade transactions and to carry on a correspondent relationship with banks in other countries. Other banks exist as a channel for paying out to enterprises and institutions the funds provided by the state budget for investment. In the event that a particular enterprise needs funds for financing new construction, it may procure these funds from a special purpose bank in the form of a nonrepayable grant. If it is practical to finance the proposal out of future earnings, a short-term, interest-bearing loan can be arranged. Agricultural banks also exist for the purpose of financing rural credit cooperatives. However, there are no longer any separate agricultural banks in most socialist countries, and their functions have been assumed by the central banks.

■ ORGANIZATION OF PRODUCTION ■ AND DISTRIBUTION

In the centrally planned economic system, most productive and distributive enterprises are under the direct control of the state. There is some place for small private enterprises, particularly in Yugoslavia, but for the most part their operation is narrowly circumscribed. Some organizations are also left to local governments to operate on the grounds that their operation is largely of local importance. Local utilities, hospitals, theaters, and housing construction would fall into this category. Nevertheless, though ownership and operation are entrusted to local governmental units, usually some agency of the central government has the ultimate responsibility for coordinating their operations within the general framework of the national economic plans.

The state exercises monopolistic control over the basic economic structure and resources of the country. It owns and operates large-scale industries, mines, power plants, railways, shipping, and various means of communication. It engages in farming on its own account through state farms, and it largely controls peasant agriculture through collective farming. It has an exclusive monopoly of banking and foreign trade, and it controls the domestic channels of distribution in its role as manufacturer, farmer, merchant, shipper, and banker. In the field of labor relations, it is the sole employer of note, and as such dominates bargaining between itself and the employees. Although trade unions are allowed, their function is purely subsidiary to the interest of the state, and strikes are illegal.

THE ENTERPRISE

The *enterprise,* which is usually an individual firm, is the basic unit of industrial production. It has its own fixed and financial capital, derived in part from the state budget and in part from bank loans and retained earnings. The enterprise is strictly subject to state planning and is managed by state appointees. Profits, if there are any, are turned over to the state treasury to be included as a part of government revenue, except for amounts assigned for retention by the enterprise earning them. Retained profits must, however, be used for specific purposes, such as bonus incentive funds. The enterprise is obligated to fulfill the production and financial plans set down by the state, which specifies targets or *success indicators* to be attained. Targets, for the most part, are in quantitative terms stated in physical or monetary units of measure. Quantity of output is often used as a success indicator. As a result quantity is often achieved at the expense of quality or by providing output that is not related to demand but that is easy to produce. Profit is also used as a success indicator.

When an enterprise is formed, it becomes an economic accounting unit with its own capital, both fixed and financial, and its own account at the central bank. It then operates as a financial entity and is generally expected to conduct its affairs in such a way that revenues will cover expenses and leave some profits. However, earning a profit is not a basic requisite for survival, as an enterprise can also operate with a planned loss. Prices of inputs and outputs are fixed, and the enterprise must operate within this constraint in fulfilling its target, covering its costs, and making a profit.

The state prescribes the ultimate objectives to be sought by the enterprise in the annual national plan, and the enterprise prepares its own annual operating plan, which is an elaboration of the targets set forth in the national plan. This operating plan contains such targets as the volume of output and the introduction of new types of products. It also contains information about the number of workers employed, cost of production, and amount of wages payable to workers. The annual operating plan requires the approval of the central authorities before it can be implemented at the enterprise level. The operating plan is then formalized in terms of control figures and resource use.

In a country the size of the Soviet Union, one can well wonder how the operations of thousands of enterprises are coordinated. Although enterprise managers have a certain degree of operational flexibility, major decisions regarding what to produce, how much to produce, and for whom to produce are made primarily by superior agencies. In the Soviet Union there is a hierarchy of agencies responsible for developing and coordinating the enterprise's plan.

In the Soviet Union there are several agencies or organizations that can exercise some sort of managerial control. The Gosbank can exercise monetary control because it holds the accounts of all enterprises. It can scrutinize an enterprise's receipts and payments to see if they conform to the objectives of the plan. The Ministry of Finance, in collecting tax receipts, can audit the accounts of an enterprise. Then, too, all Soviet industries are divided into functional groups under the control of industrial ministries that plan and control production and decide questions of technical policy, material supplies, financing, labor use, and wages. The Communist Party also exercises control over the enterprises. Each industrial enterprise has a Communist Party committee elected from the personnel who are party members. This committee is responsible for stimulating the workers to carry out the plan. The committee can also report any irregularities at the enterprise. However, as will be discussed in chapters which follow, there is also some decentralization of authority in the control of enterprises in some socialist countries, such as Yugoslavia and Hungary.

AGRICULTURE

The organization of agriculture has always presented a problem to the Communists because the peasants have always been hostile to efforts to collectivize and regiment them. For ideological reasons the Communist Party regards it as imperative that agriculture be collectivized, but early Soviet experiments with collectivization invariably ended in disaster. Eventually, after the most repressive measures were used on the peasants to enforce their compliance with Soviet collectivization policies, some sort of compromise was worked out whereby, in return for work on the collective farms, the peasants were given the privilege of farming their own private plots. This arrangement exists in other socialist countries as well. The degree of collectivization, however, differs considerably among socialist countries. In the Soviet Union there are a few individual peasants who own their land, but their numbers are exceedingly small relative to the total farm population. In Yugoslavia the opposite is true, for 80 percent of the agricultural land is privately owned; individuals are permitted to own up to 10 hectares (about 24.7 acres) of land.

In comparing the relationship of the government to agriculture in the socialist and capitalist countries, the fundamental distinction lies in the pervasiveness of government control and administration of the whole socialist system, of which agriculture forms an integral part. The communist state exercises a monopolistic control over the agricultural resources. It engages in farming on its own account through state farms, and it largely controls peasant agriculture through collective farming. Through control of the state budget and the banking system, it can control the allocation of monetary resources to agriculture. Agricultural activity is also subject to state economic planning.

Agriculture in the socialist countries is carried on by collective farms, state farms, and individual farmers. A *collective farm* is a production unit in which farm property is owned by the peasants and the produce is distributed according to their labor contribution. A certain amount of produce is also set aside for delivery to the state to be sold to consumers. A *state farm* is owned and operated by the government. Its annual budget and operating plans are prepared just like those of any state enterprise, and its equipment and machinery are owned by the state. It hires workers and pays them wages established by the state.

MARKETING

In a centrally planned economic system, the state is typically the sole producer and distributor of goods. It performs the principal marketing functions of buying and selling, transporting, storing, standardizing, and grading goods. The role of intermediaries in the exchange process was decried by the communists as a capitalistic invention designed to gain profits and was eliminated during the early stages of communist development in the Soviet Union and other countries. This, however, failed to simplify the process of exchange, and in some respects there is a distinct similarity between distribution procedures in socialist and capitalist countries. In the Soviet Union, for example, the main channel of distribution for consumer goods is from producer to wholesaler to retailer to consumer, which also holds true for the United States. However, the Soviet government owns and controls each link in the production and distribution process.

Distribution at both the wholesale and retail levels is usually the responsibility of the state trading network or the cooperative trading network. Although nominally collective, the cooperative network comes under close state control and is in fact little different from the state network. Both trading networks are governed by the annual economic plan. The plan determines the volume of goods to be distributed through the state and cooperative trading systems, and an effort is made to relate the volume of goods and services that will be made available to the income of consumers so that some sort of equilibrium is attained. Responsibility for the coordination of the distribution system is placed in the hands of a number of government agencies that perform such functions as drafting general plans for state and cooperative trade in accordance with the annual economic and financial plans and fixing wholesale and retail prices for state and cooperative outlets.

■ PRICING AND PROFIT ■
IN A CENTRALLY PLANNED ECONOMY

The problem of pricing in a socialist country is a different order of magnitude from that under capitalism. For one thing, prices do not determine the allocation of resources to the same extent as in a market economy. Moreover, pricing is not merely a question of economics, but also of ideology and politics. Value in the communist frame of reference is the amount of labor embodied in particular goods and services; that is, labor is the only factor of production with the capability of creating value. Thus the price or value of any commodity is determined by the amount of the labor required to produce it. The relative prices of two products will be in the same proportion as the amount of labor required to produce them. If two hours of labor are required to make a pair of shoes and five hours are required to build a cart, the price of the shoes on the market will be two-fifths of that of the cart.

Trying to set prices based on the labor theory of value has caused the communists all kinds of pricing problems. For one thing, the theory virtually denies the role of demand in the determination of value. The idea of marginal utility is rejected because it is in conflict with the assumption that value is objectively determined by labor content, not by subjective valuation depending on the amount used. Moreover, the factor of scarcity has been ignored. The value of a good or service in exchange for something else depends on the size of its supply and the amount of demand for it. Behind supply and demand can be a great many interdependent determinants that cannot be ignored. When scarcity and utility are considered, not only labor but capital and natural resources count as productive and value-creating.

However, pragmatism has transcended ideology in communist pricing policies, so that the actual formation and structure of prices incorporate little of the labor theory of value. In fact, actual prices are arrived at through the use of different plan variants that do recognize the scarcity of resources and the significance of demand. But the fact remains that no fully workable pricing system has been devised. Prices do not reflect all factor costs, as rent and interest are not necessarily fully accounted for. Furthermore, different criteria for price setting are used for different categories of products. As a result, prices still do not perform a rational allocative function.

PRODUCER AND CONSUMER PRICES

A dual price system operates in centrally planned economies—prices paid to producers and prices paid by consumers for retail goods. Producers' prices are those received by producing enterprises from other producing enterprises and from wholesale trading entities. The wholesale price is considered a producer price in the sense that it is the price of a product when it leaves the factory. It consists of full production costs and the profit of the producers; it does not normally include distribution costs. Producer prices are normally based on an average cost for the entire industry producing a given product. Included in average cost are wage payments, material costs, and capital charges. In some cases, producer prices are actually set by the state at levels below average cost so that enterprises operate with a planned loss that is subsidized by state revenues.

Retail prices consist of all of the components that make up the prices charged by the producer to the wholesaler plus a retail price markup. There is virtual isolation between producer and retail prices in that what happens to the former has little impact on the latter. Retail prices are set to keep supply and demand in balance within the guidelines of the economic plan. However, the setting of prices is based on the macrosocial preferences of the planners rather than on the true interaction of supply and demand affected by consumer preferences. There is a certain amount of flexibility in retail prices. For example, "free prices," prices set by supply and demand, operate in the purchase and sale of certain agricultural products. Prices also may be allowed to fluctuate within ranges above and below the levels set by the state planning authorities.

The final price of most products consists of production cost, profit of the producers, turnover tax, and wholesale and retail price markups. Profit, which is a matter for subsequent discussion, is designed to achieve a better use of resources at the enterprise level. The turnover tax occupies a distinct role in pricing in two ways. First, it is used to adjust demand to supply through the manipulation of tax rates on various goods. Typically goods in short supply or luxury goods carry a high tax. Second, the turnover tax is used to regulate profits. Since prices are fixed for the producer as well as the consumer, the tax rates in effect determine the amount of profits allowed to producers.

Determination of the final price for a product produced by a state enterprise may be described as follows: The first step is the enterprise price, which consists of two components—enterprise costs and profits. Enterprise costs include materials, wages, and social costs (education, housing, and recreation). The definition of these components differs from one country to another. One innovation in centrally planned enterprise pricing was the decision by East Germany and Hungary to permit enterprises to set their own prices to other producing enterprises, with the exception of the prices of most raw materials, which remain set by the state. This, however, has led to distortions as monopolistic sellers have increased prices. These prices were passed on, where possible, by the purchasing firm.

Profit markup is the second component of enterprise price. This markup is set within ranges permitted by the state and represents what can be considered an average for a given industry. Profits for an individual enterprise may be greater than this average through either increased production of goods that meet buyers' preferences or reduced unit costs. From profit there is a deduction that goes into the state treasury.

The turnover tax is added to the enterprise price to give an industry price. As mentioned above, the size of the turnover tax is determined by the required level of the retail price. The rate is differentiated to reflect different elasticities of consumer demand for different products. Typically the tax is arrived at residually, i.e., the retail price is fixed first to balance supply with demand, and the tax is the difference between this price and the price paid to the producer.

The wholesale price is really a margin added to the industry price to cover distribution costs. This margin is the price at which wholesale organizations sell to the retail network. In the absence of wholesaling organizations, an enterprise wholesale price may also be charged. The turnover tax is included in the enterprise wholesale price and therefore is paid by the producer.

The retail price consists of all of these components that go into the making up of the price of a product plus a retail markup added as the last element. The markup may be fixed by the state or it may be flexible within prescribed limits. Ceiling prices in which the state prescribes a maximum retail markup are sometimes used. In a few cases, free prices also are used.

A schematic presentation of the pricing policies followed by the East German clothing industry is shown below.[2]

Enterprise price (production costs and profit markup)
+ Turnover taxes
_____
Industry sales price
+ Wholesale margin
_____
Wholesale price
+ Retail margin
_____
Retail trade sale price

2. Staatsverlag der Deutschen Demokratischen Republik, "Gesetzblatt der Deutschen Demokratischen Republik," Teil 11, Nr. 24 (Berlin, May 10, 1972), p. 269.

PROFIT

Profit is an interesting phenomenon in a socialist system. At first profit was decried as one of the most basic evils of a capitalist system. Although profit has always been used in centrally planned economies, it was merely an accounting device to ensure that enterprises tried to cover their costs out of their own resources where possible and then handed the surplus over to the state. But certainly profit was not the rationale for the existence of an enterprise. However, profit has come to have a new and important role in some centrally planned economies. For one thing, it is used as a measure of enterprise efficiency. More important is the attempt to link profit with incentives. It is now common to tie the reward system to enterprise profit, for profit may be distributed in the form of bonuses to both labor and management. The share of profit distributed in this manner comes under the heading of the materials incentives fund.

In setting profit directives, state planning authorities use as the criterion, or base, average production costs in an industry producing a given commodity. Profit is expressed as a percentage of industry average cost and is set in combination with turnover tax rates and distribution markups. However, the use of a single average profit rate in the price set for a particular product does not result in a uniform rate of profit for all enterprises, because production costs vary widely among enterprises. By tying bonus funds to profit, enterprise managers do have an incentive to reduce production costs. As a result, however, some enterprises may make large profits while other enterprises may end up with a loss.

The profitability of an enterprise can be measured by comparing the profit to costs of production to obtain a profit rate. There are, however, weaknesses in this measure, and state planners are adopting other approaches. Profitability can now also be measured as the ratio of profit to the total annual average value of fixed assets and variable assets. Fixed capital allocated to enterprises is no longer free, but is subject to capital charges now representing cost. The profit rate then becomes a composite of five factors:

1. The average production cost of an enterprise, which includes wages, materials used, interest, and depreciation of fixed capital;

2. The quantity of output actually sold by the enterprise;

3. The price at which the output is sold;

4. The average annual value of fixed assets;

5. The average annual value of variable assets.

The formula for the profit rate can be expressed as follows:

$$PR = \frac{Q\,(P - C)}{F + V}$$

where PR = profit rate
      Q = quantity sold
      P = selling price
      C = average production costs
      F = average annual value of fixed assets
      V = average annual value of variable assets

DISTRIBUTION OF PROFITS

When an enterprise makes a profit, the first claimant is the state. A part of profit is allocated to the state budget, and the remainder is divided by the enterprise into a number of funds. Each fund is designed to accomplish a specific objective. There is a *production development fund* to finance capital investment for new technology, mechanization and automation, renovation of fixed assets, modernization of equipment, and other purposes designed to develop and improve production. There is also a *fund for social and cultural measures,* which has as its purpose the improvement of worker morale and productivity. It provides revenue for the construction and maintenance of child-care centers, expansion of recreational facilities, support of athletic programs, and housing construction. Finally, there is a *reserve fund,* used for the purpose of paying off long-term loans.

A simplified scheme of profit used for the individual state enterprise can be presented as follows:

Gross profits of the enterprise
– Payments to the state budget
– Interest on bank loans
_____

Net profits of the enterprise

The net profits of the enterprise are divided into:

1. Production development fund to finance fixed and working capital;

2. Social and cultural funds to improve the social and intellectual life of the worker;

3. Material incentive fund to stimulate worker productivity;

4. Reserve or amortization fund;

5. Profit residual.

A specific example of profit distribution can be provided in the case of an East German state farm. The starting point in the distribution of profits is gross sales, which is obtained by multiplying the planned volume of sales per product by the set state price. From gross sales, production costs, including the costs of seed, fertilizer, and depreciation, are deducted to get gross income. From gross income a deduction is made into the wage fund, and the remainder is called the *socially clear income.* This income may be considered as a residual that is divided between the state farm and the state. The example follows.

Total sales		$450,450.45
− Seed, fertilizer, and other costs		− 225,225.22
Gross income		$225,225.23
− Wage funds		− 90,090.09
Socially clear income		$135,135.14
− Special costs	$22,522.52	
− Production levy	$18,018.02	− 40,540.54
Gross profit		$ 94,594.60
− Land and production fund tax		− 18,018.02
Net profit		$ 76,576.58

■ INCOME DISTRIBUTION ■ IN A CENTRALLY PLANNED ECONOMY

Income distribution is detemrined by the state within the framework of the economic plan. The total amount of wages to be paid and the production counterpart to support the wage funds depend on the division of the national income between accumulation and consumption. Consumption must be divided between the social consumption fund and the wage fund. The total wage fund is partitioned into wage funds for all economic fields. In its economic planning, the government is able to determine the total wages for the economy by multiplying the planned number of workers by the wage rates it has set. Wages are changed as seems necessary to carry out government policy and achieve particular production ends. For example, to attract more workers to a given industry, its wages may be raised while other wages remain static or are allowed to decline. Direct pressure from workers would in general have little effect on wage determination.

The degree of state control over the wage fund at the enterprise level is smaller. Some latitude is allowed to enterprise managers in determining the size and the use of the fund. Typically the wage fund consists of several components, including basic wages. Basic wages is subdivided into two categories—time rates and piece rates. Both are based on work output indicators. The wage fund also provides for extra wages for more difficult work; payments for night, holiday, and Sunday work; and wages for paid state holidays, vacations, and time off to participate in public duties. In addition, bonuses may also be paid from the wage fund. As it stands, typical workers receive payments according to their work grade from the wage fund plus a bonus based on a performance standard.

Another source of worker income is provided from the material incentives fund, which is tied to enterprise profit. The significance and success of the profit criterion lie mainly in the fact that a direct link has been established between profit and incentive payment. It is in the interest of enterprise personnel—and at the same time of society—to maximize enterprise profit. The proportion of enterprise profits channeled into this fund varies in different socialist countries. For example, in East Germany up to 20 percent of net profits can be placed in the fund. In East Germany, Poland, and Romania the size of the fund is based on complicated formulas in which a distinction is made between planned and above-plan profits, and further between profits made by exceeding production targets and those achieved by reductions in costs.

■ ECONOMIC REFORMS ■

With the exception of Yugoslavia, the socialist countries of Eastern Europe were occupied by Soviet forces after the end of World War II. It was inevitable that sooner or later the Soviet Union would impose its economic system on these countries. Although this imposition did not occur at the same time for each country, by 1950 the basic rudiments of the Stalinist command type of economy had been established in Eastern Europe. This command economy was based on the ideological assumption that the only repository of human rationality is the Communist Party. Accordingly, the independent actions of individuals, groups, or institutions—which could only hinder the pursuit of rational goals—were replaced by the absolutist exercise of power by the party-state. This absolute rationality was embodied in the state plan, which prescribed practically all actions for each economic unit in the form of a state law to be carried out to the last detail. The same rigid relationship existed between the state and the individual in all walks of human life, particularly in politics, where it was seen as the only guarantee that the Party could control the economy.

The advantage of a Stalinist command economy was that it ensured the structure of production and distribution according to the priorities postulated by the Communist Party. However, there was no room for independence of decision making at the operational level. Producing units were bound by directive targets and a large number of other directive plan indicators. Economic accounting was done entirely in terms of physical units, and allocative decisions were not based on prices but on material balances. The most important defect of the Stalinist command economy was its lack of flexibility and wastefulness. Resources were not allocated in the most efficient manner. In each country under Soviet influence there was a command legacy of internal rigidity and resultant problems of economic performance. The attainment of Stalinist-type objectives reinforced traditional autarky, nonspecialization, inappropriate specialization, and small-scale economics—problems that were to plague Eastern Europe's development as a viable economic region.

To improve economic efficiency, a series of reforms were instituted by the socialist countries, particularly during the 1960s. Industrial and trading enterprises were given greater freedom to choose ways and means of plan fulfillment. Profit was accepted as the main indicator of enterprise performance, while the total number of success indicators was drastically reduced. Increased importance was attached to material as distinct from moral incentives. Centralized planning was made less prescriptive and detailed; instead, efforts were made to lay down broad targets expressed in monetary terms.

Prices were brought more in line with production costs to reduce the need for state subsidies and to enable average enterprises to be profitable. Similarly, procurement prices paid to the farms were raised in relation to industrial prices, to encourage agricultural production and to improve rural living standards. There was some overhaul of the retail and wholesale trade network, designed to improve services to consumers and to transmit customers' preferences to producing enterprises. A greater role was assigned to finance and credit, with a flexible use of interest rates.

Although economic reforms are necessary, they create problems. Changes in administrative organizations, planning methods, and performance indicators arouse the opposition of special-interest groups. There is an ambivalent attitude on the part of Communist Party leaders, who fear a lessening of their authority and control. Caution and delay are often involved in the implementation of reforms. The state, as represented by the Communist Party, is ready to take away what it has given at the first sign of real independence. Moreover, there are no political reforms to accompany decentralization of economic decision making at the enterprise level. Although there has been an effort to decentralize decision making, there is no corresponding effort to provide more political autonomy. All economic decisions are made within the constraint of a highly circumscribed political framework. Inevitably, the reforms have come into conflict with ideological and political issues.

■ HUNGARY: A CASE STUDY ■
OF ECONOMIC REFORM

A series of economic reforms, the most important of which took place in 1968, has been a distinctive feature of the Hungarian economy.[3] These reforms have been designed to promote administrative and economic efficiency. They include measures designed to establish a consumer and producer price system that better reflects actual market scarcities. Broad guidelines are provided for enterprises with respect to quality, style, and pricing. Enterprises also have been given the latitude to determine their own production resource mix on the basis of their preferences. A modified market economy is permitted in which enterprises can react to consumer preference. In 1968 enterprises were made independent economic units with the right to determine the structure of their production and sales. They were also given the right to establish direct contacts with foreign firms and engage in independent foreign trade.[4]

Reforms introduced in 1984 and 1985 were aimed at increasing the efficiency of state enterprises. The compulsory reserve fund, introduced in 1968, was eliminated. The reserve fund was a prescribed percentage of after-tax profits; as a result disposable enterprise income was reduced. In its place, reserves held from pretax profits will be allowed, based on the decisions of individual enterprises. Bonds may be issued by state enterprises and sold to the general public to raise capital. The rate of interest can be determined by the issuing enterprise.

Another reform introduced in 1985 was a new form of management. Rather than being chosen by the Communist Party, the director and management staffs of small state enterprises are to be selected by the workers,

---

3. The New Economic Mechanism of 1968 introduced the Hungarian reforms. It substantially reduced central government intervention in the economy at the enterprise level. However, the reforms were never designed to do away with a substantial government role in economic planning and decisions.

4. A number of contracts have been signed between U.S. and Hungarian enterprises. Philip Morris has a licensing agreement with Hungary to produce and sell Marlboro cigarettes. Levi Strauss has an agreement with five Hungarian partners to produce and sell blue jeans in Hungary and the rest of Eastern Europe. Coca-Cola has an agreement with Hungarian bottling plants to produce and sell Coca-Cola. American and Hungarian enterprises are producing tractors for sale in both Western and Eastern Europe.

who will also have the right to recall them. Enterprise councils were also introduced in the same year as a new form of management of large state enterprises. The councils consist of members of management and labor who are responsible for the selection of managers.

THE PRICE SYSTEM

Some prices of consumer goods are set by state authority; others, as permitted by state authority, are flexible within limits; still others are free. About 40 percent of all consumer prices are fixed, including those on basic consumer goods and services.[5] There are flexible or free prices on the remaining consumer goods and services. These prices are determined by supply and demand, but some are only allowed to fluctuate between maximum and minimum limits fixed by the State Price and Material Office.[6]

Domestic producer prices are more closely controlled and may be either fixed or flexible within limits. The prices of basic raw materials, energy, and fuels are fixed by the state; the prices on finished products sold by state enterprises to other state enterprises are not fixed. Flexible prices allow state enterprises to compete against each other for business with other state enterprises.

INCOME AND PRODUCTIVITY

An important objective of the Hungarian reforms has been to improve the economic performance of workers and state enterprises. Previously, wages of workers in very profitable and well-managed enterprises have only marginally exceeded those of the workers in unprofitable enterprises. Wages and bonuses have been linked to the performance of state enterprises—the better the performance of the enterprise, the higher the wages and bonuses. More flexible wage standards have been introduced to reward efficient workers and punish the lazy. There has also been an increased reliance on private enterprise to improve economic performance, particularly in service areas. Any private firm can employ up to five workers. This has given rise to a new class of Hungarian entrepreneurs, some of whom have become quite wealthy. One example is Anton Rubik, who invented the

---

5. Consumer prices in Hungary and other communist countries are both heavily subsidized and taxed. But low prices encourage excessive consumption at the expense of supply.

6. *Further Developments of the Economic Control and Management System.* (Budapest: Ministry of Finance, 1985).

Rubik Cube, which is sold worldwide. In addition to making Rubik quite wealthy, sale of the cube abroad brings hard currency to the Hungarian economy.[7]

AN EVALUATION OF HUNGARIAN REFORMS

Hungarian reforms have moved in alternating directions. A broad sweep in 1968 that gave much freedom to state enterprises was followed by a period of retrenchment during the 1970s.[8] The pendulum swung back toward liberalization in the 1980s, with the breakup of large monopoly enterprises into smaller competing firms, the easing of regulations on the private and semiprivate sectors of the economy, and the freeing of prices on many consumer products. The reform program has had the support of Hungary's leader and Communist Party secretary, Janos Kadar, and much of the population. The Soviet Union and the other Eastern European countries have implemented only piecemeal reforms, which usually does not mesh with their centrally planned economies. In contrast, Hungary has attempted to reform its economy on a much broader scale. In essence, Hungary developed something of a market-socialist economic system while maintaining its political allegiance to the Soviet Union. Given the emphasis that the new Russian leader, Mikhail Gorbachev, is placing on revitalizing the Soviet economy, Hungary may enjoy more latitude to experiment. It can be regarded as a laboratory for economic experimentation.

7. Hard currency is currency that is convertible into other currencies in world markets. For example, the dollar is hard currency because it is convertible into pounds, francs, and other currencies, and is acceptable as some international medium of exchange. Hungarian currency is not convertible.

8. Paul Hare, Hugo Radice, and Nigel Swain, eds. *Hungary: A Decade of Economic Reform* (London: George Allen & Unwin, Ltd., 1982).

SUMMARY

Probably the most important difference between the capitalist and socialist countries is the role of centralized economic planning in resource allocation. Fundamental to the operation of centralized planning is the public ownership of the factors of production, which joins industrial, agricultural, and trading companies into a single economic unit. Since there is no meaningful competition between rival firms, there is no price competition. In turn, the profit motive is rendered unimportant as an automatic regulator, which is its role in a market economy. In the absence of the market price system, economic planning is necessary to make the complex of state enterprises function. To organize the uninterrupted operation of these enterprises, a full and exact account must be kept of the national requirements for particular products and of the channels through which they must be distributed.

The state exercises virtual monopolistic control over all economic resources. It owns and operates large-scale industries, mines, power plants, railways, shipping, and various communication media. It engages in farming on its own account through state farms, and it largely controls agriculture through collective farming. It has an exclusive monopoly of banking and foreign trade, and it controls the domestic channels of distribution in its role as manufacturer, farmer, merchant, shipper, and banker. In the field of labor relations, it is the sole employer of note and as such dominates bargaining between itself and the employees. Although trade unions are allowed, their function is purely subsidiary to the interest of the state, and strikes are illegal.

REVIEW QUESTIONS

1. Why is it difficult to fit the socialist countries into a common economic pattern?
2. Compare the role of the national budgets in the United States and the Soviet Union.
3. Discuss the role of profit in a centrally planned economic system.
4. Compare the process of income determination in a market economy and a planned economy.
5. What are the objectives of the Hungarian economic reforms?
6. What is a turnover tax? How is it used as a control mechanism?
7. What is the difference between medium-term and annual plans?
8. How are prices determined in a centrally planned economy?

C H A P T E R   1 2

AN INTRODUCTION
TO THE SOVIET UNION

The Soviet economy depends on economic planning rather than on a market system to make the basic economic decisions of what and how much is to be produced and to whom it is to be allocated. Interaction between buyers and sellers—which determines the prices of commodities, services, and the factors of production in a market economy such as the United States—is inoperative in the Soviet Union. Land and capital are owned by the state in the name of society and the state operates almost all lines of economic activity, so it has the ability to make comprehensive economic plans and see to it they are carried out.

The Soviet economy has entered into a difficult period, with problems of declining growth in output, serious inflationary pressure, slow technological progress, and accumulated deficiencies in housing and other public needs. Attempts to alleviate these problems usually encounter resistance from party ideologues and bureaucrats. Moreover, an imbalance in the economic system is created by an orientation toward military spending. Even though the Soviet Union is one of the richest countries in the world in terms of mineral resources, resource constraints, based in part on geographic impediments to transportation, limit the growth of the Soviet economy. The costs of obtaining and using natural resources have risen as high-grade, well-located resources have been depleted and less accessible supplies must be used. New deposits of oil have not been found and developed rapidly enough to offset declines in older fields.

In land area, the Soviet Union is larger than the United States and Canada combined. Its length from east to west is 7,000 miles; from north to south it is about 3,000 miles. From the standpoint of population, the Soviet Union is a little larger than the United States. Its population in 1980 was an estimated 262 million compared to 220 million for the United States. The populations of the two countries are similar because each consists of a melange of different racial and ethnic groups. The people of the Soviet Union can be categorized as Slavic or non-Slavic or as Russian or non-Russian. The Slavic group consists of Russians, Belorussians, and Ukrainians, and they are united by similar languages.[1] The non-Slavic group consists of Estonians, Lithuanians, Tatars, Armenians, Georgians, and others. The Russian population is limited primarily to the western, or European, part of the country.

The Soviet Union consists of 15 socialist republics. The largest is the Russian Soviet Federated Socialist Republic, which comprises 79 percent of the total area and around half of the population of the country. The second largest republic in terms of land area and population is the Ukrainian Soviet Socialist Republic. Within a particular republic, there also are autonomous republics and regions that reflect the ethnic diversity of the country.[2] For example, within the Russian Soviet Federated Republic is the autonomous Soviet Socialist Republic of Yakutia, which has a land area of more than a million square miles, but is very sparsely populated and far removed from Moscow. Its autonomy is largely a matter of administrative convenience. An example of an autonomous region is the Jewish Autonomous Region, which is in the Asiatic part of the Russian Soviet Federated Republic.

■ THE POLITICAL SYSTEM ■

Perhaps the most important characteristic of the political system of the Soviet Union is the interlocking relationship between the Communist Party and the administrative units of the government. Political and governmental power in the Soviet Union is completely in the hands of the Communist

---

1. There are three subdivisions of Slavs—eastern Slavs (Russians, Belorussians, and Ukrainians), western Slavs (Poles, Czechs, and Slovaks), and southern Slavs (Serbo-Croatians, Slovenes, and Bulgarians).

2. There are, in fact more than 170 different nationalities and 200 languages and dialects spoken in the Soviet Union.

Party. In other words, the Communist Party dominates the governmental administrative structure of the Soviet Union and has its members in practically all important offices and positions. Party policies are carried out by all governmental agencies and organizations.

ORGANIZATION OF THE GOVERNMENT

The governmental administrative apparatus of the Soviet Union is a multi-tiered arrangement, with control extending from Moscow down to the rural soviets (elected government councils). The current arrangement is essentially as follows.

TERRITORIAL ADMINISTRATION From a territorial administrative standpoint, the Soviet Union can be divided into several categories. First, there is the Soviet Union itself. As a federation of constituent republics, it has its own constitution. Then there are the 15 theoretically independent union republics that form the federation. Each republic has its own constitution, government, and party hierarchy. The republics are similar to American states, though they are generally larger in size. A distinctive feature of Soviet public administration is the fact that most of these republics were formed primarily on the basis of nationality. The federalist structure of the Soviet Union can be regarded as a concession to the non-Slavic peoples' nationalistic sentiments. However, administrative safeguards modify the formal federalism of the constitutional structure of the Soviet Union. The Communist Party itself is a single, unified organization that exerts a countervailing centralism to ethnic federalism. Moreover, the highest administrative organs of the country are centralized in Moscow.

NATIONAL POLICY ADMINISTRATION The state apparatus through which national policy is administered can be divided into two pyramidal hierarchies—the Council of Ministers of the U.S.S.R. and the Supreme Soviet of the U.S.S.R. The Council of Ministers is the executive branch of the Soviet government; the Supreme Soviet, the legislative branch.

THE COUNCIL OF MINISTERS The Council of Ministers is responsible for the development of economic policy and the enforcement of laws passed by the Supreme Soviet. It is also responsible for exercising general guidance in the sphere of relations with other countries and for directing the general organization of the country's armed forces. It is elected by and is responsible to the Supreme Soviet. The Presidium of the Council of Ministers, which consists of a chairperson and six deputies, one of whom represents each of six committees mentioned below, is the policy-making body. There is also a Council of Ministers in each of the 15 constituent republics.

To assist the Council of Ministers in coordinating economic activity, there are a number of committees whose responsibilities are to provide the information needed for decision making. One important committee is the State Planning Committee (Gosplan), which is responsible for the development of the national economic plans. There are five other committees— the All-Unions Agricultural Committee, the State Committee for Science and Technology, the State Committee for Material and Technical Supply, the State Committee for Construction, and the CEMA Commission.[3]

THE SUPREME SOVIET The Supreme Soviet of the U.S.S.R. is the most important legislative branch in the Soviet Union. It is formally a bicameral legislature with coequal houses—the Soviet of the Union, whose deputies are elected on the basis of population, and the Soviet of Nationalities, whose deputies are elected on a territorial basis by nationality. The responsibilities of the Supreme Soviet are stronger in theory than in practice. In terms of real decision making it has little power; it passes the bills that are submitted to it. A law is considered enacted if passed by both houses by a simple majority vote in each. There are standing committees for each house in areas of credentials, plans and budgets, industry, transportation and communication, building and the building materials industry, agriculture, public health and social security, public education, science and culture, trade and public services, legislative proposals, and foreign affairs.

THE COMMUNIST PARTY

Control of the government machinery in the Soviet Union is in the hands of the Communist Party, which is the only political party permitted in the country.[4] Although membership in the Communist Party is limited to a small minority of the total population of the country (16 million in 1980), it maintains firm control over every aspect of Soviet life through its well-organized and disciplined organization. Communists hold key positions in all institutions and enterprises in Soviet society. In factories, offices, schools, and villages, primary units called *cells* operate. Cells consist of at least three party members and are responsible for the recruitment of mem-

---

3. The Council for Mutual Economic Assistance (CEMA) is the consultative organ that coordinates the domestic and foreign economic policies of the U.S.S.R. and the European satellite countries.

4. The Communists argue that political parties are class organs and that, if several parties were permitted, there would be a return to class antagonisms.

bers and for the selection of delegates to the local party conferences, which in turn select delegates to conferences covering a somewhat wider area, and this process continues until finally, in district and regional congresses, delegates are selected to the National Party Congress, which is supposed to be the highest body of party authority. Power actually rests in the Central Committee, the Politboro, the Secretariat, and the various staff departments of the central apparatus in Moscow.

THE CENTRAL COMMITTEE   The Central Committee is elected at the meeting of the National Party Congress. It is composed of the Politburo, Secretariat, Party Control Committee, and a number of individual sections including those called Cadres Abroad, Economic Relations with Socialist Countries, International Affairs, and Relations with Bloc Parties. The Central Committee has no effective role as a decision maker; that function is performed by the Politburo. It does, however, provide a forum for the elaboration of the major policies of the Communist Party and its top leaders. It is also responsible for the dissemination of the aims and objectives of the leaders to officials in various departments in the central apparatus and also downward to the various party committees in the republics and lower levels.

THE POLITBURO   The *Politburo* is the supreme instrument of political power in the Soviet Union. When the Central Committee is not in session, the Politburo is responsible for all phases of national life—foreign policy, domestic economic policy, and military policy.[5] There are 13 full voting members who exercise the prerogatives and responsibilities of national policy making and nine candidate members who participate in varying degrees in the policy-making process. Most members of the Politburo have collateral duties, meaning that they serve in other capacities in addition to their positions as party administrators.

THE SECRETARIAT   The Secretariat of the Central Committee ranks second only to the Politburo from the standpoint of decision making. Unlike the Politburo, which has no administrative responsibility, the Secretariat is responsible for the administration of the Communist Party. It consists of 11 members elected by the Central Committee in plenary session—a formality, since the slate is drawn up in advance by top party leaders. There

---

5. The Politburo of the Central Committee should not be confused with the Presidium of the Council of Ministers of the U.S.S.R. and the Presidium of the Supreme Soviet. The last two are involved in the operations of the government, as opposed to the Politburo, which is involved in the operation of the Communist Party.

is an overlap between the Secretariat and the Politburo in the sense that several members serve on each organization. The Secretariat is responsible for providing the leadership for the Communist Party organization, which consists of a hierarchy of subordinate secretariats at the republic and lower administrative levels. This hierarchy is responsible for insuring the implementation of state economic policy by the various governmental organs. It is also responsible for the allocation and mobilization of personnel and other resources of the Communist Party.

PARTY AND GOVERNMENT STRUCTURE   Party and government structure parallel each other. For example, at the national or U.S.S.R. level, the basic Party administrative units are the Central Committee, Politburo, and Secretariat; the basic governmental administrative units are the Supreme Soviet and the Council of Ministers with their respective presidiums. The leaders of the party are members of both units. At the union republic level, the Party administrative unit consists of the Central Committee and Secretariat, and the governmental administrative unit consists of the Republic Supreme Soviet and Council of Ministers. This interlocking relationship continues down to the rural soviet level. Although inefficiency may result at lower administrative levels because of communication problems, there is no question that the interconnection of Party and government, and Party domination of the government, confer on Soviet public administration exceptional unity of control and uniformity of ideological perspective.[6]

NOMENKLATURA SYSTEM

There is a famous quotation from George Orwell's classic *Animal Farm:* "All animals are equal, but some are more equal than others."[7] Supposedly workers are "first among equals" in the Soviet Union and the other socialist countries, but this is hardly the case. To the contrary, there is an ideological imperative that is simply that party leaders have to maintain a monopoly of political, ideological, and economic power. This is done through the *nomenklatura system.* Nomenklatura is simply patronage designed to insure party loyalty. Party leaders determine the staffing of government and

---

6. This does not mean, however, that party and government organs function as two perfectly synchronized parts of a smoothly working administrative machine. To the contrary, there are cliques within the party and the governmental bureaucracies that often cause power rivalries or power disputes. These cliques have a vested interest in maintaining the status quo.

7. George Orwell, *Animal Farm* (New York: Harcourt Brace Inc., 1954), Chap. 10.

industrial posts beneath them. In turn, those in subordinate positions exercise the same influence over those beneath them. This ensures control from the top down. Promotions and rewards are more likely attached to party membership and one's position within the nomenklatura system than to merit.[8]

Nomenklatura gives a person both power and privileges. A member of the system is able to enjoy the best things in life, to travel to Paris and New York. He or she is able to shop at special state-run stores intended for foreigners with hard currency. These stores exist not only in the Soviet Union but in other Eastern European countries as well; they are off-limits to ordinary citizens.[9] The stores contain many luxury items as well as basic consumer goods that are usually in short supply in the regular state stores. Membership in the nomenklatura elite also provides access to larger apartments and cars. Those who are higher up in the nomenklatura system have villas and summer homes. Privileges also extend to the family members. Admission to the best colleges and opportunities for better-paying jobs are examples. Even after retirement, a member of the system gets a special pension and retains the privilege of shopping at the special stores.[10]

■ THE ECONOMIC SYSTEM ■

The leaders of the Soviet Union are committed to the view that the future of the country depends upon the Soviet economy's productivity and efficiency. Emphasis is placed on the organization of production. The organization is based on two fundamental characteristics of the Soviet economy: (1) the allocation of resources is accomplished by administrative decision rather than by a market mechanism; and (2) resource allocation is governed by a priority system that over the years has given preference to capital goods and military and scientific development over consumer goods. Because of these characteristics, consumer sovereignty, which exists when the production of goods is determined by the individual decisions made in the marketplace by millions of consumers, cannot function in the Soviet Union. Through its control over economic resources, the state can manipulate the share of gross national product allocated to consumption;

8. This is also likely to hold true in the United States. Both major political parties rely on political patronage to reward the party faithful, with little attention paid to merit. However, political parties can be voted out in the United States. This is not true in the Soviet Union.

9. These stores are also called *dollar stores*. Almost anything can be bought there. The author once bought a box of Kellogg Cornflakes at a dollar store in Warsaw.

10. Michael Voslensky, *Nomenklatura* (New York: Doubleday & Co. Inc., 1984).

through its investment policies, the state can control the amount of inputs for those sectors of the economy that supply the consumer. Nevertheless, in recent years Soviet leaders have heeded to some extent the expectations of the consumer for a higher living standard.

ECONOMIC PLANNING

The distinctive feature of the economic system of the Soviet Union is that it operates on the basis of comprehensive economic planning. Fundamental to centralized economic planning is public ownership of the factors of production. Public ownership has joined the multitude of industrial, agricultural, and trading enterprises together in a single economic unit. Since there is no competition among rival firms, there is no meaningful price competition. This, in turn, renders the profit motive impotent as an automatic economic regulator, which is its role in the market system of a capitalistic country. So in the absence of the market system, economic planning is necessary to make the complex of Soviet enterprises function. To organize the uninterrupted operation of these enterprises, full and exact account must be taken of the national requirements and distribution channels for their particular products. Conversely, every enterprise must be constantly supplied with raw materials, fuel, plant and equipment, and trained workers, the amounts of which must also be commensurate with national needs.

An important principle of economic planning in the Soviet Union is the priority given to the development of industries that will contribute the most to the attainment of national economic and political goals. Economic plans provide for the maximum possible rate of development of targeted areas of the economy through priorities in investment, materials, labor, and financial resources. It is assumed that expansion of certain key industries, such as the chemical, oil, gas, and power industries, makes it possible to increase the overall rate of growth in industrial and agricultural production. Economic planning also has political as well as economic overtones in that priorities in past and current plans have been given to industries that make the Soviet Union strong from a military standpoint.

It is necessary to stress the fact that there is a difference between formal and actual economic plans. In practice plans are changed often and some plans reflect simply aspirations. Targets are constantly revised to reflect changing economic conditions. As the socialist countries enter higher stages of economic development, the number of alternative uses for resources and the complexity of economic processes have greatly increased. Consequently, the negative results of errors have multiplied, threatening the economies with greater waste and dislocation than before. So the longer the planning period, the less precision can be introduced in terms of plan targets. What happens then is that planning, particularly for periods of five years or longer, is continuous; the plans are constantly supplemented and extended in the process of their implementation.

TYPES OF PLANS   The economic plans differ in their functional character. There are physical output plans, which involve production, distribution, and investment goals; and financial plans, which are derivatives of the physical output plans. Then, too, plans differ in terms of time. Long-range plans extend for 15 to 20 years. These plans usually deal with a particular aspect of the economy, such as electrification. Medium-term plans, which cover a period of 5 to 7 years, develop targets or goals to be accomplished during this time. There are also annual plans involving production plans to be followed by Soviet enterprises and other organizational units during the year.

The annual plan can be considered an operational plan. Annual plans can be broken down further into quarterly or monthly periods. All of these plans are interconnected and related, and it is important and necessary for planning agencies to ensure their unification in order to establish a proper relationship between production and consumption and between national requirements and resources. In terms of a frame of reference for the presentation of the methodology of Soviet planning, economic planning refers primarily to physical planning, which involves product output and distribution, labor force utilization, and investment, and which is developed annually. Table 12-1 illustrates an annual physical output plan.

The organization of economic planning can be divided into the following stages.

1. Drafting of the plan in conformity with the objectives of the Communist Party and the Soviet government;

2. Endorsement of the plan by relevant government administrative units;

3. Organization and control over the execution of the approved plan.

Planning in the Soviet Union is directed by the Supreme Soviet and the Council of Ministers. The actual plans are drawn up by planning bodies that may be divided into three groups—state planning bodies, ministries and departments, and the planning bodies of enterprises and organizations. The state planning bodies are the State Planning Committee (Gos-

TABLE 12-1   1985 PHYSICAL OUTPUT PLAN FOR THE SOVIET UNION

	Units of Output
Electricity (billions of kilowatts)	1,540
Petroleum (millions of tons)	628
Coal (millions of tons)	726
Steel pipes (millions of tons)	20
Cement (millions of tons)	132
Robots (thousands)	14
Meat (millions of tons)	9
Butter (millions of tons)	1
Milk (millions of tons)	29
New railroad lines (kilometers)	700
New hard-surfaced roads (thousands of kilometers)	12
Rolled ferrous metals (millions of tons)	109
New hospital beds (thousands)	60
Irrigated land (thousands of hectares)	663
Drained land (thousands of hectares)	695
Mineral fertilizers (millions of tons)	48

Source: John L. Scherer, *U.S.S.R. Facts and Figures Annual 1985* (Gulf Breeze, Fla.: Academic International Press, 1985), p. 138.

plan), which is a part of the Council of Ministers of the U.S.S.R.; the state planning committees of the union and autonomous republics; regional planning committees; and district and city planning committees. These committees draw upon the economic and cultural plans for the country as a whole and for individual republics, regions, and districts. In the ministries and departments, plans are compiled by planning boards and sections; at the enterprise level they are the responsibility of planning departments.

GOSPLAN Gosplan is the agency that translates broad policy decisions made by the Council of Ministers and the Central Committee of the Communist Party into concrete programs. It is responsible for working out national economic plans of all kinds and for presenting them for review by the Council of Ministers. It is also responsible for the supervision of the plans. Gosplan is organized into various economic planning sections for the branches of the national economy. One section is responsible for sector planning and is divided into the following sectors: machine building, transportation and communications, consumer goods, agriculture, heavy industry, and electrification. Another section is responsible for the supply and distribution of materials, such as coal and metal products. This section monitors the supply of key materials.

Gosplan is also responsible for setting wholesale prices for industrial and agricultural products and for setting retail prices. Through an affiliated institute, the Scientific Research Institute of Economics, it also plays a leading role in theoretical economic research.[11] To check on Gosplan and its activities, various departments within the Secretariat of the Communist Party serve as watchdogs.

Since the Soviet economic plan covers the entire economy, it is necessary to have planning units extending down to the lowest administrative units of government. Below the national Gosplan, and subordinate to it in terms of planning, are the republic Gosplans. These Gosplans are responsible for the preparation of plans for all of the industries under republic supervision. They are also responsible for developing recommendations pertaining to the production plans of all enterprises located within their respective republics. There are also the Gosplans of the autonomous republics and regions. They are responsible for drawing up plans for industry and transportation, agriculture, social and cultural development, and regional housing and public construction. They base their summary plans on plans developed at the rural soviet levels. The planning bodies at the autonomous region and republic levels draft the plans for enterprises under their direct control and check to see that they are implemented. In addition, industrial enterprises, state farms, and transport and trading enterprises have planning departments. Their activities are guided by targets set forth in the national plan.

GOSSNAB Gossnab is the State Committee on Material-Technical Supplies and is responsible for handling the distribution end of the plan. It is supposed to tie customers to suppliers at both the republic and local levels. Subject to general guidelines and within the limits set by central allocation, the local units of Gossnab make detailed arrangements for supplies, sometimes from warehouses they administer. Managers of enterprises are supposed to negotiate for supplies with the local Gossnab unit. Gossnab has 22 central distribution sections and each has the following responsibilities:

1. Identify special supply needs and assign priorities to such needs.

---

11. Alec Nove, *The Soviet Economic System*, 2d ed. (London: George Allen & Unwin, Ltd., 1981), pp. 37-40.

2. Make the most economical assignment of each supplier to a group of users.

3. Decide on long-term direct supplier-user contacts among plants or enterprises.

4. Regulate the flow of products according to assigned priorities in the plan.[12]

DRAFTING OF THE PLAN   Control figures are drawn up by Gosplan before the five-year plan is drafted. These figures determine the principal trends and general scale of economic development planned for the duration of the plan. They cover the volume and distribution of national income, the overall volume of capital investment and industrial production in the more important branches of industry, the volume of output and state purchases of farm produce, the volume of retail trade, expected increases in labor productivity, and the monetary income of the population. These control figures are based on the economy's achievements in preceding time periods and on estimates of future labor availability and progress in technology and labor productivity.

STAGES OF THE PLANNING CYCLE   When the plan is designed, it is a draft plan that outlines the basic economic development tasks for the plan period. This drafting phase transforms government and party objectives into numerical targets that determine the amount of resources to be allocated for specific purposes.

When the draft plan has been completed, it is sent for approval to the Central Committee of the Communist Party and to the Council of Ministers of the U.S.S.R. After the plan is approved, it is broken down by sections and sent to the appropriate national ministry or department for consideration. It is also sent to the Gosplans of the republics, which are supposed to prepare plans for the economic programs of their particular republics and ministries. The draft plan is then sent to the regional and local planning commissions and to enterprises. The purpose of this dissemination is to provide information that can be used as a basis for plan formulation at the enterprise level and at the various local, regional, and national administrative levels. An enterprise, for example, would receive information as to the kinds, quantities, and qualities of goods it was expected to produce, quantities and kinds of labor, power, materials, and capital

12. Sumer C. Aggerwal, "Managing Material Shortages: The Russian Way," *Columbia Journal of World Business* (Fall 1980), pp. 26-37.

goods that would be supplied to it, estimates of the productivity the workers should achieve, and estimates of the workers' incomes and living standards.

After the control figures have been made available to the various economic units and the lower echelons of government, there is a plan counter-design that starts with the formulation of plans by industrial and trade enterprises, state farms, and other local economic units. These plans cover all phases of their operations in great detail. For example, plans of enterprises set forth what they are to make, in what quantities, and by what combinations of labor and capital. These are target plans that are supposed to serve as a framework for annual operating plans. The plans then travel upward to their eventual integration in the national plan by Gosplan. At each administrative stage the plans cumulate into a larger whole. From the primary producing units—industrial, agricultural, and trading enterprises—the plans move through local soviets and the various ministries and planning agencies at the union republic and national level. Gosplan has the final responsibility for the preparation of the overall national plan. The problem is reconciling all draft plans into one national plan.

The process of reconciliation is the third stage of the planning cycle. Gosplan must adjust Politburo objectives from above with the aggregation of plans from below. It is also at this stage that various financial plans are developed; they represent a counterpart to the main economic plan, which is expressed in physical terms. The major financial plans are the state budget and the cash plan and credit plan of Gosbank. Each plan exercises important control functions that will be discussed later in the chapter.[13] The financial plans are approved and developed by the Ministry of Finance and Gosbank and are reviewed by Gosplan in its preparation of the national economic plan. When the plan is prepared, it is sent to the Council of Ministers and the Central Committee of the Communist Party for ratification. Finally, the plan, with its tasks for each administrative and economic level, is passed down the line until it reaches the enterprise. The whole Soviet planning process is complex, for there has to be a flow of operational directives to the thousands of operating enterprises. Plans for various sectors must be coordinated with those of other sectors.

THE USE OF MATERIAL BALANCES   The basic method of Soviet economic planning has involved the use of material balances. These bal-

---

13. There is also the consolidated financial plan, which includes the state budget and the cash and credit plans of Gosbank. In addition, it includes the profits of all state enterprises and allowances for depreciation, increases in savings bank deposits, and other financial resources.

ances are usually presented in physical terms and represent an intended relationship between supplies and their allocation for particular commodities. Material balances are drawn up for all important types of industrial and agricultural products. An example of the use of material balances is presented in Table 12-2.

However, given the complexities of the production and distribution process, the material balance method has become cumbersome. Thus it has been replaced to some extent with input–output analysis, which consists of working out a matrix of flows. These flows represent an array of relationships between economic sectors. The economy is divided into many sectors, each supposed to achieve an annual output of a given quantity. Each sector uses a certain portion of its annual output and the remaining portion is available to be used as inputs for other sectors. That part of production over and above that used in the economic sector during the year constitutes net material production. This amount is used for production of final goods for consumption and capital investment.

Economic planning has to reconcile a number of flows, including production, consumption, and saving; the use of labor resources; the distribution of national income; and personal money income and expenditure. The total amount of wages to be paid and the production necessary to support the wages depend on the division of national income between savings and consumption, and further, of consumption between social consumption and wages. This leads to the problem of relating the total flow of wages to the total value of consumer goods and services. The maintenance of balance between incomes from work and the resources allocated to personal consumption is a part of distribution policy and especially of wage planning. As prices of consumer goods and services may change, this also involves the problem of maintenance of the purchasing power of wages and the relationship between nominal and real wages.

TABLE 12-2　MATERIAL BALANCES FOR A SPECIFIC COMMODITY

Resources	Distribution
Stocks at the start of the planning period	Production and operating needs
Production	Capital construction
Imports	Replenishment of state stocks
Mobilization of internal resources	Exports
	Other needs
	Stocks at the end of the planning period
Total	Total

CONDITIONS FOR PLANNING   The essential requirements for centralized planning are present in the Soviet Union. The state is in full control of the land, factories, transportation, and raw materials necessary for the production of all commodities. It controls the quality and quantity of the labor force, which enables it to supply the economy with the necessary labor to fill planned targets. Through control of money and credit, it finances construction and the operation of enterprises in accordance with the financial plan. The state, through Gosplan, Gosbank, and other organizations, can maintain control over the plan's execution. Gosplan in particular has the responsibility for checking on the progress made in implementing the plan. This is done through the hierarchy of planning offices that exist from the top to the lower administrative levels of government. The Communist Party also performs a control function in that its members hold positions of authority in all enterprises; they can supervise the implementation of the plan at the enterprise level.

LIMITATIONS OF PLANNING   Nevertheless, the whole process of planning has its limitations. The plan may estimate that workers, given certain supplies of machinery, land, equipment, materials, and energy, will turn out a specific number of units of product of definite quality in a given period, but the results of the workers' activities may be anything but those which were expected. There is also a certain lack of coordination and inefficiency in planning that can be attributed to the comprehensive bureaucratic structure. Enterprises are separated from the decision-making agencies at the top by a number of intermediary agencies. This means that they are separated from other enterprises by agencies that must check purchase and sales requests and disburse funds. Another defect in planning is that the setting of general production norms or indexes fails to take differences in the characteristics of various enterprises. Also, over the years since planning was developed, the Soviet Union has grown into a complex and modern industrial nation with increasingly sophisticated production techniques and greater demands for quality specifications of materials. This, in itself, has complicated the central planning process and has caused a need for more detailed microplanning.

PUBLIC FINANCE

The operation of any modern state requires the collection of large sums of money to finance public services and pay for the general administrative expenses of government. This is as true of the Soviet Union as it is of any capitalistic country. However, there are great differences in the ways in which the two forms of economic organization acquire and dispose of their revenues. Both the Soviet and Western capitalistic governments necessarily devote substantial portions of their national incomes to general administrative expenses, to war and defense measures, and to various forms of social services, but in the case of the Soviet state, additional sums must also be made available to finance industry operation.

THE SOVIET STATE BUDGET   In the Soviet Union the national budget is of paramount importance because it provides for the accumulation and distribution of so much of the national income. The national budget, or Soviet State Budget, is a consolidated budget that provides for the revenues and expenditures of the national, republic, and local units of government. It is also closely related in terms of revenues and expenditures to the national economic plan. It performs an important allocative function in that it is the major instrument for financing many types of investment and for controlling the use of investment in accordance with planning objectives. The budget is also instrumental in decisions to divide the national product between consumption and investment.

The Soviet State Budget is prepared annually by the Ministry of Finance. It includes the all-union or central budget, the budgets of the autonomous republics, and the budgets of regional, urban, and rural administrative entities. Republic and local authorities prepare their own budgets in conformation with the objectives of the national economic plan.[14] When the tentative budgets are prepared, they are transmitted upward—local government budgets to their respective republics' ministry of finance and republic budgets to the Union Ministry of Finance—and coordinated at each step with the national economic plan. When the total budget—national, republic, and local—is integrated, it is sent by the Ministry of Finance to the Council of Ministers of the Soviet Union for approval. After the Council of Ministers has made changes and recommendations, the Soviet State Budget is then presented by the Ministry of Finance to the Supreme Soviet for final approval before it becomes law and is published. The budget often provides an indication of Soviet economic policies for the coming year, for it is a part of the country's overall economic and financial plan and reflects yearly priorities for resource allocation.

GOVERNMENT REVENUES   Table 12-3 presents the principal sources of revenue for the state budget. Most of the revenue of the budget is derived

---

14. Only the principal headings or expenditures in the budgets require ultimate approval at the top of the budgetary hierarchy. Local and republic governments have some autonomy concerning expenditures for specific items such as fire protection and repairs of drains.

TABLE 12-3   PLANNED REVENUES
OF THE SOVIET STATE BUDGET FOR 1985
(billions of dollars)

Social Sector		$612.0
Turnover tax	$175.1	
Payments from profits	171.7	
Income tax from collective farmers	2.0	
Other receipts, including social insurance taxes	263.2	
Private Sector		53.5
State income taxes	$51.5	
Other receipts	2.0	
Total Revenues		$665.5

Source: John L. Scherer, U.S.S.R. Facts and Figures Annual 1985 (Gulf Breeze, Fla.: Academic International Press, 1985), p. 148.

from national output rather than from direct taxes on the incomes of individuals. The two most important sources of revenue are the turnover tax and deductions from the profits of state-owned enterprises. Revenue is obtained by setting the prices of goods at levels higher than the cost of production and appropriating the difference.

THE TURNOVER TAX   The turnover tax is the largest single source of revenue in the state budget. It was established in 1930 when Soviet industry, unable to support itself, needed additional revenue for further expansion. The tax is a flexible and varied portion of the price and is delivered directly to the state budget in accordance with sales of goods on which the tax is levied. The tax is collected by wholesale distributing organizations, individual enterprises, and procurement organizations dealing with consumer goods and foodstuffs. The burden of the turnover tax falls ultimately on the Russian consumer, so it represents a part of the flow of funds between the state and households.

The Soviet turnover tax performs several important economic functions. In addition to being a principal source of revenue for the government, it also absorbs the excess purchasing power of consumers. The national production plans provide that a given amount of goods be made available to consumers annually. On the other hand, in order to maintain incentives and partly because of errors in planning, consumers may receive more purchasing power than can be absorbed by the goods made available to them at controlled prices. This excess of purchasing power is siphoned off by the turnover tax, which has the impact of an excise or sales tax as it is applied primarily to consumer goods. It is not a fixed-rate tax, but rather a tax where the desired yield determines the rate. It is varied in response to particular supply and demand conditions. Since the turnover tax is tied to output and is collected either directly at factories or at wholesale distribution outlets, it guarantees a steady flow of funds to the government and is easy to collect and inexpensive to administer. Moreover, it is a flexible device for establishing equilibrium prices on the basis of the level of output of consumer goods and disposable income.

PAYMENTS FROM PROFITS   Another important source of revenue in the state budget is payment from profits of state-owned enterprises and organizations. In fact, the turnover tax and payments from profits account for more than one-half of the total government revenues. In 1985, for example, the turnover tax accounted for $175.1 billion and payments from profits accounted for $171.7 billion out of planned total budget revenues of $665.5 billion. Thus, most of the Soviet tax burden can be seen as equal to the total difference between production cost and final sales prices of all goods and services.

Payments from profits are paid on actual rather than planned profits of enterprises, and payments vary from industry to industry. Most state enterprises operate on the basis of what is called *khozraschet financing*. This means that they sell their products for money and use the resulting proceeds to finance normal operating expenses. However, the typical enterprise receives extensive support, including the major share of all capital investment, from the state budget. The rate for a particular enterprise is fixed on the basis of its financial plan for the year. Each enterprise has the right to retain part of its profits for such purposes as expanding its fixed and financial capital, and the government takes this into consideration. Nevertheless, the amount of profits returned to the state is high; it can be as much as 80 percent of total profits.

Retained profits can be used to finance an enterprise's material incentives fund, which is a part of the new economic reforms that have taken place in the Soviet Union. Their purpose is to provide an incentive system of bonuses to workers as a reward for increased productivity. Retained earnings are also used to finance an enterprise's social-cultural and production development funds. The former is used to support various services provided to workers by an enterprise, and the latter provides a source of revenue for the expansion of fixed capital. Depreciation deductions also provide revenue for the same purpose.

SOCIAL INSURANCE TAXES   The remainder of the revenues obtained from the operation of the national economy comes from social insurance taxes paid by enterprises, taxes levied on organizations such as collective farms, and income taxes levied on individuals. The social insurance taxes are levied as a percentage of wages and salaries and vary from industry to industry. The revenue is paid into a state social insurance budget administered by the trade unions. This budget is consolidated with the state budget, and revenue is transferred to republic and local budgets.

PERSONAL INCOME TAX   Direct taxes on the population are relatively unimportant in the Soviet revenue system. The personal income tax accounted for only 7.8 percent of the planned total state budget revenues in 1985. The tax is progressive in nature; in 1983 it ranged from a minimum of 0.35 percent to a maximum of 13 percent of monthly earnings. It is withheld by the enterpises and paid to the Ministry of Finance. The income tax is differentiated between economic groups, with certain groups, such as workers and salaried employees, paying a lower tax than others, such as doctors, lawyers, and artisans with incomes from private practice. The personal income tax was supposed to have been abolished in the Soviet Union by 1965; however this has not yet occurred. In 1983, the amount of income exempted from the tax was 70 rubles ($118) a month.

There is a rural counterpart to the income tax, a so-called agricultural tax levied on farmers who earn an income from their private plots of land. Its purpose is to discourage farmers from spending too much time on their own land at the expense of their work on collective farms.[15] The tax rate is progressive and is based on the quantity of land in use rather than on the return on the land. As a source of revenue, the agricultural tax is of little importance, but it has a control function of regulating work.

GOVERNMENT EXPENDITURES   Expenditures of the state are presented in Table 12-4. There are four main categories of expenditures—expenditures to finance the national economy, social-cultural measures, national defense, and administration. Expenditures for financing the national economy and social-cultural expenditures account for almost 90 percent of total outlays.

FINANCING THE NATIONAL ECONOMY   Expenditures to finance the national economy accounted for approximately 56 percent of planned total budget expenditures in 1985. These expenditures include allocations to enterprises for capital investments and financial capital. Capital goods and construction industries are the major recipients of budget funds for investment purposes, for the government concentrates on growth-inducing

15. If farmers fail to work the stipulated minimum number of labor-days or workdays on the collective farms, the agricultural tax can be increased by as much as 50 percent.

TABLE 12-4   PLANNED EXPENDITURES OF THE SOVIET STATE BUDGET FOR 1985
(billions of dollars)

Financing the national economy		$377.4
Social-cultural measures		210.0
Education, science, and culture	$84.3	
Health and physical culture	29.0	
Social security and social insurance	98.0	
Defense		33.3
Administration		5.1
Residual[1]		39.1
Total expenditures		$664.9
Budget surplus		$ 0.5

[1]This includes such items as budget allocations for increasing credit resources of long-term investment banks.

Source: John L. Scherer, *U.S.S.R. Facts and Figures Annual 1985* (Gulf Breeze, Fla.: Academic International Press, 1985), p. 148.

investment in areas that constitute the base of economic power. Appropriations from the state budget are used to finance the construction of transportation facilities, investment in state farms, and housing construction. State farms are government-owned and -operated and are a major recipient of budgetary funds. Housing construction also enjoys a high priority in terms of allocation of bugetary funds because there is an acute housing shortage in the Soviet Union, particularly in the larger cities. Funds are allocated to housing construction in two ways: to construction enterprises for building apartments and other dwellings and to individual home builders in the form of credits.

The state budget redistributes income within the economy. Payments from profits represent a withdrawal of income from the economy, but the funds reenter the economy through the budget as expenditures used to finance capital investment, increases in financial capital, and housing. The turnover tax can also be considered a device used to reallocate resources from consumption to investment.

SOCIAL AND CULTURAL MEASURES   Expenditures for social and cultural measures, including education and training, public health, physical culture, and social insurance benefits, accounted for 32 percent of total expenditures in the 1985 planned state budget. A wide variety of social services are financed under the three subcategories of social and cultural measures—education, science, and culture; health and physical culture; and social welfare measures.

Expenditures on education, science, and culture include building and maintaining schools, paying teacher's salaries, and providing financial support for students. Expenditures for science include the support of scientific research. Certain defense expenditures are included under this category. Expenditures on culture include support for museums, expositions, and the performing arts. Other expenditures that are financed under education, science, and culture include the costs of disseminating Soviet propaganda throughout the world.

The second subcategory of social and cultural expenditures includes spending on health and physical culture. Health expenditures cover outlays for medical and hospital facilities, training medical personnel, and medical research. Physical culture expenditures support athletic programs that are carried on throughout the Soviet Union. Unlike the United States, the Soviet Union subsidizes sports activities and provides special support for its better athletes. In fact, success in sports, particularly in the Olympic Games, is of prime value to the Soviet Union from the standpoint of propaganda. Special sports schools are maintained throughout the Soviet Union and its Eastern European satellites, particularly the German Democratic Republic (East Germany).

The third subcategory, social security and social insurance, represents expenditures for old-age and disability pensions, sickness and maternity benefits, and family allowances. The retirement age is 60 for male industrial workers with 25 years or more of work experience and 55 years for women workers with at least 10 years of work experience. Sickness and maternity benefits are also payable to all persons under the Soviet social insurance program. Paid vacations cover 15 working days as a minimum. Pensions are also paid to Russian workers, including those on collective farms, who become disabled as a result of work injuries. Temporary disability benefits are paid from the first day of injury until recovery. Finally, family allowances are paid to families with two or more children, and there is an income supplement for those whose per capita income falls below 50 rubles a month.

NATIONAL DEFENSE   Outlays for national defense account for about 5 percent of planned total budget expenditures in 1985. However, the amount of $33.3 billion understates the amount that will actually be spent for defense-related activities because a substantial proportion of military–space research is carried out under expenditures for science. These expenditures include outlays for research and development for complex military equipment such as aircraft and missiles and for nuclear energy and space activities. The general defense category includes monetary and material allowances for armed forces personnel, payment for supplies and repair of combat equipment, maintenance of military institutions and schools, and military construction. When general defense expenditures are added to outlays for scientific research related directly or indirectly to national defense, total defense expenditures have been about 20 percent of the state budget and around 14 to 18 percent of Soviet gross national product.[16]

Soviet defense expenditures have placed a burden on the economy. For one thing, the best human and material resources are channeled into defense-related activities. The huge amounts of human and material resources claimed by the military and space establishment have been particularly detrimental to agriculture. Outside of defense activities, the economy has generally been inefficient. With a labor force 45 percent larger and about equal real capital investment, the Soviet Union provides its population with less than half the goods and services available in the United States. The resources foregone for defense could have resulted in a higher standard of living for the Soviet consumer. The most apparent trade-off has been between defense weapons and producer durable goods, with decreases in the latter resulting in a smaller capital stock, one of the primary ingredients in the growth process. So it can be argued that Soviet defense expenditures have had an adverse effect on the country's economic growth rate.[17]

ADMINISTRATION   Expenditures for administration is the final major category of expenditures. It includes financing for local and central government agencies including planning and financial bodies, ministries, government departments, and the courts and judicial organs. The Soviet state budget covers a scope of activities that is much broader than equivalent activities financed in the budgets of capitalistic governments. The state budget covers the planned expenditures for all of the national, regional, and local Soviet governments.

MONEY AND BANKING

Money plays a subordinate role in the Soviet economy. To some extent this reflects the traditional Marxist view of money, which largely represented a

16. Central Intelligence Agency, National Foreign Assessment Center, *Handbook of Economic Statistics* (Washington: USGPO, 1985), p. 64.

17. Henry F. Becker, "Soviet Power and Intentions: Military-Economic Choices," *Soviet Economy in a Time of Change* (Washington: Joint Economic Committee, 1979), pp. 341-45.

reaction against capitalism, where money reaches its peak of development and influence. Moreover, primary reliance on planning is in real terms; investment funds are channeled through the state budget rather than through financial markets. As long as plan balancing is done in physical terms, there is little need for prices in planning. Since prices are generally fixed, money values rarely indicate the value of goods in terms of real cost, and are, therefore, an uncertain guide to investment decisions. Money also does not provide automatic access to goods in the capital investment market. First, there must be authorization for the goods to be produced, second, in addition to money, there must be plan authorization to acquire the goods. The Gosbank, acting as the agent of the planning authorities, allocates credit to enterprises in conformation with the plan.

This is not to say, however, that money is of no importance. Soviet money has many of the same functions as money in a market system. Within and outside the state sector, money serves as a unit of account; that is, all goods and services that are bought and sold are valued in monetary units. Money also functions as a medium of exchange in the Soviet Union in that wages and salaries are paid in terms of currency, and receivers of money can use it to purchase goods and services. However, the ownership of money does not give individuals command over the allocation of resources as it does under a market system, for resource allocation is determined by the national plan and not by the price system. Economic reforms, even to the limited extent they have been implemented, imply a more important role for money, particularly in the area of pricing.

Similar to the control over other sectors of the Soviet economy, there is a plan to control the monetary aspects—the financial plan—that parallels and is coordinated with the production and distribution plans for each period of time. The three essential components of the financial plan are the following: the state budget, which is responsible for resource allocation between consumption and investment; the credit plan, which regulates the granting of credits by the banking system to enterprises during a stipulated period of time; and the cash plan, which controls the supply of money in circulation. Through the financial plan, the planners seek to coordinate the operations of the monetary and financial aspects of the economy with the production of physical goods and services. The financial plan is calculated prior to the production plan because it determines the income and expenditure patterns of all important sectors of the Soviet economy.

The Soviet banking system has the following characteristics.

1. Banking is centralized as a monopoly of the government. Through the direct operation of the banking system, the government determines the volume of credit and hence the money supply.

2. The banking system is subordinate to the economic plan. It serves as an instrument of control through the verification of planned transactions.

3. Banks specialize according to functions. There are banks for savings and for investment. There is, however, a trend toward bank consolidation, and savings banks have become a part of the State Bank (Gosbank). For all practical purposes, Gosbank is the banking system of the Soviet Union because it provides the cash and credit needs of the country.

THE STATE BANK (GOSBANK)   The Gosbank is the keystone of the Soviet banking system. Within the framework of the centrally planned economy, it performs a number of functions.

1. It acts as the fiscal agent of the government in that it receives all tax revenues and pays out budgetary appropriations to enterprises and institutions.

2. It is responsible for granting short-term or commercial credit to all types of enterprises.

3. It carries the accounts of all business enterprises in the country. Each enterprise has an account in the Gosbank that is supposed to supply it with financial capital. When a sale is made between two industrial enterprises, the bank simply deducts the amount of the sale from the buyer's account and adds it to that of the seller. This, as will be explained later, gives the central government control over the performance of each enterprise within the economic system.

4. It is responsible for the preparation of the credit and cash plans that are a part of the financial plan prepared by the Ministry of Finance. In this capacity, the bank is exercising a planning function for currency needs and credit expansion.

5. It is also responsible for providing currency and for holding all precious metals and foreign currencies owned by the Soviet government. As the bank of issue, it can issue money and withdraw it from circulation, thereby helping to regulate the supply of money available to enterprises and individuals in accordance with the cash plan.

ORGANIZATION OF THE GOSBANK   At the apex of the Gosbank is the policy-making head office in Moscow. The administrative apparatus of this office is divided into several departments that have a variety of responsibilities. In addition to the main office, there is a network of republic, regional, and local offices of the Gosbank throughout the Soviet Union. Each republic has a principal office responsible for the coordination of policy between the main office and regional and local offices.

Regional offices are responsible for the supervision of local offices and the transmission of credit plans to the main office. They are also responsible for the dissemination of central bank policies into all areas of the Soviet Union. Local offices perform an important control function in that they possess the accounts of the various enterprises and collective farms and can enforce financial discipline in the sense that they can make sure that funds are used for only those purposes set forth in the financial plan. In addition to the republic, regional, and local offices, the Gosbank also operates savings banks responsible for the accumulation of individual savings and the sale of government bonds.

FINANCING THE GOSBANK   The funds used to support the operations of the Gosbank are obtained from several sources, including the state budget. Since the end of World War II, the state budget has annually shown an excess of revenues over expenditures. This excess is shown as the residual in Table 12-4 and used to increase the credit resources of the Gosbank. There are also other transfers of funds from the budget to the Gosbank. For example, budgetary grants are made for investment purposes. Deposits of savings by the public in the savings banks operated by the Gosbank are also a source of funds. These savings banks do not make loans to the general public. Part of the income derived by the Gosbank is obtained from the difference between the interest paid on savings deposits and interest received from loans to enterprises. The reserves of the social insurance funds also provide a source of funds. Other sources are increases in note circulation and increases in the balances of enterprises and collective farms held on account with the Gosbank.

PLANNING FUNCTION   One of the most important functions of the Gosbank involves economic planning. The Gosbank has the responsibility for the preparation of the credit and cash plans. Loans made by the bank are carried out in connection with the credit plan and are granted for the fulfillment of the production and distribution plans. Through its quarterly cash plans, the bank has a significant influence in determining the extent and composition of note issue. The purpose of the credit and cash plans is to adjust the supply of money to the real output goals of the national economic plan and to prevent expenditures outside of planning purposes. The credit and cash plans are used to implement the physical output plan and to preserve price stability. Both types of plans are used not only by the Soviet Union but by the other centrally planned economies of Eastern Europe and by China.[18]

The *credit plan* determines the amount of short- and long-term credit allocated to all enterprises and collective farms in the economy during the period of the national economic plan. Both types of credit plans involve the preparation of a statement showing the sources and use of funds.

The short-term credit plan is designed to provide loans for such purposes as financing the acquisition of inventories by enterprises. Other uses of funds include loans for the payment of wages, loans for temporary needs, loans against drafts in the process of collection, and loans for technological development. The sources of funds used to provide short-term credit are state budgetary contributions, bank reserves and profits, balances of credit institutions such as savings banks, deposit balances of enterprises, and net changes in currency in circulation. It can be seen that the purpose of the plan is to collate the short-term needs of enterprises and collective farms with the supply of credit This collation is carried down to the regional and local levels of the economy though the use of regional credit plans.

The long-term credit plan is prepared annually and is designed to provide loans for both productive and nonproductive investments with completion dates of several years or longer. The funds to finance fixed investment are obtained from three sources: loan repayments by collective farms, individuals, consumer cooperatives, and municipal enterprises; funds from the state budget, which include allocations for such purposes as construction, home building, and agriculture, and also temporary Treasury loans; and subsidies from the union republics, used to defray the cost of home building. The funds are used to provide loans to collective farms, individuals, consumer cooperatives, and municipal enterprises, and to repay temporary Treasury loans.

The *cash plan* controls the amount of currency in circulation. It is prepared quarterly and consists of a statement showing the inflows and outflows of money. The inflow of money represents deposits in the Gosbank. These deposits represent currency receipts from a wide variety of sources—tax payments, deposits to the accounts of collective farms, receipts from municipal services, receipts from retail sales, receipts from amusement and personal services enterprises, post office and savings banks receipts, and receipts from railroad, water, and air transportation. Mon-

18. The banking system of the Soviet Union is a model followed by other Eastern European Communist countries with the exception of Yugoslavia.

etary outflows under the cash plan go for wage payments, pension allowances and insurance payments, payments for agricultural products and raw materials, consumer loans, expenditures for individual housing construction, and cash disbursements by various economic organizations. The outflow side of the balance statement represents most of the money income payments of the Soviet Union. Wage payments constitute four-fifths of total monetary outflows of the cash plan. Inflows into the Gosbank represent the deposit of receipts from consumer expenditures that result from wage and other income payments on the outflow side. Thus, the cash plan is an instrument used to control the performance of the consumer sector of the Soviet economy in terms of the disbursement and use of money.

CONTROL FUNCTION The Gosbank also exercises important control over the operations of Soviet enterprises. All financial transactions of enterprises are legally required to be accomplished through the Gosbank. This affords the bank an opportunity to view the economic performance of an enterprise with regard to real and financial plan fulfillment. Inasmuch as most transactions between enterprises are concluded in terms of bank transfers, the flow of goods is necessarily accompanied by a counterflow of funds. The very status of an enterprise's account at the bank is an indicator of its efficiency and production. If it breaks even on its operation, its account should neither increase nor diminish. If it makes planned or unplanned profits, its balance at the bank will grow; but if it operates inefficiently and sustains losses, its balance will decrease.

Financial transactions must be executed through accounts established in the Gosbank where not only the transactions but also the performance of the units carrying out the transactions comes under the close scrutiny of bank officials. This procedure is not in reality basically different from capitalistic bank settlement procedures; most transactions in capitalistic countries are also carried out through bank accounts, though these transactions are not as closely examined by capitalistic commercial banks. In the Soviet Union, every purchase or sale of goods and raw materials must be reflected in changes in the accounts of the enterprises involved. This settlement process gives the Gosbank its unique position to carry out many of its control functions.

PROVISION OF CREDIT Short-term credit accounts for an overwhelming percentage of the total credit granted by the Gosbank. The most important purpose of short-term credit is to finance accumulations of inventories by enterprises. Another important use of short-term credit is to finance accounts receivable, which provides financial capital to the seller of goods while payments are being collected. Short-term loans must be secured by real assets, such as goods in process or finished goods, and must carry a fixed maturity date.

Interest rates, which are practically uniform as to borrower, are applied to all short-term loans, and penalty rates are charged on overdue loans. Interest proceeds are a source of revenue to cover the operating expenses of the Gosbank. Since short-term loans can be made only for purposes consistent with the credit plan, interest does not play an important role as an allocator of resources in the Soviet Union.

THE INVESTMENT BANK The Investment Bank is an agent for the disbursement of budgetary funds in the form of grants to enterprises in accordance with their investment plans. Although most of its financing is long-term, it provides short-term working capital loans to the construction industry. The Investment Bank derives its funds from state budget grants, which constitute the bulk of its investment assets, and from depreciation allowances and profits of enterprises. It is also responsible for the following functions.

1. Financing cooperative housing construction and the long-term credit for individual housing construction and repair of houses in urban areas;

2. Financing the construction of schools, hospitals, and the like in urban areas;

3. Investment financing in all state-owned sectors of the economy, except agriculture, transportation, communication, and state-owned housing construction;

4. Providing short-term credit for contract organizations working on construction projects for which it handles budget grants;

5. Controlling the accounts and expenditures of funds for capital repair and maintenance by contract organizations in the construction field.

THE FOREIGN BANK Another Soviet financial institution is the Foreign Bank, which has been in operation since 1924. It is responsible for financing Soviet foreign trade and for carrying out a large part of Soviet international settlement operations. It is also designated as an agent for the Gosbank in many dealings with regard to gold and foreign exchange. It provides the state budget with any surplus of export proceeds over the amount export producers would receive based on the domestic value of their products and pays subsidies to producers when export prices are below domestic costs. The Foreign Exchange Bank is organized as a shareholding bank with the Gosbank owning two-thirds of the shares. It has few offices of its own in the Soviet Union and, therefore, carries out its operations in the offices of the Gosbank; abroad, it carries out its business through local correspondence banks.

S U M M A R Y

In their structural arrrangement, both the Soviet government and the Communist Party resemble a pyramid with its apex representing control by a central government and party hierarchy. There is an interlocking relationship between government and the Communist Party, with party officials controlling the administrative structure of each organization. This merging of authority at the top continues with parallel lines of party and government organizations extending downward through the whole Soviet system. In addition to its control and supervision over the government administrative apparatus, the party is organized in every Soviet institution.

In the Soviet Union central economic planning is responsible for resource allocation based on the public ownership of the factors of production. However, the size and complexity of the Soviet Union make it difficult for planning to operate efficiently. Economic planning consists of a system of plans. There is a single national plan for the economic development of the country and a subset of plans for different sectors of the economy and for different geographic areas.

Economic planning can be divided into long-term and annual planning. The basic form of long-term planning is the five-year plan, in which important targets are established. The long-term plan is the principal form of state economic planning. Long-term economic planning is essentially investment planning, and annual planning is basically production planning. These operational plans are particularly important at the enterprise level.

Public finance in the Soviet Union occupies a much more prominent role in the economy than it does in the economies of the United States and Western Europe. The state budget is very important, for through it flows a large part of national income. The budget is related to the financial plan of the Soviet Union, which it uses primarily as a check on the operation of the basic plan, which is expressed in physical value terms. The two main sources of state budget revenues are the turnover tax and payments from the profits of state-owned enterprises. The turnover tax is used to regulate profits and to maintain a balance between aggregate demand and the available supply of consumer goods. Budgetary expenditures include allocations for capital investment and for financial capital for enterprises. Expenditures on social welfare measures also constitute a major expenditure item in the state budget.

Gosbank is the principal instrument of the banking system in the Soviet Union and can be called a monobank because it performs the functions of both central and commercial banks. It is the collection agent for the payment of taxes and other revenues by state enterprises and other organizations. It also serves as a control mechanism to assure that the flow of funds between enterprises is in accordance with the objectives of the national plan. Gosbank plays an important role in economic planning in that it prepares the credit and cash plans, which are a part of the financial plan.

REVIEW QUESTIONS

1. Distinguish between the roles performed by the Council of Ministers and the Supreme Soviet of the U.S.S.R.
2. Discuss the interlocking relationship maintained between the Communist Party and the administrative units of the Soviet government.
3. Distinguish between Gosplan and Gossnab.
4. What is the role of the state budget in the Soviet economy?
5. The turnover tax performs several important economic functions in the Soviet Union. What are those functions?
6. Discuss the role of money in the Soviet economy.
7. In addition to performing central and commercial banking functions, Gosbank also performs control functions. Discuss.
8. What is the purpose of the credit plan?
9. What is the purpose of the cash plan?

RECOMMENDED READINGS

Goldman, Marshal I. *U.S.S.R. in Crisis: The Failure of an Economic System*. New York: W.W. Norton & Co. Inc., 1983.

Huffman, Erik P., ed. *The Soviet Union in the 1980's*. New York: Academy of Political Science, 1985.

Klose, Kevin. *Russia and the Russians*. New York: W.W. Norton & Co. Inc., 1984.

Kolbin, Vyacheslav V. *Macromodels of the National Economy of the U.S.S.R.* Dordrecht, Holland: D. Reidel, 1985.

Lane, David Stewart. *Soviet Economy and Society*. Oxford: Basil Blackwell, 1985.

Lee, Andrea. *Russian Journal*. New York: Random House Inc., 1982.

Nove, Alec. *The Soviet Economic System*. 2d ed. London: George Allen & Unwin, Ltd., 1981.

Shepler, David K. *Russia, Broken Idols, Solemn Dreams*. New York: Times Books, 1983.

Voslensky, Michael. *Nomenklatura*. New York: Doubleday & Co. Inc., 1984.

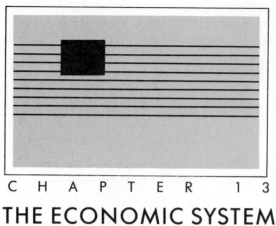

C   H   A   P   T   E   R   1   3

THE ECONOMIC SYSTEM
OF THE SOVIET UNION

The organization of production and distribution is a fundamental concern of all economic systems. Production involves decisions about the types and quantities of goods to be produced. Production also involves the allocation of scarce resources among competing alternatives to attain maximum output. Once the goods have been produced, the problem of their distribution arises. Distribution, or *marketing*, refers to the process by which physical goods are brought from producers to consumers. It involves the organization of channels of distribution: transportation, storage, finance, and inventory planning. These functions have to be performed regardless of the economic system involved. In the Soviet Union, they are performed by the government, which owns, administers, and controls all wholesale and retail distribution facilities.

Distribution also refers to the division of national income in terms of money, real goods, and services among the factors of production. Most of the Soviet national income is distributed to workers in the form of wages. The Soviets use monetary incentives, such as wage differentials and bonuses, as key devices for motivating workers. Profits are also a part of national income. Enterprises in all fields of economic activity can make both planned and unplanned profits, but the significance of these profits is quite different from that of profits in the United States. They belong to the government and are used for capital development and other purposes. As mentioned in the preceding chapter, deductions from profits constitute a major source of income for the state budget. Profits are also used as an index of the production effectiveness of Soviet enterprises. The extent of profit retention by enterprises depends on the promotion of greater productivity through better organization of production and through economies in the use of raw materials and energy. Interest also figures in the national income to some extent, particularly in the form of payments on the savings deposits of individuals.[1]

In this chapter the organization of industry and agriculture in the Soviet Union will be discussed. In looking at this organization, it is necessary to examine the macroeconomic structures of industry and agriculture and their relationship to economic planning. To enforce planning in a country the size of the Soviet Union, there has to be a system of surveillance imposed by both government and party organizations. It is also necessary to examine the operation of individual industrial and agricultural enterprises, for they are the focal point of the primary, critical function of production. However, the production process in itself is incomplete until goods are distributed from producers to consumers. The role of unions in the Soviet Union and the process of income distribution among various types of workers will also be discussed in this chapter.

■ ORGANIZATION OF INDUSTRY ■

The organizational structure of Soviet industry is complex because an immense bureaucratic apparatus is necessary to plan and administer production and distribution policies in a country that is almost three times the size of the United States. There has, however, been a continual reorganization of the Soviet economic-administrative structure. Soviet leader Mikhail Gorbachev is currently working to consolidate ministries to improve the flow of information between Gosplan and the enterprises.

ADMINISTRATION OF INDUSTRY

The administrative and policy-making framework of Soviet industrial organization resembles a pyramid, with the top being the Politburo of the

---

1. Interest also takes the form of a rental charge for the use of capital. This charge is supposed to be levied only at the end of the period during which the capital has been used. Short-term credits provided by Gosbank to finance inventory accumulations of enterprises usually carry an interest rate of 2 percent.

Central Committee of the Communist Party and the bottom being the industrial enterprise. The Politburo is responsible for making major policy decisions, including those that affect industry. Next there is the Council of Ministers of the U.S.S.R., the most important governmental executive and administrative body in the Soviet Union, and Gosplan, which is directly subordinate to the Council of Ministers and is responsible for the development of the long-term and annual economic plans. There is also Gossnab, the State Committee for Material and Technical Supply, which is also under the supervision of the Council of Ministers. This committee is responsible for implementing national material and technical supply plans and for ensuring that ministries, departments, and enterprises fulfill their delivery plans on time.

However, the direct links in the organization of industrial production are the all-union and union republic ministries, the ministries of the autonomous republics, regional and district departments and boards, and the enterprises.[2] The all-union and union republic ministries are responsible for the allocation of material and technical resources to different industries. These resources are distributed according to plan through various central and regional supply organizations. Each ministry is divided into a number of administrative units called *sectoral boards* that are responsible for the administration of different industrial sectors within an industry. For example, the all-union Ministry of Machine-Tool and Instrument Industry has the following sectoral boards: heavy and custom-built machine tools; automatic lines and universal machine tools; precision machine tools; woodworking equipment; forging, pressing, and foundry equipment; cutting and measuring instruments; technological equipment; abrasive and diamond tools; hydraulic apparatus; general machine parts and items; and casting, forgings, punchings, and welded structures.

THE SOVIET ENTERPRISE

The enterprise is the basic link in the general system of Soviet production management and operates as a legal entity engaged in production activity under the national economic plan. It is obligated to fulfill its own production plan, which contains certain targets or success indicators that should be attained. It is required to operate under a profit-and-loss accounting system, and it has fixed and financial capital that form the basis of its statutory fund, the size of which is shown on its balance sheet. It can decide

---

2. In 1985, there were 39 all-union ministries and 46 union republic ministries.

how best to use the fixed and financial capital assigned to it, providing that each is used for purposes stipulated in the production plan. An enterprise also has the right to make capital investments from funds that are set aside for amortization purposes and to fix the prices of its products within the limits set by the economic plan.

ORGANIZATION OF AN ENTERPRISE   In general a Soviet enterprise is organized along the following lines.[3] There is a director appointed by the state to run the enterprise. This director is governed from above by directives and rules of behavior that guide all decisions. However, the director is not rigidly circumscribed as to what can be done, but rather is somewhat free to operate in any manner so long as it is within the general framework of the national economic plan and the enterprise's operating plan. The director can influence the contents of the operating plan through familiarity with the resource needs and product specifications of the enterprise. The Soviet planning system, of necessity, has to permit a certain degree of managerial autonomy, for it is impossible to supervise in detail the operation of thousands of enterprises. Caution, rather than risk taking and innovation, appears to be an important characteristic of Soviet enterprise directors; it is easier and safer to work within established production procedures in the fulfillment of the operating plan.

Since the Soviet reward system has favored directors who fulfill or overfulfill their plans, there have been frequent unfavorable results. Directors often have claimed overall plan fulfillment, when in fact the production included subquality output, incomplete items, or an incorrect assortment of goods. To fulfill their plans, directors often have concentrated on goods of high value or items that are easy to produce. This subterfuge is fairly difficult to detect, but the Soviet authorities are aware of it. Economic reforms have drastically reduced the number of targets or success indicators with which a director has to contend. Nevertheless, there is a community of interest, which tends to favor plan fulfillment regardless of the method involved, that binds the director and others who are directly associated with the enterprise.

THE TEKHPROMFINPLAN   Each Soviet enterprise has to prepare what is called a *tekhpromfinplan*, which is its operating plan for the year.[4] The

---

3. The Communist Party controls all appointments to important positions through the nomenklatura (patronage) system, meaning appointees have to be either members of the Communist Party or in good standing with the party.

4. David Lane, *Soviet Economy & Society* (London: Basil Blackwell, 1985), p. 21.

tekhpromfinplan is a consolidated plan that includes the financial, output, and investment plans of the enterprise. It is prepared twice. The first is a preliminary draft and the second is a formally approved economic document. It is supposed to be developed within the framework of the long-term or five-year plan, which is not only developed for the economy as a whole, but for each enterprise as well. However, operational targets and the allocation of resources for an enterprise are determined for the most part in the annual plan. The plan also functions on a quarterly and monthly basis.

The tekhpromfinplan contains a number of assigned indexes or success targets to be achieved by an enterprise. These indicators are as follows:

1. The volume of output to be produced and sold,

2. The total value of sales,

3. The fulfillment of planned delivery contracts,

4. The amount of profits and level of profitability,

5. Payments to and allocations from the state budget,

6. The amount of funds to be spent on the expansion and improvement of production,

7. The introduction of new techniques and automation,

8. The volume of inputs in the form of material and technical supplies.

In terms of success, an enterprise is judged primarily by the volume of its sales and amount of its profit, which includes savings made from economies in production. Constraints are placed on an enterprise in the form of fixed prices for both inputs and outputs and in limitations in the selection of inputs allocated to it. All prices, with the exception of those in the free agricultural market, are set by the government. In setting prices, an allowance is made for profits expressed as a percentage of average production cost for an entire industry. Individual enterprises will have differing rates of profits because of differences in production costs. *Profits*, then, can be defined in terms of the Soviet enterprise as the difference between its total income from sales and its cost of production. In its annual operating plan, an enterprise lists its expected or planned profits as a percentage of total production costs. Its planned profits may be more or less than its actual profits.

ROLE OF COMMUNIST PARTY   The Communist Party plays a role in the operation of an enterprise. There is a local unit of the party in all enterprises that is supposed to act as the custodian of the nation's interest as opposed to the more narrowly circumscribed outlook of the industrial manager. Most managers are members of the Communist Party, but, despite this fact, the party maintains its own independent hierarchy in each enterprise. At the head of this enterprise hierarchy is the party secretary, who shares responsibility with the director for plan fulfillment. The secretary is also supposed to keep the party informed of any adverse developments in the enterprise. There is some ambiguity in defining the secretary's relationship with the director and with the party. The secretary can neither interfere excessively in the decisions of the director, nor be too lax from the standpoint of control.

CHANNELS OF DISTRIBUTION

In the Soviet Union the government owns and controls every distribution outlet in the production process. There are two networks through which goods move—a material and technical supply network, which is responsible for moving supplies and intermediate goods to and from industrial enterprises, and a state trading network through which consumer goods are sold. The key state agencies responsible for distribution are Gosplan, Gossnab, and the Ministry of Trade. Requirements are written into a plan for material supplies which is a part of the national economic plan. Gosplan is responsible for the development of this plan, and Gossnab (the State Committee of the U.S.S.R. Council of Ministers for the Supply of Materials to the National Economy) is responsible for carrying out plans for supplying materials and equipment drawn up by Gosplan. Gossnab is also responsible for the distribution of production that is not distributed by Gosplan. What all of this means is that materials and equipment are centrally allocated, and material transfers to enterprises must be authorized by the government and must be accompanied by payment from the enterprise.

MATERIALS SUPPLY PLAN   A materials supply plan is developed annually to balance production with consumption. The plan is divided into three sections.

1. A materials balance between consumer needs based on the preceding year's supply and the currently available production capacity is prepared. Items covered in this balance are food,

shoes, other consumer goods, and appliances. Side by side, a production balance is developed in terms of need versus available capacity of machines, raw materials, and fuel.

2. Distribution plans that show the detailed allocation of each product from production centers to distribution centers are prepared.

3. Interstate and interregional plans specify the volume of production to be obtained within the republic or region, the volume to be provided by other republics or regions to each republic or region, the volume to be contributed by each region or republic to national needs, and the volume needed for exports.[5]

DISTRIBUTION The actual distribution of supplies is carried out by various supply agencies attached to the ministries. These agencies function at both the national and republic levels. An enterprise estimates its output targets and input norms based on its proposed production plan and makes its requests for materials to a supply agency that is part of the ministry that has ultimate jurisdiction over the enterprise. It is the responsibility of the supply agency to ascertain whether or not the requests of the enterprise are legitimate, for in many cases enterprises pad their orders to enhance their chances of fulfilling their production plans. A fact of economic life for the director of a Soviet enterprise has been the inadequate provision of resources necessary to fulfill the production plan. An unsteady flow of supplies causes work stoppages and jeopardizes plan fulfillment; the disruptions spread through the economy in a chain reaction. In fact, the planning and distribution of supplies is a severe weakness in the Soviet economic system; in spite of the many organizational reforms that have been introduced, uncertainty in resource allocation still remains a critical problem for enterprise directors.

Consumer goods also go through various stages of distribution. At each stage, the characteristics of centralized allocation of resources are all present—estimation of needs, requests by enterprises, determination of delivery orders, and the transfer of funds. It is not until the final stage—retail trade—that goods are freely sold to the consumer. As is also true for the distribution of industrial supplies, planning of consumer goods involves a

---

5. Sumer G. Aggarwal, "Managing Material Shortages: The Russian Way," *Columbia Journal of World Business*, Fall 1980, pp. 26-28.

reconciliation of requests from wholesale or retail enterprises at the lower levels with the production and distribution plans at the higher levels. For example, a wholesale outlet may receive requests from retail stores for a certain commodity. These requests are transferred to the Ministry of Trade in the republic in which the wholesale and retail outlets are located. The requests eventually are transmitted upward to Gosplan. The allocation of consumer goods is determined in the overall national plan, and the amount of the particular commodity is allocated to the Ministry of Trade in the republic and also to the republic Gosplan, which are responsible for delivery to the wholesale outlet. It, in turn, is responsible for the final delivery of the commodity to the retail stores.

RETAIL STORES   The Ministry of Trade, which is a union-republic ministry, is at the apex of the consumer trade network. It is responsible for the operation of a network of government stores located in urban areas. There is a Ministry of Trade in each republic, which has control over a number of wholesale outlets. Typically, government retail stores are under the control of a local city trade organization. The trade organization has departments responsible for supplying goods to the city and supervising the operation of the retail store system. Warehouses are also attached to the trade departments.

Retail stores represent the ultimate link with the consumer. Retail prices are, for the most part, by the government at levels that attempt to equate supply with demand. The retail price consist of several elements: production cost, profit of the producer, the turnover tax, and wholesale and retail markups. In other words, it consists of all of the components that make up the price charged by the seller to the retailer plus a retail markup.

In addition to the network of government stores, there is a consumer cooperative store network. Consumer cooperatives operate primarily in the rural areas. Like other organizations in the Soviet Union, they are structured as a pyramid, with local outlets at the base and the decision-making agencies at the republic and all-union levels at the apex. Prices are set by the Ministry of Trade and are usually higher than those set on consumer goods in the urban areas to compensate in part for higher transportation costs. Distribution is performed by government wholesale distributing units called *trade warehouses*. Residents of a village or state farm are organized into consumer cooperatives and become shareholders. They are supposed to elect a governing board, a director, and an inspection committee, though actually there is little autonomy granted to local cooperatives.

■ LABOR UNIONS ■
AND THE SOVIET WORKER

Labor unions exist in the Soviet Union, and workers are not only permitted but are encouraged to belong to one. Unlike their counterparts in the industrial countries of the West, unions do not enjoy a significant sphere of autonomous action. They do not have the right to strike, and decisions on wage rates, output norms, hours of work, and similar matters are prerogatives of government. These decisions are made on a national scale by the State Committee on Labor and Wages, which is a part of the Council of Ministers of the U.S.S.R.

The powers that unions do possess in the Soviet Union are in relationship to the operation of an enterprise. Although it was originally intended that important managerial decisions would be made by a troika of management, union, and party representatives, the role of the union has declined in importance as the drive for industrial efficiency strengthened managerial authority. It can be said that in terms of power, the union ranks behind both management and party in an enterprise. The union does have certain functions, which can be enumerated as follows:

1. It has the right to participate with management in the development of the economic plan for an enterprise.

2. It is responsible for the maintenance of worker discipline by discouraging tardiness, absenteeism, and worker turnover and by promoting measures to encourage productivity.

3. Management is required to obtain its permission in assigning workers to wage categories and in introducing regulations on piecework and bonus systems.

4. It plays an important role in the area of social insurance and carries out a variety of activities in connection with vacations, education, recreation, and culture. It is responsible for the collection of social security contributions from the enterprise and the disbursement of cash benefits.

5. It has the right to express opinions on candidates nominated for management positions and to oppose discharges of workers that are initiated by management.

■ A G R I C U L T U R E ■

In the period immediately prior to World War I, agriculture in the Soviet Union underwent some dramatic changes. Under the Stolypin reforms of 1906, a large number of peasants were given legal title to the land they worked. The large land-owner declined in importance and even disappeared from the economic scene. However, the deep-seated aspirations of the Russian peasantry to own and manage their own land were to be thwarted when the Communists came into power. It was inevitable that an effort would be made to socialize agriculture, for many communists believed that communism would never succeed in the Soviet Union as long as agriculture remained a small-scale, capitalistic enterprise.

By the end of the First Five-Year Plan, the basic structure of Soviet agriculture had been determined. The structure was based on two forms of collective enterprises—the state farm and the collective farm. A state farm was (and is) the full property of the Soviet government. It represents the main communist objectives for agriculture—the peasants are truly proletarians with no property of their own.[6] The collective farm, as the name implies, is supposed to be a self-governing cooperative made up of peasants who voluntarily pool their production and divide the proceeds. At first, there were two types of collective farms—collectives in which all livestock and implements were held in common by the peasants, who lived in communal buildings; and collectives in which the peasants were allowed to own lifestock and a small plot of land privately as well as live independently of other members of the collective farm. The latter has become the prevalent agricultural unit in the Soviet Union.

Agriculture is controlled by the government through national economic planning. The supply and price of inputs, the share of output marketed, and the prices paid for agricultural output, as well as farm income and expenditures, are regulated by the plan. Overall output goals are established for agricultural products that are to be delivered to the government. These goals are disseminated downward by Gosplan to the Ministries of Production and Procurements in each republic and to lower administrative units in the provinces and districts. Given the goals, which are supplemented by local requirements, each state farm and collective farm has to formulate a production plan. When this is done, each plan goes up

---

6. According to Marx, the ideal agricultural organization would be state farms where private ownership, no matter how insignificant it might be, could not exist and where all of the workers were to be paid by the government on the same basis as factory workers.

the administrative line—district, province, and republic—to be examined and combined with other plans. Finally, the combined plans reach Gosplan for approval. Gosplan also is responsible for the determination of the production and use of such agricultural inputs as machinery and fertilizer.

STATE FARMS

State farms, as mentioned previously, are owned by the government and operated as regular industrial establishments with managers and hired workers.[7] Their annual budgets and operating plans are developed by the government, which is also responsible for the determination of wages paid to the workers and for the provision of livestock and equipment.

As originally set up, the state farms were extremely large. They were intended to increase agricultural production through economies of scale by utilizing modern, efficient farming techniques and by serving as experimental stations and model agricultural centers. The state farm remains the highest form of a socialized agricultural unit and enjoys a favored position in Soviet agriculture. In recent years the number of state farms has increased considerably because some collective farms have been converted into state farms. Also, a number of specialized meat, dairy, and vegetable state farms have been created around major urban centers. In terms of physical output, they account for one-fourth of total agricultural output— an amount which is adversely affected by the fact that many state farms are established in areas of low productivity.

State farms sell their produce to the government for processing and distribution through state stores, for stockpiling, and for export. The arrangement between state farms and the government is a contract that specifies the price to be paid for the commodity produced and the delivery date. There is usually a basic procurement price, subject to some regional variation, for each commodity. Prices are used as incentives for changes in production. For example, if an increase in the production of dairy products or meat is desired, prices are raised. In this way, prices perform a function in allocating resources that is similar to their role in a market economy. Prices are also set at levels that reflect, at least in part, differences in average production costs on state farms operating in different areas of the country. Lower prices are paid in areas with more productive land, reflecting the fact that no charge is made for land rent.

---

7. In 1982 there were 21,600 state farms in the Soviet Union. The average size of a state farm is approximately 8,700 acres.

State farms are managed by directors who have the right to determine the total number of workers to be used on the farm, the planned production costs, the planned labor productivity, and other general factors of management control. Although this has meant greater independence of state farm management from central control, the basic policies to be followed are determined by the government, and directors must operate according to these policies.

Since state farms are entirely owned and operated by the state, workers are direct employees of the state and are paid wages. The wages vary according to the type and quantity of work done. Payments are usually piece rates that vary according to the classification of the worker. Specialists, such as agronomists, are paid on a monthly basis. Wages are paid from a general wage fund that is included in the state farm's overall operating plan. In addition, a bonus arrangement is provided by the material incentives fund, which is separated from the wage fund.

The starting point in the distribution of profit is gross sales, which is obtained by multiplying the planned volume per product by the set state price. Production costs, including the costs of seed and fertilizer and depreciation, are deducted from gross sales to get gross income. From gross income a deduction is made into the wage fund, and the remainder is called the *socially clear income*. Special costs and production levels are deducted and paid to the state. There is a deduction for profit taxes that also goes to the state. Remaining income is divided into various funds. An example of the determination and use of profit of a state farm is shown in Table 13-1.

COLLECTIVE FARMS

The collective farm is a form of agricultural organization in which varying numbers of individual peasants combine their resources and talents and operate collectively.[8] The land occupied by a collective farm is secured to it without payment and without time limit, and the livestock, implements, and public structures in its possession are considered to be its property. Each collective farm household, in addition to its basic interest in the collective property, is entitled to a small plot of land for private cultivation, housing, and such auxiliary items as productive lifestock, poultry, and minor agricultural implements.

---

8. In 1982 there were 25,900 collective farms in the Soviet Union. Their average size is 2,470 acres.

TABLE 13-1 ROLE OF PROFIT AT A STATE FARM

Total sales		$1,300,000
Less seed, fertilizer, and other costs including depreciation		−650,000
Gross income		$ 650,000
Less wage funds		−260,000
Social clear income		$ 390,000
Less special costs	$ 65,000	
Less production levy	52,000	−117,000
Profit		$ 273,000
Less profit taxes		−52,000
Net profit		$ 221,000
Less investment funds	$104,000	
Less enterprise funds	3,900	
Less social and cultural funds	48,100	−156,000
Profit residual		$ 65,000

DIFFERENCES FROM STATE FARMS   Members of a collective farm are not paid wages, but share in the income of the individual collective farm. This income depends directly upon the crops produced. After certain deductions are made from the harvest, the remainder is distributed in kind among the collective farmers or is sold for cash, which is then distributed. However, with recent agricultural reforms, there has been a shift to a regular cash wage paid on a monthly basis. This reflects an attempt on the part of the government to use similar methods of wage payments for both collective and state farm workers.

Investment in collective farms is not financed out of the state budget, but from the income of the individual collective farm. From this income, the collective farm must pay an income tax and various current expenses, including those for administrative, educational, and cultural purposes. An undivided surplus must also be set up to cover necessary capital expenditures.

DISTRIBUTION OF INCOME AND PRODUCTION   There are three claimants to the income and output of a collective farm—the state, the collective farm itself, and the members of the collective farm. The state has first claim on production. Prior to 1958, collective farms had to deliver to the government certain specified quantities of crops and animal products. (To acquire farm products cheaply had always been one of the main goals of

Soviet economic policy.) Also, payment in kind of a certain amount of produce had to be made to the Machine Tractor Stations. In 1958, however, the government introduced a single system of procurement prices, and agricultural products are now purchased from collective farms at a basic price for each product. Currently there is a wide variety of prices for most commodities, depending on such factors as the type of market, quality, location, and the season when the commodity is marketed.

There are two agricultural marketing systems in the Soviet Union—the state system and the private market system. Under the state system, the state assumes the responsibility for transporting and marketing all products it produces. For example, state-owned processing plants receive raw materials at a specified price, which is established by the government, and deliver the finished products to state stores and other outlets at specified prices, which are also set by the government. These products are then distributed to the consumer through state stores. The state marketing system has proven to be inefficient, so the collective farms are now allowed to deliver their produce to stores and other retail outlets; in return, the collective receives the retail price less a discount.

The revenue derived by collective farms from the sale of their produce is used for several purposes. First of all, a number of general expenditures have to be met. These include contributions to a sociocultural fund, production costs for such items as fuel and fertilizers, insurance on the collective farm's physical assets, and contributions to a fund for the purpose of acquiring capital goods. Prior to 1965, a standard 12.5 percent tax was levied against the gross income of collective farms. However, in order to improve production incentives, changes were made in the tax. The tax is now calculated on the basis of net income, which is the difference between gross income and production costs plus deductions to the social insurance fund. A portion of net income (which is equal to a profit rate of 15 percent) is exempt from the tax. A tax of 12 percent is levied on the remaining net income.[9]

Wages paid to collective farm workers come out of a wage fund. The standard method of payment has involved the use of workdays. The *workday* is an abstract unit based on such factors as the quality and quantity of work performed and the type of work involved. Each worker must work a minimum number of workdays a year. The total number of workdays ac-

9. For example, assume a gross income of 2 million rubles and total costs of production plus social insurance contributions of 1.5 million rubles. Net income is 500,000 rubles. Net income that would provide a profit rate of 15 percent (1,500,000 × 15% = 225,000 rubles) is exempt from taxation. Taxable net income is 500,000 minus 225,000, or 275,000 rubles. The tax is 12 percent of 275,000 rubles, or 33,000 rubles.

cumulated by the workers is divided into the amount of income available in cash or in kind for distribution at the end of the year. This system has been erratic over the years, and incomes of collective farm workers have lagged behind those of state farm workers. To remedy this defect, measures have been taken to raise incomes of collective farm workers to parity with incomes of state farm workers. A guaranteed minimum income, which was 80 rubles (or $130) a month in 1985, was made applicable to collective farm workers. A monthly wage system has been introduced. This places the workers' claim on a part of the income ahead of the claim of the collective farm instead of the other way around.

PRIVATE PLOTS

Private plots represent the third form of agriculture in the Soviet Union. To a certain extent, they are almost an anachronism in that they represent the only substantial form of private enterprise in the country. However, the fact that they do exist can be attributed to the fact that the Russian peasants have never completely converted to the idea that land should belong to the state and not to them. The typical private plot is 1.5 acres. Although dwarfed in terms of physical size by the state and collective farms, the private plots account for an inordinately large share of agricultural output. Although private plots account for only 3 percent of all land in cultivation, they contribute substantially to the production of livestock, dairy, and truck garden products. Most of the products produced on the private plots are high-value products. In 1980 the private sector produced 30 percent of the total meat supply, 35 percent of the milk, 35 percent of the eggs, 59 percent of the potatoes, 34 percent of the vegetables, and 44 percent of the fruit in the U.S.S.R. Sales of products from private plots represent a substantial amount of the income of collective farms.[10]

The private sector of Russian agriculture can be classified into three categories—private plots held and operated by members of the collective farms, private plots operated by state farm workers and by other state employees, and private land held by individual peasants. The last category is rare in the Soviet Union. The few individual peasants who own and operate their own farms are located primarily in sparsely populated regions where the formation of collective farms is not economically justifiable. Ownership of private plots on collective farms represents a partial retreat from the complete collectivization attempts of the 1930s, which had disas-

10. Lane, *Soviet Economy*, p. 178.

trous results. Although, in general, the attitude of the government toward private farming has ranged from encouragement to hostility, individual ownership and use of farmland is legal according to Articles 7 and 9 of the 1936 Constitution of the Soviet Union, providing it does not involve the use of hired labor. Collective farm private plots are allowed as an entitlement under a 1935 statute.[11]

■ DISTRIBUTION OF INCOME ■

In a socialist country, income is limited primarily to wages and salaries because, under communist doctrine, labor is the only factor of production endowed with the capability of creating value. Therefore, labor should be remunerated to the exclusion of land and capital. The total amount of wages to be paid and the production counterpart to support wages depends on the division of socialist national income between accumulation and consumption, and further, of consumption between the social consumption fund and the wage fund.

NATIONAL INCOME

National income in a centrally planned economy begins with the concept of the *net material product*, which can be defined either as the net contribution of the productive sectors of the economy (that is, gross production less the value of intermediate products and depreciation charges) or as the total income realized by the productive sectors. To put it more simply, the socialist concept of national income is that of national income produced and national income distributed. National income produced covers those activities that create material goods or help in the productive process—for example, gathering raw materials and processing them into finished products. National income distributed refers to the distribution of the income of the labor force, enterprises, and society by financial flows. This income can be divided into two categories. The first category of income is distributed to individuals and consists of gross money income before taxation of workers employed in production, money income and income in kind of farmers, and the value of net production from private activity. The second category of national income distributed consists of gross profits before taxa-

---

11. The plot is given to the household for its personal use only. The land cannot be sold or rented; if not used, it is taken away.

tion of production enterprises, the turnover tax, and contributions of enterprises to social insurance.

The distribution of national income may be shown as follows.

INCOMES OF INDIVIDUALS

1. Wages and salaries of workers in the state sector of productive industries,

2. Wages and salaries of workers in producer cooperatives,

3. Incomes of cooperative farmers from cooperative activities,

4. Incomes of cooperative farmers from private plots of land,

5. Incomes of individual farmers,

6. Incomes, private or otherwise, from other activities.

INCOMES OF THE SOCIAL SECTOR

1. Gross profits before taxes of productive enterprises,

2. Turnover taxes,

3. Contributions of enterprises to social insurance.

PERSONAL INCOME

The main difference between national income and personal income in a socialist system of national income accounts lies in the fact that only incomes of individuals and firms generated in the productive sectors—industry, agriculture, and others—are counted in national income, while personal income takes into account income earned in the nonproductive sectors as well. These sectors are education, health, justice, finance, and public administration. These sectors are considered nonproductive not because they are not useful, but because they do not contribute directly to the creation of material production. Thus, personal income in a country such as the Soviet Union would consist of wages and salaries of all workers employed in both productive and nonproductive industries, incomes of self-employed persons and independent entrepreneurs, and income from other sources including, for example, the income from the sale of agricultural products grown on private plots of land. Personal income would also include transfer payments of various types, including family allowances and old-age pensions.

Personal income can be regarded as income generated in the process of redistributing the national income. This process is effected by transfers between the state and society and between different sectors of society. These transfers are realized mainly through the state budget, which is the most important instrument in modifying income flows in a socialist economy, and through a system of credits. Many transfers are payments by the state for which no service is provided in return, but which redistribute income to various groups. Examples are old-age pensions and family allowances. Personal outlays include personal consumption of goods and services, taxes, and other payments. The result is an economic balance that relates total money income of the population to their total outlays. An example of this balance is shown in Table 13-2.

As mentioned before, wages constitute the bulk of personal income distributed in a socialist economic system. Although labor itself enjoys some freedom from central planning, there is a high degree of centralization and control over the determination of wages. The total amount of wages to be paid is set in the wage fund, which provides gross payments for all work done: basic wage rates, payments based on piece-rate norms, basic salaries, payments for overtime, and payments for night work and work on Sundays and holidays. The wage fund is linked to private consumption. Consumption, both collective and private, has to be planned in advance because it constitutes an integral part of the national economic plan, which cannot be constructed and balanced unless the size and structure of

TABLE 13-2   PERSONAL INCOME AND OUTLAYS
IN A CENTRALLY PLANNED ECONOMY

Income	Outlays
Wages and salaries	Consumption goods
Income of cooperative and individual farmers	Services
Supplementary income from enterprises	Consumption of goods in kind
Imputed rent	Consumption of services in kind
Other labor and rental income	Total private consumption
Total income from work and property	Personal contributions
Government transfer payments	Personal tax payments to institutions
Total income	Total outlays

consumption are laid down. The planning of consumption necessitates the planning of the wage fund.

WAGE DETERMINATION   Wages are determined by government fiat. In the Soviet Union, there are several state agencies that play a role in wage determination. Within the organizational framework of the Council of Ministers of the U.S.S.R., there is the State Committee on Labor and Wages. This committee is responsible for examining prevailing wage structures and practices within the Soviet Union. Within the committee there is the Institute of Labor, which does research on wage questions and policies. The committee takes this information and makes recommendations concerning changes in wages for various occupational groups. Gosplan and the Ministry of Finance also participate in the calculation of wages, which are a part of the national economic plan. The total amount of wages for a given industry or enterprise would depend upon changes in the size and composition of the labor force, expected changes in the availability of consumer goods, and output and labor productivity plans. Once the total amount of wages has been determined for a particular industry, it is subdivided among the enterprises on the basis of the criteria mentioned above. Each enterprise, then, has its own wage fund from which it pays its workers.

Soviet economic reforms have provided a set of incentives to increase worker performance. Worker incomes come from two main sources—the regular wage fund from which wages are paid to all workers and the material incentives fund from which bonuses are paid. Money for the material incentives fund comes out of profits in accordance with standards prescribed by the state. The amount of the bonus is set by Gosplan and implemented by ministries responsible for individual enterprises. The planned size of the material incentive fund is fixed for each year. Actual incentive funds may deviate from the planned funds, with the funds increased or decreased based on enterprise performance, which includes, among other things, the quality of the product produced and the production of new products.[12] The incentive funds are also tied to the government's efforts to produce more consumer goods.

WAGE DIFFERENTIALS   Considerable wage and salary differentials exist in the Soviet Union. These differentials are based on several factors.

Within the factories, there are wage differentials based upon skills. In most industrial plants, there are six skill grades that are differentiated ac-

---

12. In the past, bonus funds encouraged enterprise managers to stress the volume of total output and quality was neglected.

cording to variations in skill from unskilled to highly skilled. The requirements for each grade are determined by the State Committee on Wages and the All-Union Central Council of Trade Unions. Differentials between the lowest and highest grade can vary according to the industry. These ratios, however, involve only the basic standard wage rate for each grade and do not take into consideration the fact that the use of piece rates and bonuses can cause considerable differentials in earnings among workers within the same grade.

Wage differentials are also based on conditions of work, with hard or hazardous work commanding a higher premium than less arduous working conditions. Rates for work under hazardous conditions would carry a premium of as much as 30 percent above the basic wage rate.

The form of wage payment use also is responsible for wage differentials. Piece-rate workers are generally better paid than time-rate workers because under piece rates there is a direct correlation between output and payments.

There are also regional differentials in wage and salary payments. To attract workers to less desirable areas of the country where labor shortages are endemic, additional payments ranging from 10 to 100 percent of the base wage are added to all grades.

Salary differentials also exist for engineers, economists, and white-collar employees. These differentials are based on the skill requirements of the job, the complexity of work, and the economic importance of the industry. There are various salary categories, similar to the wage grades used for plant workers.

WAGE SYSTEMS   There are several systems of wage and salary compensation used in the Soviet Union. These systems usually combine time rates or piece rates with bonus payments and cover most industrial wage earners. The rationale of the bonus is to tie personal interests of workers more closely to the interests of production. Bonuses may be awarded on the basis of individual or collective performance. Individual bonuses are based on the performance of each worker as measured against other workers, while collective bonuses reward a group of workers as a whole and are divided uniformly among the workers. Bonuses, however, are not always tied to the output performance of the enterprise, but may be awarded for other reasons. For example, workers can get bonuses for reducing waste or for coming up with suggestions that contribute to the efficient operation of an enterprise. In 1986 new pay scales were put into effect in a number of industries in order to increase productivity. The pay scales permit wages for outstanding workers to be 50 percent above the average. Those workers who invent new techniques to improve productivity will be given patent royalties that could make some of them millionaires.

The economic reforms have intensified the incentive role of bonuses as a lever for increasing worker productivity and the rate of economic growth. As it now stands, Soviet workers receive fixed payments according to their grades from the wage fund of an enterprise plus a bonus that can come from the wage fund and from the material incentives funds. Workers could fall under one of three compensation categories.

TIME RATE PLUS A BONUS   In this compensation system, wages are based on hourly rates set for each skill grade. In addition, bonuses are paid either individually or collectively. These bonuses are usually based on quantity standards such as output quotas, cost reduction, and material usage. Workers receive bonuses for the fulfillment and overfulfillment of individual or collective targets.

PIECE RATE PLUS A BONUS   The piece rate can be progressive, which means that earnings rise more than in proportion to output above the standard task. However, progressive piece rates have declined in importance and have been replaced primarily by straight piece rates, in which earnings vary in direct proportion to output. Bonuses are paid when an enterprise exceeds planned production targets.

STRAIGHT TIME RATES   Straight time rates, usually monthly, are paid to professional workers, such as doctors, teachers, and employees of various government agencies. Salaried workers for enterprises, such as engineers, managers, and technicians, are also paid time rates, but receive a bonus as well, provided that the enterprise achieves its targets. Under the reforms, bonuses to salaried workers come from the material incentives fund, the amount of which depends upon the profits an enterprise earns.

TRANSFER PAYMENTS AND SPECIAL BENEFITS   Money wages are only one course of a Russian worker's income. When various subsidized consumer services, such as medical benefits and transfer payments, are taken into consideration, total money and real income can be increased considerably for the average Russian worker. Free goods, which include education, medicine, and health care, and subsidized food and housing are estimated to account for more than a quarter of the average Russian worker's income.[13] Then there are special benefits for certain elites. These include foreign currency, which is used for the purchase of superior quality goods in foreign currency shops; other specialty shops and restaurants

13. Lane, *Soviet Economy*, p. 178.

reserved for senior officials; and special holiday and medical facilities for certain management and executive groups. Occupational groups have access to housing that favors the academic, industrial, and political elites; access to cars is also given to people in high-level posts.

Comparisons of income distribution in the Soviet Union and the United States are difficult to make. One would conclude on an a priori basis that incomes are distributed more equally in the Soviet Union. Various forms of property income that would favor the rich in the United States have been eliminated in the Soviet Union. The state also exercises complete control over the determination of wages, which are generally distributed more equally than in the United States. However, it is necessary to factor in the various benefits received by the Soviet elite—the access to cars, travel, spacious apartments, and summer villas—that are not available to the Russian masses. One estimate places the top incomes in the Soviet Union, including the various benefits, as 60 times higher than the minimum wages.[14] Another estimate gives a differential of 100 times the average income in the Soviet Union.[15] There is a greater disparity between top and bottom income earners in the United States. However, the progressivity of U.S. personal income tax does reduce this disparity somewhat.[16] In the Soviet Union, income taxes would have no effect on income redistribution.[17]

■ AN APPRAISAL ■
OF THE SOVIET ECONOMY

The economic performance of the Soviet economy was generally good during the period 1950–1975. During this period the Soviet leadership was able to pursue successfully a policy of guns and butter as well as economic growth. The Soviet Union developed into one of the two major superpowers of the world and proved itself capable of creating a military-industrial complex rivaling that of the United States. In the field of space technology, the Soviet Union has made very important contributions, indicat-

14. The minimum wage in 1984 was 80 rubles a month. Sixty times the minimum would give a monthly income of 4,800 rubles.

15. Lane, *Soviet Economy*, p. 181.

16. This is more likely to hold true for Sweden than the United States. Comparisons of income distribution in Sweden and the Soviet Union indicate that after-tax income differentials are higher in the Soviet Union.

17. For a comparative study of income distribution, see Peter Wiles, *Distribution of Income: East & West* (Amsterdam: North Holland Publishing Co., 1974).

ing the ability of the leadership to mobilize resources to accomplish certain objectives. The Soviet Union increased its influence in the international arena and at the same time witnessed the economic and political decline of its chief adversary, the United States. The Soviet leadership dealt successfully with unprecedented dissent movements among the intelligentsia and assured relatively great political and social stability in the country.

However, the Soviet Union has developed some serious problems that its new leader, Mikhail Gorbachev, will have to confront. Agriculture is one problem. A country that was once the world's largest grain exporter has become the world's largest grain importer. There is also an enormous waste of agricultural production. It is estimated that up to 25 percent of some crops are left to rot in the fields because of equipment shortages.[18] Second, there is a problem of more efficient resource allocation. The Stalinist model used in the past was able to mobilize the necessary resources for the establishment of a powerful industrial base with a strong defense sector by diverting resources from nonpriority sectors such as housing, consumer goods, and agriculture. The model has outlived its usefulness, but resources are still being allocated to the heavy industrial sector at the expense of consumer goods and agriculture. Third, the Soviet Union has lagged far behind the West in technology, particularly in the production of computers and software. Fourth, the economic system, with its bureaucratic centralization, has become increasingly more difficult to manage.

ECONOMIC GROWTH

Table 13-3 presents the growth rate of the Soviet economy for the period 1961–1984. The growth experience of the Soviet Union during the 1960s was generally good, averaging around 5 percent a year. During the 1970s the growth rate declined, averaging around 3.4 percent a year. The early 1980s witnessed a further decline in the rate of economic growth to around 2.5 percent for the period 1980–1984. There are specific reasons for the decline in the Soviet growth rate. Military expenditures absorb resources that could be made available for capital formation. There are resource constraints, both human and material, that inhibit the growth rate. Factor productivity, as measured by inputs of labor, capital, and land, has shown a decline. Several factors have contributed to the decline of factor productivity.[19] One is the depletion of the raw material base of oil, coal,

18. Marshall I. Goldman, *U.S.S.R. in Crisis* (New York: W.W. Norton & Co. Inc., 1983), p. 2.

19. Herbert S. Levine, "Possible Causes of the Deterioration of Soviet Productivity Growth in the Period 1976–1980" in *Soviet Economy in the 1980's: Problems and Prospects*, Part 1, U.S. Congress, Joint Economic Committee, 97th Cong., 2d Sess., 1982, pp. 155-161.

TABLE 13-3 GROSS NATIONAL PRODUCT
AND FACTOR PRODUCTIVITY
IN THE SOVIET UNION, 1961–1984
(percentage increase or decrease)

| | Gross National Product | Factor Productivity | | |
		Labor	Capital	Land
1961–1965	5.0%	3.4%	−3.5%	4.4%
1966–1970	5.2	3.2	−2.0	5.6
1971–1975	3.7	2.0	−4.0	2.9
1976–1980	2.6	1.5	−4.0	2.7
1980	1.7	0.6	−4.6	2.1
1981	1.9	1.1	−4.2	3.2
1982	2.6	1.7	−3.5	2.2
1983	3.7	2.8	−2.5	3.3
1984	2.5	1.9	−3.5	2.5

Source: Central Intelligence Agency, *Handbook of Economic Statistics 1985* (Washington: USGPO, 1985), p. 68.

and iron ore on the major industrial regions. A second is the aging of the Soviet capital stock. When labor is combined with old capital, labor productivity is lower than it would be if combined with newer capital.

AGRICULTURE

Agriculture is an area of concern for the Soviet Union. There are many problems confronting Soviet agriculture. Geography and nature have not been kind to the country. Despite the largest land area in the world, only a small fraction of the country has a long-enough growing season and enough moisture to support agriculture. Storage and transportation facilities are inadequate. The overwhelming majority of Soviet farms have no paved roads at their disposal to bring in supplies and to take out their harvests.

Agriculture has also turned out to be expensive to the Soviet government in that annual subsidies amount to around $50 billion a year. Food products are bought from the farms at a price that is much higher than the fixed retail price to consumers. The retail price of meat is about half of the procurement price paid by the government to the farms that produce it.

Table 13-4 presents grain production in the Soviet Union for the period 1975–1984. During the period, the Soviet Union was an importer of grain.

TABLE 13-4 GRAIN PRODUCTION IN THE SOVIET UNION
(million metric tons)

1975	140.1	1980	189.1
1976	223.8	1981	160.0
1977	195.7	1982	180.0
1978	237.4	1983	195.0
1979	179.2	1984	170.0

Source: U.S. Department of Agriculture, *Foreign Agriculture Circular: Grains* (December 11, 1984), p. 8.

In 1984 the Soviet Union imported 19.4 million metric tons of wheat.[20] There is considerable variation in output, with the period 1979–1981 being affected by a drought. In addition to the drought, other factors—including poor farming technology and inadequate chemical techniques—were responsible for the generally poor grain production.[21] A general lack of pesticides and herbicides allowed losses to weeds, rodents, and insects. Soviet fertilizer-handling techniques are primitive; fertilizer delivered to railroad sidings often sits there undiscovered. A lack of farm machinery is another problem. There is also a labor shortage because of the strong out-migration created by the lure of the cities.[22]

CONSUMPTION

As Table 13-5 indicates, consumption is given a lower priority in the Soviet Union than it enjoys in capitalist countries. In the United States, for example, consumption expenditures constitute around 70 percent of gross national product. In the Soviet Union investment priorities have favored heavy industry and defense. These priorities, coupled with a rigid and cumbersome system of distribution, have created a consumer sector that

20. John L. Scherer, *U.S.S.R. Facts and Figures Annual 1985* (Gulf Breeze, Fla.: Academic International Press, 1985), p. 225.

21. Anton F. Malish, "The Food Program: A New Policy or More Rhetoric" in *Soviet Economy in the 1980's: Problems and Prospects*, Part 2, U.S. Congress, Joint Economic Committee, 97th Cong., 2d Sess., 1984, pp. 45-47.

22. The words of a popular American song in World War I were: "How're you going to keep them down on the farm after they've seen Paree?" Moscow is not Paris, but it beats life on a collective farm. The state has tried to stop migration to the cities by setting average rural wages higher than average urban wages.

T A B L E 1 3 - 5   PERCENTAGE OF SOVIET GROSS NATIONAL PRODUCT ALLOCATED TO CONSUMPTION, INVESTMENT, AND DEFENSE

	1960	1970	1980	1984
Consumption	58	54	53	53
Fixed investment	20	23	26	28
Other investment	4	5	7	8
Defense	18	18	14	13
Gross national product	100	100	100	100

Source: Central Intelligence Agency, *Handbook of Economic Statistics 1985* (Washington: USGPO), p. 64.

lags far behind not only the Western countries but most of the Eastern European satellite countries as well. Low-quality goods and services, queues, and shortages are a way of life to Soviet consumers. Although there has been an upward trend in the well-being of the Russian consumer, expectations of more have been built into the Soviet system. In view of other claims on resource allocation, it may be difficult for the Soviet leaders to continue a policy of consumption growth during the 1980s, particularly with a decline in the growth rate.[23]

The standard of living of the Soviet consumer has been changing over time; except for food, it generally improves each year. The number of apartments and the stock of consumer goods continue to increase each year. However, there are problems. Although food prices are heavily subsidized by the state, food quality is low and certain products are in short supply. Many food products, including fruits and vegetables, can be bought only at private markets. Basic consumer products, such as toothpaste and soap, are often unavailable, reflecting in part an inefficient distribution system. State-supplied services are hard to find and unpleasant to use.[24] It is often very difficult and time-consuming to find someone who can repair an automobile or the plumbing. This has led to the creation of what has been called the "secondary economy," where consumer needs can be satisfied for a price. For example, an auto mechanic or plumber can be hired after-hours, often with parts stolen from the regular job.[25]

23. The Eleventh Five-Year Plan, 1981–1985, called for a lower rate of increase in consumption than did the previous five-year plan.

24. Goldman, *U.S.S.R. in Crisis*, p. 97.

25. David K. Shepler, *Russia, Broken Idols, Solemn Dreams* (New York: Times Books, 1983), pp. 172-173.

Table 13-6 compares consumer standards of living in Moscow, Washington, DC, and London for 1982. The standards are calculated by using costs in terms of working time. Although disposable income is much higher in Washington, DC, and London than it is in Moscow, Soviet citizens are faced with a different pattern of prices. Many services are provided at no charge by the government, and the prices of others do not reflect their scarcity value. In the Soviet Union, rent is very cheap, and food and medical care are highly subsidized. However, other consumer goods are far more expensive relative to disposable income than they are in the market economies. An example is cars. The table also does not take into consideration the quality of the product being compared. The quality of most products made in the Soviet Union is far inferior to that of products made in the market economies.[26]

INDUSTRIAL PRODUCTION

The Soviet Union has achieved some quantitative successes in industrial production. Steel production in 1984 amounted to 1.54 million metric tons, which made the Soviet Union the largest producer of steel in the world.[27] The steel industry has been the cornerstone of Soviet industrial production since the time of Stalin and continues to lay claim to a disproportionate share of capital at a time when technology is rapidly changing throughout the world. Still, the Soviet steel industry has its problems. Each year 15 to 17 million tons of steel are wasted in the production of poorly designed equipment.[28] Rolled steel is limited in its variety, easily corroded, and of poor quality. Ninety percent of the casting iron used for machine building is produced in antiquated, inefficient furnaces. Only about 13 percent of steel production in the Soviet Union involves continuous casting (compared to 80 percent in Japan).

In a world that has become increasingly dominated by high-technology industries, the Soviet Union is lagging behind in the production of computers.[29] Soviet computer equipment has lagged behind what has become standard in the United States and Japan. The Soviet Union produces 9 percent of world computer output, compared to 43 percent for the

26. For that matter, they are inferior to goods made in Poland, East Germany, and Hungary. Russians go to Warsaw and Budapest to buy goods; Poles and Hungarians don't go to Moscow to buy goods.

27. Central Intelligence Agency, *Handbook of Economic Statistics, 1985* (Washington: USGPO, 1985), Table 113, p. 150.

28. Scherer, *U.S.S.R. Facts and Figures*, p. 209.

29. Ibid., p. 208.

TABLE 13-6 COMPARATIVE COMMODITIES COSTS IN TERMS OF WORK TIME

	Moscow	London	Washington, DC
Minutes of work time to purchase 1 kilogram[1]			
White bread	17	25	16
Beef	123	115	69
Potatoes	7	3	7
Butter	222	50	55
Hours of work time			
Apartment rent month	12	28	51
Color TV	701	132	65
Months of work time			
Small car	53	11	5

[1]Kilogram = 2.2. pounds

Source: Keith Bush, "Retail Prices in Moscow and Four Western Cities in March, 1982," *Radio Liberty Research* (June 1982).

United States, 28 percent for Western Europe, and 11 percent for Japan.[30] Many Soviet computers have been imported from Hungary, which provides the experts to run them. Few schools in the Soviet Union offer training in computers, and computer literacy is low.

The Soviet Union is also far behind the developed countries of the West in the production and use of industrial robots and computer-aided manufacturing techniques. In 1985 the Soviet Union had 25,000 industrial robots, compared to 70,000 for Japan.[31] Most robots are first-generation fixed-program manipulators unable to adapt to a changed environment. The Soviets lack ready access to digital and computer circuitry, which hinders research in advanced robotics.

MIKHAIL GORBACHEV AND ECONOMIC REFORMS

A dramatic change has taken place in the leadership of the Soviet Union. The septuagenarian leaders of the past have been replaced by a much

30. Stuard Gannon, "The Soviet Lag in High-Tech Defense," *Fortune*, November 25, 1985, pp. 107-118.

31. Scherer, *U.S.S.R. Facts and Figures*, p. 207.

younger and more dynamic leader, Mikhail Gorbachev, who aims for a complete reformation of the Soviet economy. He has many problems to overcome, one of which is an entrenched bureaucracy that has resisted previous efforts at economic reform. Another problem is to make Soviet state enterprises more efficient. Under the present system, Soviet ministries allocate capital to successful and unsuccessful enterprises alike. Many plants that are now considered obsolete must be modernized. Another problem is the system where prices are set by the state to cover production costs and allow some profit. Demand plays no role, and shortages do not lead to higher prices and more production, as in a market economy. Labor shortages and declining hard currency earnings from oil exports create problems. Without hard currency, it becomes more difficult to import the machinery necessary to improve industrial efficiency.

Since he has been in office, Gorbachev has undertaken several initiatives. To reduce alcoholism, which has become a serious problem in Soviet society and is responsible for much worker absenteeism, he has restricted the hours during which alcohol can be sold. He has cracked down on corruption, which has been a problem in the Soviet Union. He has set a goal to almost double national income and output by the end of the century. To do this, he plans to give more autonomy to state enterprises by allowing them to retain and reinvest more of their earnings. There is a modest attempt at price reform in that enterprises are allowed to increase the price of top-quality goods by as much as 30 percent. The central planning agency (Gosplan) and the various ministries have reduced the number of plan indicators or goals that state enterprises are required to meet to three: output, production, and the fulfillment of contract obligations.[32]

32. Bruce Steinberg, "Reforming the Soviet Economy," *Fortune*, November 25, 1985, pp. 90-96.

SUMMARY

The cornerstone of the Soviet economy is the industrial enterprise, which operates on the basis of an annual production plan integrated into the national economic plan. Its performance is based on a series of success indicators. Enterprises operate under a profit-and-loss accounting system, and their success is supposed to be judged primarily by the volume of their sales and profits. Each enterprise is run by a director or manager whose responsibilities are similar to those of managers of American enterprises. However, the government prescribes the policies all enterprises are to follow in the national economic plan, and managers are confined by the targets and resource limits prescribed in it. There is a government and party hierarchy that plans and administers Soviet industry and, for that matter, the entire economy.

Agriculture has long been a problem in the Soviet Union. It has suffered because of underinvestment, excessive central direction, and lack of incentives. In terms of production and performance, it lags well behind agriculture in the United States. The United States uses more capital to achieve a greater output. Most equipment used on Soviet state and collective farms is not used at an optimum level because there is a chronic shortage of technical personnel. There has been a large-scale migration of younger workers, especially those who are trained, from rural to urban areas. To arrest this urban migration and to promote greater efficiency in agriculture, economic reforms were introduced with the objectives of raising rural incomes and living standards and increasing capital investment. Guaranteed minimum monthly payments to collective farmers have been introduced, and state farm workers have been put on the same wage system as that used for industrial workers. Although managers of state and collective farms have been given more autonomy, pricing of farm products remains in the government's domain.

A number of problems confront the Soviet economy in the middle 1980s, not the least of which is agriculture. Production has been erratic and there has been much wastage of output. Imports of grain crops have increased. The Soviet Union has lagged behind the West in the development of high-technology industries. Central planning has created a centralization of economic authority that works against enterprise efficiency. Enterprises must be made more efficient by allowing managers more latitude in making decisions. The efficiency of the labor force also has to be improved by providing more incentives to be productive. The new Soviet leadership, headed by Mikhail Gorbachev, has set a new agenda to improve the performance of the Soviet economy.

REVIEW QUESTIONS

1. Why are wage differentials used in the Soviet Union?
2. Discuss the supply system of the Soviet Union.
3. Distinguish between state farms and collective farms.

4. How are state farms financed?
5. What are the functions of labor unions in the Soviet Union?
6. Income distribution in the Soviet Union is, theoretically, based on the Marxist concept of "from each according to his ability; to each according to his need." Do you agree? Explain.
7. What is the role of the Communist Party in the Soviet enterprise?
8. As you see it, what are the strong and weak points in the Soviet economic and political system?
9. Discuss the economic problems of the Soviet Union in the 1980s. What are the particular problems of Soviet agriculture?
10. What role do private plots play in Soviet agriculture?
11. Although consumer living standards have increased in the Soviet Union, many problems still remain. Discuss.

RECOMMENDED READINGS

Bailer, Seweryn. "The Harsh Decade: Soviet Policies in the 1980's." *Foreign Affairs* (Summer 1981), pp. 990–1020.

Bergson, Abram, and Herbert L. Levine, eds. *The Soviet Economy: Towards the Year 2000*. London: George Allen & Unwin, Ltd., 1983.

Berliner, Joseph. "Managing the U.S.S.R. Economy: Alternative Models." *Problems of Communism* (January–February 1983), pp. 40–56.

Lane, David. *Soviet Economy and Society*. London: Basil Blackwell, 1985.

Moore, Thomas. "Managers: Russia's New Elite." *Fortune* (November 25, 1985), pp. 98–104.

Nove, Alec. *The Economics of Feasible Socialism*. London: George Allen & Unwin, Ltd., 1984.

Scherer, John L., ed. *USSR Facts and Figures Annual, 1985*. Gulf Breeze, Fla.: Academic International Press, 1985.

Steinberg, David. "Reforming the Soviet Economy." *Fortune* (November 25, 1985), pp. 90–96.

U.S. Congress, Joint Economic Committee. *Allocation of Resources in the Soviet Union and China, 1984*. 98th Cong., 1st Sess., 1984.

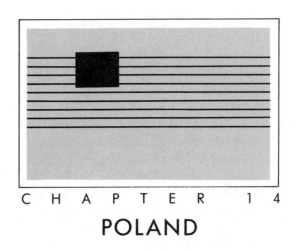

C H A P T E R   1 4

POLAND

"The Winter is yours, the Spring belongs to us."[1]

In December 1981 the Polish government, under pressure from the Soviet Union, imposed martial law on Polish society. Thousands of workers, intellectuals, and dissidents were arrested and the independent Solidarity union was dissolved. The government was put in the anomalous position of repressing the very workers it claimed to represent. Tanks ringed factories and mines, and soldiers and police used force to clear out resisting workers. In the coal-mining area of Katowice, workers who resisted were killed or injured. The lesson that can be learned is that the last thing a communist state will tolerate is any move that would cause its decline or that would mitigate the dictatorship of the Communist Party. Lenin once reduced the past and future alike to two pronouns and a question mark: "Who—whom?" He meant: Who would prevail over whom? To the Communist Party the answer was never in doubt: Lenin and those who have followed him in the Soviet Union would prevail over "whom"— whoever they were.

The tragedy of Poland is its geographic location. Poland has the unique misfortune of being located between Germany and the Soviet

1. Sign in the Lenin Shipyard in Gdansk.

Union. A historian once wrote: "It is easier to lecture the Poles than to live their lives between Berlin and Moscow."[2] However, long before Germany and the Soviet Union became countries, Poland was a common battle-ground for invaders ranging from the Mongol hordes of Genghis Khan to the Magyars and Swedes. In addition to suffering repeated foreign inva-sions, Poland was partitioned in the eighteenth century and eliminated as a political organization until 1918. From 1918 to 1939 Poland was recre-ated as a country out of territory that had been taken from Germany, the Austro-Hungarian Empire, and Russia. During World War II Poland was again partitioned between Germany and the Soviet Union. When Ger-many invaded the Soviet Union in 1941, much of the early fighting was done on Polish territory held by the Soviet Union. During the German re-treat from the Soviet Union in 1944, many battles were again fought in Poland. Some 6 million Poles were killed during World War II, the highest casualty rate for any country involved in the war.[3]

Successive occupations have given the Poles a deep-seated resentment of foreign-imposed rule of any form.[4] Long ago the Poles developed a sense of national unity tinged with romantic fatalism. Poles have revolted count-less times against their oppressors, these revolts usually ending in failure. In 1978 the election of the first Polish pope, John Paul II, helped to create a psychological climate that eventually resulted in the creation of an inde-pendent labor movement that challenged the existence of the communist state.

This chapter will break somewhat from the form followed in the pre-vious chapters on individual countries. Sections covering banking, public finance, and central planning are not included because Poland follows the same procedures as the Soviet Union in these areas. The historical back-ground and events leading to the current instability in Poland are explored as an example of problems faced by command economies.

■ RELIGION, HISTORY, ■ AND ECONOMICS

Modern Poland was created as a result of agreements reached at the Yalta conference of 1945. At the end of World War II there were two rival fac-

---

2. Salvador de Madariaga, *Victors Beware* (London: Jonathan Cape, 1946), p. 214.

3. Poland at that time had a population of 30 million.

4. While visiting in Warsaw in 1985, the author was told the following joke: A sergeant in the Polish army asked a new recruit, "If the Germans and Russians invaded Poland at the same time, who would you shoot first, a German or a Russian?" The recruit replied, "The German." "Why?" the sergeant asked. "Business before pleasure," the recruit replied.

tions in Poland, both of which had been resistance groups during the German occupation. One faction was the so-called National Army of Liberation, and the other was the Communist People's Army.[5] The agreements of the Yalta conference allowed the Soviet Union to extend its sphere of influence over Poland. Although free elections were called for, the Soviet Union had already created a provisional government, and it was only a matter of time before Communist Party influence was firmly established. When free elections were finally held in 1946, the outcome was preordained. The Communist Party and its affiliated groups received 89.8 percent of the vote. Members of the National Army groups were either eliminated or left the country. In 1949 the Communist Party became the only political party in Poland, and in 1952 a constitution based on the Soviet constitution was promulgated.

After the war, the immediate need was to reconstruct the Polish economy, which had largely been destroyed.[6] The institutions of a Soviet command economy were introduced by degrees. During the period 1945–1948, industry, trade, and finance were nationalized and a two-year plan aimed at reconstruction of the economy was introduced. The direction and structure of the Polish economy was designed primarily to accord with Soviet economic and strategic priorities at considerable cost to Poland's own economic development.

Consumption was given short shrift. In the late 1940s the Polish regime, under strict Soviet tutelage, began trying to control consumption through detailed planning and administrative rationing in order to hasten the building of an industrial state. Once adequate supplies of basic necessities had been restored, the expansion of heavy industry took precedence over further increases in consumption. The distribution of food and housing was governed by administrative rationing. Prices were relied upon to govern the distribution of meager supplies of food, clothing, and consumer durables, but these prices were held below equilibrium levels, with the result that shortages and waiting lines were commonplace.

Certain contradications developed in the Polish economy and society despite attempts to impose a Soviet-type economic and social model. In the Soviet model, agriculture is collectivized, management and labor relations are controlled by the state, and resources are allocated on the basis of centralized economic planning. Religion was regarded by Marx as the opiate of the masses, so it would be eliminated (or at least severely discouraged). The application of the Soviet model was more difficult to implement in

---

5. The National Army of Liberation was a part of the Free Polish group that was based in London during World War II. During the Warsaw uprising against the Nazis in 1944, the Russian army, though just across the Vistula river from Warsaw, did nothing to help the Poles.

6. Warsaw was 95 percent destroyed by the end of World War II.

Poland than in the other Eastern European countries. For one thing, Poland is a larger country in both population and physical size. Poland is a Roman Catholic country, with strong attachments to the Church that go back a thousand years. The tradition of Polish agriculture runs counter to the establishment of collectivized agriculture. The Polish farmer has a deep-rooted sense of private property, individual freedom, religious feeling, and family farming. Attempts by the state to alter these institutions have not been successful.

RELIGION

The Catholic Church has been an integral part of Polish life ever since the baptism of the nation's first ruler, Prince Mieszko I, in 966. It helped to keep the Polish language and culture alive during periods of occupation. After the communist takeover of Poland in 1945, religion remained largely untouched. The Roman Catholic Church was too much a part of Polish history and a repository of its culture for the state to eliminate. A policy of accommodation developed between Church and state in Poland. The Church did not criticize the communist regime directly, and the regime ignored the Church as best it could. The primate of Poland from 1948 to his death, Stefan Cardinal Wyszynski, set Church policy, which was based on moral criticism and ethical guidance to the faithful. The essence of the Church was its religious mission. It would not identify itself directly with any opposition movement, but would also defend every persecuted opposition movement. However, the Church was not submissive to the state. Bishop Karol Wojtyla, who later became Pope John Paul II, was a critic of the temporal power of the state. The viability of the Catholic Church is evidenced by fact that 88 percent of the people of Poland are communicants today.

POLAND FROM 1950 TO 1970

Aside from religion and agriculture, the Polish socioeconomic system is similar to that of the Soviet Union. What makes Poland unique are the people and their actions under Communist rule. The three main social classes are the intelligentsia, the workers, and the peasants. Real political power is exercised by the top leadership of the Communist Party. In times of stress such as in 1956, 1970, and 1981, the party merely reshuffles the leadership and demotes a few bureaucrats. The Poles are adept, through long years of experience with foreign rule, at frustrating the objectives of any authority. When denied other means of political opposition, they withdraw into tight circles based on family and friends and there preserve their own traditional system of values.

THE 1956 REVOLT   In 1956 an event of historic significance broke down the pretense of worker support for the Communist regime. Industrial workers of the city of Poznan went on strike, demanding bread, freedom, free elections, and the departure of the Russians. The strike escalated into armed attacks on police headquarters; it was suppressed, with much bloodshed, by the army and punished by massive arrests. Threatened Soviet intervention led to worker and student demonstrations throughout much of Poland. Various factions in the Communist Party blamed each other for the riots. The Stalinist faction wanted tighter controls placed on the press, intellectuals, and workers, but also wanted to increase workers' wages as a palliative for their discontent. Another faction wanted to implement economic and political reforms. Wladyslaw Gomulka, who was not identified with either faction, became party boss.

THE GOMULKA PERIOD, 1956–1970   Gomulka enjoyed tremendous initial support because he was never identified with the pro-Russian faction. His immediate task was the restoration of order in the country. Anti-Soviet feeling was high, and political activists threatened to vote the Communists out in a general election, which would have meant immediate Soviet intervention. Gomulka made a number of concessions to workers, farmers, intellectuals, and the Catholic Church to lessen discontent. He succeeded in reestablishing Communist Party rule over the country, but his popularity began to decline as he began to eliminate workers' councils and other forms of democratic self-expression. A closer working relationship with the Soviet Union also caused him to lose popularity within the country. Tension also developed with the Church, the intellectuals, and students at Warsaw University. Student demonstrations in 1968 led to arrests and an attempt by the party to blame the unrest on the Jews.[7]

Gomulka's economic policies were based on a continuance of industrialization based on the Soviet industrial model. Resources were directed to such industries as iron and steel, heavy machinery, and chemicals—industries that are typical of nineteenth-century industrialization and sensitive to technological change. The development strategy was wrong for Poland because it is totally different from the Soviet Union in resources and size.

---

7. Poland has never been a model of religious tolerance. Anti-Semitism runs deep in Polish history.

Profitable industries had to subsidize unprofitable ones, and high operating costs made many plants and industries unprofitable. The consumer and agricultural sectors, whose resources went into the forced industrialization policy, suffered accordingly, and by 1968 the Polish economy was stagnant.

POLAND IN THE 1970s

After riots in 1970, Gomulka was replaced by Edward Gierek as party secretary. Gierek faced several major economic problems, the most important of which was a high level of consumer unrest, attributed to chronic shortages of meat and quality consumer goods. Gierek promised dramatic gains in the nation's standard of living, mainly through a massive influx of foreign investment. Poland imported large amounts of new capital goods from the West, paid for with credit from Western banks and governments.

The Poles expected to pay off their debt with expanded exports to the West in the form of goods produced with their new technology. Industrial cooperation agreements involving a considerable amount of money were concluded with Western firms. For the most part, these agreements accomplished little or nothing in terms of enhancing the ability of the Poles to earn hard currency in order to finance Polish debt payments to Western banks.

PROBLEMS OF AGRICULTURE   Poland is the only centrally planned economy that relies principally on private farming.[8] Unlike any other Eastern European country, the Communists never succeeded in collectivizing the bulk of Polish agriculture; even at the outset of Communist Party rule, its hold on the allegiance of the people, especially in the heavily Catholic countryside, was simply too tenuous. Communist efforts to collectivize all forms of agriculture, often against the armed opposition of the farmers, resulted in many deaths. In 1956 the government formally postponed the political efforts required to enforce the collectivation of agriculture. The result is that today approximately 75 percent of the country's arable land is farmed by 3.5 million independent small farmers, who account for 75 percent of the country's agricultural output.

There are two factors responsible for the erratic performance of Polish agriculture. First, most private farms are too small to achieve economies of scale. Incomes are too low on most farms to afford investment in equip-

8. Yugoslavia also has private ownership in agriculture, but it does not fall within the mold of the centrally planned economy.

ment for mechanizing farm tasks. Second, government policy toward agriculture has not been consistent. The government has subsidized consumers at the expense of farm income. Investment in agriculture has generally been low, as the government has favored development of the industrial sector. For years, private farming suffered from neglect and government policies discouraged expansion and limited growth in productivity.

During the 1970s, poor agricultural harvests and government inefficiency played havoc with agricultural production in one of the premier agricultural countries in Europe. Meat consumption, a critical element of the Polish diet, declined to the point where rationing was imposed as early as 1977. Meat exports to the West, which were an important source of hard currency earnings, declined to the point where meat eventually had to be imported. A shortfall in the potato crop, a major source of feed for hogs, forced farmers to purchase livestock feed from the state. This resulted in an increase in Polish grain imports, which heavily affected the trade deficit with Western countries. The cost of the grain imports was passed on to farmers, but it was not matched by higher prices for livestock.

The state's pricing system, designed to hold down food costs to consumers, was an invitation to disaster. The state was paying farmers 10 zlotys for a liter of milk that it sold in the store for 4 zlotys.[9] Live hogs were bought from farmers at 130 zlotys per kilogram and sold as butchered pork for 70 zlotys per kilogram. Farmers bought bread and fed it to their livestock because it was cheaper than the wheat from which it was made. The state began to lose in two ways. First, price subsidies began to absorb more and more of national budget expenditures. Second, farmers felt that prices offered by the state for meat and other food products were too low. They began to withhold meat and other products from state buyers, preferring to sell them in private markets or use them for personal consumption. When it became necessary to raise food prices to prevent a continuing drain on the state budget, major riots occurred.

THE INCREASE IN THE POLISH FOREIGN DEBT The growth of exports to the West did not keep pace with the growth of imports and the increase in foreign debt. As borrowing increased, Poland became more and more dependent on private credit from Western commercial banks. In 1970 debt to Western commercial banks and governments amounted to $1.3 billion; by 1981 the amount of debt owed to Western commercial banks and governments had increased to $25.5 billion. Servicing and repaying the loans consumed all of Poland's hard currency export earnings, estimated at $6.5

9. The zloty exchanged at 130 for $1 in 1985. It is not convertible outside Poland.

billion in 1981.[10] The increase in debt service payments, which resulted from a rising debt, forced Poland to seek easier credit terms in the West and to appeal to the Soviet Union for financial assistance. Soviet aid took the form of financial loans, shipments of grain and crude oil, and the provision of certain consumer goods. But this assistance, by itself, was not sufficient to solve Poland's balance-of-payments problems and debts to the West, nor did it resolve consumer unrest.

The significance of the Polish debt to the West is reflected in the comparison of debt services to exports. A debt service-to-export ratio of 0.25 is considered by bankers to be a signal for lending caution. The ratio for Poland reached 0.81 in 1980, which means simply that for every $1.00 earned from exports, $.81 is paid out in debt service payments. The Polish capacity for handling the debt was exacerbated by agricultural problems, which required increased imports of food products. Overemployment, generally low productivity in most industries, and an emphasis upon meeting quantity targets as expressed in the economic plan also worked against Poland's capacity to increase its exports.

The debt has placed Western banks and the Soviet Union in a dilemma. The banks are reluctant to lend more money to Poland. Yet at the same time, the banks would lose billions of dollars if Poland defaulted on existing loans. A Polish default would also have an impact on Western lending to other Eastern European countries and the Soviet Union. Both Eastern Europe and the Soviet Union depend upon Western banks to finance large capital projects. The Russians may be put in the position of having to pay off the Polish debt in order to keep their own lines of credit open to the West.

EXTRANEOUS FACTORS   There were also factors over which Poland had no control that contributed to the decline of the Polish economy. One such factor was a decrease in the demand for Polish coal. Poland is the second largest coal-exporting country in the world; half of Poland's coal shipments go to hard currency countries. During the late 1970s, a lessening of demand for coal in the West, which resulted from a slowdown in economic activity, worked to the detriment of Polish exports of coal. The growth in hard currency earnings from the export of coal became highly dependent on world economic recovery and increases in world coal prices.

REVISED ECONOMIC PLAN   The 1976–1980 economic plan had to be revised to placate consumers, with increased priority attached to invest-

---

10. *Time*, January 4, 1982, p. 69. U.S. banks had made about $1.8 billion worth of loans to Poland. West German banks have been the largest lenders to Poland, with $2.7 billion in loans as of 1981.

ments in food, housing, and commercial service. An important aspect of the revised plan was greater reliance on the Polish private sector to increase the output of consumer goods and services. Many concessions were made, including reduced taxes on private businesses and raising the tax-free limit on private service income by 500 percent. Credit was increased to private enterprises, private artisans, and private craftspeople. Efforts were made to attract foreign investments to improve the service sector in order to attract foreign tourists with their hard currencies.

■ THE SOLIDARITY MOVEMENT ■

In 1980 the most important development since the beginning of the modern communist state occurred in Poland with the formation of the Solidarity union and its subsequent challenge to state authority. Before that time unions were state-controlled groups that were little more than passive organs of the state. Workers were forbidden to strike, for to do so would be striking against the state that claimed to be the representative of the proletariat. Therefore, workers would be striking against themselves. Solidarity, which was formed in the Lenin Shipyard in Gdansk, was more than a union. It became a national movement representing workers and intellectuals, and at its peak claimed 10 million members.

FACTORS RESPONSIBLE FOR THE RISE OF SOLIDARITY

The spark that united the Solidarity movement was a government decree that raised meat prices in 1980. However, forces were already at work to create worker discontent. These forces were built into the expectations of workers as to how their economic system should function. There were major differences between promises and performance. Since 1945 the workers had been promised a communist paradise of milk and honey, but the paradise had not arrived. As one teacher said, she got tired of being told how good she had it and how bad off the capitalist countries were.[11] Visits to the West had convinced her otherwise. There was much evidence to convince even the most gullible Polish workers that the economy was not functioning the way it should.

Standing in line to buy things is very much a way of life in Poland. (For that matter, it is also a way of life in the Soviet Union, but Soviet citizens are more malleable and have been doing it longer than their Polish

11. Conversation with a Polish professor.

counterparts.) It is often necessary to stand in several lines in order to get meat at a meat market, bread at a bakery, and milk at still a third store. Many important products are in short supply. Soap, for example, has become largely unobtainable in the larger Polish cities. To make matters worse, there are several types of retail outlets. The first type of outlet is the PEWEX store, which sells imported goods for hard currency. Although Poles may shop there if they have hard currency, this type of store is designed for the foreign visitor. Then there is the state store, which is characterized by low prices, negligible stocks of goods, and long lines. Finally, there are the open markets, which are usually on the periphery of a city, where almost anything can be obtained for a price. There are also barter arrangements where, for example, a haircut can be exchanged for a sack of potatoes.

SOLIDARITY AND LECH WALESA

In July 1980 workers in the Lenin Shipyard in Gdansk walked out in protest of the government's decision to raise meat prices. The protest appeared to be going nowhere when an unemployed electrician named Lech Walesa, who had been fired for trying to create an independent union, climbed over the shipyard fence and became the catalyst in a labor movement that was to shake Poland and the world. That he was able to do what he did in a shipyard named for one of the saints of communism has some irony, for the last thing in the world that Lenin wanted, or would tolerate, was any movement that would mitigate the dictatorship of the Communist Party.

Walesa assumed control over the protesting shipyard workers and the protest movement began to spread to other parts of Poland. A link was formed between intellectuals and workers that led to the creation of Solidarity.[12] The Lenin Shipyard became the focal point of the Solidarity movement; in August, 1980, Walesa and other Solidarity officers met with members of the Gierek government to hammer out the Gdansk agreement. The government agreed to allow the workers the right to strike—something unheard of in a communist state, where Marxist theory holds that there are no contradictory class interests to cause labor conflicts. Workers were also given the right to form their own unions. Censorship was reduced and access to the state broadcasting networks was given to the unions and the Catholic Church.

---

12. The Committee for Social Self-Defense was a precursor of Solidarity. It was formed by dissident intellectuals to oppose political oppression.

After the Gdansk agreement, the Solidarity movement spread like wildfire across Poland. Solidarity evolved into a loose-knit federation to which some 10 million Poles belonged. Everyone from coal miner to college professor belonged to Solidarity, which was divided into 30 semiautonomous regional chapters throughout the country. Problems of policy and strategy developed because some members wanted a union federation concerned with labor goals, while other members wanted to mount opposition to the state. Cross-currents were at work in Solidarity, and the federation was increasingly forced into the path of contentious political activism by its various factions. Elements within Solidarity eventually gave the government the excuse it was looking for when they called for a national referendum on the future of the communist government in Poland and reexamination of Polish military ties with the Soviet Union. In December 1981, martial law was declared in Poland and Lech Walesa and thousands of other Poles were arrested.

GOALS OF SOLIDARITY

During its brief existence, Solidarity accomplished a number of things that were later abrogated by the state. Recall that the root causes of the upheaval that created Solidarity were economic. The Communist Party and the government had fallen into a state of near-terminal paralysis. But Solidarity was concerned with political goals as well as economic ones. It wanted a democratization of the political process. The goals and accomplishments of Solidarity are briefly summarized here.

WORK WEEK   Solidarity won a concession from the government for a five-day work week after decades of a six-day work week. This concession was a mixed blessing. Although the workers gained in terms of leisure time, the economy incurred a loss in production, particularly in the output of coal. In 1979 total coal production in Poland amounted to 240 million tons; in 1981 coal production had decreased to 168 million tons.[13] In 1979 Poland exported 40 million tons, yielding a hard currency profit of $3 billion. In 1981 exports of coal dropped to an estimated 10 million tons. The government offered coal miners triple pay to work on Saturdays; the workers refused because there was nothing to buy in the shops. Poland lacked the hard currency to import consumer goods and food from the West. In early 1986, the government restored Saturday workdays for industry, eliminating a major gain achieved by Solidarity.

---

13. Lawrence Weschler, "A Reporter in Poland," Part II. *New Yorker*, November 16, 1981, p. 199.

NOMENKLATURA   Solidarity mounted an attack on nomenklatura, the system whereby the Communist Party exercises the right to appoint bureaucrats, administrators, and managers in Poland. Nomenklatura in Poland and the other communist countries really involves a position of privilege attained on the basis of nepotism, favoritism, service to the Communist Party, and other factors that have little to do with merit. Most galling to many Poles were the special privileges that accrue to those who were a part of the nomenklatura system—villas, yachts, special stores—privileges that were handed down by the ruling elite to their families and cronies.[14] Solidarity wanted the complete elimination of the nomenklatura system, but nothing has come of that effort.

WORKERS' COUNCILS   Solidarity wanted to create workers' councils similar to those in Yugoslavia. These councils would appoint managers on the basis of their skills, not on their loyalty to the party, and the managers would be subject to worker recall. The state would exercise a normative influence by setting regulations and pollution standards, and an economic influence by using monetary and fiscal policies. There would be reliance on free markets to allocate resources. Free unions would represent workers. There are some contradictions here. Why would unions be necessary since workers would perform the functions of both labor and management? Workers' councils were introduced in a few enterprises before martial law was proclaimed by the government.

CENSORSHIP   Solidarity wanted a relaxation of press censorship and more free expression on television and in the theatres. (Note again that Solidarity was a broad-based movement, including workers, intellectuals, and even disillusioned members of the Communist Party.) It wanted history books to reflect true Polish history, not a distortion of it. An example of distortion was the claim that only Communists were a part of the underground movement during World War II.

■ THE POLISH ECONOMY: ■
POST-SOLIDARITY

The performance of the Polish economy in the 1980s has been poor. The level of industrial production is lower than it was in 1975. Communist

---

14. The author has seen the villas, yachts, and special stores. A member of Solidarity told the author that what was so bad about nomenklatura were the special privileges. She would stand in line for meat that was rarely available, and then see party favorites and their friends come out of the special stores with plenty of meat.

Party leaders blame this poor performance on the general unrest created by Solidarity, but Solidarity was a result, not the cause, of the problem. The simple fact is that after 40 years with a monopoly on power, the Communist regime has not been able to fulfill its economic promises to the people of Poland. On numerous occasions it has had to use force on the very workers it claims to represent.

The Communist ideology contains imperatives that, though they render impossible the solution of important problems, the Polish leadership cannot discard. At its back are the Soviet leaders, who are concerned above all that Poland and the other Eastern European countries be ruled by a party of the Leninist-Stalinist type. This means that the party must maintain a monopoly on political, ideological, and economic power through central planning, centralized control over industrial production, and the elimination of beliefs that compete with Marxism-Leninism. In November 1985 the government announced that it had discharged 1500 rectors and other administrators at the Polish universities for a lack of support of government policies.

Table 14-1 presents the performance of the Polish economy from 1970 to 1985, using indices of agricultural and industrial production. It is evident that the country was headed for a major crisis long before Solidarity was created. The index of industrial production, which was 144 in 1975, had increased to only 148 by 1980. Drastic shortages of consumer goods have existed for years. In 1977 Polish citizens had to forego the consumption of meat once a week. Capital and labor productivity also showed sharp declines in the late 1970s. By 1982 the index of industrial production had fallen to 126. Although it increased in 1983 and 1984, the index for 1985 is still below the index for 1975. The index of agricultural production showed a sharp decline for 1982, but has shown subsequent increases. Construction declined by 10.5 percent in 1980 and 19.8 percent in 1981.[15] It has shown a marginal increase since 1982. The hard currency debt of Poland to the West increased from $8 billion in 1975 to $28.1 billion in 1984.[16]

Table 14-2 presents real per capita growth rates for Poland and Eastern Europe for selected periods. The rate of real per capital growth for Poland during the 1971–1975 period was much higher than real per capita rate of growth for Eastern Europe. However, it declined sharply for the period 1976–1979. The growth rates for 1980, 1981, and 1982 were negative. The 6.3 percent decline in 1981 was by far the worst for any

15. Ebigniew M. Fallenbuchl, "Poland's Economic Crisis," *Problems of Communism*, March–April 1982, p. 6.

16. Central Intelligence Agency, *Handbook of Economic Statistics 1985* (Washington: USGPO, 1985), p. 48.

TABLE 14-1   INDICES OF AGRICULTURAL AND INDUSTRIAL PRODUCTION FOR POLAND AND EASTERN EUROPE, 1970–1985
(1970 = 100 percent)

	Agricultural Production		Industrial Production	
	Poland	Eastern Europe	Poland	Eastern Europe
1970	100	100	100	100
1975	118	119	144	130
1980	126	127	148	147
1981	128	124	130	144
1982	121	127	126	144
1983	125	128	131	148
1984	137	134	138	152
1985[1]	135	138	136	154

[1]Estimates

Source: Central Intelligence Agency, *Handbook of Economic Statistics 1985* (Washington: USGPO, 1985), pp. 44, 46.

TABLE 14-2   REAL PER CAPITA GNP GROWTH RATES FOR POLAND AND EASTERN EUROPE
(average annual rate of growth)

	Poland	Eastern Europe
1961–1965	3.2%	3.2%
1966–1970	3.3	3.2
1971–1975	5.5	4.2
1976–1979	0.5	1.5
1980	−3.3	−0.8
1981	−6.3	−1.5
1982	−1.8	0.5
1983	3.7	1.2
1984	2.5	2.7
1985[1]	1.8	2.2

[1]Estimates

Source: Central Intelligence Agency, *Handbook of Economic Statistics 1985* (Washington: USGPO), p. 40.

developed economy in the world. The per capita growth rate rebounded to 3.7 percent in 1983, but fell again in 1984 and 1985.

■ THE FUTURE DIRECTION ■
OF THE POLISH ECONOMY

As of early 1986, First Secretary Wojciech Jaruzelski, who has governed Poland since the military crackdown on Solidarity, appears quite secure in his position. He has succeeded in restoring some stability to the Polish economy and steered a moderate course between Communist Party hard-liners who wanted a crackdown on all dissidents and elements of Solidarity who wanted more political and economic freedom. The economy improved in 1983 and 1984, with industrial production and personal consumption increasing. Some economic reforms were introduced. For the most part, the reforms involve the use of economic incentives to increase productivity.[17] One reform involves managerial independence. Enterprises are supposedly free to make decisions on employment and output, except in cases where the output is considered of national importance. A second reform allows more use of free prices as opposed to state-fixed and regu-lated prices.[18] However, this and other initiatives as well as new forms of planning are in the experimental stage and do not seem to portend any fundamental economic change in the economy.

There are several directions in which Poland can go. There could be a somewhat modified return to conditions that existed before martial law was imposed, when freedom within state-imposed limits was permitted. More oppressive state control of the type that exists in Czechoslovakia and East Germany could be adopted. Finally, a more flexible economic policy of the type that is used in Hungary could be adopted. (However, it is nec-essary to point out that reforms in Hungary exist only within circum-scribed limits.) Regardless of the approach, the government has to con-vince the Poles that it is capable of improving their economic lot. This may prove somewhat difficult to do, for in 1985 shortages of many goods con-tinued, and living standards were no better than they were in 1977.[19]

---

17. John P. Hardt and Richard F. Kaufman, "Policy Highlights: A Regional Economic Assessment of Eastern Europe" in *East European Economies: Slow Growth in the 1980's*, Vol. 1, U.S. Congress, Joint Economic Committee, 99th Cong., 1st Sess., 1985.

18. See Stanislaw Gomulka and Jacek Rostowski, "The Reformed Polish Economic System 1982–1983," *Soviet Studies*, July 1984, pp. 386-405.

19. The author was in Poland in 1977 and 1985. There appeared to be more goods available in 1977 than there were in 1985. Many food products, particularly meat, appeared to be in short supply.

FACTORS AFFECTING THE POLISH ECONOMY

Poland and the other Eastern European countries have experienced a transition from rapid growth to low growth and austerity. This poses some policy issues for the future that may prove difficult to resolve.

RELATIONS WITH THE SOVIET UNION The new leader of the Soviet Union will have a profound impact on Poland and other Eastern European countries. Mikhail Gorbachev has announced his intention to make many economic changes in the Soviet Union. He has committed himself to an increase in Soviet consumer living standards and the rate of economic growth. It remains to be seen how much of a gap there is between rhetoric and performance. Many Eastern European countries argue for more diversity in their systems of planning and management to improve the efficiency of their economies. It remains to be seen how willing the new Soviet regime is to allow its satellites to experiment with reforms. If true economic reforms occur in the Soviet Union, then the movement toward reform will probably accelerate in Eastern Europe.

RELATIONS WITH THE WEST Poland and the other Eastern European countries are caught in a dilemma when it comes to dealing with the West. The goods and services of the West are necessary for furthering economic modernization, which is crucial to foreign trade competitiveness and improving consumer living standards. However, any significant change in the global economic environment will affect the Eastern European economies.[20] Prosperity in the Western economies will lead to increased imports from Eastern Europe; a recession will decrease imports from Eastern Europe. High interest rates in the West have had an impact on the costs of debt service. In Poland most of the country's export earnings have to be used to meet interest payments on its $29 billion debt to Western banks. The political environment also affects Polish trade. For example, under the Reagan administration, the United States has imposed trade sanctions on Poland.

INTEGRATION WITHIN CMEA Poland and the other Eastern European countries could turn away from the economic uncertainties of trade with the West toward more integration within CMEA.[21] This would link the Eastern European countries much closer to the economy of the Soviet

---

20. Daniel Bond and Lawrence R. Klein, "Impact of Changes in the Global Environment on the Soviet and Eastern Economies" in *Eastern European Economies*.

21. Council of Mutual Economic Assistance. The members are Bulgaria, Czechoslovakia, East Germany, Hungary, Poland, and Romania.

Union and increase their dependence on Soviet energy supplies. It would, however, also reduce their capacity to import technology from the West necessary to improve their economies. Moreover, the CMEA countries probably would not be able to satisfy Poland's export and import requirements.

S U M M A R Y

Joseph Stalin said that it is easier to saddle a cow than it is to impose communism on Poland. Although Stalin has been dead for many years, subsequent events have proved him to be right. There are several reasons why the Poles have proved to be so intractable. First, Poland had no tradition of communism before World War II. In East Germany and Hungary, Communist Parties were well-established between World Wars I and II. Second, Poland has been occupied by foreign powers throughout much of its history. There is a resentment of any outside power—including the Soviet Union. Third, the Roman Catholic Church has always been a viable part of the life of Poland and bulwark against change. Finally, there is the Polish national character itself—a romantic fatalism created by many centuries of being the battleground for neighboring powers.

A major upheaval occurred in the Polish economy in 1980 when popular discontent with state management of the economy coalesced into the Solidarity movement. Solidarity posed a direct challenge to the state and the authority of the Communist Party. Solidarity was crushed and martial law was imposed in Poland.

The Polish economy continues to have its problems, including a decline in overall living standards and high external debt to the West. Some efforts were made by Jaruzelski to improve the efficiency of the Polish economy, but they have proved to be largely unsuccessful. The Polish hard currency debt to the West remains a major problem, as does a general shortage of consumer goods.

R E V I E W   Q U E S T I O N S

1. What were the goals of Solidarity?
2. Why did the Solidarity movement revolt against the communist system in Poland?
3. What is the significance of the Polish debt to the West?

4. What role has religion played in the life and history of Poland?
5. Discuss the problems of Polish agriculture.
6. What were some of the factors that led to the military crackdown on Poland?
7. Comment on the role the Jaruzelski regime has played in Poland.
8. What is the future of the Polish economy?

RECOMMENDED READINGS

Askers, Anders. *Private Enterprise in Eastern Europe: The Non-Agricultural Private Sector in Poland and the GDR*. New York: St. Martins Press, 1985.

Bond, Daniel, and Lawrence J. Klein. "Impact of Changes in the Global Environment on the Soviet and Eastern European Economies." In *East European Economies: Slow Growth in the 1980's*. Vol. 1. U.S. Congress, Joint Economic Committee, 99th Cong., First Sess., 1985, pp. 7–21.

Fallenbuchl, Zbigniew, M. "The Polish Economy Under Martial Law." *Soviet Studies* (October 1984), pp. 513–527.

Gomulka, Stanislaw, and Jacek Rostowski. "The Reformed Polish Economic System 1982–1983." *Soviet Studies* (July 1984), pp. 386–405.

Landau, Zbigniew. *The Polish Economy in the 20th Century*. New York: St. Martin's Press, 1985.

"Poland Today at Rock Bottom and Crawling." *U.S. News and World Report* (December 9, 1985), pp. 40–42.

Terry, Sarah M. "The Implications of Economic Stringency and Political Succession for Stability in Eastern Europe in the Eighties." In *East European Economies, Slow Growth in the 1980's*. Vol. 1. U.S. Congress, Joint Economic Committee, 99th Cong., First Sess., 1985, pp. 502–540.

Wanless, P. T. "Inflation in the Consumer Goods Market in Poland, 1971–1982." *Soviet Studies* (July 1985), pp. 403–416.

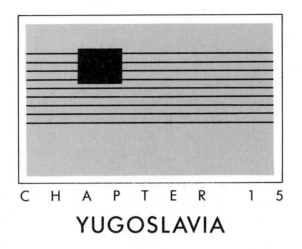

C H A P T E R   1   5

YUGOSLAVIA

The Federal Republic of Yugoslavia represents a rather distinct brand of socialism that is different from that in the rest of Eastern Europe and the Soviet Union. The Yugoslav economy is a synthesis of central planning and a market economy. It contains many features of a market economy, including decentralized management, small-scale private enterprises, advertising associations to promote the distribution of products, and personal incentives to accomplish desired economic objectives. There is also a constitutional guarantee of private peasant landholdings of up to 25 acres of arable land. There is decentralized economic decision making and virtual autonomy of individual producing units, which leads to the use of the term *decentralized socialism* to describe the economy of Yugoslavia.

Yugoslavia was formed in 1918 from the countries Serbia and Montenegro. The population included five Slavic groups—Serbians, Croats, Slovenes, Macedonians, and Bosnians—as well as Hungarians and Albanians. A centralized monarchy was created with the support of the dominant Serbian elements in the population and against the wishes of the Croats, who wanted a federal system of government with a certain amount of regional and ethnic autonomy. Antagonism between the Serbs and Croats characterized the internal history of Yugoslavia between the two world wars. Although considerable autonomy was given to the Croats by the time of World War II, rivalries persist between Serbs and Croats which even today the present government finds difficult to dissipate.

During World War II, Yugoslavia was occupied by the Germans. Resistance forces were split into two groups—the Chetniks, representing the exiled monarchy of King Peter, and the Partisans, led by Tito, a member of the Communist party.[1] The Partisans emerged as the stronger of the two groups and received the bulk of Allied (including Soviet) military support. Those forces that had identified with Tito formed an independent base for the establishment of a communist regime in Belgrade at the end of the war. Since the liberation of Yugoslavia owed nothing to the Russian army but much to Tito and his supporters, there was no reason to be grateful or subservient to Moscow. For this reason, Tito could assert the independence of his regime from Russian domination. In 1948 Yugoslavia was expelled from the Soviet-dominated Cominform for pursuing both domestic and foreign policies independently of Moscow's influence.

After the split with Moscow, Yugoslavia effected a rapprochement with the Western countries based on trade and aid and the desire to secure an alliance in the event of Russian aggression. However, in terms of foreign policy, it has pursued an independent line between East and West and has attempted to project itself as the leader of nonaligned nations, eschewing proximity to either the Eastern or Western military bloc. Although relations with the Russians have improved since the hardline Stalinist days, Yugoslavia's economic ties are primarily with the West, and Yugoslavia participates in such Western economic organizations as the Organization for Economic Cooperation and Development (OECD) and the European Economic Community.

Politically, the country is divided into six republics and two autonomous regions. Each has a president, republic assembly, and numerous specialized administrative agencies. Over the years, greater authority has been given to republics, as the federal government has sought to decentralize decision making and to encourage wider popular participation in economic affairs.

The commune (which has nothing in common with the Chinese institution of the same name) is a local government unit that forms the basic self-governing entity in Yugoslavia. It would roughly correspond to a small city or county in the United States and has three basic responsibilities: guiding economic affairs, including planning, investment, and supervision of enterprises; providing municipal services; and managing various social welfare activities.

---

1. The *Chetniks* were Serbian nationalists who desired an independent Serbia. The *Partisans* were primarily Croats and were led by Josip Broz (Tito), a Croat who was a Communist. Although Communists controlled at the top, considerable support was obtained from people and groups of differing political opinions who believed in Tito's call for national unity.

Yugoslavia is a communist country, and the Communist Party (League of Communists of Yugoslavia, LCY) is the only political party. Despite the institutional arrangement of the Yugoslav economic and political system, the LCY is the final authority over and above all other decision makers. It participates directly in the institutions of the state and of self-management, all the way down to the lowest level of enterprise organization. In these respects the LCY is no different from communist parties in the Soviet Union and the People's Republic of China.

■ THE ECONOMIC SYSTEM ■

Yugoslavia has a unique, complex economic system combining elements of both a centrally planned and a free market economy. One special feature of the Yugoslav economy is the workers' council, which is elected by all workers in each enterprise. The worker's council has extensive management powers concerning the operation of an enterprise. It approves the production plan, the hiring and firing of workers, the distribution of income to workers, and the annual financial statement. It also has control over the division of production and the use of investment funds from outside sources. The workers' council functions through a management board, which it elects from its members to perform the necessary decisions involving the day-to-day operations of the enterprise.

Other unique characteristics of the Yugoslav economic system are the use of decentralized economic decision making and dependence on the free market to allocate resources. Within the limits dictated by national and international competition, enterprises are free to set prices, to decide what and how much to produce, and to distribute revenue from sales from their products. Enterprises are legally independent in that their property is not owned by the government, but the property is held in trust by the enterprises for society as a whole.

ECONOMIC PLANNING

Yugoslavia has moved from centralized planning, which copied that of the Soviet Union, to decentralized planning. The process of decentralization began at the time of the political split with Russia in 1948 and has continued to the present. During the first Five-Year Plan (1947–1951), the dominant theme was the elimination of the market system and its replacement by a system of central economic planning. The early economic plans gave definite instructions to each Yugoslav enterprise pertaining to the methods and scope of production and distribution. Subsequent economic plans shifted from a centralized command arrangement to a more decentralized form of planning that came to resemble French economic planning more than Russian economic planning. The system of fixed production quotas and prices was abandoned, and planning control was transferred to local authorities. Enterprises were given more latitude in price setting and in the distribution of their income.

The current plan provides for certain measures designed to control the distribution of the output of enterprises and cooperatives. Within the plan, the government relies on the individual interests of the workers and enterprises to produce in compliance with the desired social objectives and national income. The federal government does not make detailed decisions concerning production, but leaves them to the various production units. The economic plan serves as a guide for the production and distribution decisions of enterprises.[2]

FORMULATION AND IMPLEMENTATION OF YUGOSLAV PLANS There are actually three levels of plans in Yugoslavia—national, republic, and commune plans. Communes are subunits within the republics. The Yugoslav national plan lays down the basic guidelines, targets, and aims of economic policy. Within the guidelines and objectives determined by the national plan and plans of the republics and communes, Yugoslav enterprises and other economic organizations are free to formulate their own production plans. This is in keeping with the decentralization policies of the government and reflects the Yugoslav view that it is necessary to turn more and more economic authority from the government to the enterprises and communes. It also reflects the view that the workers, rather than the state, must decide on the allocation and use of the goods they produce. This is done, as will be discussed later in the chapter, through the election of the workers' councils, who have vested control over the operations of all enterprises. Worker self-management fits in with the process of decentralized planning.

The national plan is prepared by the Federal Planning Institute and is approved by the Federal Assembly. The Federal Planning Institute consists of a number of technical divisions, each of which is responsible for the preparation of a certain part of the plan. These divisions include agriculture; forestry; transportation and communication; regional development; personal consumption and social welfare; investment; domestic trade and tourism; industry, power, and mining; and national income.

---

2. There are annual and middle-term (five-year) plans and also a ten-year plan. The fundamental elements of the policy of Yugoslav development are expressed in the five-year plans.

The republic plans set the same objectives embodied in the national plan, allowing for special features of the republic economies. Republic plans refer only to segments of the economy and do not involve national concerns such as foreign trade or balance of payments. The republics are free to set goals that go beyond the scope of the federal plan and are under no legal obligation to harmonize their plans with the federal plan. As the commune has emerged as the basic unit of government, republic plans have come to play a more limited role.

After the republic plans are completed, the communes prepare plans. The plans of the communes are more comprehensive and detailed than the republic plans and are prepared after consultations with various workers' organizations. They encompass such concerns as planned tax policies and social welfare services. The communes, as well as the federal government, can influence compliance with planning objectives through control over policy instruments in the fields of credit, finance, and taxation. Neither the republic nor the commune plans must agree in detail with the national plan; nevertheless, the lower administrative units are expected to consider the overall frame of reference provided by the national plan.

PUBLIC FINANCE

During the period just following World War II the state was preeminent in all economic activities. All phases—production, distribution, exchange, and consumption—were included in government planning. Of all instruments of control available to the state during this period, the general state budget was the most important. It was composed of the federal budget, the budgets of the national republics, and local commune budgets. The general state budget was, for all practical purposes, one fund established by one authority, the national government. The general state budget served as the main distributor of investment funds. Its main sources of revenue were the sales tax, a form of profits tax for the socialist sector, and an income tax from the private sector. The state budget has become less important relative to the budgets of the republics.

Over the years, the Yugoslav budgetary system has been decentralized and jurisdiction for expenditures has been transferred from higher to lower administrative units. As a result, the size of the budgets of the communes has been increased. All sociopolitical units, with the exception of the autonomous provinces and districts, are independent in determining their revenue needs and the required tax rates.

Government units in Yugoslavia rely on several types of taxes as revenue sources. The sales tax is an important source of revenue for the operating budget of the federal government. A general tax rate of 14 percent is normally charged at the time of purchase of all items bought at the retail level. Special taxes on luxury goods can range up to 100 percent of the purchase price, while some essential goods are not subject to taxation. Communes and republics also levy sales taxes. The sales tax imposed by both is confined to retail trade, is uniform within each territorial district, and has a maximum limit prescribed by federal regulation.

There are also fixed capital and income taxes. The fixed capital tax is levied on the fixed assets and buildings owned by an enterprise. The federal government is the sole recipient of revenue from this tax source and uses the revenue to finance economic development in the less developed areas of the country and to finance infrastructure (social overhead capital) investments that benefit the nation as a whole. Income taxes are levied by the federal government and are shared with communes and republics. The range of tax rates varies; the average Yugoslav worker pays at a rate of 12 percent and private enterprises pay as high as 35 percent.[3] Foreign firms, which are allowed to have joint ventures with Yugoslav enterprises, are also subject to a 35 percent federal income tax. The rate is reduced to 10 percent if the income is reinvested in Yugoslavia.

Social welfare taxes and expenditures are excluded from budgetary accounts and are collected and distributed by the communes and autonomous districts. Yugoslav workers have to pay various social security taxes, which average about 25 percent of their gross income. The social security system itself includes old-age and survivor's pensions, sickness and maternity benefits, unemployment compensation, work injury disability benefits, and family allowances. All wage and salary earners are eligible for full coverage under the social security system, while limited benefits are available to the remainder of the population. Although private farmers, craftspeople, and shopkeepers are eligible for health and old-age benefits, they are not eligible for family allowances.

THE BANKING SYSTEM

Banking laws passed in 1976 and 1977 applied the provisions of the 1974 constitution to the banking system. The current system includes the National Bank, which is responsible for general central banking operations; regular banks; and specialized banks. Regular and specialized banks are not intended to function as profit-making institutions, nor are they instruments of the state. Accordingly, banks may be funded by enterprises, but

---

3. Private enterprise is permitted in Yugoslavia. Business owners are allowed to employ up to five workers. Private enterprise is important in the service areas—restaurants, dry cleaning, and hotels. There are also craftspeople.

not by local governments or government agencies. Each organization or member association with a bank has a delegate in the bank's assembly. Management of the bank is entrusted to the bank assembly. Apart from participating in the bank management, the members also have the right to share in any profits of the bank. The members also jointly carry the liability for all bank obligations.

THE NATIONAL BANK OF YUGOSLAVIA   The National Bank is the central bank of Yugoslavia. It has branches in the republics and autonomous provinces, and governors of these banks constitute the Board of Governors of the National Bank. In addition to issuance of bank notes as legal tender, it is also responsible for the monetary policy of Yugoslavia. The National Bank is authorized to regulate the money supply by using minimum reserve ratios and by conducting open market operations in treasury and commercial bills. It utilizes instruments of qualitative credit control, such as rediscounting, to exert a selective influence on the structure of short-term investments by basic and associated banks. However, it cannot extend long-term loans, except to the national government to finance budget deficits or to guarantee foreign loans.

REGULAR BANKS   There are three kinds of regular banks: internal, basic, and associated. *Internal banks* are established by groups of enterprises for their own use and do not serve the general public. They can perform all banking transactions for their members. Since they do not deal with the general public, they do not create money and are not subject to monetary regulation. Their main function is to facilitate pooling of resources among the member enterprises. *Basic banks* are conventional commercial banks that can be created by enterprises, communes, and other social legal entities. They are all-purpose banks largely continuing the activities of the former commercial banks, which were eliminated by new bank laws.[4]

Associated banks are formed by basic banks for tasks that exceed their legal responsibilities and are authorized to engage in foreign exchange operations. They specialize in loans for investment to increase foreign trade in particular sectors such as manufacturing or mining. Interest rates on loans extended by the associated banks are determined by individual agreements with the borrowers, while interest rates on deposits are determined by interbank agreements. Each republic and autonomous region also has its own associated bank.[5]

---

4. Martin Schrenk, Cyrus Ardalan, and Nawal E. Tatawy, *Yugoslavia: Self-Management Socialism and the Challenge of Development* (Baltimore: Johns Hopkins University Press, 1979), pp. 140-41.

5. Ibid.

SPECIALIZED BANKS   In addition to the main banking system, there are three specialized financial institutions. The Yugoslav Foreign Trade Bank is responsible for holding foreign exchange and providing long- and short-term foreign exchange credits. The United Agricultural Bank is responsible for extending long-term agricultural loans. The Yugoslav Bank for International Economic Cooperation is authorized to finance exports of capital goods as well as the construction of overseas projects, to provide export insurance against noncommercial risks, and to promote cooperation between Yugoslav and foreign firms in third-world markets. The bank's operations are financed by other banks and enterprises, but not by the federal government.[6]

THE ROLE OF INTEREST   Under a capitalistic system, when quantities of capital funds are available for investment, the question of how they should be allocated is determined by the amounts of interest firms in various fields of production are willing to pay for their use. The rate of interest will be determined in the market by the forces of supply and demand, and the rate plays the role of an allocator of resources. The underlying assumption is that if an economic entity is willing to pay more for the use of capital resources, the productivity of that entity is expected to be higher.

In Yugoslavia interest is also used as a device to allocate investment funds. Enterprises have to pay interest on borrowed funds as well as on their fixed and financial capital. Almost all real capital is owned by society, and enterprises are only entrusted with its use. It is to society's benefit to have full and efficient utilization of these capital resources. This is ensured by charging interest for the use of fixed and financial capital, the idea being that those who have no use for the capital will hesitate to hold it if they have to pay a certain price to do so. By granting loans to those who are willing to pay the highest rate for the privilege, the rate of interest plays the role of allocator of financial and capital resources. This role of interest is not only applicable at the enterprise level, but also at the personal level for consumer credit.

AGRICULTURE

Agriculture in Yugoslavia (and Poland) departs from the typical pattern found in the Soviet Union and its Eastern European satellites. The ownership and management of farms in Yugoslavia remains overwhelmingly in private hands, organized in many small family farm units. State farms and

---

6. Data provided by the U.S. Embassy in Belgrade, Yugoslavia, April 1982.

collective farms, which are the dominant forms of agricultural production in the Soviet Union, control only about 16 percent of the productive farm land in Yugoslavia.[7] The Yugoslav government has actively supported private farming by providing a number of incentives to stimulate the expansion of farm output:

1. Increasing prices paid by government to farmers for their products,

2. Expanding agricultural loans to private farmers on favorable terms,

3. Greatly expanding the use of fertilizers by private farmers,

4. Encouraging specialization and interfarm cooperation in the use of machinery, and

5. Abstaining from further forced collectivization of agriculture.

STATE FARMS   Those farms that are managed by the government in Yugoslavia emphasize large-scale production of grains and potatoes. Both state-supported and private agricultural sectors can be regarded as largely complementary: The state sector produces the bulk of industrial crops and grains, while the private sector produces most of the vegetables, fruits, and meat products that supply the population with food. The private sector is important during the current plan period because of the continuing emphasis on livestock breeding to achieve both improved domestic diet and export goals. The goal of the plan is to shift the national diet away from cereals and toward higher quality foodstuffs, especially meat. In the state sector, which accounts for around 25 percent of real agricultural output, more intensive efforts are to be placed on the production of grain.

COLLECTIVE FARMS   Land on the collective farms is state owned and is worked by the farmers in common. The produce is distributed according to the contribution of each member. They function and operate in a fashion similar to Russian collective farms. The government encourages cooperation between the collective farms and private farmers; in some instances, private farms are worked by a collective farm on a sharecrop or cash basis. In this way farmers may retain possession of their land and benefit from the use of agricultural machinery, fertilizer, and farming techniques provided by the collective farm.

---

7. Gregor Lazarcik, "Comparative Growth of Agricultural Output, Inputs, and Productivity in Eastern Europe, 1965–1982" in *East European Economies: Slow Growth Rate in the 1980's*, Vol. 1, U.S. Congress, Joint Economic Committee, 99th Cong., 1st Sess., 1985, pp. 389-393.

COOPERATIVES There are also general agricultural cooperatives jointly managed by the farmers and their own employees. The land is owned by the cooperatives and farmed by private farmers who are paid in cash. The cooperatives provide the machines, implements, seed, and fertilizer. They are also responsible for the marketing and sale of farm produce produced on cooperative land. The private farmers neither subscribe to business shares in a cooperative nor are they liable for its debts. Cooperatives and individual farmers may produce jointly, with profits shared in proportion to the contribution made by each partner, or the cooperatives may be responsible only for participation in the production process—furnishing services and equipment—and, in return, receive a fixed share of the profits of the farmers. In most cases, the cooperatives and the private farmers conclude, in advance, contracts on production and the purchase of farm produce at fixed prices or at prices found on the market at the date of delivery.

The Yugoslav agricultural sector is caught in a bind. Productivity is lower than it would be with larger-scale operations, but ideology and inheritance customs in the country have caused private farm holdings to be too small to effect economies of scale. Private farms are limited by law to a maximum of 10 hectares (24 acres), but most private farms are smaller. Farmers have subdivided their farmland between their heirs, constricting the size of private farm holdings. Also, private enterprise, including private farms, is constrained by rules limiting the number of hired workers they may employ. Attempts by the state to encourage the movement of farmers from their private holdings into labor-managed collective farms have failed. The difference in ownership rights evidently has discouraged many farmers from leaving their own farms, no matter how small they are.

THE YUGOSLAV ENTERPRISE

The Yugoslav enterprise is the basic economic unit and may be started or expanded in several ways.

1. It may be formed by any governmental unit—commune, republic, or the national government.

2. It may be formed by a group of five or more individuals who have pooled their assets.

3. It may be formed by the division of an existing enterprise or by the merger of two or more existing enterprises.

When the enterprise starts operation, it acquires an independent status even though its sponsors have committed considerable resources to its formation. Its assets become social property and the people that it employs have the right to self-government and to participate in the income of the enterprise on the basis of work done. It may merge with another enterprise provided that a majority of workers in both enterprises approve the merger. As a matter of economic policy, mergers have been encouraged in order to improve productivity and make Yugoslav firms more competitive in international markets.

Yugoslav enterprises have certain similarities to their U.S. counterparts. Profit is the basic criterion of success for enterprises in both countries, and each enterprise acts independently in the pursuit of its business and development policies. Each can determine the volume and assortment of production according to its assessment of the market, and each can determine its pricing policies. Although economic planning exists in Yugoslavia, the government does not direct that specified quantities of products have to be provided by each enterprise, but instead relies on more indirect controls, including relying on money incentives (wages and bonuses), to encourage compliance with national economic objectives.

MANAGEMENT OF AN ENTERPRISE   Management of all Yugoslav enterprises was given to their workers under terms of a law passed in 1950. That is, all factories, mines, and other enterprises that had been under state ownership since the Communist Party came to power in Yugoslavia were turned over to the workers of these enterprises to manage. The ownership passed from the state to society in general. Enterprises were defined not as state property, but as social property, and workers were given the right to manage them, but not to own them. The key instrument through which this management would be accomplished was the workers' council that, in essence, became the trustee of social wealth and the method of self-management for an enterprise. Through the system of workers' councils, the workers, in principle, exercise ultimate control over economic policy, including the formulation of economic plans.

Figure 15-1 presents the organization and the process of decision making of a Yugoslav enterprise. At the top is the workers' council, which decides on all of the most important matters affecting strategic planning and the operation of the enterprise. The management board, elected by the workers' council, is responsible for drafting the operating plan of the enterprise. Its jurisdiction includes the tactics involved in running the enterprise and the enforcement of the plan. The general manager implements the decisions of the workers' council and the management board.

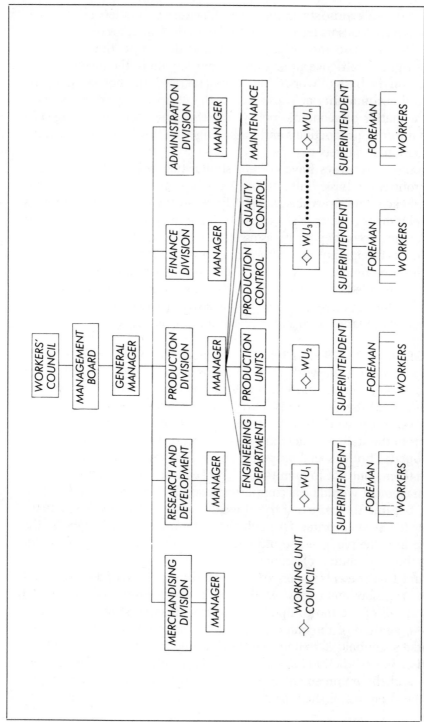

FIGURE 15-1 ORGANIZATION OF A YUGOSLAV ENTERPRISE

Source: D. Zelenovich, "The Basic Characteristics of the Management System and Decision-Making Process in Yugoslavia's Enterprises," unpublished, September, 1985, p. 6.

The working unit councils consider the plans and tasks of each work unit and implement the policies of the workers' council.

WORKERS' COUNCILS   Workers' councils are composed of delegates elected by secret ballot from within the work organization and from a list of candidates prepared by unions.[8] The authority of workers' councils is substantial. Within the limits set by the government, they have the right to decide what to produce and in what quantity, and they are also responsible for setting prices, determining wages, and distributing profits. The last responsibility is one of their most important functions. They distribute enterprise profits in the form of wage bonuses to the various investment and social welfare funds of the enterprises. They also choose a management committee, which is their executive organ. The management committee is responsible for the development of the production plans of the enterprise, the appointment of workers to important administrative positions, the specification of wage and production norms, and the development of methods designed to increase productivity.

COUNCIL OF THE WORKING UNITS   This body is elected by members of each work unit within the enterprise. For example, an integrated textile mill could be divided into work units for spinning, weaving, finishing, final processing, and retail supply. The council represents workers linked together by a common working interest. To be valid, the plan of each enterprise must be accepted by all constituent councils. Profits to be distributed are computed for each work unit in the enterprise on the basis of its business success and by the contribution of each work unit as determined on the basis of an agreement between its council and the enterprise.

ENTERPRISE MANAGERS   Administration and management of the enterprise is the responsibility of the manager (or management board), who is appointed by the workers' council and the Communist Party of the local commune. Management positions must be publicly advertised, and the manager (or management board) is appointed on the basis of a competitive examination. Friction between the workers' council and the management often arises over the distribution of profits; the workers' council tends to favor higher wages out of profits, while the manager or board strives for increased investment. Management is responsible for carrying out the decisions of the workers' council and for handling the day-to-day affairs of the enterprise according to its plan and business policy. Manage-

8. The Communist Party is heavily represented on each workers' council.

ment is subject to recall at any time by either the workers' council or the assembly of the local commune. It is excluded from personnel relations in that it does not have the right to hire or fire workers, take disciplinary action, or determine the final internal distribution of income.

THE OPERATION OF AN ENTERPRISE An enterprise can draw up its own plans for production independent of the national plan, but within limits prescribed by the plan of the commune. The production plan is approved by the workers' council after being put forward by the management committee of the enterprise. Once passed, the plan may be amended by the workers' council. Usually the enterprise is free to make its own decisions pertaining to what to purchase and what to sell, and it can establish prices for its products unless they are subject to some form of price control. Distribution is not regulated, and an enterprise can offer its goods in a comparatively free market.

In a Yugoslav enterprise wages are not deducted from revenue as a cost of production. Instead, after raw material costs and other operating expenses are deducted, the resulting net income is divided between a fund for personal income (wages) and a fund for reinvestment. Income set aside in the wage fund is shared among the workers as base pay and supplements in accordance with a wage schedule adopted by the workers' council. To start with, a guaranteed minimum wage is assured all workers, and no worker can be paid less than this amount. Actual earnings, however, normally exceed the guaranteed minimum by a substantial amount, and the minimum assumes importance only when it cannot be covered out of the earnings of an enterprise. If this situation occurs, then the commune is required to make up the difference between the actual wage and the guaranteed minimum wage.

However, the use of workers' councils in decision making in Yugoslavia also has its drawbacks. In particular, because workers receive a share of the firm's profits only as long as they are members of the organization, the incentive of workers to invest in capital with long-term payoffs decreases as they approach retirement or anticipate leaving the enterprise for some reason. The bias is toward projects with short-term payoffs to the exclusion of some investment projects that would be socially beneficial. This is not a problem in capitalist firms because the potential value of long-term investments will be reflected in the value of the firm's stock, which owners can sell to capitalize the value of current investments. In addition, since all workers must share in the residual profits of the Yugoslav enterprise, the incentive for a single individual to innovate or institute a new production idea is substantially reduced.

■ AN APPRAISAL ■
OF THE YUGOSLAV ECONOMY

Yugoslav socialism is unquestionably more liberal and humane than the socialism of the Soviet Union and its satellites. The reforms and the general attitude of the government indicate flexibility and willingness to experiment that is lacking in other socialist countries. In order to honor promises to workers and to stimulate production, the government has decentralized management and has introduced workers' councils in economic enterprises. There are, however, certain problems confronting the Yugoslav economy.

From the beginning of its history, Yugoslavia has been confronted by a seemingly insoluble nationality problem. It is really a confederation of diverse ethnic groups that are difficult to weld into a homogeneous unit. Rivalries exist between regions and are exacerbated by extremely uneven economic development between regions. The hope that surplus capital would flow to the less developed regions of the country has not been realized. Neither Croatia nor Slovenia, which are among the most developed and richest republics of Yugoslavia, has shown much interest in investing in the underdeveloped areas of the south. Chauvinistic sentiment is a key deterrent to the free flow of capital between regions.

Much of Yugoslavia's success over the last several decades was derived from the unifying force of President Tito's leadership. Tito's charisma helped prevent the country's political disintegration into a number of regional special-interest groups. His death in 1980 has intensified regional rivalries that appear to be an ineradicable feature of the Yugoslav political and economic system. The problem the current leaders of Yugoslavia have is to prevent a renewal of regional nationalism and separatism. To achieve this goal, they must create a viable economy that continues to improve living standards and reduce the income disparities between prosperous and less prosperous republics. Antagonisms, ethnic differences, and other sources of discord in Yugoslavia are likely to continue in the future because even adherence to communism as a unifying factor has not united the people.

ECONOMIC PROBLEMS

The economic problems of Yugoslavia are similar to those present in many other economies, both socialist and capitalist, in the 1980s. The rate of economic growth is low, productivity has declined, and there are marked variations among regional rates of development within the country. Import restrictions imposed in 1981 to conserve hard currency resulted in a short-age of many food products and food prices increased by as much as 40 percent.[9] Agricultural production decreased by 2.1 percent in 1983, a rate well below the 4 percent annual increase projected in the 1981–1985 plan. The economic growth rate for 1983 was −1.3 percent, and the forecast for 1985 is 2 to 3 percent.[10] These rates impact more heavily upon the poorer regions of the south than the more wealthy northern republics.

UNEMPLOYMENT Unemployment has become a serious problem for Yugoslavia. The transition from an agricultural to an industrial economy has not been smooth, with the result that many workers have migrated to jobs in more advanced industrial countries in Western Europe. However, as economic growth slowed and unemployment increased in Western Europe, Yugoslav and other foreign workers were the first to be laid off. As a result the unemployment rate in Yugoslavia rose to 13.6 percent in 1985.[11] The employment of Yugoslav workers abroad cut both ways. The emigration eased unemployment problems in Yugoslavia, and hard currency earnings of the workers were remitted home, which had a favorable impact on the Yugoslav balance of payments. However, the social and political attitudes of Yugoslav workers were affected by foreign employment, making them less patient with economic and political conditions at home.

INFLATION Probably the most important problem confronting the Yugoslav economy is inflation. The period since the reforms of 1965 has been highly inflationary as a result of the gradual lessening of control over the economy and the move to a freer price structure. During the period 1965–1973, consumer prices increased at an annual average rate of 11 percent in spite of the imposition of wage and price controls and attempts to limit the money supply.[12] From 1973 to 1983 inflation increased at a rate of 23 percent. In June 1980 the government announced a price freeze in an effort to reduce inflation, but the measure was largely unsuccessful. In 1984 the rate of inflation, as reflected by the consumer price index, registered 65 percent, leading to a further price freeze and the reduction of subsidies on food.[13] For the sixth year in a row, real income of Yugoslav workers declined.

9. Mark Baskin, "Crisis in Kossovo," *Problems of Communism* (March-April 1983), pp. 61-74.

10. Josef Adamek, *Centrally Planned Economies: Economic Overview* (New York: The Conference Board, 1985), p. 36.

11. Data provided by the U.S. Embassy in Belgrade.

12. The World Bank, *World Development Report 1985*, p. 175.

13. Central Intelligence Agency, *Handbook of Economic Statistics 1985*, p. 53.

ECONOMIC GROWTH   The Yugoslav economy is one of contrasts. With a mixture of a planned and market economy and a policy of accelerated industrialization, the government has transformed Yugoslavia from an agrarian society to a position just short of the less developed Western European countries such as Spain.[14] The average annual growth rate of GNP per capita was 4.7 percent for the period 1965–1983.[15] However, there have been wide variations in the rates of economic growth. In 1974 it was 9.8 percent, but by 1976 it had fallen to around 3 percent. The rate of economic growth during the 1980s has been poor, ranging from a -2.0 percent to a high of 1.8 percent in 1985.[16] This performance was below the average for all of the OECD countries, of which Yugoslavia is a member, but about on par with the average for the Western European countries.

FOREIGN DEBT   The foreign debt of Yugoslavia at mid-1985 was $19.5 billion.[17] This debt creates a burden for the Yugoslav economy in that some 45 percent of its hard currency earnings have to be used to meet principal and interest payments, thus severely limiting the ability to import critically needed materials and capital. Moreover, in 1985 the trade deficit with the Western European countries, which are the major source of hard currency earnings, increased. This is a serious problem because increased exports to the hard currency countries is a key component of Yugoslavia's long-term strategy for reducing foreign debt. In the first half of 1985, Yugoslavia concluded an agreement with the International Monetary Fund for a short-term loan of $100 million. A debt rescheduling arrangement was concluded with Western banks to extend the debt that becomes due in 1985 to a later period.

ECONOMIC REFORMS

Economic reform in Yugoslavia has occurred without the direct influence of Soviet military power, and the country has been able to move farther and farther away from the Soviet model of economic and political development. The main goal of the Yugoslav economic reforms has been the development of a decentralized economic system, in part for political reasons and in part to promote economic efficiency. The reforms have reflected a

14. Ibid., pp. 39-40.
15. *World Development Report 1985*, p. 178.
16. *Economic Statistics 1985*, p. 40.
17. Data provided by the U.S. Embassy in Belgrade.

need for changes in resource allocation and administration in order to promote economic performance, while recognizing the interests of various nationalist groups within the country.

Steps to decentralize the economy and establish the socialist market system were intensified in the 1960s as economic problems, quantitatively expressed by an erratic growth rate and decreasing productivity, developed. Moreover, the fact that Yugoslavia had limited domestic markets and resources meant foreign trade was indispensible for promoting technological progress. However, dependence on imports of raw materials and machinery created large deficits in the balance of payments. Recurring crises led to constant government intervention in the economy.

The economic reforms of 1965 accelerated the decentralization of economic management. Administrative elements of central control were greatly reduced and transformed in terms of content and methods of intervention. It was felt that greater autonomy on the part of state enterprises would improve efficiency. There were two basic objectives of the reforms: improvement of the productivity of capital and labor, and a more balanced rate of economic growth. The reforms ushered in a phase in Yugoslavia's economic development referred to as *market socialism*. The price system was reformed with the objective of eventually allowing the free determination of prices by market forces. Prices of goods and services were allowed to increase to bring them into harmony with those that prevailed in the international markets and also to use them as instruments of internal economic development policy.[18]

The 1965 reforms had some adverse affects on the economy. Under decentralization of state control, some of the state's effective policy instruments were dismantled—notably those for fiscal policy, resource allocation, and the compulsory coordination and implementation of plans. Policy making was regionalized, but there was no attempt to introduce alternative mechanisms for coordinating diverse economic objectives. In the opinion of many political and economic leaders, the market system failed to live up to anticipations: growth over the 1965–1970 period was disappointing, and inefficiencies in the use of capital and labor remained. In addition, there was an increase in the rate of inflation and a perceived concentration of power in the hands of financial institutions, a managerial elite, and wholesale, retail, and foreign trade enterprises.[19]

---

18. Schrenk, Ardalan, and El Tatawy, *Yugoslavia: Self-Management Socialism*, pp. 26-28.

19. Laura D'Andrea Tyson and Gabriel Eichler, "Continuity and Change in the Yugoslav Economy in the 1970's and 1980's," in *East European Economic Assessment*, Part 1, U.S. Congress, Joint Economic Committee, 97th Cong., 1st Sess., 1981, pp. 141-43.

PERFORMANCE OF THE ECONOMY

Table 15-1 presents consumer price indexes and growth in real per capita GNP for Yugoslavia for selected periods. As the table indicates, inflation as measured by changes in the consumer price index has become a major problem in Yugoslavia during the 1980s. In 1985 the currency unit, the dinar, was devalued 38 percent against the European Community currencies and price controls were imposed on the sale of agricultural products.[20]

Yugoslavia is a country that can be considered in the middle stage of economic development. It is comparable to Brazil, Mexico, South Korea, Portugal, and Hungary in its level of industrial development, per capita income, and the percentage of its labor force employed in agriculture. A comparison can be made between income distribution in Yugoslavia and other countries in similar stages of development. As Table 15-2 indicates, income distribution is more equal in Yugoslavia than it is in the developing countries of Latin America and Asia, but less equal than in Hungary.

TABLE 15-1 GROWTH IN REAL PER CAPITA GNP AND CONSUMER PRICE INDEXES IN YUGOSLAVIA, SELECTED YEARS

	Growth in Real Per Capita GNP	Consumer Price Index
1970	—	100
1971–1975	5.1%	—
1975	—	241
1976–1979	5.5	—
1980	1.7	561
1981	0.7	789
1982	0.0	1,039
1983	−2.0	1,464
1984	1.0	2,246
1985[1]	1.2	2,940

[1]Estimates

Source: Central Intelligence Agency, *Handbook of Economic Statistics 1985*, pp. 40 and 53; estimate for 1985 is based on information provided by the U.S. Embassy in Belgrade.

20. Data provided by the U.S. Embassy in Belgrade.

TABLE 15-2 INCOME DISTRIBUTION IN YUGOSLAVIA AND COUNTRIES IN SIMILAR STAGES OF ECONOMIC DEVELOPMENT
(share of total household income by quintiles)

		Lowest Quintile	Second Quintile	Third Quintile	Fourth Quintile	Fifth Quintile	Top 10 Percent
South Korea	1976	5.7%	11.2%	15.4%	22.4%	45.3%	27.5%
Brazil	1972	2.0	5.0	9.4	17.0	66.6	50.6
Argentina	1977	4.4	9.7	14.1	21.5	50.3	35.2
Portugal	1974	5.2	10.0	14.4	21.3	49.1	33.4
Mexico	1978	2.9	7.0	12.0	20.0	57.7	40.6
Israel	1980	6.0	12.0	17.7	24.4	39.9	22.6
Yugoslavia	1978	6.6	12.1	18.7	23.9	38.7	22.9
Hungary	1982	6.9	13.6	19.2	24.5	35.8	20.5

Source: The World Bank, *World Development Report 1985*, p. 229.

COMPARISONS WITH SOCIALIST ECONOMIES

Comparisons of Yugoslavia with the socialist economies of Eastern Europe are somewhat difficult to make. For one thing, there are differences in the kind of economic development and resource availability. Moreover, some countries were more adversely affected by World War II than others. East Germany had a pre-World War II industrial base on which to rebuild its economy. Czechoslovakia was also an advanced industrial country, particularly in comparison to Bulgaria and Romania. Soviet influence over the economic process also affects comparisons. Soviet control and influence over industrialization policies fall more heavily on countries that are closer to its sphere of influence. Additionally, comparisons can be difficult because a comparatively good performance in one area of the economy may be achieved at the expense of a concurrent or postponed weaker performance in another area.

Table 15-3 presents the growth rates of real per capita GNP for Yugoslavia, the Soviet Union, and Eastern Europe for selected periods. The performance of the Yugoslav economy during the 1960s and 1970s was quite good in comparison to the Soviet Union and Eastern Europe. During the 1980s, Yugoslavia has encountered the same problems that have affected other socialist countries—declining growth rates, large hard currency debts, and falling investment. Since Yugoslavia's foreign trade is linked to Western Europe, it was affected by the recession that hit Europe during the latter part of the last decade and continued up to 1985.

TABLE 15-3   GROWTH IN REAL PER CAPITA GNP
(average annual rate of growth)

	Yugoslavia	Soviet Union	Eastern Europe
1961–1965	5.6%	3.5%	3.2%
1966–1970	5.4	4.3	3.2
1971–1975	5.1	2.8	4.2
1976–1979	5.5	2.0	1.5
1980	1.7	0.9	−0.8
1981	0.7	1.1	−1.5
1982	0.0	1.7	0.5
1983	−2.0	2.7	1.2
1984	1.0	1.5	2.7
1985[1]	1.2	1.6	2.8

[1]Estimates

Source: Central Intelligence Agency, *Handbook of Economic Statistics 1985*, p. 40.

Agriculture, as measured by its contribution to total GNP, is important
to the economies of Yugoslavia and the Eastern-bloc countries. From 1975
to 1982 the greatest increase in agricultural output was achieved by Yugoslavia, with an increase of 25 percent, followed by Hungary and Romania
with an 18 percent increase. In 1982, agriculture accounted for 19.5 percent of the GNP of Yugoslavia, compared to 24.9 percent in Hungary,
26.6 percent in Poland, and 22.6 percent in Bulgaria.[21] Table 15-4 compares combined factor (land, labor, and capital) productivity in agriculture for Yugoslavia, Hungary, Poland, and for Eastern Europe for the
period 1970–1982. As the table indicates, factor productivity increased the
fastest in Yugoslavia, while Poland had the poorest performance.

**TABLE 15-4   COMBINED FACTOR PRODUCTIVITY,
1965–1982**
(three-year moving average with 1965–1967 as base)

	Yugoslavia	Poland	Hungary	Eastern Europe
1965–1967	100	100	100	100
1970	109	92	104	103
1975	127	95	111	111
1976	131	93	111	111
1977	134	94	112	112
1978	136	93	114	113
1979	137	90	114	112
1980	141	85	113	112
1981	145	82	115	112
1982	149	82	115	112

Source: Gregor Lazarcik, "Comparable Growth of Agricultural Output, Inputs, and Productivity in
Eastern Europe, 1965–1982," in *Eastern European Economies; Slow Growth in the 1980's,*
Vol. 1, U.S. Congress, Joint Economic Committee, 99th Cong., 1st Sess., 1985, pp. 418-419.

21. Lazarcik, "Comparative Growth," pp. 391-392.

SUMMARY

The fundamental feature of the Yugoslav economic system is not state
ownership of the means of production, but the self-management by
workers and other direct producers of the operation of all economic

organizations. The Yugoslav concept of communism is that society is a community of working people who create material wealth through their work. Thus, it is these working people who must decide on the allocation and use of the goods they produce. If working people are the leading social group, then the basic question concerns the construction of an economic system in which the active role of the producers and their associations will be strengthened and the economic and social role of the state will decrease and gradually disappear. According to the Yugoslav concept, the state, with its bureaucratic organization, represents an obstacle to progress, for it encroaches on the rights of workers to distribute income and to participate in the operation of the economy. The state is simply an institution that has replaced private capitalism in the socialist countries, but it imposes a new set of restraints upon the working people so that true communism is never achieved.

A Yugoslav enterprise is managed by its workers through a body called the "workers' council." Workers' self-government and social management are supposed to encourage initiative and bring about a combination of centralized and decentralized decision making. The workers' council is responsible for the development of the plan and work schedule of an enterprise. It also makes decisions concerning basic matters of business policy and the use of the resources and funds of the enterprise. The workers' council selects a management board, which has the responsibility for enforcing decisions made by the council. Every enterprise also has a managing director who executes the decisions of the workers' council and the management board. The manager is elected by the workers' council on the basis of public competition and is responsible to the council and to the management board for the performance of specific duties.

Yugoslavia has a socialist regulated market economy rather than a socialist centrally planned economy. Yugoslav economic planning differs considerably from the centralized command plans of the Soviet Union and the Eastern European countries. It is closer to the French type of planning in that it does not mandate rigid targets for industries. The performance of the Yugoslav economy has been somewhat erratic. There have been wide swings in the rate of real economic growth, but the rate compares favorably to that of the Eastern European socialist countries. It has achieved a level of economic development comparable to Spain among the Western European countries. Inflation is a problem in Yugoslavia, as in unemployment. The Yugoslav external debt to the West also creates something of a problem because it increases the need for export earnings of hard currencies.

REVIEW QUESTIONS

1. Compare the roles of economic planning in Yugoslavia and the Soviet Union.
2. What are the responsibilities of a workers' council?
3. Discuss the role of the Bank of Yugoslavia in the monetary system.
4. Compare the agriculture situation in Yugoslavia and the Soviet Union.
5. How may Yugoslav enterprises be formed?
6. What role does interest play in allocating funds in Yugoslavia?
7. What is the role of the commune in the Yugoslav economic and political systems?
8. Yugoslavia has a problem of national identity. Discuss.

RECOMMENDED READINGS

Baskin, Mark. "Crisis in Kossovo." *Problems of Communism*. March-April 1983, pp. 61–74.

Estrin, Saul. *Self-Management: Economic Theory and Yugoslav Practice*. New York: Cambridge University Press, 1984.

Gruenwald, Oscar. *The Yugoslav Search for Man: Marxist Humanism in Contemporary Yugoslavia*. South Hadley, Mass.: J.F. Bergin, 1984.

Lazarcik, Gregor. "Comparative Growth of Agricultural Output, Inputs, and Productivity in Eastern Europe, 1965–1982." In *East European Economies: Slow Growth in the 1980's*. Vol. 1, U.S. Congress, Joint Economic Committee, 99th Cong., 1st Sess., 1985, pp. 388–425.

Lydell, Harold. *Yugoslav Socialism: Theory and Practice*. New York: Oxford University Press, 1984.

Meier, Viktor. "Yugoslavia's National Question." *Problems of Communism*. March-April 1983, pp. 47–60.

Singleton, Frederick, B. *The Economy of Yugoslavia*. New York: St. Martin's Press, 1982.

Stankovic, Slobodan. *End of the Tito Era: Yugoslavia's Dilemmas*. Stanford, Calif.: Hoover Institute Press, 1981.

PART 5

ECONOMIC SYSTEMS OF THE LESS DEVELOPED COUNTRIES

16
PROBLEMS
OF THE
LESS DEVELOPED COUNTRIES

17
THE PEOPLE'S
REPUBLIC OF CHINA

18
MEXICO

19
NIGERIA

C H A P T E R   1   6

PROBLEMS
OF THE
LESS DEVELOPED COUNTRIES

The countries of the world can be classified into more developed and less developed, or haves and have-nots, and there are a few that are somewhere in between. Unfortunately, a majority of countries can be classified as less developed, including China and India, which have more than a third of the world's population between them. Mass poverty exists in the less developed countries and basic consumption needs remain unfulfilled. The magnitude of poverty is all too apparent. We read about it in newspapers and see it on television. A drought in Ethiopia and other parts of Africa was responsible for the death by starvation of thousands of people. Anyone who has been to a less developed country is struck by the squalor and the number of beggars in the large cities. The enormous gap between more and less developed nations increases the potential for social conflict in the world.

This chapter is divided into several parts, the first of which examines the subject of economic development. The second part discusses the characteristics of the less developed countries. It looks at population—the causes and consequences of population growth and its link to economic development and performance. The third part explores some theories of economic development. Many economists are concerned with the conditions necessary for economic development. The fourth part presents some of the obstacles to economic development confronting the less developed countries, and there are many. Possible solutions to the problems of economic development make up the last part of the chapter—but solutions will not come easily. The problems of the less developed countries can be attributed in part to the economic and financial policies of the developed countries.

■ ECONOMIC DEVELOPMENT ■

Economic growth and economic development are often used interchangeably. However, the two terms have different meanings. *Economic growth* can be defined most simply as the ability of a nation to expand its capacity to produce the goods and services its people want. It represents an increase in the real output of goods and services. *Economic development* means not only more real output but different kinds of output than were produced in the past.[1] It includes changes in the technological and institutional arrangements by which output is produced and distributed. There can be economic growth without economic development. For example, a country that relies on the production of oil for export can have its growth rate increase as greater inputs lead to greater output of oil, while its economic development may be minimal. However, the process of economic development almost necessarily depends on some degree of simultaneous economic growth.

There are a number of requisite factors that must exist before economic development can take place in any country. Most of the developed countries in the world have at least several of them, which are listed here.

1. The quantity and quality of a country's labor force has an impact on its economic development. However, the existence of a large labor force does not guarantee economic development. India is an excellent case in point. A labor force has to have education and job skills, both of which are lacking in India because it is a poor country.

2. The quantity and quality of real capital is important for economic development. Real capital is capital goods or inventories in the form of raw materials, machines, and equipment used for the ultimate purpose of producing consumer goods. The

1. Bruce Herrick and Charles F. Kindleberger, *Economic Development*, 4th ed. (New York: McGraw-Hill Book Co., 1983), pp. 21-23.

supply of real capital depends upon the level of savings in a country, which is the difference between its income and its consumption. In countries at a subsistence level, there is little difference between income and consumption.

3. The level of technological attainment in a country has to be considered. Technology as a concept deals more with the productive process than with the introduction of new goods. It involves the relationship between inputs of economic resources of land, labor, and capital. The combination of these inputs will determine both the level and type of technology.

4. The quantity and quality of a country's natural resources is also important. Great natural resources contributed to the economic development of the United States. However, it is possible to develop without adequate natural resources. Japan has attained a high level of economic development by importing what it needs.

5. Sociocultural forces also affect economic development. Religion is an example. The role of religion as an economic force can vary considerably among countries. The theocratic society of Iran offers a case in point, where modern ways are resisted. Other sociocultural forces are the underlying competitive nature of an economy, the distribution of income and wealth, the pattern of consumer tastes, dominant forms of business organization, and the organization of society.

■ CHARACTERISTICS ■
OF THE LESS DEVELOPED COUNTRIES

Three-fourths of the world's population live in the less developed countries. Most of the nations of Latin America, Africa, and Asia fall into this category.[2] However, the less developed countries are by no means all alike, for some countries are in different stages of economic development from others. There is a vast degree of difference in life between, say, the typical

---

2. The United Nations classifies countries on the basis of more developed and less developed. More developed regions comprise all of Europe and North America, plus Australia, Japan, New Zealand, and the U.S.S.R. All other regions are classified as less developed. Note that there is not much difference between per capita income of Portugal, which is considered more developed, and the per capita income of Mexico, which is considered less developed.

slum dweller of Mexico City and that of an average peasant in Bangladesh or Ethiopia. Although Mexico's per capita income is one-sixth that of the United States, it is 15 times that of Bangladesh or Ethiopia. Nevertheless, the less developed countries possess some common characteristics and a discussion of each is in order.[3]

PER CAPITA INCOME

Whether a country can be classified as developed or less developed is sometimes determined by the size of its per capita gross national product (GNP), which is a rough measure of the value of the goods and services produced and available on the average to each person. Among the poorest countries of the world are China, India, Bangladesh, Ethiopia, and Pakistan, which account for almost 40 percent of the world's population but less than 2 percent of the world's gross national product. The GNP per capita for these countries is less than 5 percent of the annual United States figure, which was $14,090 for 1985, and the average of $10,870 for the developed market economies. Bangladesh had a per capita GNP of $130 in 1985, which is about one percent of that of Sweden. The poverty this figure represents shows up in tangible ways in nutritionally inadequate diets, primitive and crowded housing, an absence of medical services, and a general unavailability of schools.

Table 16-1 presents a breakdown by categories of per capita GNP for some of the less developed countries. The first category includes the poorest countries in the world, those with per capita incomes of $500 or less. China and India, the two largest countries in the world, fall into this category. Then there are poor countries such as Indonesia and Nigeria that have a per capita GNP between $500 and $1,000, but are not much better off than China and India. Sixty percent of the world's people live in countries with a per capita income of $1,000 or less. A third category of countries includes Mexico and Brazil, which are relatively better off in terms of per capita income, have some industrial base, but are at the lower stage of development. A fourth category of countries includes those in the upper stage of economic development. Spain and Singapore are examples. The last category includes the developed countries. The Soviet Union qualifies even though its per capita GNP is not much higher than that of some countries in the upper stage of development.

3. See Harvey Leibenstein, *Economic Backwardness and Economic Growth* (New York: Macmillan, 1957), pp. 40-41.

TABLE 16-1 PER CAPITA GNP FOR SELECTED COUNTRIES BASED ON DEGREE OF DEVELOPMENT

Poorest Countries		Poor Countries		Lower-Stage Development	
Bangladesh	$130	Indonesia	$ 560	Malaysia	$1,870
Ethiopia	140	Egypt	700	Chile	1,870
Zaire	160	Ivory Coast	720	Brazil	1,890
India	260	Philippines	760	South Korea	2,010
China	290	Nigeria	760	Argentina	2,030
Kenya	340	Thailand	810	Portugal	2,190
Pakistan	390	Nicaragua	900	Mexico	2,240
Sudan	400	Guatemala	1,120	Algeria	2,400

Upper-Stage Development		Developed	
South Africa	$2,450	U.S.S.R.	$ 6,350
Yugoslavia	2,570	U.K.	9,050
Greece	3,970	Japan	10,106
Venezuela	4,100	France	10,390
Spain	4,800	W. Germany	11,420
Israel	5,360	Canada	12,000
Hong Kong	6,000	Sweden	12,400
Singapore	6,620	United States	14,090

Average all developed countries $9,380
Average all less developed countries   700

Source: Mary M. Kent and Carl Haub, *1985 World Population Data Sheet* (Washington: Population Reference Bureau, Inc., 1985).

OVERPOPULATION

Although the overall rate of population growth in the world has been declining since the late 1970s, annual world population figures have increased each year. In 1985 the world population increased by 83 million persons, bringing the total to 4.8 billion, or twice the level of 20 years ago.[4] Given current projections of population increase, the world population is estimated to be around 6.5 billion by the end of this century, with almost all the population increase taking place in Latin America, Africa, and Asia, where birth rates are high and mortality rates are declining. Moreover, the bulk of the population increase will take place in the countries that can afford it the least. For example, the populations of China and India, two of the poorest countries in the world, are projected to increase by 450 million persons each by the year 2,000, and the populations of Bangladesh and Pakistan are projected to increase by 150 million each.

Table 16-2 presents the population, birth and death rates, and population doubling time for selected less developed countries that together have over half of the world's population. (Population doubling time is found by dividing 70 by the population growth rate.) It is well to remember that for these countries the more people there are, the less will be the real capital and natural resources per capita. India, which is one of the poorest countries in the world, had a 1985 population of 762 million and will double its population in 32 years. Mexico, with a birth rate of 32 per 1,000 persons and a death rate of 6 per 1,000 persons, will double its population in 27 years. China will double its population in 65 years, while Nigeria, with one of the highest birth rates in the world, will double its population in only 22 years. Conversely, the United States, with a birth rate of 16 per 1,000 persons and death rate of 9 per 1,000 persons, will double its population in 100 years. West Germany, with a negative rate of population growth, will never double its population.

AGRICULTURE

One of the most fundamental characteristics of the less developed countries is that a very high percentage of the population is employed in agriculture. There is absolute overemployment in agriculture; that is, it would be possible to reduce the number of workers and still retain the same total output. The level of agrarian technology is low; tools and equipment are

---

4. "Population Bulletin of the United Nations," (New York: United Nations, 1985), p. 1.

TABLE 16-2 POPULATION DATA FOR 1985

	Population (millions)	Birth Rate (per 1,000)	Death Rate (per 1,000)	Population Doubling Time at Current Rate (years)
Bangladesh	101	45	17	25
Ethiopia	36	43	22	33
India	762	34	13	32
China	1,042	19	8	65
Pakistan	99	43	15	25
Kenya	20	54	13	17
Sudan	22	46	17	24
Philippines	57	32	7	28
Egypt	48	37	10	26
Indonesia	168	34	12	32
Nigeria	91	48	17	22
Malaysia	16	29	7	32
Burma	38	37	15	32
Thailand	53	25	6	36
Brazil	138	31	8	30
Mexico	80	32	6	27
United States	239	16	9	100
Sweden	8	11	11	6,930
W. Germany	61	10	11	—

Source: Mary M. Kent and Carl Haub, *1985 World Population Data Sheet* (Washington: Population Reference Bureau, Inc., 1985)

limited and primitive. Opportunities for sale of agricultural products are limited by transportation difficulties and the absence of local demand. Agricultural output in the less developed countries is made up mostly of cereals and primary raw materials, with relatively low output of protein foods. The reason for this is the conversion ratio between cereals and meat production; that is, if one acre of cereals produces a certain number of calories, it would take more than one acre to produce the same number of calories from meat products.

Table 16-3 presents the percentage of the labor force employed in agriculture, industry, and services for less developed countries with a per capita gross national product of less than $500 a year, other less developed countries, and, as a frame of reference, such developed countries as the United States and West Germany. In Chad, the poorest country in the

TABLE 16-3   LABOR FORCE PARTICIPATION IN AGRICULTURE, INDUSTRY, AND SERVICES FOR SELECTED COUNTRIES, 1981

	Per Capita GNP (1983)	Agriculture	Industry	Services
Chad	$ 65	85%	7%	8%
Bangladesh	130	74	11	15
Ethiopia	120	80	7	13
India	260	71	13	16
China	300	69	19	12
Niger	240	91	3	6
Pakistan	390	57	20	23
Kenya	340	78	10	12
Sudan	400	78	10	12
Indonesia	560	58	12	30
Thailand	820	76	9	15
Syria	1,760	33	31	36
Brazil	1,880	30	24	46
Mexico	2,240	36	26	28
Yugoslavia	2,570	29	35	36
Japan	10,120	12	39	49
W. Germany	11,430	4	46	50
United States	14,110	2	32	66

Source: The World Bank, *World Development Report 1985*, pp. 174-175 and 214-215.

world, 85 percent of the population of working age is employed in agriculture (compared to 2 percent in the United States and 4 percent in West Germany). Note also that as countries develop industrially they eventually reach a point where employment in the service industries exceeds employment in manufacturing. The United States is an example of what is called a *postindustrial country*, with employment in services far exceeding employment in industry and agriculture.[5]

INCOME DISTRIBUTION

Incomes are distributed far more unequally in the less developed countries than in the developed countries. There is generally no middle class, particularly in the poorest of the less developed countries, and an enormous income gulf between rich and poor that creates a potential for economic and political instability. El Salvador is a case in point. Low incomes in the less developed countries can be explained by the large agricultural labor force and the absence of skilled workers in manufacturing. Economic growth and the development of technology leads to a greater equality in the distribution of income and wealth over an extended period. However, time is one thing the less developed countries do not have on their side, and rapid population growth and other factors make economic development extremely difficult.

Table 16-4 compares the distribution of household income for selected less developed countries. Although statistical comparisons of income distribution by countries are difficult to make, the table does indicate that incomes are distributed far more unequally in the less developed countries than in the developed countries, some of which are used as a comparison in the table. In Brazil, for example, 50.6 percent of total household income was received by the top 10 percent of all households, compared to 16.4 percent of total household income for the bottom 60 percent. Moreover, the statistics do not show the enormous difference in living standards between the few at the top and the many at the bottom of the income ladder. The absence of a comprehensive welfare system does little to transfer income from the haves to the have-nots in the less developed countries.

5. Daniel Bell, *The Coming of Post-Industrial Society* (New York: Basic Books, Inc., 1976). An industrial society is defined by the quantity of goods as marking a standard of living; a postindustrial society is defined by the quality of life as measured by the services and amenities—health, education, and the arts—deemed desirable for everyone.

TABLE 16-4 INCOME DISTRIBUTION FOR SELECTED COUNTRIES
(share of total household income by quintiles)

		First Quintile	Second Quintile	Third Quintile	Fourth Quintile	Fifth Quintile	Top 10 Percent
India	1976	7.0%	9.2%	13.9%	20.5%	49.4%	33.6%
Kenya	1976	2.3	6.6	11.5	19.2	60.4	45.8
Peru	1972	1.9	5.1	11.0	21.0	61.0	42.9
Malaysia	1973	3.5	7.7	12.4	20.3	56.1	39.8
Panama	1970	2.0	5.2	11.0	20.0	61.8	44.2
Brazil	1972	2.0	5.0	9.4	17.0	66.6	50.6
Mexico	1977	2.9	7.0	12.0	20.4	57.7	40.6
Argentina	1970	4.4	9.7	14.1	21.5	50.3	35.2
United Kingdom	1979	7.0	11.5	17.0	24.8	39.7	23.4
Japan	1979	8.7	13.2	17.5	23.1	36.8	21.2
Finland	1981	6.3	12.1	18.4	25.8	37.6	21.7
West Germany	1978	7.9	12.5	17.0	23.1	39.5	24.0
Sweden	1981	7.4	13.1	16.8	21.0	41.7	24.8
Norway	1982	6.0	12.9	18.3	24.6	38.2	22.9
United States	1980	5.3	11.9	17.9	25.0	39.9	23.3

Source: The World Bank, *World Development Report 1985*, pp. 228-229.

TECHNOLOGICAL DUALISM

Technological dualism is a prominent feature of many less developed countries. It is the coexistence in a society of two modes of production. One is generally categorized as modern, capital-intensive, export-oriented, and often foreign-owned and managed; the other is traditional, labor-intensive, dedicated to producing for the home market or for the family itself, and domestically owned. The second mode may involve small cottage industries where each worker performs all of the production operations. The first mode of production operates in a sector of the economy that is technically well advanced with high productivity, while the second mode of production involves a sector that has old technology and low productivity. Technological dualism can lead to social dualism because new products and production methods often cause people to change their beliefs and ways of living. Workers accustomed to the two different modes of production will have different and often conflicting social values.

■ THEORIES ■
OF ECONOMIC DEVELOPMENT

Economic development involves changes in the composition of a country's outputs and inputs. Economists have been concerned with the conditions necessary for economic development, and over time a considerable number of economic development theories have developed.[6] The "big push" theory is seen as a way to break the circle of low income resulting from low productivity, which is caused by a low rate of capital formation, which in turn comes from a low rate of saving from low income. According to this theory, a large, balanced wave of investment in different industries will enlarge markets, create support industries, increase growth because the industries will buy from each other, and lead to increases in income and saving. Thus the circle will be broken.

The "dependency" theory of economic development is in a way related to colonialism and imperialism. Most less developed countries were at one time possessions of Spain, England, France, or other European countries. These countries hindered the development of their colonies by exploiting

---

6. Herrick and Kindleberger, *Economic Development*, chapter 2.

their natural resources and denying them access to technological development. When independence was achieved, these former colonial possessions remained economically and psychologically dependent on their former owners.

MARXIST THEORY OF ECONOMIC DEVELOPMENT

One approach to explaining economic development is the Marxist theory of development. Marx contended that economic conditions were the basic causal forces shaping the nature of society. Economic development occurs in stages, beginning with the evolution of medieval feudalism into industrial capitalism. Marx considered technological change the prime mover in the process of development. The transition from feudalism to capitalism is a result of technological change. But capitalism is merely a stage in the evolution of society toward the communist state, which is the inevitable final form of economic and social organization. According to Marx, economic development under capitalism results from technological progress, which depends on investment. The latter depends on profit, which, in turn, is affected by wages. The key proposition in Marxian economics is that all value comes from labor; for that reason, the profits of capitalists arise from the exploitation of labor. Capitalists pay a subsistence wage to the workers and claim the surplus value, i.e., the value created by the workers less their wages. This eventually causes consumption to decline and economic crisis to develop.

The buying power of the home markets decreases because the workers are earning subsistence wages and their purchasing power is insufficient to take all of the goods that the capitalists produce. Inventory accumulates, which causes the rate of profit to fall for the amount of money invested. The capitalists must turn to foreign markets to absorb their excess goods. But foreign markets are limited in number and imperialistic wars result. Eventually, within the colonies, liberation movements will occur that are directed against the mother country. India, Kenya, and Rhodesia (now Zimbabwe) are examples of former British colonies that have achieved their independence.

The result of imperialist wars and liberation movements, the Marxists say, will be the downfall of capitalism. Then the less developed countries will develop along Marxist lines. In the Marxist scheme of things, the less developed countries are simply precapitalist and would have to go through the capitalist phase before they could enter the optimum state of communism.

ROSTOW'S THEORY OF ECONOMIC DEVELOPMENT

Probably the most recent prominent theory of economic development is Walt Rostow's "take off" theory.[7] According to Rostow, in the process of economic development nations pass through five stages:

1. *The Traditional Society.* In the first stage, the nation's society is traditional (or feudal). All societies before the Renaissance were traditional societies, with little upward social mobility. Most resources were concentrated in agriculture. A crucial attribute is the absence of any cumulative, self-reinforcing process of material improvement.

2. *Prerequisites for Takeoff.* In the second stage, the prerequisites for sustained and systematic change are created. Chief among the prerequisites is an abandonment, by at least part of the population, of the philosophy of fatalism and determinism. There must be entrepreneurs in finance and manufacturing who are willing to take risks. Other changes in attitude and philosophical values must take place, including a respect for the individual, not on the basis of inherited status, but because of economic efficiency. Finally, a leading sector, e.g., mining, petroleum, is necessary for the takeoff.

3. *The Takeoff.* In this stage, which lasts for 20 to 30 years, the pace of social and economic change suddenly accelerates. An important part of this acceleration is an increase in the percentage of the gross national product that is saved and invested in capital goods. Another important step is the establishment of manufacturing. There is also continued change in such things as customs of the people, governmental forms and practices, and kinds of economic units in existence.

4. *Drive to Maturity.* This stage is a period of self-sustaining increase in both total and per capita gross national product. During this stage of some 60 years, industry comes to employ the most advanced technology available anywhere and becomes capable of producing whatever it wishes, being constrained only by market conditions and availability of resources.

---

7. Walt Whitman Rostow, *The Stages of Economic Growth: A Non-Communist Manifesto* (New York: Cambridge University Press, 1971).

5. *Mass Consumption.* The last stage is mass consumption of consumer durable goods and services. The production of these goods and services enables the majority of the population to attain high living standards.

CRITICISMS   Rostow's theory of the stages of economic growth has been criticized on a number of counts. Included among these is the charge that it fails to fit with historical fact. Some countries did not have a takeoff at all; rather, they developed steadily over a long period. The theory is also criticized because it fails to specify what makes each of the stages peculiarly distinctive relative to each of the others. It is further criticized for its failure to include forces that may be important to causing growth. However, Rostow's theory does indicate that important changes must occur before a nation in the traditional stage can advance in its development.

■ OBSTACLES ■
TO ECONOMIC DEVELOPMENT

Economic growth and development have been occurring slowly or not at all in many of the less developed countries. In Chad, for instance, the average annual economic growth rate was negative for the period 1960–1982; for Bangladesh, the average annual economic growth rate was 0.3 percent. Per capita income is not only very low, but it is not increasing very much. The people of the less developed countries want higher living standards. Given the communications revolution that has been developing throughout the world, people in even the remotest villages in Latin America and Africa have some idea of what the good life is. However, it turns out that economic development is an extremely elusive objective. The obstacles to its achievement are many, and the task of converting backward, poor people into at best moderately well-off ones is far from easy. There are many obstacles to economic development, and a review of some of them is in order.

POPULATION

In 1798 the English clergyman Thomas Malthus published his book *An Essay in the Principles of Population.*[8] His world outlook was pessimistic;

---

8. London: J.M. Dent & Sons, 1951.

it suggested that population grows faster than the food supply. Based on scattered empirical evidence, including the colonizing of North America, Malthus calculated that population tended to double every 25 years in a geometric progression, whereas food supplies tended to increase in an arithmetic progression. An example is shown in Table 16-5.

His proposition was based on two assumptions: Technological change could not increase food supply faster than population, and population growth would not be limited by fewer births, only by more deaths. Although both assumptions have proved to be wrong, there is an element of truth in his predictions. It took more than 4,000 years of recorded history for China to have its first 500 million people, but only a little more than three decades to increase the population to one billion. Regardless of a country's size, natural resources, or level of development, countries with large populations and high birth rates face increasing problems. At current rates of population increase, the population of developed countries will double in 118 years and the population of less developed countries will double in 34 years.[9]

URBANIZATION Urbanization and congestion are population-related problems. Often peasants are driven off the land into the cities by poverty or takeovers of the land by rich landowners or foreigners. Overcrowding can lead to increased population, unemployment, stress, and a demand for human services that can be greater than the capacity of the urban area to provide. Overcrowding can lead to an increase in health costs, not only from communicable diseases, but also from heart disease, cancer, and other ailments caused by a stress-related breakdown in the body's immunity. Urbanization problems are particularly acute in less developed countries because they lack the financial resources to provide the necessary services to cope with their problems. By the end of the century, at least 22

TABLE 16-5

Year	0	25	50	75	100	125	150	175	200
Population size	1	2	4	8	16	32	64	128	256
Food supply	1	2	3	4	5	6	7	8	9

9. Mary M. Kent and Carl Haub, "1985 World Population Data Sheet" (Washington: Population Reference Bureau, Inc., 1985).

cities in the world will have a population of more than 10 million; 60 will have more than 5 million. Most are located in the less developed countries. Mexico City, which has become the largest city in the world, is projected to have a population of 27 million by the end of the century.[10]

FOOD SHORTAGES   The larger the population of a country, the greater the demand for adequate food. Both a rural overpopulation and a rising tide of urban consumers compete for a limited agricultural output. In most less developed countries the need to satisfy the demand for food has prevented the allocation of resources to economic development. As a result, the inability to industrialize reduces the potential to earn money from exports to pay for the import of food products. It is a vicious cycle of hunger.

Food shortages can also have a deleterious effect on the health of a country's workers. A case in point is Ethiopia, where famine has resulted in the death of countless thousands of persons. Other African countries have also been affected by famine. Nutritional deficiencies in the less developed countries lead to a lower level of worker productivity, with subsequent lower agricultural and industrial output as a result.

Although food production in the less developed countries has increased in recent decades, it has just kept pace with population growth in some countries and has failed to do so in others, including 27 African countries. In Nigeria, the largest country in Africa, the average annual rate of agricultural production declined during the period 1970–1980.[11] The output of food in China and India has exceeded population growth, but only by a narrow margin.

Moreover, in the less developed countries, increases in agricultural acreage have been relatively small over the last two decades. In the main, further growth of the land frontier is constrained in many countries. In Africa, for example, the expansion of farm land is limited by the Sahara desert, rivers, jungles, and mountains, and also by diseases that destroy livestock and farm products. Insecticides used to try to control the diseases have had undesirable effects on the environment.[12] In India the number of rural households and people trying to earn a living in agriculture has increased at a rate far in excess of cultivated land.

---

10. United Nations, Department of International and Social Affairs, *Population Bulletin of the United Nations*, No. 14, 1984, p. 24.

11. The World Bank, *World Development Report 1984*, pp. 84-88.

12. Ibid., p. 90.

INFRASTRUCTURE

Capital can be classified in two ways—social overhead capital and physical capital. The former includes the structures and equipment required for shelter, public health, and education, and the latter consists of plant and equipment used in industry and agriculture. Poor countries are deficient in both forms of capital because saving and income are low. They cannot afford the medical services and educational facilities necessary to improve the quality of the labor force. This fact becomes evident in Table 16-6. In Bangladesh, for example, there is one physician for every 10,940 persons; in the United States there is one physician for 520 persons.[13] In Uganda, only 5 percent of people of secondary school age are in school and only one percent of those in the higher education age group are in some form of college. In Japan, the corresponding statistics are 92 percent and 30 percent. Only one percent of the relevant age group attends college in China; however, this is a legacy of the Cultural Revolution, when universities were closed down.[14]

Infrastructure, or social overhead capital, is a descriptive economic concept that refers to the existence of highways, railways, airports, sewage facilities, housing, schools, and other social amenities that indicate the development or lack of development of an area or region. Once an infrastructure is in place, it encourages both economic and social development. Developed countries have developed infrastructures; less developed countries generally do not. This creates a problem for economic development, for industry will normally not locate plants in areas where there is a poor infrastructure. In particular, mass consumption products require the existence of skilled labor, sewage disposal facilities, transportation and communication facilities, and other amenities for their marketing.

EDUCATION Education facilities are a key component in the infrastructure of any area or region. Education itself is directly related to the quality of life and constitutes a form of human capital. Literacy, or rather the lack of it, is not as directly related to a country's population as it is to the country's stage of economic development. There is a positive correlation between a lower standard of living and a higher rate of illiteracy. It has been estimated that one-third of the world is illiterate. Most of this illiteracy is

13. In Chad there is one physician for every 47,530 persons. Only 3 percent of the secondary school age group are in school and less than one percent are in college.

14. The colleges were closed during the Cultural Revolution for ideological reasons and professors and students were put to work in the fields alongside the peasants to learn humility and to ponder socialist ideals. Working side-by-side in a manure pile was considered a good way to eliminate class distinctions.

TABLE 16-6　HEALTH- AND EDUCATION-RELATED
INDICATORS FOR SELECTED COUNTRIES

	Population Per Physician	Percentage of Age Group in Secondary Schools	Percentage of Age Group in Higher Education
Bangladesh	7,810	15%	4%
Ethiopia	69,390	12	1
Uganda	26,810	8	1
India	3,690	30	8
China	1,740	35	1
Pakistan	3,480	14	2
Kenya	7,890	20	1
Indonesia	11,530	33	4
Nigeria	12,550	16	3
Guatemala	8,610	16	7
Italy	340	74	25
Japan	780	92	30
United States	520	97	58
Sweden	490	85	38
U.S.S.R.	270	97	21
Canada	550	98	39

Source: The World Bank, *World Development Report 1985*, pp. 220-221 and 222-223.

concentrated in countries with high birth rates, large populations, and the least to spend on education. A lack of educational opportunities maintains the distinction between the haves and have-nots in society and perpetuates class differences. It also reduces the base of educated labor upon which the economic development of the country depends.

ROADS　A requisite for the economic and social development of a country is an adequate system of roads. Few countries can depend exclusively on other forms of transportation. Air transportation is too expensive to be used for the shipment of most products, and railroads are limited to specific routes between main access points. Poor countries usually do not have the resources to maintain an adequate road system. Physiography also works against the development of an adequate highway system. Most of the less developed countries are located in geographic areas of the world with barriers to transportation. For example, the Sierra Madre and Andes mountains have inhibited the east-west development of Mexico, Bolivia, and Peru. Transportation is also hard to develop in countries dominated by tropical jungles because vegetation overtakes roads in only a short time.

OTHER FACILITIES   Dams, bridges, sewage disposal, and other facilities are a vital part of a region's infrastructure and are usually inadequate in the less developed countries. Dams control flooding and provide the water supply and electric power necessary for economic and social development. Bridges create more efficient transportation by linking areas that are separated by bodies of water. Inadequate sanitary facilities can result in the spread of communicable diseases such as cholera and typhoid fever. Garbage and waste materials dumped in city streets attract rats and other animals, which increases the possibility of epidemics. Communication facilities have to be adequate to handle the needs of a region. The cost and efficiency of service have to be considered. Government-owned telephone and postal services in less developed countries are notoriously inefficient.

LOW SAVINGS RATE

As mentioned above, there is an extreme imbalance in the distribution of income in less developed countries, exacerbated in part by the existence of a large component of unskilled labor. The vast majority of workers do not earn enough to do any saving; moreover, a minority of households get most of the income. In Mexico, for example, in 1977 the top 10 percent of income earners received 40.6 percent of national income; in Brazil in 1972, the top 10 percent received 50.6 percent of national income. This group should provide much of the saving necessary for capital formation. However, savings are usually invested out of the country or in real estate, where there is a quick and high rate of return. Political instability provides a good reason to invest one's income, say in Swiss bonds, where it will be safe from possible expropriation by a new government. El Salvador is a case in point.

Savings is a necessary requisite for capital formation, for without it investment for capital formation cannot take place. Inadequate amounts of capital and the inability to increase the capital are obstacles to economic development. It can be said that less developed countries are caught in a vicious circle. Because savings is small, investment is low and the capital stock is small, and the real gross national product is small. Nations that save little grow slowly and are locked into a circle of poverty.[15]

LIMITED RANGE OF EXPORTS

Less developed countries usually depend on the export of agricultural products, fuels, minerals, or metals such as oil or copper. Many depend on

15. Ragnar Nurkse, *Problems of Capital Formation in Underdeveloped Countries* (New York: Oxford University Press, 1953).

the export of a single product for the bulk of national income. Nigeria depends on the export of oil for around 80 percent of its total export earnings. Thus the drop in the world market price of oil has created problems for the Nigerian economy. When oil prices were high during the early 1970s, Nigeria benefitted. It ran a surplus in its balance of payments, and it could use foreign earnings to improve its living standards. Government spending increased to improve the infrastructure of the Nigerian economy. However, during the early 1980s, the world demand for oil declined, and oil prices fell from a peak of $35 a barrel in 1980. Revenues from oil exports declined, Nigeria had a deficit in its balance of payments, and it now has a problem of a large foreign debt incurred when oil prices were high and earnings were good.

Countries that depend on exports of agricultural products and minerals are usually subject to a disadvantage in trade with the developed countries. The terms of trade, the real quantity of exports required to pay for a given amount of real imports, favor the developed countries. Brazilian coffee and Mexican oil are much more subject to shifts in world prices than are American computers and Japanese cars. When prices decline for coffee or oil, Brazil and Mexico will have to give up more income to import computers and cars. Conversely, America and Japan will have to give up less income to acquire coffee and oil. There is an inelastic demand for many products exported by the less developed countries. When prices for the product fall, there is no offsetting increase in revenue resulting from a more than proportionate increase in demand.

SOCIOCULTURAL FACTORS

Sociocultural factors can also provide an obstacle to economic development.[16] Culture involves interaction between individuals and groups. It consists of behavioral patterns and values of a social group. It is culture that influences individual and group behavior and determines how things will be done, at least in theory if not in practice. It includes a number of features such as the status distinction, based on education, caste, politics, religion, or sex, between members of a social group. Culture may also assume the form of language differences identifying a group or region. It also may extend to production, with the use of machinery and equipment in an industrial society creating a culture that is alien to agrarian societies. Cultures need a certain amount of conformity to keep groups of people working together, but they also need new ideas to promote progress.

16. For a discussion of sociocultural factors and their impact on development see Edmund Leach, *Social Anthropology* (New York: Oxford University Press, 1982).

RELIGION   Religion can provide the spiritual foundation for a culture. It can also exacerbate the problems of economic development. Cultural conflicts in the area of religion can be quite serious, as anyone familiar with the Middle East can testify. Conflicts between Hindus and Moslems created such severe problems in governing India after it gained its independence from the United Kingdom that Pakistan was made a separate Moslem country. The assassination of Indian Prime Minister Indira Gandhi involved a religious conflict between Hindus and Sikhs culminating over the alleged defiling of the latter's holy temple at Amritsar by Indian troops. Several days of rioting resulted in threats and destruction of property. The revolt against the Shah of Iran was largely led by fundamentalist Moslem clergy who felt that traditional religious values were being replaced by Western values of materialism. Religion can place moral and economic norms on a culture by prescribing limits, particularly the subordination of impulse, on acceptable conduct.

FATE   A fatalistic view of life is one of the differences between Western and Eastern cultures. Fate is called *karma* in the Hindu and Buddhist religions and *kismet* in the Moslem religion. Karma holds that every action carries with it a reward or punishment. One literally has little control over one's life; it is controlled by destiny. Good fortune is the result of some action in the past, even in a previous life, that was good. Conversely, bad fortune is also the result of some bad act committed at some time in the past. A person is unaware of past actions, good or bad; it is simply his or her karma at work.

SOCIAL ORGANIZATION   The social organization of a society also can have an impact on economic development. It refers to the roles of men, women, and children within a system. Employment, manners, dress, and expectations are virtually dictated by each culture to its members. Certain actions may be permitted or denied through a legal process, but the majority of actions are learned through interaction in the culture or from the training of those familiar with the culture. A social organization functions within the cultural system of the society in which it is located. The component parts—that is, the people—function and work together through patterns of interaction that develop among the members. These interactions take many forms of interpersonal relationships that can have an effect on economic development. Examples of these forms are as follows.

CLASSES   Each social system has a demarcated class system. Class distinction may be based on religion. An example is the Hindu religion, with its caste system. At the top are the Brahmins, who are members of the priestly class; at the bottom are the untouchables. Social classes may achieve distinctiveness based on hereditary titles or through being arbiters of taste and refinement. Class may be based on educational attainment, particularly in societies where education is limited to the select few. Class systems can inhibit economic development; in some societies, business is regarded as a lowly occupation, something done by the lower class or foreigners.

FAMILY   In all cultures, men, women, and children live together in families. The family is the one basic institution found everywhere. It represents a sort of social insurance and insulation against the trials and tribulations of life. However, the role of the family varies in different countries. In Japan it represents stability in a country that prizes consensus. It is probable that the group ethic, including family solidarity, has contributed to the economic development of Japan. The role of the family can also work against economic development. Large families are regarded as an economic asset in many parts of the world. The children can be put to work in the fields when they are young and contribute to family income. They are also expected to take care of their elderly parents. Birth control methods designed to limit family size are often resisted in the less developed countries, even though the population is greater than the food resources available to feed it.

PHYSIOGRAPHY

The physiography of a country can have an impact on its economic and social development for better or worse. Flat, fertile soil, supported by water and a suitable climate, provides the basis for agriculture. Dense forests provide a renewable resource in the wood, and also furnish a refuge and habitat for wildlife as well as a root base that prevents soil erosion. Fast-running rivers and streams offer a potential for hydroelectric development. Water is vital to the support of life and forms a primary source of transportation. Deserts, which were once a barrier to economic development, are now more malleable, given the state of world technology. In many of the less developed countries, a combination of physical forces has had an adverse effect on economic and social development.

SOIL   Because humans must eat in order to survive and because nearly all of our food is either directly or indirectly a product of the soil, agriculture is probably the most important activity on the earth. A shortage of productive land is one of the major problems facing the world and its rapidly growing population. Although this problem hardly exists in the United States, it is endemic in most of the less developed countries. The ratio of arable lands to people is basic to agricultural productivity and consumption rates. As the maximum productivity per unit of agricultural land is achieved, the per capita amount of food available must decrease as the population continues to increase. Maintenance of soil fertility, vital to productivity, is a growing problem as soils are becoming more and more exhausted throughout the world.

Less than 5 percent of the total land area of Latin America and Africa has the combination of climate and physiographic conditions necessary for agricultural production.[17] The mountainous nature of Bolivia and Peru makes cultivation of most of the land impossible. In most of Latin America, climatic variations run to the extremes of either too much or too little rain; the Amazon basin of Brazil, for example, receives too much rainfall, resulting in the rapid leaching of nutrients from the soil. The tropical lands of Africa have sufficient moisture and are very fertile, but the presence of human and botanical tropical diseases results in low agricultural productivity. The remaining lands, which occupy an enourmous expanse, are semidesert or desert and can produce little without irrigation.

MOUNTAINS While mountains provide a basis for tourism and winter sports, they are a barrier to economic development. Mountainous terrain makes farming difficult, if not impossible; makes mining expensive and hazardous; and inhibits the construction of transportation facilities. The forests that cover many mountain slopes are a valuable resource, but harvesting is difficult. Transportation is hard to develop in countries such as Guatemala, Bolivia, and Peru that are dominated by mountain ranges. In Asia, the Himalaya range makes a large land area inaccessible and unavailable for development. In China, economic development of the whole country is difficult because much of the land area is isolated from the main population centers by insurmountable mountains.

■ SOLUTIONS ■
FOR ECONOMIC DEVELOPMENT

There are no easy solutions that will enable less developed countries to become developed. Many have nothing of value to export and little potential

---

17. Bernard Gilland, "Considerations on World Population and Food Supply," *Population and Development Review* (July, 1983), pp. 203-211.

for industrial development. They are hamstrung by hostile social, cultural, and political institutions. The average annual growth rate of the poorest countries in the world, those with half of the world's population and with a per capita income of $390 or less, was 3.0 percent over the period 1960–1982.[18] The average annual growth rate of India was 1.7 percent, and its per capita income for 1982 was $260. At that rate of growth, it would take more than 50 years for India's per capita income to double. The rate of investment in India and other of the poorest countries is constrained in three ways: the capacity of the country to absorb additional capital; the level of domestic savings; and foreign exchange rates that affect trade with other countries. Even so, India is far better off then Bangladesh, which had an average annual growth rate of 0.3 percent for 1960–1982, or Chad, which had a negative rate of growth and a negative rate of investment for the same period.

FOREIGN AID

Foreign aid involves a transfer between the more developed nations and less developed nations for the purpose of promoting economic development. The transfer may be in the form of grants that do not have to be repaid or loans that carry lower rates of interest and longer periods of repayment than normally would prevail for the borrowing country. Foreign aid may also come in a variety of physical forms. Technical assistance and supplies of foods are examples of physical aid.[19] However, foreign aid cannot be considered a panacea for economic development. It may concentrate benefits in a few hands and may fail to change incentives and responses needed for broad economic development. Foreign aid can be used for consumption purposes, generating a one-time increase in well-being for those lucky to get it and leaving no lasting benefits. Many foreign aid projects have long gestation lags before their output is directly marketable. This can conflict with public expectations of immediate success.

INTERNAL POLICIES

Certain development policies that do not involve outside assistance have been used with varying degrees of success by a number of countries. These

18. World Bank, *World Development Report 1984*, pp. 218-219.

19. The World Bank makes loans to less developed countries to improve their economic and social infrastructures. The United States and other developed countries have their own programs of capital and technical assistance for the less developed countries.

policies rely on the notion that a less developed country can pull itself up by its bootstraps. The communist countries have followed a policy of unbalanced growth, where resources are channeled away from the production of agriculture and consumer goods and into the development of heavy industry. The Soviet Union, by following this policy, was able to transform itself from an agricultural to an industrial country, although at considerable cost.[20] Then there are policies based on trade to achieve development. The inward-looking, or import-substitution policy, promotes the development of home industries by restricting the import of outside products.[21] This policy has its drawbacks, but has been used by some countries, notably Mexico and Brazil, to achieve some economic development. There is also an outward-looking trade policy that relies on exports of products to achieve development. Internal resources are used to develop export industries and exports are subsidized by the government.

GOVERNMENT MONETARY AND FISCAL POLICIES   Government monetary and fiscal policies are also used to promote economic development. Central banks use monetary policy to control the level of national output and the price level through changes in the money supply. Increasing the money supply can have a stimulative effect on an economy, as witnessed by the development of Spain as the world's leading country during the sixteenth century. The flow of gold and silver from the New World stimulated the economic development of Spain and provided the base for "easy money" policies in the Dutch and German banking houses of Western Europe.[22] However, the problem with an "easy money" policy is that less developed countries are inflation-prone. Shortages of goods develop as a result of bottlenecks in production, and prices rise. Investment on the part of the rich is directed toward speculative holdings, such as real estate, rather than toward the creation or expansion of productive enterprises. A constantly rising price level tends to aggravate this tendency by making speculation all the more profitable.[23]

---

20. This industrialization was achieved in its early stages, largely at the expense of the landowners and the peasants. The former were liquidated and the latter were literally starved, to provide a surplus of foodstuffs for the support of workers in the factories.

21. For example, to build a domestic automobile industry, one could restrict the import of automobiles.

22. It might be added that gold and silver proved to be the ruination of Spain. The Spanish kings spent the wealth on military conquests. Gold and silver increased the money supply in Spain, creating inflation that eventually destroyed the economy.

23. Inflation also worsens income inequality between rich and poor and increases the potential for social unrest.

Fiscal policy affects aggregate demand through changes in government spending and the level of taxation. An expansionary fiscal policy can stimulate economic growth and development through an increase in government spending, various tax breaks, or both. The problem with fiscal policy is that it is far more adaptable to the developed countries, where income, output, consumer spending, taxation, and investment are high enough to be manipulated. Many less developed countries rely on sales taxes as a major source of revenue. Income taxes are often not feasible because there is little income to tax or tax avoidance is easy. Countries may also resort to deficit financing—expenditures that are greater than revenues—to stimulate the economy. The deficit is financed by borrowing from the central bank or through the sale of debt to the public. However, in the less developed countries, there are no money markets for the sale of the debt and the public does not have the money. Thus borrowing is done primarily through the central bank.

MARKET MECHANISMS　　Some economists feel that the problems of the less developed countries can be solved by market forces coupled with a nineteenth-century government policy of laissez faire. All developed countries began by being underdeveloped; they developed naturally without state intervention through the market application of capital, entrepreneurial and technical skills, and labor. Essentially, market mechanisms consist of permitting individual buyers and sellers to make economic decisions for themselves and letting things be as they are or will be. Market mechanisms can play an important role in the conversion of a less developed country into a developed one. The ideas of how they can do so have been formulated from the British experience and from other developed countries such as the United States and Japan. But it is unlikely that market mechanisms alone will achieve economic development for the less developed countries. Moreover, there are tremendous differences between the situations of England and the United States over the last two centuries and the less developed countries of today. Some of them may be summarized as follows.

1. Sociological forces favored development of the United States and other Western countries. The Protestant work ethic emphasized thrift.[24] This attitude helped produce a flow of savings sufficient to finance the introduction of new commodities and new techniques brought on by the Industrial Revolution.

---

24. R.H. Tawney, *Religion and the Rise of Capitalism* (New York: Harcourt, Brace and World, 1926), chapters 1 and 2.

2. Technological factors were more favorable to development in the Western world than they are to the less developed countries of today. The simplest of these factors is the extent of resource endowment. If one compares the resource endowment of the United States to that of Bangladesh or Pakistan, the contrast is apparent. The proportions in which land, labor, and capital are available are a drag on development in the latter two countries. The proportions favor agriculture against industry; labor is abundant, land is relatively limited, and capital is very scarce.[25]

3. Political factors also favored economic development of the Western countries. In the United States, for example, nationalism did not manifest itself in a hostility toward the inflow of foreign capital. There was a large and continuous flow of foreign capital into the country during the period 1865–1900, when the United States became a world industrial power. In many of the less developed countries today, foreign investment may be threatened with outright expropriation. Foreign investment is limited because risks of unpredictable government action, often based on nationalistic sentiment, are added to the normal risks attendant in investment abroad.

SUCCESS IN EAST ASIA

Although there are many factors over which the less developed countries have no control, some East Asian countries, notably South Korea and Singapore, have succeeded in developing their economies through a combination of government policies and private enterprise initiative.[26] Exports have been promoted by keeping exchange rates competitive. This has enabled South Korea and Singapore to expand exports, while restricting imports on the basis of price. Second, these countries have maintained high real interest rates, which has encouraged domestic savings and insured that investment is directed into the areas of highest return. Third, they have relied on market mechanisms for resource allocation.

In the following chapters, three countries will be examined from the standpoint of their approaches to economic development. They represent

---

25. Colin Clark, *The Conditions of Economic Progress* (London: Macmillan & Co., Ltd., 1951).

26. Japan is the prime example of a successful East Asian country. However, Japan was a developed industrial nation before World War II.

Asia, Latin America, and Africa. China is the largest less developed country in the world and is also one of the poorest. It is a socialist country in the process of experimenting with market mechanisms of capitalism to increase productivity. Mexico is at a lower middle stage of economic development. Its per capita income is one-sixth that of the United States, but is eight times larger than China's. Nigeria, the largest country in Africa, has a per capita GNP higher than most African countries, but lower than most Latin American countries. It is a country in the lower stages of economic development.

SUMMARY

Almost half of the world's people live in countries with a per capita gross GNP of $500 a year or less; another 500 million people live in countries with a per capita income between $500 and $1500 a year. These countries are at the lowest stages of economic development. Many countries with higher per capita incomes, such as Mexico and Brazil, can hardly be called modern industrial economies. This is also true of the oil-exporting countries, whose per capita incomes are high, but whose level of economic development is low. These less developed countries are committed to economic development as a way to improve living standards, but face many obstacles in achieving a rate of investment that will provide a satisfactory rate of economic growth. One major obstacle is the lack of an adequate infrastructure to provide the services necessary for industrial development. Sociocultural factors can also inhibit development. Probably the most important obstacle to economic development is population. When population grows rapidly, the bulk of domestic investment is simply devoted to maintaining the current level of per capita income.

REVIEW QUESTIONS

1. Upon what basis is a country classified as less developed?
2. What are the typical economic features of a less developed country?
3. Distinguish between economic growth and economic development.
4. What is Rostow's theory of the stages of economic development?
5. In traditional societies, what is the typical attitude toward family size? Why does this attitude exist?

6. What do you regard as the paramount obstacle to economic development in less developed countries? Why?
7. What are some examples of sociocultural factors that block economic development?
8. Discuss the concept of technological dualism.
9. Why do less developed countries have a disadvantage in their terms of trade with the developed countries?
10. When and how are more people a detriment rather than a benefit in achieving economic development?

■ —— RECOMMENDED READINGS —— ■

Gilland, Bernard. "Considerations on World Population and Food Supply." *Population and Development Review* (June 1983), pp. 203–211.

Hagen, Everett E. *Economic Development,* 3rd ed. Homewood, Ill.: Richard D. Irwin, 1980.

Herrick, Bruce, and Charles P. Kindleberger. *Economic Development.* 4th ed. New York: McGraw-Hill Book Co., 1983.

Kent, Mary M., and Carl Haub. *1985 World Population Data Sheet.* Washington: Population Reference Bureau, Inc., 1985.

Newman, James L., and Gordon E. Matzke. *Population: Patterns, Dynamics, and Prospects.* Englewood Cliffs, N.J.: Prentice-Hall, Inc., 1984.

Rostow, Walt W. *Why the Poor Get Richer and the Rich Slow Down.* Austin: University of Texas Press, 1980.

World Bank. *World Development Report 1985.* New York: Oxford University Press, 1985.

C H A P T E R   1   7

THE PEOPLE'S REPUBLIC OF CHINA

China is the most populous country in the world based on a population of more than one billion and is third in terms of land size. The land area, though slightly larger than the United States, presents a serious problem in that much of it is uninhabitable mountains and deserts. Only one-tenth of China's land area is suitable for cultivation, with the result that millions of Chinese depend upon small allotments of land for their subsistence. More than 90 percent of the population is concentrated in the eastern and central parts of the country, an area roughly half the size of the United States. The sheer size of the population creates problems of food, housing, employment, and transportation for those who manage the economy.

China is also one of the poorest countries in the world. Its per capita GNP in 1985 was $290.[1] Its per capita GNP was about the same as Haiti's, which is the poorest country in the Western Hemisphere. Any increases in food production are largely offset by increases in population. Per capita food consumption is only about what it was during the 1950s, and the

1. The World Bank, *World Bank Atlas 1985*, p. 6.

average daily consumption is between 2,400 and 2,500 calories per person.[2]

Despite efforts to industrialize the country, 69 percent of the Chinese were employed in agriculture in 1982. Some 800 million Chinese still live in rural areas. In 1982, only 44 percent of those persons of secondary school age were enrolled in school, and only one percent of the college-age population were in college.[3] The overall infrastructure of the country is poorly developed; housing and sewage facilities are inadequate and there is no transportation system.

Since 1949, which marked the fall of the Nationalist Chinese government, the Chinese Communists have tried to promote economic development. At first, the Chinese looked to the Russians to provide the expertise and guidance necessary to transform China into a planned economy along Soviet lines. This approach was eventually discarded in favor of idealistic extremism. In the late 1970s, more moderate thinking and planning prevailed; by 1980 some experimentation with the free market was permitted in agriculture. In October 1984, a major break occurred when the *People's Daily*, the newspaper of the Communist Party, stated that orthodox Marxism could not be depended on to solve China's economic problems.[4]

Thus reforms incorporating the use of free markets and other elements of capitalism have been introduced or are being introduced in China. In agriculture, for example, the commune system has largely been abandoned and private plots have increased in importance. Chinese farmers are required to sell a specific amount of their produce to the state; they are allowed to sell anything over this amount in the free market. The standard of living for many farmers has improved to the point where they can afford television sets and other consumer products.[5] A second reform involves renunciation of egalitarian wages and the adoption of a wage system linked to productivity. Enterprises will have the right to fine unproductive workers. A third reform is to establish a rational price system. Currently, the

---

2. The World Bank, *World Development Report 1984*, p. 264. The average daily calorie supply of the Chinese is above the average for the low-income countries. In Chad, for example, the average daily calorie supply for 1982 was 1810. The average daily calorie supply for the United States was 3,647. However, five-sixths of the caloric intake of the Chinese is derived from grains such as rice, wheat, and corn, rather than from other richer and varied sources such as meat, fish, eggs, vegetables, and sugar.

3. The World Bank, *World Development Report 1984*, p. 266. The Cultural Revolution deemphasized the role of education in Chinese society. Most universities were closed and professors and students were put to work in the fields and factories.

4. "Communique of Third Plenary Session of the 12th Central Committee of the Chinese Communist Party," October 20, 1984.

5. Orville Schell, *To Get Rich Is Glorious: China in the Eighties* (New York: Pantheon Books, 1985), pp. 20-27.

prices of most products reflect neither their value nor the relation of supply and demand. Greater attention is to be placed on a free-floating price system. A fourth reform will include competition between state enterprises. They are to be put to the test of direct judgment by consumers in the marketplace so that only the best survive.

■ DEVELOPMENT ■
OF THE ECONOMIC SYSTEM

At the end of World War II, China was split into two factions, the Nationalists and Communists, both of which had resisted Japanese incursions since the begining of the Sino-Japanese War in 1937. Japan's defeat set up a struggle for control of occupied China extending from Manchuria in the north to Canton in the south. Mediation was attempted by the United States, and a tripartite committee consisting of Nationalists, Communists, and the United States was set up to work out conditions for coalition government. These efforts proved short-lived and a civil war broke out in 1946. The Nationalists' initial advantages in territory and logistics were lost, and the Nationalist government was driven from the Chinese mainland to Taiwan by the Communists in 1949.

THE PERIOD OF CONSOLIDATION, 1949–1952

When the Communists formally announced the creation of the Chinese People's Republic on October 1, 1949, they were able to begin the consolidation of power and the development of a new type of economic system. Certainly the task was not easy. Years of fighting and inflation had debilitated the economy. Widespread corruption had been rampant under the Nationalist government. The masses of the people were illiterate and had to be trained and educated to fit into an industrial base that was to be the fountainhead for the development of the communist economic system.

Upon gaining control of the country, the Communist regime began a series of nationwide reforms that attempted to control nearly every aspect of Chinese life. Of paramount importance was the redistribution of land to the peasants and the elimination of landlords as an economic class. This marked the first step toward collectivization of agriculture.

During this period, Chinese industry was also placed under the control of the government. In 1949, the Communist government took over those state organizations it identified as bureaucratic capital. During 1951 and

1952, the government took over all foreign-owned businesses. In 1952 and 1953, private enterprises were placed under government control.[6]

THE FIRST FIVE-YEAR PLAN, 1953–1957

The First Five-Year Plan marked the second stage in the economic development of the People's Republic of China. To implement the plan, the Chinese relied heavily on Russian expertise. Soviet technicians were imported to develop the plan and to run the factories. Agreements were reached providing for Russian aid in building or expanding electric power plants and supplying agricultural, mining, and chemical equipment. Soviet financial aid took the form of low-interest loans. The Russians also contracted for the construction of factories producing a wide variety of products, including chemicals, synthetic fibers and plastics, liquid fuel, and machine tools. The Soviets built modern iron and steel complexes, nonferrous metallurgical plants, refineries, and power stations and trained Chinese technicians to operate them. Sets of blueprints and related materials giving directions for plant layouts were also provided for the Chinese.

The land reforms of 1949–1952 were followed by a series of organizational reforms beginning with the simplest form of social enterprise, the *mutual aid team,* and progressing through successive stages of producer cooperatives to complete collectivization of the farms in 1957. At that time the peasants lost all title to the land. This same organizational pattern was followed for craftspersons and small retailers. By 1957, practically all industrial enterprises were state-owned or collectives.

THE GREAT LEAP FORWARD, 1958–1960

In 1958 the Chinese departed from the pattern of economic development set by the First Five-Year Plan and moved to a new approach that relied on the idealistic fervor of the masses of workers and peasants to drive the economy ahead much more quickly. This approach was called the *Great Leap Forward.* It is an example of idealistic extremism that substituted zeal for the material incentives developed under the First Five-Year Plan. China's enormous population was regarded as an economic asset and not a liability—the more people, the more hands to build to communism. Emphasis was placed on indigenous methods of production and the development of labor-intensive investment projects. To put the basic objective of

---

6. Gregory Chow, *The Chinese Economy* (New York: Harper & Row, Publishers, 1985), p. 134.

the Great Leap Forward simply, the population was to be harnessed to increase production and make China a world power.

AGRICULTURE   In agriculture, economic policy involved the formation of communes. The communes marked the final stage in the transition of agriculture from private enterprise, which had existed during the first years of Communist rule. Under communal organization, all vestiges of private property were eliminated. The peasants were not only deprived of the private plots, livestock, and implements that had been left to them through previous collectivization, they also had to surrender their homes. The purpose was to turn the peasants into mobile workers ready for any task in any area to which they might be assigned.

INDUSTRY   In industry, economic policy emphasized the use of labor to create thousands of tiny industrial units throughout the country. Again, the Communists planned to capitalize on the presence of a large labor surplus to accomplish rapid industrialization, particularly in rural areas. During that part of the year when the rural population was underemployed, labor could be used for useful output. Small indigenous industrial plants were created to harness the energies of the labor force. These plants included handicraft workshops, iron and steel foundries, fertilizer plants, oil extraction, machine shops, cement manufacture, coal and iron ore mining, and food processing. The capital used to build the small plants came from the local communes and from taxes on state enterprises. Labor, however, was the key factor employed in the development of local industry.

Top priority was given to the iron and steel industry. Lack of technology and equipment was replaced by mass fervor. This has been called facetiously "the steel mill in every backyard" policy. Some 80 million people were involved in an attempt to create a do-it-yourself steel industry. Two million backyard furnaces were developed throughout China. Many millions of Chinese worked day and night turning out steel, while millions of others labored in the extraction of iron ore and coal. The result was the development of labor-intensive, small-scale steel production with a low capital-output ratio. Although the output of iron and steel was increased by the backyard furnace method, much of it was of poor and often unusable quality, reflecting the absence of quality-control standards and the necessary technical expertise. Production in other areas suffered as well because more than one-tenth of the population was diverted from other pursuits into the production of steel.

FAILURE OF THE GREAT LEAP FORWARD   The Great Leap Forward was not a success. Although industrial and agricultural output rose sharply in

1958, much of the gain was spurious. The output was often of such poor quality that most of it had to be scrapped. Production costs were high, reflecting an indiscriminate development of small plants in almost all industries. There was also a disregard for cost considerations at the level of the local plant because the most important success indicator was the degree to which the local cadre (leaders) could fulfill or overfulfill physical quotas. Output was maximized at the expense of quality and cost, and inputs of labor and raw materials could have been more effectively employed elsewhere. A shortage of fuel and raw materials caused by the waste involved in the backyard furnace method of production and a lack of adequate transportation facilities were responsible for the demise of many plants.

SINO-RUSSIAN RELATIONS   The Great Leap Forward also caused a rift in the relationship between the Chinese and the Russian advisers and technicians that had been sent to help them. In essence, the Russian blueprints for making China a self-sufficient world power were set aside in favor of a development program that made little economic sense. The Chinese persisted in ignoring the advice of their Russian technicians despite the fact that Russia intimated that support would be withdrawn unless the Great Leap Forward was discontinued. In 1960 the Soviet technicians were withdrawn from China. With them went the equipment, financial aid, and blueprints that had played a paramount role in the development of the Chinese economy during the First Five-Year Plan. This *en masse* departure of the technicians had a negative effect on China because it could not supply the expertise to replace them.

ECONOMIC AND SOCIAL READJUSTMENT, 1961–1965

The period 1961–1965 marked a return to more orthodox economic and social policies. Economic planning, which was largely superseded by the Great Leap Forward, was resumed, and agricultural policy was modified. For all practical purposes the commune was abandoned. Various forms of material incentives were restored, and farmers were again able to have private plots of land for their own use. Agriculture was given priority in terms of investment, while overall industrial investment suffered a retrenchment in favor of certain high-priority industries, in particular those that contributed to the development of agriculture. Foreign trade, which previously had been tied to the Soviet Union, turned toward exchange of basic raw materials for Western and Japanese machinery, technology, and grain.

PROLETARIAN CULTURAL REVOLUTION, 1966–1969

The Third Five-Year Plan, which began in 1965, was eclipsed by a political aberration of the first magnitude called the *Proletarian Cultural Revolution*. This was an attempt by Mao Tse-tung to mold Chinese society into his prescribed pattern. It placed primacy on ideological cant over scientific expertise and reverted to the Great Leap Forward period in its attempt to replace material incentives with political ideology and to denigrate any emphasis on technical excellence.[7] It aimed at annihilating, throughout China and particularly in the universities, any tendency towards a moderate or revisionist viewpoint concerning the role of communism in world affairs. Intrasigence toward the Western countries in general and the United States in particular was to be maintained until Western influence was eliminated from Asia. The Russians also did not escape the general opprobrium that the Chinese engendered toward the West, because Mao was furious with them for drawing back from war and subversion with the West in the interest of coexistence.

The rationale of the Cultural Revolution was political as well as economic. It involved Mao's attempt to develop a new socialist morality that would place public interest above private individualism. He believed that Stalin had permitted the development of a new class structure in the form of a state bureaucracy that differed little from a capitalist class structure. Soviet claims of egalitarianism ignored the special privileges for this small bureaucratic and technical elite. Moreover, Mao believed that Russia and other socialist countries had moved away from the utopian idea of an egalitarian society by introducing material incentives and bonuses, which tended to differentiate among workers. An ethical revolution was needed, for people had to be changed in order to create a new order of society.

The Cultural Revolution represented a step backward in terms of economic growth. The average annual rate of growth of gross national product during the period 1966–1968 was -2.5 percent, reflecting a general decline in industrial output of around 15 to 20 percent in 1967. More importantly, the Cultural Revolution encouraged an ideological polarization within the regime and weakened consensus on the nation's fundamental values and priorities. The regime faced the task of rebuilding a stable institutional structure and working out a new pattern of relationships among various groups.

---

7. A poster in a Peking park proclaimed, "We do not need brains! Our heads are armed with the ideas of Mao Tse-tung."

THE POST-CULTURAL-REVOLUTION PERIOD, 1970–1976

The end of the Cultural Revolution ushered in another stage of Chinese economic development. For one thing, central economic planning in the form of a Fourth Five-Year Plan was reintroduced. Both the Second and Third Five-Year Plans were largely shunted aside by sudden shifts in Chinese ideological policies—the former by the Great Leap Forward and the latter by the Cultural Revolution.

The Fourth Five-Year Plan (1971–1975) had several objectives. In industrial development, priority was given to the production of sophisticated electronic instruments, including computers. Continued effort was given to increase the output of heavy industry, particularly iron and steel, hydrocarbons, and chemical fertilizers. Agriculture, however, still remained the basis of the economy, and agricultural policy under the plan aimed at making rural areas more self-sustaining. Investment was increased in various water management programs, including the construction of dams, dikes, reservoirs, and irrigation canals.

However, there were additional political interruptions during this period. The leaders began jockeying for power as it became evident that both Chairman Mao and Premier Chou En-lai were in failing health. Radical elements in the Communist Party wanted to continue the Cultural Revolution. They denounced material incentives, orderly economic planning, and reliance on foreign technology; and they brought disorder into production by opposing rules and regulations. Toward the end of 1975 and the beginning of 1976, the radicals increased their attacks on government bureaucrats and party leaders who were in favor of economic modernization. Serious riots occurred in some of the larger Chinese cities.

POST-MAO DEVELOPMENTS   The year 1976 was a momentous one for China. Premier Chou died in February and Chairman Mao died in September. With the death of the two major political leaders, a struggle for succession developed between those who wanted to maintain a rigid ideological status quo, with collective behavior and control and a closed door to the outside world, and those who wanted to modernize the economy and increase the rate of economic growth. The latter faction won out, and Deng Xiaoping was elected party leader.[8]

In December 1978, the Central Committee of the Communist Party convened in Beijing (Peking). The session declared that if China were to develop successfully, it must turn from class struggle to modernization and completely restructure its economy. The *Four Modernizations Program*,

---

8. The so-called "Gang of Four," including Mao's widow, wanted to continue the Cultural Revolution. In a showcase trial in 1978, they were found guilty and imprisoned.

originally started by Premier Chou in 1975, was incorporated into a Ten-Year Plan, which called for increases in grain output, steel production, and capital construction through the purchase of foreign plants and technology. The Program emphasized the development of four major economic sectors: agriculture, industry, science and technology, and national defense. The centerpiece of the program was to be the creation of the massive Baoshan steel complex that would turn out 6.7 million tons of steel a year with the most advanced technology imported from Japan, West Germany, and the United States. However, Baoshan was an expensive failure, caused in part by China's inability to assimilate foreign technology and in part by an unrealistic emphasis on the role of heavy industry in developing the Chinese economy.[9] A period of retrenchment and reappraisal of Chinese economic goals set in.

1980 TO THE PRESENT

The 1980s have marked a liberalization of the Chinese economy from state control and direction. The ambitious goals of the Four Modernizations Program have been scaled down, and the government has turned its attention to more immediate objectives such as improving productivity and increasing output. It has introduced more competition into the economy, not only by permitting private business to exist but also by turning over small, unprofitable state-owned enterprises to private collectives. A measure of private enterprise has also been introduced into agriculture. Ability to produce rather than ideological purity has become the measure of success. In October, 1984, a number of reforms were announced by the Central Committee of the Communist Party that are aimed at improving the structure of the Chinese economy. These reforms include:[10]

1. Creation of a national price system. The prices of many products reflect neither their value nor the relation of supply and demand. Prices will be restructured away from uniform prices set by the state and toward a floating price system for some products and free prices for others based on the relation of supply and demand.[11]

9. Robert F. Dernberger, "The Chinese Search for the Path of Self-Sustained Growth in the 1980's: An Assessment," Vol. 1, U.S. Cong., 2nd Sess., 1983, pp. 27-29. A basic feature of any Communist economic policy, be it in Poland or China, is the development of a steel industry.

10. These reforms were reported in various news releases by the Chinese news service XINHUA.

11. On May 9, 1985, the government announced that the price of meat, fish, and eggs would be raised by an average of more than 50 percent. The higher prices are aimed at eliminating government-subsidized food prices and subjecting these products to the forces of supply and demand.

2. Separation of government from enterprise functions. The purpose here is to give state enterprises more autonomy over their operations. More competition between state enterprises will be encouraged to stimulate improved use of technology and management.

3. Use of reward system based on work. In enterprises, differences in wages between various trades and jobs will be widened, so as to apply fully the principle of awarding the diligent and punishing the indolent.[12]

4. Promotion of diversified forms of economic organization. During the 1980s there has been an increase in the number of private industrial and commercial enterprises licensed to operate.[13] The reforms stress the continued need for diversity in forms of production, with some state enterprises leased to individuals or collectives.

5. Expansion of foreign and domestic economic and technical exchange. Using foreign funds and attracting foreign investors for joint ventures or exclusive investments in enterprises is necessary for the modernization of the economy.[14]

6. Training of management personnel for the economy. Measures are to be taken to train engineers who can promote technological progress and accountants who can uphold financial and economic discipline.[15]

■ THE ECONOMIC SYSTEM ■

The institutional arrangements in China are basically the same as those for all socialist countries. There is, of course, the Communist Party hierarchy and its all-pervasive influence in economic and political activity. The state

12. It is reported that one worker didn't show up for his job over a period of 20 years, but continued to draw his salary.

13. Schell, *To Get Rich*, p. 21.

14. On May 8, 1985, Ingersoll-Rand, an American manufacturer of machine tools, pneumatic drills, and other manufacturing equipment, and the Chinese government announced a joint venture to produce these products in China. Modern Western-style hotels have been built by foreign investors to attract tourists.

15. The Chinese government has entered into exchange agreements with a number of American universities to train engineers, managers, and accountants. Virginia Tech is one of those universities.

prescribes the ultimate objectives to be achieved by all Chinese. Society is controlled for the purpose of accomplishing specific economic and social goals. Although it is true that many changes are taking place in China, including a much greater reliance on private enterprise and the market mechanism, changes occur only with the approval of party leaders. Another swing of the pendulum, even back to a more rigidly controlled society emphasizing political ideology before everything else, however, is always a possibility. The following sections present the institutional arrangements of the Chinese economy as they existed in 1985.

ECONOMIC PLANNING

The Chinese have developed seven formal five-year plans, the latest of which is to run from 1986 to 1990. The goals of each plan have varied, and many of them were not completed. The current economic plan emphasizes an increase in output by both the agricultural and consumer goods sectors of the Chinese economy.

FORMULATION OF ECONOMIC PLANS   The State Planning Commission has overall responsibility for economic planning, including the drafting of the five-year plans and the annual operating plan. An Economic Commission reviews the fulfillment of the annual economic plans and institutes economic reforms. Both are responsible to the State Council, which is the executive branch of the government. It, in turn, is responsible to the National People's Congress, the highest elected organ of the Communist Party.

The five-year and annual operating plans can be broken down into sectoral plans that indicate what and how much individual enterprises should produce. In agriculture, specific goals are set for consumption within the agricultural sector and for distribution to other sectors. In transportation, the plan covers the construction of facilities, with particular emphasis placed on the development of the railroad system. Then there is a plan that covers capital formation for individual economic sectors and is concerned with resource allocation. There is a labor plan involving the allocation of labor inputs to the various sectors of the economy. Plans for foreign trade, social and cultural development, and regional development are also used. The foreign trade plan covers export and import commodity targets and the use of foreign exchange. Finally, a set of financial plans controls government income and expenditures. The objectives are to regulate resource allocation between consumption and investment and to regulate the flow of credit from the banking system.

IMPLEMENTATION OF THE PLANS   The State Council, through its various ministries, is responsible for implementation of the economic plans. There are 27 ministries, each dealing with different segments of the economy. These ministries also operate at the intermediate levels of Chinese government. The central government prepares its economic plans through the administrative units at the different levels. Directions pass downward through the various administrative levels to the factories and enterprises.

PUBLIC FINANCE

The function of taxes in China is to ensure control through the state budget over a part of the incomes of state enterprises as well as over the financial and economic activities of those engaged in private enterprise. The state budget itself is very important to the national economy because a very large part of all investment is undertaken with funds allocated through it. In addition, such normal government expenditures as national defense and social welfare expenditures are financed through it. Local governments have some autonomy in levying certain taxes, including a profits tax on enterprises directly under their jurisdiction. The economic reforms have changed the tax system of China to some extent.

GOVERNMENT REVENUES   Revenue is obtained from both tax and non-tax sources. In the tax revenue category, industrial and commercial taxes comprise the bulk of tax receipts. Taxes are collected at various levels of government by a system of collection agencies and are deposited in the People's Bank of China.

THE TURNOVER TAX   This tax, which is common to all socialist countries, is the difference between the producer price and the retail price, excluding the wholesale and retail margins for trading enterprises. These taxes are levied on most consumer goods and some consumer services. The government imposes a turnover tax to separate retail prices from producer prices, and so is in fact redistributing money incomes. Some consumer goods, such as foodstuffs sold by peasants to consumers directly, are free from turnover taxes. Whatever the basis of fixing this tax, the rates are highly differentiated. The size of the turnover tax does not determine the level of prices—on the contrary, the magnitude of these taxes depends on the predetermined price level.

AGRICULTURAL TAXES   Agricultural taxes are usually levied in kind rather than in monetary amounts. One reason for this type of levy is that a problem that has faced the Chinese government is not a lack of adequate revenue, but rather the lack of marketable agricultural products. The tax is levied on the most important crop in each region—usually a grain crop, such as wheat or rice. There is also a pastoral tax levied on live-stock. The agricultural taxes have declined in importance as the economic reforms have emphasized allowing farmers to keep more of their output as an incentive to increase production.

OTHER TAXES   The economic reforms have had an impact on the Chinese tax system in several ways. First, a corporate income tax went into effect in June, 1983. There are now many private enterprises from which the state hopes to derive revenue. Business firms that make more than $100,000 in annual profits must now pay a 55 percent tax to the Ministry of Finance. Smaller businesses are also taxed based on an eight-bracket scale. Secondly, most state-owned enterprises no longer have to hand their profits directly over to the state. Previously, a certain percentage of profits had to be remitted to the national government by each enterprise. These state enterprises will also be taxed at the maximum rate of 55 percent on profits over $100,000. Individuals pay a personal income tax, but are allowed an exemption of $400 a month.

GOVERNMENT EXPENDITURES   Expenditures in the Chinese state budget are categorized according to their role in the creation of national income. In the past, more than one-half of total expenditures was devoted to finan-cing material production, including allocations to state enterprises for cap-ital investment and financial capital. However, under the economic re-forms, enterprises now may retain their earnings for direct reinvestment in capital and use as financial capital. Appropriations from the state budget are also used to finance the construction of transportation facilities, invest-ments in state farms, and housing construction. Social security benefits consisting of old-age and disability pensions, sickness and maternity benefits, and work injury compensation are also financed out of the state budget.

BANKING

The banking system in the People's Republic of China represents a finan-cial control mechanism for carrying out economic planning. All state en-terprises and cooperatives have accounts with the central bank, and con-trol can be exercised because most transactions are in terms of money through bank transfers. Purchases and sales of goods by each enterprise can be matched against authorized payments and recepits. Government control over income and expenditures is also expedited through the credit and cash plans of the banking system.

THE PEOPLE'S BANK OF CHINA The People's Bank of China was formed in 1959 as the central bank of the country. It is under the jurisdiction of the Staff Office for Finance and Trade and is responsible for the supervision of financial transactions that correspond to the physical production plans. All state enterprises have accounts in branch banks under its direct jurisdiction. In this way, the People's Bank can exercise control because all expenditures and transfers made by the enterprises come under its scrutiny.

The People's Bank, as the central bank of China, has the following responsibilities.

1. Issuing Chinese currency.

2. Financing credit to state enterprises. Funds to support credit expansion are obtained from the national budget, from retained profits, and from customer deposits.

3. Supervising expenditures of state enterprises to see that they conform with national planning objectives.

4. Developing the Credit Plan and the Cash Plan, which are financial counterparts of the physical economic plans.

5. Monitoring the performance of state enterprises.

The Credit Plan involves the amount of short- and medium-term credit that is to be provided to state enterprises and agricultural communes by the People's Bank. Funds can be allocated only for purposes that conform to the national plan. The Cash Plan consists of a set of cash inflows and cash outflows essentially in the form of a balance sheet. Cash inflows include retail sales receipts, savings deposit receipts, repayment of agricultural loans, deposits of communes, and public utility receipts. Cash outflows consist of wage payments by state enterprises and communes, government purchases of industrial and agricultural products, government administrative expenses, transfer payments by the state to individuals, management expenditures of state enterprises, new loans to agriculture, and withdrawals of savings deposits.

The Credit and Cash Plans are coordinated with the physical production plans to provide financing for expenditures required by the production plans. This means that the People's Bank can supervise the operations of state enterprises to enforce conformance with production plans because purchase and sales of goods can be matched against authorized payments and receipts.

OTHER FINANCIAL INSTITUTIONS   There are several specialized financial agencies that also provide money to finance the transactions of enterprises in certain areas of production. These specialized financial institutions, like the People's Bank, do not allocate funds independently of national planning objectives and thus have no influence on resource allocation, as they would in a market economy.

The Agricultural Bank provides agricultural loans. It also controls the allocation of rural savings to rural credit cooperatives that provide credit to communes and to individual members of communes. Loans are also made to individuals for sideline undertakings involving private plots of land. The Agricultural Bank is under the jurisdiction of the State Council and is operated independently of the People's Bank. It has provincial branches and also branches that operate at the municipal level.

There are several specialized banks under the jurisdiction of the Ministry of Finance. One bank, the People's Construction Bank, is responsible for providing investment funds to enterprise. These funds are obtained from the national budget and do not have to be repaid. It is also responsible for providing short-term loans to enterprises for capital construction projects.

Interest has no significant role in resource allocation in the Chinese economic system. Interest rates are charged on all loans by the banks to industrial enterprises, communes, and individuals, but the rates are far below those that would prevail under a free-market system. Also, the interest charges are mostly offset by a reduction in the enterprise's profit tax liability. Grants provided by the People's Bank to enterprises for capital investment are interest-free.

ORGANIZATION OF INDUSTRY

Although agriculture, providing the raw materials for industry and food for a growing population, remains the foundation of the Chinese economy, any meaningful move to a greater power status must be based on the development of industry. The process of industrialization has been difficult, and the Chinese people have paid a price in terms of resources sacrificed to achieve this end. At present, the Chinese have a long way to go before they can match the industrial potential of the Soviet Union or any of the Western industrial nations. Even within their own sphere of influence, the Chinese do not come close to rivaling the industrial base of Japan; they are behind South Korea on overall economic development. Moreover, undue emphasis has been placed on the development of heavy industry, in particular steel manufacturing.

ECONOMIC REFORMS IN INDUSTRY

Sweeping economic reforms have been introduced by the Chinese to improve economy efficiency and increase output in industry. Prior to 1979, factory managers were essentially cogs in a machine controlled from above. A factory would be allotted a certain amount of raw material and told to produce a certain number of units by the appropriate ministry in Beijing. Any profit had to be remitted to the central government. It was then up to the ministry to determine how much profit would be returned to the factory. In 1978 the Central Committee of the Communist Party called for the abandonment of the old Stalinist model of production, which rigidly maintained all planning and decision-making authority in the hands of the central ministries. Since that time, much of this authority has been dispersed downward, so that state-owned enterprises have become more independent economic units and their managers have become responsible in large measure for planning, use of capital, and distribution of profits.

THE ECONOMIC RESPONSIBILITY SYSTEM   A very important component of the industrial economic reforms is the economic responsibility system. There are two parts to this system.[16] First, responsibility is given to the state enterprise by the government in the form of a lease that provides it with a certain degree of autonomy.[17] The enterprise is responsible for finding its own raw materials, setting its own production targets, and hiring and firing its own labor force. It no longer has to remit its profits to a ministry; it retains them, after paying a tax, and makes its own decisions about how the profits should be reinvested or spent. The second major component of the economic responsibility system is a policy of paying workers according to the results of their labor. Workers for years had received a flat salary no matter whether they worked or not; now workers find their pay geared to the amount and the quality of their work.

PRIVATE ENTERPRISE   Probably the most dramatic aspect of the economic reforms is the rebirth of private enterprise in China. A private sector has been introduced where market forces are at work. Most private enterprise is small scale, ranging from family-owned restaurants to chicken farms.[18] There are privately run repair shops for television sets and radios, bicycles,

---

16. Chow, *Chinese Economy*, pp. 150-151.

17. Some 6,000 state enterprises have been given autonomy in their operations. This is still a small percentage of the total number of enterprises.

18. Private enterprise in China does not exist to the extent that it does in Hungary and Yugoslavia.

and motorcycles. Private barbers and shoemakers are commonplace, and street vendors sell a wide variety of products. Private enterprises have to be licensed by the state to operate, but their number increased from 2.6 million in 1982 to 5.9 million in 1984. Although few in number, they accounted for 10.2 percent of all national retail sales in 1984.[19]

PRIVATE COLLECTIVES   The reforms permit the formation of collectively owned enterprises. A group of citizens can take the initiative to establish a collectively owned enterprise subject to regulation by the government. Collective enterprises can be set up by workers from their own funds. The means of production are neither private property nor state property, but the property of the collective. Many state enterprises that were losing money have been turned into private collectives in the hope that autonomous management and capitalist incentives might revive them. The collective has the exclusive right to own, control, and handle its means of production and products. It keeps its own accounts and is responsible for its own profits or losses.[20] State administrative agencies may apply economic levers to influence and guide the operational activities of collective enterprises, but they cannot interfere with their internal affairs.

FOREIGN INVESTMENTS   For many years China was isolated from outside influences. During the time of Mao, ideology was supposed to solve economic problems; Western, particularly United States, influence was regarded as degenerate. The current Chinese leaders have adopted a much more pragmatic approach to the solution of the country's economic problems. During the 1970s, little was invested in modernization, so most of China's factories have machinery 10 to 40 years old. Much of its industry was built with Soviet aid during the 1950s; the technology was already obsolete by the time the Chinese received it. The Chinese entered the 1980s with an industrial base that was 50 years behind the rest of the industrial world. To accomplish industrial modernization, they are willing to accept infusions of foreign capital and foreign technology. These infusions may take several forms.

1. Joint ventures. A joint venture is simply an arrangement where a foreign company and a host country agree to provide a product or a service jointly.[21] In China, joint ventures between the

---

19. Schell, *To Get Rich*, p. 30.

20. Lin Wei and Arnold Chao (Eds.), *China's Economic Reforms* (Philadelphia: University of Pennsylvania Press, 1982) pp. 160-169.

21. Joint venture can also involve two companies. An example is the General Motors–Toyota joint venture in California to produce subcompact cars.

Chinese and Western corporations have been permitted since 1980. In 1985, Occidental Petroleum signed an agreement with China to develop and jointly operate what could become the world's largest open-pit coal mine. China is responsible for providing the site and construction of railways, highways, and power facilities. Occidental is to provide the equipment and personnel. Profits from the sale of coal are to be divided evenly for five years, after which China is to get 60 percent.

2. Foreign loans. The Chinese, unlike Mexico and Nigeria, have been rather circumspect when it comes to borrowing from abroad. However, economic modernization is one of the basic goals of the economic reforms. China has signed loan agreements with several capitalist countries, notably Japan. It provided loans to finance projects for the construction of railroads, ports, and a hydroelectric station. Belgium has granted an interest-free 30-year loan to purchase power-generating equipment.

3. Licensing agreements. A number of American firms are licensed to produce and sell products in China. A prime example is Coca-Cola, which has the exclusive right to produce and sell Coca-Cola in China. Coca-Cola provides the syrup and the authorized use of the trademark, and the drink is bottled in China and sold to foreign tourists.

4. Direct investment in China. Foreign investment in China can be channeled to certain priority areas such as hotel construction and operation, which are designed to attract foreign tourists who bring hard currency to spend. A number of hotels have been built with foreign capital, including the Great Wall Hotel, a part of the Hyatt Regency chain.

REDUCTION IN THE NUMBER OF ADMINISTRATIVE UNITS Economic planning has been cumbersome, with layer upon layer of administrative units responsible for its implementation. Industrial enterprises have always been the last link, with ultimate authority concentrated in a hierarchy of bureaus and ministries. Bureaus in charge of production had no authority over personnel, finance, and material supplies of state-owned enterprises, while bureaus in charge of the latter functions had no control over production. Thus, enterprises have had to deal with many bureaus, particularly at the provincial and local levels of government.

Many countries and cities have now abandoned their bureaus and have replaced them with economic commissions that have been given authority over all functions of state enterprises.[22] The planning directors go from the national ministry to their regional and local counterparts to the commissions to the enterprises. Managers of the enterprises have been given more discretion over production, sales, bonuses, hiring and firing workers, and distribution of profits.

ORGANIZATION OF AGRICULTURE

Agriculture is the foundation of the Chinese economy. At least 80 percent of the people work in agriculture, which furnishes the raw materials necessary for the performance of the planned economy. Unfortunately for the Chinese, most of the land area is not suitable for agricultural production. Much of China is mountainous and dry, and unfavorable soil and climate inhibit agricultural development in other areas. In addition, the ratio of population to cultivable land is very large. The country has had to operate at a margin that is very close to a minimum subsistence level. It also means that the Communists have to face the problem of a growing population and a technically backward agricultural base while at the same time trying to build up an adequate industrial base in order to become a major world power.

THE COLLECTIVIZATION OF AGRICULTURE   Agriculture has gone through several distinct phases of collectivization since the Communists came to power in 1949. At that time the farms were privately owned either by landlords or by peasants. To win the support of the masses of the peasants, landless or otherwise, the Communists redistributed millions of acres of land and eliminated landlords as a class. Once the land was redistributed, peasants were allowed to operate the land as private owners.[23]

PRODUCERS' COOPERATIVES   Agricultural producers' cooperatives were established in 1955. Peasants were organized into these cooperatives and had to pool their lands for cultivation. The land, however, was still held privately, and the cooperatives paid rent for its use. The cooperatives were run by central committees and were divided into production teams. The agricultural output was distributed by the cooperatives and the peasants were compensated on the basis of labor contributed.

---

22. Chow, *Chinese Econonmy*, pp. 150-151.

23. Marion B. Larsen, "China's Agriculture under Communism," in *An Economic Profile of Mainland China*, Vol. 1, U.S. Congress, Joint Economic Committee, 90th Cong., First sess., 1967, pp. 212-218.

COLLECTIVE FARMS   The next stage in the socialization of agriculture occurred in 1956.[24] The agricultural producers' cooperatives, which had retained many of the elements of private property ownership, were consolidated into collective farms. On these collective farms the peasants were supposed to pool their land, animals, and livestock. Land now was no longer privately owned; it was collective property. However, the peasants were permitted to own small plots of land to be used for their own purposes. Similarly, domestic livestock and small farm implements were left in private hands. The peasants were formed into brigades, with brigade leaders given the responsibility for assigning workers their tasks.

COMMUNES   In 1958 communes replaced the collective farms. A commune was a multipurpose unit that would perform administrative as well as economic functions. The transition to the commune system was rapid. The decision to form communes was announced in August, 1958. By the end of the year, some 750,000 collective farms representing virtually all of the peasant households had been formed into 26,578 communes.[25] All vestiges of private property ownership were removed. The peasants ate in mess halls, and the distribution of food was based in part on the needs of individuals and in part on work performed. Workers had to perform tasks that were by no means limited to agriculture, such as producing steel and mining coal.

By the end of the Great Leap Forward there was a shift in agricultural policies with respect to the communes. The complete collectivization of nearly all production and consumption had not achieved the desired results. Private plots of land were restored to the peasants, and the free market was permitted in which the peasants could sell their produce for income. Pigs were in short supply as a result of mismanagement during the Great Leap Forward, and peasants were given incentives to raise pigs for sale to the government. However, communes remained the highest level of collective organization in China until the end of the 1970s.

AGRICULTURAL REFORM   Probably the most important aspect of the current economic reforms has been the decollectivization of farmland. The communes have ceased to exist. Although still owned by the state, land has been divided into small plots and contracted out by the production teams to be farmed privately under a program referred to as *baochan dasho*, or "fixing farm-output quotas for individual households." The production

24. Ibid., pp. 218-220.
25. Ibid., pp. 213.

team also assigns to each farm family the necessary inputs—including land, cattle, farm equipment, and machinery. A farmer's only binding obligation, besides paying rent and a small agricultural tax, is to deliver a fixed amount of produce to the team as a contribution to the production quota. This is sold to the state at a fixed price. Any amount produced in excess of the fixed amount belongs to the farm family to consume, to sell to the state at a higher price, or to sell in the free market. Both compulsory delivery and land rental are fixed costs that do not affect the willingness of the individual farmer to increase output. The relevant marginal cost calculation of the farm household applies to the extra output after the delivery has been made. As a result of individual incentive, agricultural output has grown significantly.

PRIVATE PLOTS   Private plots have come to play a more important role in Chinese agricultural production. Before the reforms, small private plots consisting of around 5 percent of the cultivated land were allowed in certain areas.[26] They served an important role in the economy by providing most of the poultry, pigs, and vegetables consumed in China. The private plots have been expanded under the reforms and account for larger fractions of the total cultivable land—as much as 10 to 15 percent—in some areas.[27] Private plots are often the most productive tracts of land in China, in part because the farmers are strongly motivated to maximize output in order to increase family income. From the point of view of the state, while these activities do not have a central place in large-scale agricultural production, they are a practical way of obtaining the intensive use of peasant labor for the production of some highly valued items.

INCOME DISTRIBUTION

The Chinese have oscillated between extreme egalitarianism and material incentives to motivate people. The former relied on exhortations and some form of external approval (prestige, power, public honors, and acclaim) to provide motivation to work harder, and the latter relied on differences in income and occupational status to motivate workers. For example, during the Cultural Revolution egalitarianism was the goal. There was an attempt to eliminate class differences based on wage differentials and occu-

---

26. A. Roak Barnett, *China's Economy in a Global Perspective* (Washington: Brookings Institution, 1981), p. 341.

27. Chow, *Chinese Economy*, p. 54.

pational status.[28] Educators and bureaucrats were required to work side by side with peasants in the rice fields, and shoveling manure was considered as a good way as any to eliminate one's elitist impulses. Income differentials for all types of labor were reduced and reliance was placed on such slogans as "Serve the People" to provide incentives. Time and experience proved this approach to be ineffective. Workers had no reason to be efficient, for they received the same wages whether they were productive or not.

ECONOMIC REFORM   During the Cultural Revolution, someone who was interested in monetary gain or who exhibited privatistic tendencies was labelled a "capitalist roader," or worse, a "counterrevolutionary," and was chastised publicly or sent off to work on the manure piles to learn to be a true "socialist man." This has changed considerably, and the title of a new book on China, *To Get Rich Is Glorious*, encapsulates the current economic mood of the country. There is a privatization in certain sectors of the Chinese economy and entrepreneurs are free to earn what they can. The class struggle is over, at least for the present, and it is now acceptable to be prosperous. Many Chinese have done that, and it is reported that some have succeeded in earning $10,000 a year or more, which is very high for a country with a per capita income of $300 a year. The idea of working for one's own benefit rather than for the abstraction of socialism is supposed to increase production and promote efficiency. To quote Premier Deng Xiaoping, "It makes no difference what color a cat is as long as it catches mice."

WAGE DIFFERENTIATION   However, most Chinese continue to work for state enterprises. The Chinese have maintained the eight-wage classification system for both production and white-collar workers that they borrowed from the Soviet Union. Classes 1 and 2 are for unskilled and part-time workers; classes 3 and 4 are for semiskilled workers; class 5 is for skilled workers who have passed a special examination, but who have no work experience; classes 6 and 7 are for skilled workers with work experience; and class 8 is for workers with extensive knowledge. Thus Chinese industrial workers are paid according to variations in skill from unskilled to highly skilled workers. There are also wage scales within classes. Wage scales by classes are also differentiated by industrial branch in line with the Chinese regime's priorities for different industrial occupations. Manager-

---

28. William L. Parrish, "Egalitarianism in Chinese Society," *Problems Of Communism*, Vol. 30 (January–February 1981), pp. 41-45.

ial, professional, technical, and political workers receive income payments that are higher than those of industrial workers. They also have access to special privileges, including the ability to travel abroad.[29]

PRICING POLICIES

A major goal in China has been to keep prices stable because that is essential for state economic planning. In particular, the prices of basic necessities have been kept low. On the other hand, wages have also been subject to little change over time. For example, the average annual wage of all state-employed workers was $223 in 1952 and $406 in 1981. The general retail price index was 111.8 in 1952 and 150.4 percent in 1981.[30] The overall cost of living index increased from 115.5 percent in 1952 to 162.5 percent in 1981. Prices of basic necessities, such as food and shelter, are subsidized by the state. This has created problems. In many cases, the sale price of goods to consumers is less than the purchase price the state pays to farmers. This means losses that must be covered out of the state budget, losses that were estimated to be $16 billion in 1981.[31] Arbitrary price setting by the state also makes it difficult to appraise the performance of state enterprises in terms of production and costs.[32]

ECONOMIC REFORMS AND PRICING POLICIES   The economic reforms now include four types of prices.[33]

1. State prices. These are uniform subsidized prices for goods and services that are considered basic necessities. However, the price of foodstuffs was increased by 15 percent in 1985 to reduce the subsidies paid out of the state budget.

2. Floating prices. These are applied to producer prices and retail and wholesale prices for consumer and industrial products. Prices may fluctuate around a standard price within lower and upper limits.

29. Traveling abroad is one of the most important privileges afforded to party officials and other members of elite groups in most communist countries. The traveler has the opportunity to bring hard currency and goods back to the home country.

30. Chow, *Chinese Economy*, p. 143. The base of the index is 1950 = 100 percent.

31. Wei and Chao, *Economic Reforms*, p. 229.

32. A good return for an enterprise could be the result of high prices set by the state rather than the performance of the enterprise. The variance of price from value makes it difficult to compare investment returns. Good returns may be close to the favorable prices on the products.

33. Wei and Chao, *Economic Reforms*, pp. 230-231.

3. Negotiated prices. These are prices negotiated between the buyer and seller on certain farm products and industrial goods, for which the state sets no standard price. Farm products left over after state purchases may be bought by state agencies at negotiated prices.

4. Free market prices. These prices are regarded as a supplement to the other prices and cover farm products not subject to state purchases and a wide variety of consumer goods and services that are not considered basic necessities.

■ AN APPRAISAL ■
OF THE CHINESE ECONOMY

Change and the impermanence of any particular form of economic and social organization have been the dominant features and realities of Chinese life since 1949. There has been a struggle between two factions—between "experts" and "reds"—that has involved debate over whether to stress economics or politics, professional competence or egalitarian goals, material or ideological incentives, orderly incremental changes or sudden dramatic leaps. The "reds" measure costs and gains in ideological terms. Their goal is the transformation of the Chinese soul, and they lean toward the drama of struggle as the preferred engine of rapid social change.[34] Conversely, the "experts" favor expertise over ideology. They prefer that an educated elite maintain control of the process of change, in which compromise rather than struggle results in evolutionary, not revolutionary, change. At the risk of delaying rewards for the masses, they prefer to concentrate limited resources on planned economic and political development.

The contrast between the two factions can be made by comparing the goals of the Cultural Revolution of 1966–1969 and the Four Modernizations Program of 1978. In the Cultural Revolution, political objectives were given greater prominence than economic objectives. One goal was to destroy the elitism of the bureaucracy and the technicians by, among other things, making them work on the farms. Higher education was denigrated because it supposedly created technicians who were above the masses. Enrollment in colleges was sharply curtailed and some colleges were closed. Material incentives were rejected in favor of nonmaterial incentives. Man-

---

34. William W. Whitson, "The Political Dynamics of the People's Republic of China," in *Chinese Economy Post-Mao*, Vol. 1, U.S. Congress, Joint Economic Committee, 95th Cong., 2nd sess., 1978, pp. 68-70.

agers in factories were replaced by revolutionary cadres whose idea of running factories was to read quotations from Mao Tse-tung. The Cultural Revolution aimed at mass participation in the political and economic process. Americans were called "foreign imperialist devils."

The Four Modernizations Program had diametrically opposite goals.[35] Introduced by Premier Deng Xiaoping, the program involved a commitment toward modern economic growth. Schools and universities closed during the Cultural Revolution were reopened to produce a large supply of technocrats, scientists, and managers. Academic excellence, which was considered elitist in the Cultural Revolution, was reinstated, along with entrance exams as performance criteria. There was an attempt to link effort and reward through material incentives. China also began to purchase more plants and equipment from Western countries, with particular leanings toward Japan and the United States for technology, credit, and trade. By obtaining foreign capital and technology from the West, the Chinese hoped to revitalize their economy. Economic reforms have continued to be implemented, with changes made in agriculture, industry, and the price system.

ECONOMIC GROWTH

The average annual rate of growth of China's gross national product has been around 6 percent throughout the nation's 35-year history of Communist rule. However, this growth rate has been erratic and has fluctuated with shifts in economic and political policies. The average annual rate of growth was 8.8 percent during the 1950s, but was negative for the period 1960–61, reflecting the excesses of the Great Leap Forward. Then there was a rapid rate of growth for the period 1962–1966, averaging around 12 percent a year. This performance was offset by a negative rate of growth during the period of the Cultural Revolution. During the period 1970–1975 the rate of economic growth averaged around 8.0 percent. As is indicated in Table 17-1, the rate of economic growth has fluctuated widely during the period 1974–1984.

AGRICULTURAL PERFORMANCE

Agriculture is the mainstay of the Chinese economy and serves many purposes. It is needed to feed the people and to provide raw materials for in-

35. Ramon H. Myers, *The Chinese Economy Past and Present* (Belmont, Calif.: Wadsworth Publishing Co., 1981), p. 245.

TABLE 17-1   CHANGES IN GROSS NATIONAL PRODUCT IN CHINA

1974	3.6%	1978	11.6%	1982	5.5%
1975	7.0	1979	5.4	1983	7.1
1976	0.0	1980	2.8	1984[1]	5.8
1977	8.1	1981	2.1		

[1]Estimate.

Source: Central Intelligence Agency, *Handbook of Economic Statistics, 1984,* p. 42.

dustry. In addition, the Chinese agricultural goods used as export commodities are extremely valuable as a source of hard currency. Without these earnings, the Chinese would not be able to buy much of the Western equipment and technology needed for economic modernization.

Improvement of agriculture is the linchpin of the current economic reforms. Most important is the adoption of a flexible system that allows different ways of organizing and remunerating farmers, based on the principle that whoever brings in a greater output should truly earn more. This system, which is called the economic responsibility system, has been introduced to about 90 percent of rural households. It has contributed to a marked increase in agricultural production, with output increasing at an average annual rate of 7.5 percent during the period 1979–1983.[36] However, the absence of a developed transportation system and antiquated farming methods impinge upon any dramatic increase in agricultural production.

INDUSTRIAL PRODUCTION

To improve industrial production, the Chinese have made a number of changes. There has been a shift to enterprise management by professional managers. To promote efficiency, more emphasis has been placed on profits and quality of production, and prices are beginning to be based on realistic calculations of costs. Years of political upheaval have resulted in erratic industrial development in China, and it is too early to ascertain the impact the economic reforms will have on industrial production. Table 17-2, which presents percentage changes in industrial production, does indicate an improving performance for the period 1981–1984. However, the

36. Schell, *To Get Rich*, pp. 58-59.

TABLE 17-2   CHANGES IN INDUSTRIAL PRODUCTION,
             1974–1984

1974	1.8%	1978	13.7%	1982	9.1%
1975	15.1	1979	7.8	1983	10.6
1976	−0.3	1980	3.2	1984[1]	8.5
1977	14.1	1981	7.5		

[1]Estimate.

Source: Central Intelligence Agency, *Handbook of Economic Statistics, 1984*, p. 60.

percentage change is extremely erratic for the time period. Moreover, there has been a dichotomy of priorities concerning heavy and light industries, with the former getting most of the resources allocated by the state. Production was not geared for the consumption needs of society. Capital construction projects were undertaken blindly all over the country with no norms for material consumption and no profit requirement.

SUMMARY

The Chinese economy is in a state of flux. A number of economic reforms have been introduced to improve output and productivity. While China's economy remains basically a planned socialist economy, the market mechanism has been introduced to improve resource allocation and provide incentives. Agricultural reform has been significant. Urban private markets for the sale of agricultural products have been developed and sideline income-earning opportunities encouraged. In addition, there has been a move to increase the amount of land allocated to private plots.

The urban and industrial economy has also been the subject of economic reforms. State enterprises have been provided with more incentives to produce efficiently. They can retain a greater share of profits for their own use, and they can engage in production for the market, once the target for state plan output. Enterprise managers have been given more latitude in making management decisions, particularly under the economic responsibility system. A manager can pay wages based on productivity and discharge workers who do not perform. Emphasis has also been placed on the import of technology from Western capitalist countries.

■——————————————— R E V I E W   Q U E S T I O N S ———————————————■

1. Discuss agricultural policy during the Great Leap Forward.
2. Chinese economic policy between 1949 and the present has oscillated between economic rationality and idealistic extremism. Discuss.
3. What was the goal of the Cultural Revolution?
4. Evaluate the performance of the Chinese economy in terms of living standards and economic growth.
5. What was the purpose of the Four Modernizations Program?
6. Discuss the current industrial economic reforms that have been introduced in China.
7. What is the "economic responsibility system"?
8. Discuss the current economic reforms as they have been applied to agriculture.
9. Discuss the various types of prices that are currently used in China.

■——————————— R E C O M M E N D E D   R E A D I N G S ———————————■

Cheung, Steven S. *Will China Go Capitalist?* London: The Institute of Economic Affairs, 1985.

Chow, Gregory. *The Chinese Economy*. New York: Harper & Row, Publishers, 1985.

Johnson, D. Gale. *Progress of Economic Reforms in the Peoples' Republic of China*. Washington: American Enterprise Institute, 1982.

Rosen, Stanley. "Prosperity, Privatization, and China's Youth." *Problems of Communism* (March-April 1985), pp. 17–24.

Schell, Orville. *To Get Rich Is Glorious: China in the Eighties*. New York: Pantheon Books, 1985.

Wei, Lin, and Arnold Chao (eds.). *China's Economic Reforms*. Philadelphia: University of Pennsylvania Press, 1983.

U.S. Congress, Joint Economic Committee. *Allocation of Resources in the Soviet Union and China*. Washington: USGPO, 1984.

U.S. Congress, Joint Economic Committee. *China Under the Four Modernizations*. Parts 1 & 2. Washington: USGPO, 1982.

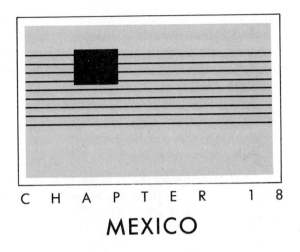

C H A P T E R   1   8

MEXICO

Mexico is a land of contrasts. There is extreme wealth and extreme poverty; there are vast natural resources and little arable land. It has many of the advantages necessary to become one of the world's most prosperous nations, yet 40 percent of the labor force is either unemployed or underemployed, and the population continues to grow at a rate of 2.5 percent a year. It is one of the *nearly industrialized countries* that are still struggling with the problem of economic development, but that have emerged as important economic powers. Moreover, it has a strategic location next to the world's largest consumer market, the United States. However, prices increased by more than 300 percent during the period 1982–1985, and the peso lost more than 80 percent of its value against the dollar. Mexico's foreign debt is, along with Brazil's, the highest of any developing country in the world, which places a burden on the development of the Mexican economy.

Mexico has a characteristic common to many less developed and developing countries: reliance on one major export product. In Mexico's case it is oil. In 1985 oil exports accounted for 75 percent of the total exports of the Mexican economy. Since its discovery in 1863, oil has been both a blessing and a curse to the Mexican economy. It could be the foundation for the development of the Mexican economy, but, unfortunately for Mexico, wide swings in the world price of oil have also created problems. Oil has come to play an important role in Mexican politics, particularly in its relations with the United States. The oil industry, which is a state-owned monopoly, is the largest expense item in the Mexican budget, but its revenues, particularly from exports, are the single most important contributor to total government revenues.

■ HISTORY OF MEXICO ■

Spain has had a greater influence on the political and social development of both North and South America than any other country. All of South America, with the exception of Brazil, was discovered and colonized by Spain. Christopher Columbus, sailing under the aegis of the Spanish crown, discovered America; and Spanish explorers, among them Ponce de Leon, had explored the southern and southwestern United States 100 years before the Pilgrims landed at Plymouth Rock. Hernan Cortez conquered Mexico in 1519; by 1600 the Spaniards had colonized that part of North America, or New Spain, that extends from southern Mexico to Texas and to California as far north as San Francisco. Mexico achieved its independence from Spain in 1821.

Spanish culture has had a far more lasting impact on the Latin American countries than British culture had on the United States. There is the common denominator of the Spanish language, and there is a common heritage in the Roman Catholic religion. Much of the political structure of Latin America is still retained from the days of Spanish colonization. Architecture, arts, and literature all have a Spanish influence.

The Mexican dictator Porfirio Diaz once remarked: "Poor Mexico, so far from God and so close to the United States." He was right in many respects. The common border of the two countries has shaped much of Mexican history for the past two centuries. In the midnineteenth century, the population of the United States expanded westward, helped in no small part by an annexation of Mexican territory after the Mexican War of 1847–1848.[1] In the later part of the last century, much of Mexico was exploited by the United States and other foreign business interests. Large amounts of resources were taken out of the country without any benefit to the Mexican people. On many occasions, the United States has either overtly or covertly interfered in the internal affairs of Mexico in support of

---

1. Under the terms of the Treaty of Guadalupe Hidalgo, Mexico had to cede to the United States half of its territory. Included were the states of Texas, New Mexico, Arizona, and California. In 1853 Mexico was forced to sell more of its territory to the United States. This was the Gadsden Purchase.

its own political interests. The terms "Yankee imperialism" and "gunboat diplomacy" had their genesis in U.S. involvement in Mexican political and economic affairs. To this day, there continue to be disputes between the two countries over political, economic, and social issues.

THE MEXICAN REVOLUTION OF 1910

The Mexican Revolution of 1910 profoundly shaped the current economic, political, and social structure of Mexico. The original objective of the revolution was to depose the dictator, Porfirio Diaz, who had ruled Mexico for 35 years. Three groups were the main beneficiaries of his rule—the Roman Catholic Church, which owned most of the wealth in the country; the landed aristocracy, which ran the government; and foreign business interests, in particular American and British, to whom Diaz gave lucrative concessions on mineral properties. Once Diaz was deposed, the revolution continued as rival factions competed for power. The United States was very much involved in protecting its commercial and political interests in Mexico, supporting one faction over others, and usually the wrong one. By 1917 political conditions in Mexico had stabilized to the point that a president was installed and a formal constitution promulgated. The constitution has had an important impact on the political, economic, and social development of Mexico in the following ways.

SEPARATION OF CHURCH AND STATE   The constitution provides that the Catholic Church cannot acquire, hold, or administer real property. Land held by the church was taken by the state and redistributed to the peasants. The constitution provides for the complete separation of church and state; priests are not allowed to hold political office. Article 33 of the constitution gives the president the right to expel without judicial process any foreigner whose presence is considered detrimental to the interests of Mexico. This article gave the Mexican government an excuse to banish many priests who had been appointed by the Vatican. Anticlerical sentiment prevailed in Mexico for many years after the revolution, and to this day, the church has had little influence on Mexican political affairs.

STATE OWNERSHIP OF NATURAL RESOURCES   A law giving foreign investors ownership rights to any mineral resources found in the subsoil of properties had been passed during the Diaz dictatorship. As a result of this law, most of the mineral wealth went out of the country, with Mexico benefitting very little. The 1917 constitution states that ownership of land and any mineral resources found in it belong to the state. This provision proved to be a bone of contention between the American and Mexican

governments for a number of years, particularly concerning U.S. oil holdings in Mexico. In 1937 American and British oil interests were nationalized by the Mexican government. To administer the oil properties, the
government created a state-owned monopoly, Petroleos Mexicanos, or
PEMEX. Today, PEMEX is the largest state-owned corporation in Mexico.

LAND REDISTRIBUTION   Probably the most sweeping result of the constitution of 1917 was the redistribution of farm land that was once held by
the church or wealthy landowners. This land was given to the peasants in
the form of the *Ejido*, which was an import from Spain during the period
of colonization. In the ejido system, title to the land is vested in the village
as a whole. The ejidatario, or farm laborer, has the right to farm a maximum of 10 hectares of irrigated land or 20 hectares of dry land. After
assignment, an ejido must be worked within at least two consecutive years
or the land is taken back and assigned to someone else. The ejido system is
an important part of Mexican agriculture, involving 40 percent of all cultivable land. Financial support to the ejidos is provided by the Mexican
government in the form of a National Ejido Bank of Credit, which provides low-interest loans to farmers. The ejido system has had mixed success
in producing the agricultural output necessary to feed the rapidly growing
population.

THE POLITICAL SYSTEM   The current political system of Mexico is also a
result of the Mexican Revolution of 1910. Mexico has a rather unique arrangement; it has been governed by one political party, the Institutional
Revolutionary Party (PRI), for more than 50 years. The PRI cannot be
compared to the monolithic communist parties of Cuba and Eastern Europe or to the military juntas that have dominated politics in most Latin
American countries. Instead, it is an amalgam of many diverse elements in
the Mexican political system. It began as a coalition of military leaders,
small landowners, workers, and peasants committed to the reforms of the
Mexican constitution of 1917, and was originally called the Party of the
Mexican Revolution. The PRI was formally organized as a political party
in 1929. Since that time, its candidates have won every presidential election, usually getting more than 75 percent of the popular vote. The PRI
represents all elements of Mexican society on a spectrum of left to right—
labor unions, government workers, farmers, and business leaders.
      There are advantages and disadvantages in a one-party political sys-
tem. The main advantage of the PRI is that it has been able to achieve
political stability. Some two million Mexicans were killed during the Revolution; Presidents Carranza and Obregon were assassinated while in of-

fice. The PRI represents a coalition of compromise between disparate political and social factions. However, the cost to Mexico is high because genuine pluralism does not exist.[2] Concentration of power in a single political party has created a vast system of patronage in which political debts are routinely paid off in cash or favors. The PRI has come to represent the party of the bosses, the bureaucracy, the spoils sharers, and the status quo. It runs not only the federal government, but state governments as well. The mayor of Mexico City, the capital of Mexico and the second largest city in the world, is appointed by the PRI, as are the members of the city council.

■ THE ECONOMIC SYSTEM ■

The Mexican economic system is a mixed system consisting of both public sector and free market arrangements. Private foreign investment has been important in promoting economic development. Most production in Mexico is conducted by private enterprise. Mexico has one of the fastest growing steel industries in the world. A large part of the agricultural system is organized as private commercial firms. The transactions of most economic units in Mexico are basically motivated by the desire to maximize profits and incomes in response to market forces. Rewards in income and wealth have gone in great measure to those units that act efficiently in response to market opportunities. There has been very little comprehensive central planning by the government.

Table 18-1 presents a percentage breakdown of the main components of Mexico's gross national product for 1984. The most important component is private consumption expenditures on goods and services, which accounted for 60.5 percent of gross national product. In total, the government or public sector generates around 25 percent of the Mexican GNP and the private sector contributes around 75 percent.

AGRICULTURE

Agriculture has been called the Achilles heel of the Mexican economy with good reason. Mexico is highly unsuited for agriculture. Much of the north is desert, two mountain ranges run the length of the country, tropical jungles cover the southern region, and much of the top soil of the country

---

2. Susan Eckstein, *The Poverty of Revolution* (Princeton, N.J.: Princeton University Press, 1977).

TABLE 18-1   MEXICAN GROSS NATIONAL PRODUCT
EXPENDITURES BY SECTORS, 1984

Government consumption	12.5%
Private consumption	60.5
Fixed capital formation	
Public	12.8
Private	13.2
Exports of goods and services	13.0
Less: Imports of goods and services	−12.0
	100.0%

Source: Banco de Mexico, *Informe Anual 1984*, p. 175.

is so thin that little can grow. Only 15 percent of the total land area of Mexico is cultivable. Most of Mexico's agricultural land depends exclusively on rainfall for moisture, and all during the 1970s, rainfall was significantly below the national average. Agriculture employs one-third of the Mexican labor force, while accounting for less than 9 percent of Mexico's gross national product.

Of major significance to the Mexican economy is the fact that the real growth in agricultural output has declined over time while the population has increased. Agricultural production increased at an average annual growth rate of 4.5 percent during the period 1960–1970 and at a rate of 3.4 percent for the period 1970–1982.[3] During the latter period, the average annual increase in agriculture barely exceeded the average annual increase in population. Mexico has also experienced a decline in self-sufficiency in agriculture and must import more farm products. There are several factors that contribute to the problems of agriculture in Mexico.

First, there is no adequate transportation network to allow quick and cheap transportation of agricultural products within Mexico. The major railroad and highway systems follow a north-to-south route from the United States to Mexico City. There is little east-west rail and highway transportation because mountains provide a barrier to construction. Many of the larger Mexican cities are served by only one major highway each. Inadequate transportation facilities have hampered the efforts of the Mexican government to restrain rises in the cost of food production. Moreover, the transportation problem is not just internal. Mexico has considerable problems in maintaining adequate distribution channels for imported

3. Banco de Mexico, *Informe Anual 1984*, p. 165.

foodstuffs as well. Port and storage facilities are inadequate and roads leading from the seaports to the major urban areas are poor.

As is true of other developing countries, agriculture has generally been neglected by the government in favor of industrial development. The latter offers more tangible results, from both political and economic standpoints. However, neglect of agriculture has encouraged urban migration, which has put more pressure on food production. Some price supports have been initiated to increase farm income and stem the tide of rural-to-urban migration, or, for that matter, rural-to-the-United-States migration. The Mexican government has also imposed export restrictions on the sale of beef abroad to lower the price of beef to domestic consumers. However, export restrictions lower the price of beef and discourage beef growers from producing more cattle, which then necessitates subsidies from the government.

The organization of agriculture is a third factor that contributes to low agricultural productivity. Mexican agriculture is typified by three different types of land holdings: communal, public, and private. The communal, or ejido, land holding is unique to Mexico, dating back to the time of the Aztecs. The land is held by the ejido and farmed by ejidatarios, or farm laborers, who share in the proceeds. The ejidos are considered inefficient and are criticized on the grounds that not allowing private property ownership weakens attachment to the soil and separates efforts from rewards. The bulk of Mexican agricultural output comes from the private farms, 4 percent of which produce more than 50 percent of total output and one percent of which produce all of the agricultural exports.

Only 12 percent of the land area of Mexico is under cultivation, yet almost one-third of the Mexican labor force is still employed in agriculture. This means that labor productivity is low. There is also an imbalance between cultivable land, population centers, and water resources. Only 10 percent of water resources are located in the central plateau around Mexico City, the area that contains half of Mexico's population and the greatest concentration of small farms. The bulk of water resources are in the underpopulated areas, and the larger, more productive farm holdings are also in the same areas.

GOVERNMENT OWNERSHIP OF ENTERPRISE

The Mexican government has intervened directly and indirectly to promote economic expansion in all sectors of the economy. Since the 1930s, when foreign oil properties were nationalized, the state has been involved in the economy to a greater extent than in most Latin American countries.

In 1982 the government nationalized the banking system. It owns most of the electrical power industry and has established government enterprises in direct competition with private ones in the same industry, such as steel production. It exercises considerable control over access to credit through state-owned financial institutions and constructs social overhead facilities, such as ports and roads, with the clear intention of influencing the geographical location and other characteristics of new private investment. The government emphasizes economic nationalism through legislation designed to discourage industrial imports, through exchange controls, and through import licensing.

PEMEX   Oil production is the most important sector in the Mexican economy and is run by a government monopoly, Petroleos Mexicanos (PEMEX). This monopoly is the only entity legally entitled to extract, refine, and distribute oil and oil products. The final distribution of gasoline products is made through a national network of privately owned gasoline stations that must comply with PEMEX regulations. PEMEX regulates the final prices of gasoline products, which cannot be changed by the station owners under any conditions. It also sets the hours for selling gasoline, the amount of gasoline to be sold, the architectural design of the gas stations, and the number of pumps allowed to operate in each station. The importance of PEMEX is demonstrated by the fact that its director has the status of a government minister and is a member of the Mexican cabinet.

Domestic price and oil extraction policies are set by PEMEX and are dictated by government economic development policies. Oil pricing policies for the international market follow those set by Saudi Arabia and other OPEC countries. The Arab oil embargo of the early 1970s and the energy crisis that developed afterward encouraged the management of PEMEX to adopt a faster rate of extraction and a more aggressive exploration policy. By 1984 Mexico was the fourth largest oil producer in the world. The increase in the rate of oil extraction required large investment expenditures, mainly for imported capital goods. As a consequence, PEMEX represents the single largest expenditure in the Mexican national budget, accounting for almost a third of total expenditures in 1984.[4]

BANKING   Banking is the second area where the Mexican government plays an important role in the Mexican economy. The Central Bank (Banco de Mexico) is a government entity and is responsible for the implementation of monetary policy through control over interest rates and reserve

4. Ibid., p. 177.

requirements of Mexican banks. It supervises foreign transactions and is the sole issuer of paper currency. Its monetary policy has been a part of Mexican government economic development strategy. During the 1970s and early 1980s, it pursued an expansionary policy of increasing the money supply to stimulate the Mexican economy.[5]

The Nacional Financiera is the second most important government-owned bank. Its function is to promote industrial development by allocating credit to industries, both public and private, that are a part of the government's program for economic development. Nacional Financiera holds a controlling interest in the country's largest steel producer, Altos Hornos de Mexico. It also holds substantial financial interests in pulp and paper, fertilizer, electrical equipment, sugar, films, textiles, food, beer, chemicals, cement, glass, and motels. Its main sources of revenue are from the government budget and from interest on loans.

There are also other specialized government lending institutions, such as agricultural banks, that lend to specific sectors. Finally, government control over the banking system was increased in 1982, when the privately owned commercial banks were nationalized.

PUBLIC FINANCE

There are several points that can be made about the Mexican fiscal system. First, the federal budget is an important part of government economic development policy. The fiscal policy of the Mexican government has been to foster economic expansion by running a deficit in the budget. Although Mexico's financial markets are relatively sophisticated by Latin America standards, they are not developed to the extent that large-scale financing of the budget deficit is possible through government bonds. The Banco de Mexico finances the deficit primarily through increases in the money supply. Also, large amounts have been borrowed from U.S. banks and the International Monetary Fund. Second, on the revenue side of the budget, the income tax has declined in importance as a source of revenue, accounting for only 12 percent of government revenue in 1984. The major sources of revenue in the Mexican budget are borrowing and income from state-owned enterprises. Since 1980, PEMEX has provided about half the national government's revenue. Third, the bulk of government expenditures are on infrastructure and housing investment, which is a large and growing sector of the Mexican economy.

5. Francisco Carrada-Bravo, *Oil, Money and the Mexican Economy* (Boulder, Col.: Westview Press, 1982), pp. 37-38.

ECONOMIC DEVELOPMENT

In terms of economic production and diversification, Mexico, by international standards, is at the lower-middle stage of economic development. It is far more developed than either China or Nigeria, but not as developed as South Africa or Venezuela. Its economy is less autonomous and more vulnerable to external economic forces than the economies of the more developed countries, but more autonomous and less vulnerable than the economies of subsistence and single-export countries. Its economy is extractive-oriented in that oil is far and away its most important export. When world oil prices were high during the late 1970s, the oil wealth of Mexico not only generated the foreign exchange necessary to finance internal economic development, but also enhanced the country's attractiveness in foreign capital markets. However, the decline in world oil prices in the early 1980s has had a deleterious impact on the Mexican economy, which by that time had incurred a large foreign debt.

ECONOMIC DEVELOPMENT STRATEGIES   It is evident that economic development has brought substantial economic and social progress to Mexico and to many other countries that were at one time poor. In general this development has come about through the use of one or more of three different growth policy approaches. The first approach is to rely on the export of a primary product, such as copper or oil, to raise living standards. This approach may not involve an attempt to achieve industrialization. For example, the Arab countries have used revenue from oil exports to achieve higher living standards, but there has been very little attempt to achieve widespread industrial development. Oil revenues have been used to improve the infrastructure of these countries through the construction of education facilities, roads, and hospitals. Venezuela, on the other hand, has used revenue from its oil exports to accomplish more broadly based industrialization.

A second approach to economic development is to achieve inward industrialization through import substitution. This has been the development strategy of Mexico, Brazil, Argentina, and several other Latin American countries. Restrictions on imports increase the demand for local consumption and are supposed to encourage the development of domestic industries. Both Mexico and Brazil have established consumer and capital goods industries that provide for local consumption. This strategy is not without its costs; protection from import competition often raises the prices of local goods and limits selection for consumers.

The third approach is that which has been followed by Japan, Singapore, South Korea, and other Asian countries since the end of World War

II. This is outward industrialization and involves the export of manufactured goods ranging from clothing to automobiles. Measures to increase exports are, for the most part, likely to develop rather slowly; it is a matter of improving production techniques, labor skills, and managerial methods, and introducing new industries. An export surplus also involves sacrifices; it means sending more abroad than one gets in return—using labor and other resources to provide goods and services for foreigners.

MEXICO'S DEVELOPMENT STRATEGY   In pursuing inward industrialization through import substitution, Mexico relies heavily on state intervention in the economy.[6] Exchange controls,[7] import quotas, and other restrictions designed to limit imports are used by the government to promote the development of home industries by making imports more expensive. This compels Mexican consumers either to pay higher prices for imported goods or to buy domestic products. In effect, consumers have been forced to subsidize the development of Mexican industry through the substitution of domestic products for imported products.

Capital investment is stimulated through tax policies and government subsidies to aid business. The government has intervened directly to promote the development of certain industries. For example, the Automobile Manufacturing Law of 1963 required foreign automobile companies operating in Mexico to increase the share of locally manufactured components to 60 percent of each car produced. This law was designed to stimulate local manufacturing through import substitution and to make the auto industry a primary source of employment.[8]

The world oil shortage of the 1970s caused a new rebirth of the Mexican oil industry and a change in development strategy away from import substitution to the use of oil for export expansion. New oil discoveries returned Mexico to the status it had enjoyed earlier in the century as a major world oil producer. Two important government development policy decisions were made. The first was to push for increased oil production; and the second was to base export policy on the sale of oil to the United States and other oil-importing countries. Earnings from oil exports were used to improve the infrastructure of the Mexican economy and to increase social welfare expenditures to the lower income groups in the population.

6. Robert E. Looney, *Development Alternatives of Mexico* (New York: Praeger Publishers, 1982).

7. Exchange controls involve the decision of a government agency as to what and how much will be imported from abroad. The government allocates foreign exchange to importers, which, in effect, controls imports.

8. Jorge I. Dominguez, *Mexico's Political Economy* (Beverly Hills, Calif.: Sage Publications, 1982), pp. 142-144.

Earnings from oil exports were also used to promote the capital goods industry in Mexico. Tariffs and import quotas were placed on imported capital goods to promote substitution of locally produced capital goods for those that were foreign produced. Import controls on capital goods and the promotion of oil exports were the main instruments of Mexican economic development strategy during the late 1970s and early 1980s.

ECONOMIC PLANNING

Economic planning is relatively new in Mexico and is quite similar to the indicative planning that was made popular by France. The length of the economic plan is linked to the six-year presidential cycle, and thus the economic planning process is aligned closely to the political and economic objectives of the incumbent president. Although succeeding presidents are from the same political party, their economic policies are not the same. The policies of the Lopez Portillo administration (1976–1982) were totally different from the policies of the current Miguel de la Madrid administration (1982–1988). Economic planning was initiated during the Portillo administration and set forth as objectives to increase oil exports, to create more jobs, to raise living standards of the poorest strata of the population, and to increase the rates of saving and capital formation in both the public and private sectors. However, the collapse of world oil prices has had an adverse effect on the Mexican economy, and the economic planning of the de la Madrid administration, of necessity, has reversed most of the goals of the previous administration.

■ AN APPRAISAL ■
OF THE MEXICAN ECONOMY

Mexico's prosperity has come rather recently. For many years Mexico was a somnolent country, locked into a circle of poverty caused by a lack of savings and social capital and by monopolistic foreign exploitation of local natural resources. The Mexican Revolution of 1910 brought changes in the economy. Between 1917 and World War II, emphasis was placed on agricultural reform. The feudal system of land ownership, with its absentee holdings, was abolished and the land was redistributed in a manner permitting the use of modern agricultural techniques. Investments in social overhead capital include literacy campaigns and technical schools. A national bank for agricultural credit was created in 1926; and an industrial bank, the Nacional Financiera, was created in 1934 to provide loans to business firms. Through these banks, the government became responsible for a large share of the financing of economic development.

The Mexican economy expanded rapidly after World War II. There was a 10-fold increase in gross domestic product between 1949 and 1978 that propelled Mexico from the rank of a poor, less developed country to a developing country.[9] Mexico's real output in constant prices increased at an average rate of 6.2 percent a year, well ahead of the annual population growth rate of 3.3 percent. Most of the gain in real output occurred in the industrial sector, which increased at an average annual rate of 7.8 percent for the period. Manufacturing increased from 19 percent of total output in 1949 to 33 percent in 1978. Mexico began to exhibit many of the key features of a large modern industrial nation, with domestic oil promising to guarantee it abundant energy at least until the end of the century. A middle class has developed, particularly in the cities, that provides an element of political stability. Moreover, it has expanded over a period of time, as the process of industrialization has continued.

Nevertheless, Mexico has both economic and social problems. A downturn in the economy occurred during the early 1980s. In 1982 and 1983 the index of industrial production decreased at a rate of 10 percent, but it increased 5 percent in 1984 and 3 percent in 1985. Inflation is a major problem. The consumer price index, which has a 1978 base of 100 percent, increased to 1,075 percent by the end of 1985.[10] It hit Mexico's poorest people, particularly those who live in the cities, with the heaviest burden. Price inflation accelerated far above U.S. levels, stimulating imports and discouraging exports. Oil prices have dropped significantly, further decreasing export revenue.

However, there are more deep-seated problems than the current performance of the economy. They are excess population, extreme income inequality, a large foreign debt, corruption that has become endemic in the political system, and inefficient agriculture, which was discussed earlier in the chapter. These social and economic problems present obstacles to the future development of Mexico.

POPULATION

Demographers estimate that the population of Mexico will exceed 100 million by the end of the century. The country is already hard-pressed to produce enough jobs to absorb the 800,000 new entrants into the labor

9. Looney, *Development Alternatives*, p. 2.

10. Banco National de Mexico, *Examen de la Situacion Economica de Mexico*, December 1984, p. 5.

force each year. Millions of Mexicans have emigrated or are in the process of emigrating, usually illegally, to the United States, where even the most menial jobs provide more money and a better life than the alternative in Mexico. For most countries, more people not only means more labor and output, but also more consumers to share the output. More people also means there will be less real capital and natural resources per capita, and labor productivity may actually fall.

URBANIZATION Mexico City had a population of 3.1 million in 1950. By 1984 the population had grown to 17.6 million, which made Mexico City the largest city in the world, and by the year 2,000 the population is projected to be 26 million.[11] Most of the population increase has resulted in migration to the city by jobless peasants. They stream in from the countryside at a rate of 1,000 a day in search of a higher standard of living. The migration problem is part of a rural unemployment problem that can be linked to a decline in agricultural employment. Unfortunately, this has created a combustible mixture of urban pollution, poverty, unemployment, disease, crime, and corruption, which manifests itself in the following statistics.[12]

1. More than two million people in Mexico City have no running water in their homes.

2. More than three million residents have no sewage facilities.

3. Mexico City produces about 14,000 tons of garbage every day, but can process only 8,000 tons. Most of the rest is left to rot in the open air, thus contributing to the potential for communicable diseases.

4. Mexico City, which is located in a bowl surrounded by mountain ranges, is one of the most polluted cities in the world. Half of Mexico's industry is concentrated in a land area smaller than the state of Rhode Island. The daily total of chemical air pollution is estimated to be 11,000 tons.

5. The combination of chemical and biological poisons kills an estimated 30,000 children each year through respiratory and gastrointestinal diseases.

11. Elaine M. Murphy, *World Population: Toward the Next Century* (Washington: Population Reference Bureau, Inc., 1986), p. 2.

12. *Time* (August 20, 1984), pp. 26-27.

6. Unemployment runs at an average annual rate of 12 percent and underemployment runs to nearly 40 percent. Many Mexicans are employed in a menial capacity; there are probably more shoeshiners in one block than there are in the entire city of New York. Each street has its collection of beggars.

Problems of urbanization are not limited just to Mexico City. Monterrey, an industrial city in northern Mexico, had its population increase from 200,000 in 1950 to 3 million in 1985. Guadalajara, Juarez, Puebla, and other Mexican cities have seen similar population increases. The increased population puts a strain on the infrastructure of those cities, which is often inadequate to begin with. The tax revenues of these cities are not large enough to provide the services necessary to support an ever-increasing population. Moreover, slowing internal migration does not offer a real solution to the rate of Mexican population growth. More than half of the population growth in the cities is due to the excess of births over deaths. Despite extensive rural-to-urban migration, population growth in the rural areas has not decreased; in fact, the rural birth rate is higher than it is in the cities.

EMIGRATION TO THE UNITED STATES   It is estimated that some 19 million Mexicans have entered the United States either legally or illegally since 1945.[13] There are a number of reasons for this immigration, the most important of which are the following.[14]

1. There is an enormous difference between the two countries in both money and real wages. The real wage differential between the United States and Mexico is about 7 to 1 for unskilled jobs and 13 to 1 for agricultural jobs.

2. The rate of inflation is much higher in Mexico than in the United States. Inflation further depresses the level of real wages for the average Mexican worker.

3. The Mexican labor force is increasing at a faster rate than the capacity of the Mexican economy to create jobs. Many of those who emigrate to the United States are impoverished rural workers from the poorest agricultural states of Mexico: Oaxaca, Morelos, Guerrero, and Michoacan.

---

13. Dominguez, *Political Economy*, p. 194.

14. Denis Goulet, *Mexico: Development Strategies for the Future* (Notre Dame, Ind.: University of Notre Dame Press, 1983), p. 39.

Mexican migration to the United States can be considered a safety valve for Mexico in that it reduces pressures of unemployment. At least two-thirds of the emigrants remit money to Mexico. For most of the Mexican households involved, these remittances are their primary source of income. Because most of the migrants come from northern and central Mexico, the Mexican government would face a severe regionally concentrated income and employment problem if the border with the United States were closed. Although migration may reduce unemployment in Mexico, it may increase unemployment in the United States. There is pressure, particularly from U.S. labor unions, to restrict the flow of migrants from Mexico.

INCOME INEQUALITY

"The thing is, there is no equality here. Everything is disproportionate. The rich are very rich, and the poor are infamously poor. The poor stick to the poor, and the rich, well, they go to the Hilton. The day I dare go to the Hilton Hotel, I'll know there has been another revolution!"[15]

This statement was made by one of the people quoted in Oscar Lewis' book *The Children of Sanchez,* written more than 25 years ago. Nothing has changed. In Mexico's case, the chosen strategy for economic development seems to have worked against social improvement. Not only has the economy been unable to create sufficient jobs—the most effective remedy for the amelioration of social problems—but it also has permitted an inordinate concentration of income and wealth in the hands of a few people. Mexico's very rich live in a style that would put all but a few American millionaires to shame, while the majority of its population lives in degrees of poverty that range from mere survival to outright misery. Mexico and Brazil, the two Latin American countries that have enjoyed the fastest economic growth since the 1950s, display the most skewed distribution of income and wealth in the Americas.

Table 18-2 presents the distribution of income in Mexico for 1977. In that year the top 10 percent of Mexican households in terms of income received 40.6 percent of total household incomes, compared to 42.3 percent for the bottom 80 percent. The average household income of those in the top 10 percent of household was 31 times that of families in the bottom 20 percent.[16] About 45 percent of Mexican families have an income that is

---

15. Oscar Lewis, *The Children of Sanchez* (New York: Random House, Inc., 1961), pp. 339-340.

16. David Felix, "Income Inequality in Mexico," *Current History* (March, 1977), p. 11.

TABLE 18-2   DISTRIBUTION OF HOUSEHOLD INCOME IN MEXICO, 1977

Lowest 20 percent	2.9%	Highest 20 percent	57.7%
Second quintile	7.0	Highest 10 percent	40.6
Third quintile	12.0	Highest 5 percent	27.7
Fourth quintile	20.4		

Source: The World Bank, *World Development Report 1985*, p. 229.

less than half the national average. The Gini coefficient for Mexico is about 0.6 percent, indicating one of the world's most unequal income distributions.[17] Contrary to patterns exhibited by other countries in similar stages of economic development, the income gap between rich and poor has widened.[18]

Moreover, there are geographic disparities in the distribution of income that are far greater than those in developed countries such as the United States. The average per capita income in Mexico City is six times that of the state of Oaxaca, a factor that promotes internal migration and contributes to overcrowding in Mexico City.

There are a number of reasons for income inequality in Mexico, most of which are common to other less developed economies. However, there are several reasons that are the result of conditions particular to Mexico.

1. The economic growth policies of Mexico have benefitted the upper and middle classes. Import substitution has kept foreign imports out and stimulated Mexican business. Emphasis was placed on industrialization, which did create jobs but particularly benefitted a small number of large Mexican-owned firms that are capital-intensive.

2. The Mexican tax system is probably more regressive than progressive. The personal income tax, though progressive, is evaded by many persons and social welfare benefits are low.

3. Much of Mexican wealth is concentrated in real estate.

17. As was pointed out in chapter 1, the Gini coefficient is a measure of income inequality. It can range from 0 to 1. The coefficient for the United States is around .36, which indicates that there is less income inequality in the United States than in Mexico. The coefficient decreases as a country develops an industrial base and adopts policies of income transfers and progressive taxation.

18. Woulter van Ginnekin, *Socioeconomic Groups and Income Distribution in Mexico* (London: Groom Helem, 1980), chapter 1.

4. Corruption is a factor. One of the more recent presidents of Mexico is alleged to have pocketed one to three billion dollars while in office. Corruption is not new to Mexico; it goes back to the time of the conquistadores.

5. Income inequality is another carryover from the *latifundio* system of the last century when a few families controlled much of the land of Mexico. Even though the Revolution of 1910 broke up the latifundio system, most families retained their wealth.

Income inequality can also be translated into inequality in the distribution of wealth. Much of the wealth is concentrated in real estate or is invested in foreign holdings, particularly in the United States. Wealthy Mexicans devise elaborate schemes to put their wealth beyond the reach of Mexican tax collectors and give themselves a safe haven outside of Mexico.[19]

The extreme dichotomy in income and wealth between rich and poor increases the potential for social unrest in Mexico. The Mexican fiscal system includes thousands of subsidies and controls that are supposed to benefit low-income groups, but often do not. The income tax, though progressive, does very little to reduce income inequality among groups, for there are many loopholes. A developed welfare state like the one in the United States and Western Europe that has narrowed income differences between rich and poor does not exist in Mexico. Only 35 percent of the population is covered by social security.

FOREIGN DEBT

The external or foreign debt of Mexico was around $97 billion at the end of 1985. This debt was incurred at a time when world prices for oil were high. As mentioned previously, Mexican industrial development strategy during the late 1970s was predicated on oil, which represented about 80 percent of total exports. As long as there was a world demand for oil and prices remained high, the Mexican government could afford to mortgage the future by borrowing against the expected revenue from oil exports. These loans went to finance a wide variety of development schemes, including a national system of supports for basic agriculture and a plan to build 20 nuclear reactors. However, the Mexican government ignored the consequences of the global oil glut that began to develop in early 1981 and

19. Capital outflows from Mexico amounted to $33 billion during the period 1977–1984. Around $20 billion came to the United States.

continued to borrow from foreign banks, using anticipated future oil revenue as collateral.

Falling world prices for oil and rising interest rates in the United States exacerbated the difficulty the Mexican government had in meeting payments on the debt it had contracted with foreign banks. Exports declined as a result of the world oil glut, while the price of imports, particularly those from the United States where the dollar gained in value relative to the peso, increased. To correct a negative balance in Mexico's balance of payments, the government devalued the peso in 1982.[20] This did little to stop the flight of Mexican money out of the country because Mexicans had lost faith in the value of the peso. In September, 1982, the government nationalized Mexico's private banks, blaming them for the exodus of Mexican money to the United States. The devaluation of the peso made Mexico's imported goods more expensive, further lowering living standards for many Mexicans. Inflation contributed to a further decline in the value of the peso, which by early 1986 exchanged at 400 to the dollar.

High interest rates in the United States increased interest payments on Mexico's foreign debt at the same time that Mexico's earnings from oil exports were declining. In 1984, for example, Mexico's interest payments on its foreign debt amounted to about 40 percent of its total export earnings and 3 percent of its gross national product.[21] This means that Mexico was having a hard enough time meeting its interest payments, much less returning any part of the principal. The situation worsened as oil prices continued to fall. In an effort to improve its foreign debt position, the government introduced austerity measures. Taxes were raised and government spending was cut, while domestic interest rates were increased.[22] To further help cut imports and promote exports, foreign exchange controls were imposed, making it more difficult for Mexicans to buy products made in the United States. These austerity measures have had mixed results. In early 1986, with oil down to $15 a barrel, Mexico has been forced to limit interest payments on its debt.

20. Currency devaluation refers to a downward adjustment of a currency's official exchange rate relative to other currencies. It has both external and internal effects on a country's economy. The external effect is to increase exports as a result of lower export prices in terms of foreign currencies. The internal effect is to decrease imports because import prices increase in terms of domestic currency. The export advantages of devaluation presuppose no immediate retaliation on the part of other countries.

21. Banco National de Mexico, *Indicadores Economicos* (February, 1985), p. 24.

22. For example, the interest rate on 90-day notes averaged 48.02 percent for 1984. This rate can be compared to an average rate of 10.95 percent on 90-day certificates of deposit in the United States. The prime interest rate charged by Mexican banks averaged around 52 percent in 1984 compared to a U.S. prime rate of around 12.5 percent. However, the rate of inflation in Mexico was much higher in 1984 than the rate of inflation in the United States. The real rate of interest, i.e., the money rate of interest less the rate of inflation, was negative in Mexico in 1983 and 1984, while it was positive in the United States for both years. This would attract capital from Mexico to the United States.

CORRUPTION

"I don't know about political things. The first time I voted was in the last election, but I don't think there is much hope there. The men in the government always end up rich and the poor are just as badly off."[23]

Corruption is endemic in Mexico.[24] It has long been an article of faith that any politician worth his or her salt will amass at least a minor fortune before leaving office.[25] A new president is elected every six years even though the same party remains in office, and has 45,000 patronage jobs to fill. Each patronage job involves some sort of a political payoff, and there are benefits to be gained. From ministers and directors of goverment agencies down to the workers on garbage trucks, civil servants have the opportunity to make money. The average minister or director may amass a small fortune during a term in office. It is reported that some ministers leave office with amounts 30 or more times as much as their original salary.[26] Even garbage collectors can demand bribes from the households they serve, threatening to leave the garbage in the streets. In turn, the garbage collectors have to pay off the head of the garbage collectors' union.

Nepotism is always a fact of life in Mexican politics. For example, one former president of Mexico, Jose Lopez Portillo, appointed his son, his mistress, two cousins, and his sister to ministerial positions. Another sister was given the job of his personal secretary, and his wife was appointed head of cultural affairs. All enjoyed an extravagant lifestyle. Lopez Portillo himself constructed a five-mansion complex, with tennis courts, swimming pools, stables, and a gymnasium. He bought a two-million dollar villa in Acapulco for his mistress, and, to show no favoratism, built one equally expensive for his wife. One sister built a 36,000-square-foot mansion on government property. It is estimated that Lopez Portillo and his family enriched themselves to the extent of $11 billion during his term in office.[27]

Corruption simply exacerbates the differences between the haves and the have-nots. It is a result of 56 years of one-party rule in which widely diverse constituents have been allowed easy access to the government. Mexicans have socially and cynically accepted corruption as a part of

---

23. Lewis, *Children of Sanchez*, p. 342.

24. It is necessary to emphasize the fact that Mexico has no monopoly on corruption. Bribery and other forms of corruption are an accepted way of life in many countries.

25. A classic example involves a former police chief of Mexico City, who acquired two mansions, property in Acapulco, twelve Mercedez-Benz, two helicopters, two airplanes, and $12 million in cash during his term of office.

26. Alan Riding, *Distant Neighbors* (New York: Alfred A. Knopf, Inc., 1985), p. 117-119.

27. Ibid., p. 128.

everyday life. The 1985 earthquake that devastated a part of Mexico City revealed that many buildings collapsed and lives were lost unnecessarily because building contractors had used poor quality materials on government buildings.[28] Corruption, particularly as flagrant as it is in Mexico, has the potential for creating social unrest. A system that never worked smoothly without corruption is no longer working smoothly because of corruption. As an historical note, a major reason for Castro's overthrow of the Batista regime in Cuba was the extent of corruption that existed in the country at that time. Although the current president of Mexico, Miguel de la Madrid, has vowed to eliminate corruption, it will be impossible to destroy completely, for it is too much a part of the system.

28. "A Nation in Jeopardy," *The Wall Street Journal* (October 15, 1985), p. 1.

SUMMARY

Mexico is one of the largest countries in the world, both in population and land size. Although it is not nearly as rich as the United States and Canada, it has experienced a rapid growth in economic development and ranks as one of the more successful developing countries in the world.

Its economy is mixed in that both the private and public sectors are important. Agriculture is a problem to Mexico for several reasons: inadequate transportation, neglect by government, low labor productivity, and lack of adequate water. Mexico has relied extensively on government intervention in the economy, intervening both directly, with controls on investment and trade, and indirectly through taxes, subsidies, and other measures affecting the prices in both factor and product markets. Its internal economic development policy has relied on import substitution. This policy was used to develop the Mexican oil and steel industries. When oil increased in importance in world markets, Mexico used its earnings from its oil exports to subsidize the development of its capital goods industries.

Nevertheless, Mexico faces a number of problems, most of which are common to other less developed and developing countries. One is overpopulation. The population of Mexico is growing at a rate faster than the country's capacity to support it. One result is a mass migration of Mexicans to the United States, which has put a strain on the relations between the two countries. The external debt of Mexico is a second problem. It places pressure on government policy to earn more from exports while encouraging austerity at home. Oil exports account for most of Mexico's export earnings, and the world price for oil has declined. A third problem is corruption, which permeates much of Mexican life. Income distribution, which is one of the most unequal in the world, is a fourth problem. The enormous income disparity between rich and poor creates a potential for social unrest. The final problem is low productivity in agriculture.

REVIEW QUESTIONS

1. Discuss the importance of oil to the Mexican economy.
2. Discuss some of the problems of Mexican agriculture.
3. What is an import substitution approach to economic development?
4. What are the three approaches to economic development? Which one has Mexico used?
5. Mexico represents a lower middle stage of economic development. It is far more developed than either China or Nigeria, but far less developed than the United States. Discuss.
6. Discuss the relationship of population growth to economic development in Mexico.
7. What problems does its foreign debt create for Mexico?
8. Population growth has increased more rapidly in the cities of the less developed and developing countries than in the cities of the developed countries. Why is this so?

RECOMMENDED READINGS

Aspra, Antonio. "Import Substitution in Mexico: Past and Present." *World Development*. January-February, 1977, pp. 111–124.

Barken, David, and Gustavo Esterva. "Social Conflicts and Inflation in Mexico." *Latin American Perspectives*. Winter 1982, pp. 48–64.

Bergsman, Joel. *Income Distribution and Poverty in Mexico*. Working Paper No. 395. New York: The World Bank, June 1980.

Carreda-Bravo, Francisco. *Oil, Money, and the Mexican Economy*. Boulder, Colo.: Westview Press, 1982.

Dominguez, Jorge I. *Mexico's Political Economy*. Beverly Hills, Calif.: Sage Publications, 1982.

Eckstein, Susan. *The Poverty of Revolution*. Princeton, N.J.: Princeton University Press, 1977.

Gallagher, Charles F. *Population, Petroleum & Politics: Mexico at the Crossroads*. Reports Nos. 19 and 42. Hanover, N.H.: American Universities Field Staff, 1981.

Goulet, Dennis. *Mexico: Development Strategies for the Future*. Notre Dame, Ind.: University of Notre Dame Press, 1983.

Looney, Robert E. *Development Alternatives of Mexico*. New York: Praeger Publishers, 1982.

Riding, Alan. *Distant Neighbors*. New York: Alfred A. Knopf, Inc., 1985.

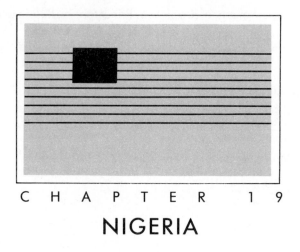

C H A P T E R   1 9

NIGERIA

Nigeria is one of a number of African countries that have achieved their independence from colonial rule in the last 30 years. However, before Nigeria can be discussed in terms of economic development, the characteristics of Africa, which is the poorest and most diverse of all the continents, must be understood. What is applicable to Africa is applicable to Nigeria as well.

■ CHARACTERISTICS OF AFRICA ■

The majority of African countries have three things in common. First, with few exceptions, they were once colonies of a European country; second, they are poor; and third, uncontrolled population growth limits their potential economic development and creates enormous social problems.

COLONIALISM

For centuries, Africa was called the "dark continent," unknown to all outsiders except a few explorers. All of this changed when the European powers decided at the Berlin Conference of 1885 to divide up Africa into enclaves or spheres of influence. Five countries shared in the division of African territory—Belgium, England, France, Germany, and Portugal. Belgium got that area of Africa known as the Congo, which became one of the largest copper-producing areas in the world. England, which was already established in Egypt and the Cape of Africa, acquired the Sudan, southern Africa, and part of southwest Africa. France, which had already conquered Algeria, was given West Africa. Germany was given the right to parts of East Africa and southwest Africa, including that area known as the Tanganyika territory.[1] Portugal, the smallest of the five European countries, was given what was left in southern East and West Africa, including the areas that are now the countries of Angola and Mozambique.

The African colonies served two purposes. First, they provided a source of wealth for their owners in the ruling country. Private companies were given monopoly rights by their governments to operate in the colonies and became the general media of commerce. The South Africa Chartered Company, owned by Cecil Rhodes, was given the right to develop the resources of southern Africa. The discovery of gold in the South African Rand and diamonds at Kimberley made Rhodes one of the richest men in the world.[2] Second, the African colonies served as markets for the products of the ruling countries. Until 1870 British-manufactured goods found a market in other European countries. After 1870 Germany, France, Belgium, and other countries were able to satisfy their home markets and began to produce a surplus for sale abroad. With increasing saturation of European markets, all looked for more markets overseas and for this purpose, Africa served admirably. Thus, the race to acquire colonies began.

The colonies were governed by administrators sent down from London, Paris, Berlin, Brussels, and Lisbon. The colonial civil service and military were run by the ruling countries, and the middle-class merchants were either European nationals, Indians, or Chinese. Native Africans were given little opportunity for self-government and were given no positions of authority in the colonial governments. As a result, when the colonies achieved their independence and became self-governing nations, there was a leadership vacuum. Most of the foreign civil servants, engineers, and merchants who had comprised the backbone of government and commerce returned to their home countries. Their positions were filled by persons who had little training in government or who had no technical

1. Germany lost its colonies after the end of World War I.
2. Cecil Rhodes is the man who established the Rhodes scholarships.

experience. Animosity toward anything foreign also resulted in the forced departure of Indian and Chinese merchants from some African countries. Unfortunately, the locals did not have the entrepreneurial skills to run the businesses vacated by the Europeans and Asians.

POVERTY

Africa is the poorest of the world's continents. Its per capita GNP of $750 in 1985 was less than 5 percent of that of the United States, and it contains most of the poorest countries in the world. Chad had a 1985 per capita GNP of $80, the lowest in the world; in fact, 28 of the 35 countries with a per capita GNP of $500 or less in 1985 were located in Africa.[3] Only two countries, Algeria and South Africa, would qualify as being in the same stage of economic development as Brazil and Mexico. Libya, which has the highest per capita GNP of all of the African countries, derives its income from oil exports. Moreover, the average annual growth rate of per capita GNP is lower for the African countries than it is for the countries of other continents. The average annual growth rate for the 26 African countries with a 1983 per capita GNP of $500 or less was 0.2 percent for the period 1965–1983, and seven of the countries had a negative rate of growth.

Table 19-1 presents the per capita GNP and average annual rate of growth per capita for selected African countries. Most of the countries have per capita GNPs of $1,000 or less; all, with the exception of Ethiopia, were former colonies of England, France, Belgium, Germany, or Portugal. It is in these low-income countries that slow income growth does most to perpetuate poverty. The rate of savings for most African countries is low—in some countries it is negative. Chad, for example, had a negative rate of savings of 25 percent in 1983 and Lesotho had a negative rate of 77 percent.[4] Income distribution is more unequal than it is for the developed countries of the world. In Kenya, for example, the highest 10 percent of households received 45.8 percent of total household income, compared to 39.6 percent for the bottom 80 percent.[5]

---

3. The World Bank, *World Development Report 1985*, pp. 174-175.

4. Ibid., p. 226.

5. Ibid., p. 272. The data for Kenya are for 1976. There are no data for most African countries, but Kenya probably can be considered typical. In the poorest African countries, notably Chad, there may be less income inequality because there is little income to distribute.

TABLE 19-1   PER CAPITA GNP FOR SELECTED AFRICAN COUNTRIES

	Per Capita GNP, 1983	Average Annual Growth Rate 1965–1983
Chad	$ 80	−2.8%
Ethiopia	140	0.5
Mali	150	1.2
Zaire	160	−1.3
Burkino Faso	180	1.4
Uganda	220	−4.4
Tanzania	240	0.9
Niger	240	−1.2
Madagascar	290	−1.2
Ghana	320	−2.1
Kenya	340	2.3
Sudan	400	1.3
Zambia	580	−1.3
Egypt	700	4.2
Nigeria	760	3.2
Morocco	750	2.9
Cameroon	800	2.7
Ivory Coast	720	1.0
Tunisia	1,290	5.0
Algeria	2,400	3.6
South Africa	2,450	1.6
Libya	7,500	0.9

Source: The World Bank, *World Development Report 1985,* pp. 174-175.

POPULATION GROWTH

Africa's population is growing faster than the population of the other continents. In addition, its population is outstripping food production. Famines in Sudan and Ethiopia have been publicized on national television, but other African countries have also had famines. The number of hungry and malnourished Africans has increased to 100 million, which represents almost one-fifth of the continent's population. Moreover, the population increase has put pressure on medical care, housing, and the overall infrastructure of the African countries. Infant mortality rates are much higher than those for other developing and developed countries, but the birth rates are the highest in the world. The average African woman has 6.9 children, the average American woman has 2.2 children, and the average West German woman has 1.9 children. Africa's total population will double in 24 years. Western Europe's will double in 729 years.

Their large populations create a burden for most African countries in terms of resource allocation. Most resources must be used for consumption. Incomes are low, so human and physical capital is less developed.[6] This population growth affects both the demand for and the supply of savings. Household savings—usually the largest component of domestic savings—is reduced by the high dependency burdens associated with rapid population growth. At any given level of per capita income, greater numbers of dependents cause consumption to rise, so savings per capita will fall. Governments can, within limits, use fiscal and monetary policies to change a country's rate of savings, irrespective of demographic conditions. However, the effectiveness of fiscal and monetary policies is predicated on the existence of a well developed system of public finance and banking, which most African countries do not have.

Table 19-2 presents population, birth and death rates, and population-doubling time for selected African countries, many of which can be expected to double their population in less than 25 years. The implication is clear, particularly from the standpoint of education. More school-age children require increased spending on education, even if the objective is just to maintain current enrollments and standards. In a world of rapid technological change, these countries need to improve their schools both quantitatively and qualitatively. They will have to generate more national savings, or curtail other investments in, for example, power and transport. But the latter are also an important part of a country's infrastructure and are necessary for economic development. If a country is unwilling or, more likely, unable to make these sacrifices, spending must be spread over a large group of school children to the detriment of the quality of their education; otherwise, a growing number of children have to be excluded.

POLITICAL AND SOCIAL INSTABILITY

Political and social instability create economic development problems for many of the African countries. In the spring of 1985 the Sudan was wracked by civil war and political discontent over the economic austerity measures

---

6. Human capital represents the skills that people use in combination with their labor effort. These skills are the result of education or training carried out some time in the past and used for future production. A long period of schooling lowers a society's quantity of labor resources, but the lost working time is offset by the greater productivity that results from the knowledge and skill gained from the education. Physical capital, such as factories and machines, makes it possible for countries to produce more efficiently than they can without them.

TABLE 19-2 POPULATION DATA FOR SELECTED AFRICAN COUNTRIES, 1985

	Population (millions)	Birth Rate (per 1,000)	Death Rate (per 1,000)	Population-Doubling Time at Current Rates (in years)
Chad	5.2	44	23	33
Ethiopia	36.0	43	22	33
Mali	7.7	49	21	25
Zaire	33.1	45	16	24
Burkino Faso	6.9	48	22	27
Uganda	14.7	50	15	20
Tanzania	21.7	50	15	20
Niger	6.5	51	23	25
Madagascar	10.0	45	17	25
Ghana	14.3	47	15	22
Kenya	20.2	54	13	17
Sudan	21.8	46	17	24
Zambia	6.8	48	15	21
Egypt	48.3	37	10	26
Nigeria	91.2	48	17	22
Morocco	24.3	41	12	24
Cameroon	9.7	44	18	27
Ivory Coast	10.1	46	18	25
Algeria	22.2	45	12	21
South Africa	32.5	35	14	33
Africa	551.0	45	16	24
Developed Countries	1,174.0	15	9	118

Source: Mary M. Kent and Carl Haub, *1985 World Population Data Sheet* (Washington: Population Reference Bureau, Inc., 1985).

of President Gaafar Nimeiri, who was eventually deposed. In South Africa, rioting by blacks over the government's apartheid policies is a daily occurrence. All too frequently, the African countries have become hostage to leaders intent solely on gaining and holding political power.[7] Vast amounts of money and resources are spent for these purposes.

In the past 25 years, more than 70 leaders in 29 African countries have been deposed by assassinations, purges, or military coups.[8] Most African countries are run either by the military or by one political party that permits only token opposition. Zambia's President Kenneth Kaunda was the sole candidate in his nation's presidential election, when he was elected to a fifth four-year term. In Nigeria, a military coup ousted President Alhaji Shehu Shagiri, who had been reelected to office in an election where candidates representing several political parties had participated. Genuine political democracy, with several competing political parties, exists in only a small number of African countries.

There are a number of factors that contribute to the political and social instability of Africa. Poverty is obviously a very important factor, and uncontrolled population growth is another. Corruption is another factor. Politicians and bureaucrats line their pockets at the expense of the public. Even in countries as poor as Chad, ownership of a Mercedes-Benz by government officials is very common.[9] As often as not, large amounts of foreign food, cash, and equipment aid never reach their intended destinations. Tribal conflicts are another major factor inhibiting political stability. In all but a handful of African countries, tribal loyalties still predominate, especially in rural areas where nationalist sentiment has not penetrated.[10] Savage warfare between tribes is common. The bloodiest war in postcolonial Africa was fought in Nigeria from 1967 to 1970, when the predominantly Ibo region of southeastern Nigeria seceded and formed the independent state of Biafra. The civil war cost a million lives before Biafra was brought under control.

The Sudan is a microcosm of the problems of Africa. It is a poor country, with few natural resources. Its birth rate is high, and it can be expected to double its population in less than 25 years. In the spring of 1985,

---

7. The most infamous leader was Idi Amin, who was dictator of Uganda and who practiced tribal genocide, systematically killing people who were members of tribes other than his own. He patterned himself after Adolf Hitler, whom he greatly admired.

8. *Time*, January 16, 1984, p. 26.

9. A Mercedes-Benz costs around $50,000. The per capita GNP of Chad is less than $100.

10. Zaire has 200 tribes speaking some 75 languages, from the Pygmies to the Baluba. Tribal conflicts may be the reason for the emergence of one-party states in Africa. The ruling tribe simply exterminates other tribes.

it was on the verge of internal collapse. Four years of drought had reduced agricultural production below basic subsistence level. Food and other forms of aid had to be obtained from the United States. Its population, enlarged by refugees from Ethiopia, was on the edge of starvation. There was discontent in Khartoum, the capital city, over government austerity measures. Government officials rode around in high-priced limousines, while gas was rationed for ordinary citizens. There were conflicts between Christians and Moslems, and a civil war that was largely based on geographical and racial divisions threatened to pull the country apart.[11]

■ THE DEVELOPMENT OF NIGERIA ■

At the beginning of the twentieth century, Nigeria did not exist as a national entity, and it was notable in world commerce chiefly as a supplier of a few tropical products, such as palm oil and spices. During earlier centuries, its commercial history was very largely dominated by the slave trade. It became a formal British colony in 1860 and was recognized by other European powers as a British enclave at the Berlin Conference of 1885.

British colonial rule provided a mixed blessing for Nigeria. Its main direct contributions were building railroads and developing harbor facilities. Administrative measures were also used to encourage and regulate the production of cotton and other crops for export.[12] Trade and banking were run by companies chartered in England. Barclay's Bank ran the banking system and the Royal Niger Company was responsible for the development of crops for export. Rules, attitudes, and monopolistic practices by the British colonial administration, churches, and firms excluded Nigerians from any participation in government and commerce.

The economic and social orientation of the British colonial government in Nigeria changed dramatically after World War II. It moved from maintaining the existing colonial economy to a new approach that allowed more Nigerian participation in the economy. Priority was placed on the development of industry and trade that would be run by Nigerians. An increasing degree of local self-government was embodied in successive constitutions of 1951, 1954, and 1957; by then, Nigerian control over the government apparatus was substantial. A colonial-nurtured capitalism devel-

---

11. The government was overthrown by a military coup in May, 1985.

12. Gavin Williams, *Nigeria Economy and Society* (London: Rex Collings, 1976), pp. 18-19.

oped, particularly in the areas of trade and light industry. The British–Nigerian colonial relationship came to mean planned economic development, the spread of industrialization, and better social services for the Nigerian people. England systematically extended the rights of self-government, so when Nigeria achieved its independence in 1960, it had a bureaucracy that had some experience with government and a small, but expanding, business class. The British had also spent money on developing agriculture and transportation systems and on extending medical and educational services.[13]

THE NIGERIAN ECONOMY

In 1985 Nigeria had a per capita GNP of $760, which placed it in the upper one-third of the African countries. Its 1985 population of 91.2 million makes it the largest country in Africa, and its fertility rate of 6.3 is about average for the African countries.[14] The population-doubling time for Nigeria is projected as 22 years, compared to an average of 24 years for all of Africa taken together. Despite the fact that Nigeria is more industrialized than most of the African countries, more than two-thirds of the labor force is employed in agriculture. However, agriculture contributed only 26 percent of gross domestic production in 1983. Industry accounted for 34 percent of gross domestic product. In terms of value added by manufacture, Nigeria ranked third among the African countries in 1983, behind Egypt and South Africa, and far ahead of two Asian countries, Bangladesh and Pakistan, that are comparable in population size.[15] It qualifies as a country in the lower stage of economic development.

OIL

Oil, especially in a developing country, can be a decisive factor in economic development. It is an easily negotiable source of wealth for the producer, an efficient source of energy for the user, and a good base for indus-

---

13. It should be pointed out that the post-World War II England was far different from the England that was the dominant world power of the last century. Imperialism led to the development of the British empire. However, by the end of World War II, the empire was a thing of the past, and the colonies no longer served the purpose of providing markets and raw materials.

14. Mary M. Kent and Carl Haub, *1985 World Population Data Sheet* (Washington: Population Reference Bureau, Inc.). The fertility rate indicates the average number of children that would be born to each woman who lived during her childbearing years. A fertility rate of 2.1 to 2.5 indicates a replacement level.

15. The World Bank, *World Development Report 1985*, p. 179.

trialization because of the variety of products needed by petrochemical industries.

Nigeria is a major oil-producing country and a member of the OPEC oil cartel. It ranked seventh in world oil exports in 1984, and oil accounted for more than 80 percent of its export earnings. Apart from being the major source of foreign exchange, the Nigerian oil industry contributes significantly to government revenues in the form of royalties, rents, license fees, and a petroleum profits tax. In 1985 oil revenues accounted for 62 percent of total revenue in the national government budget. Nigerian oil production is based on concessions made to a number of world oil companies that pay royalties to the Nigerian government. There are also joint ventures involving the state-owned National Oil Corporation and international oil companies.

The worldwide oil glut of the early 1980s has had a disastrous effect on the Nigerian economy. Earnings from exports of Nigerian oil declined from a high of $26 billion in 1980 to $10 billion in 1985, and oil production declined from 2.1 million barrels a day in 1980 to 1.1 million barrels a day in 1985. Conversely, Nigerian imports increased over the same period, and the terms of trade, which is the ratio of export prices to import prices, became more unfavorable. Imports increased in price at the same time oil prices were falling. The result was that Nigeria had to finance the higher levels of imports by drawing down its foreign exchange reserves, which declined from $10 billion in 1980 to $1 billion by the end of 1984. To illustrate the importance of oil exports to the Nigerian economy, its GNP fell from $76 billion for 1980 to $65 billion in 1984. There was also a decline in per capita GNP of more than 10 percent for the same time period. The government had contracted foreign debt of around $22 billion by the end of 1984, the repayment of which was predicated on increased earnings from oil exports. In 1984 interest payments alone required the use of 40 percent of Nigeria's foreign exchange.[16]

THE ROLE OF THE GOVERNMENT

Nigeria is a federal republic consisting of 19 states. Although the states have a certain amount of autonomy, they receive most of their money from the federal government, which derives its revenue from taxes and oil exports. The most important taxes are a petroleum profits tax and excise taxes. A personal income tax is used, but the rate of avoidance is high.

16. Ibid., p. 202.

There are three ways in which a government can intervene in a mixed economy. First, intervention can occur through fiscal and monetary policies. Second, there can be a more direct intervention through economic planning where government policies are designed to affect resource allocation and business conduct and performance. Third, there can be government ownership and control of the means of production. All are used by the Nigerian government, which plays a dominant role in the economic development of the country. It is the largest single employer, and it is the principal exporter and importer. It is responsible for the development of the national economic plans and the setting of planning priorities. It grants subsidies and makes loans to various sectors of the economy and implements foreign trade policy.

FISCAL AND MONETARY POLICIES   The fiscal policy of the Nigerian government is effected in two ways: through the national budget, which amounted to $13 billion in 1984, and oil revenues, which amounted to $11 billion in the same year. The combined oil and tax revenues amounted to approximately one-third of the gross national product of Nigeria for 1984. Essentially, fiscal policy is used by the government to alter the level of aggregate demand either directly by changing the level of its own expenditures or indirectly by changing tax rates.

Fiscal policy is also used to stimulate economic development. Funds from the national budget are channeled into various development funds used to finance capital expenditures. Special tax breaks are used to stimulate the private sector of the economy. The government has also used deficit financing to increase the rate of capital formation. However, the use of deficit financing has proved to be at best a mixed blessing. The proceeds have been spent to finance projects that were often never completed and that have provided little or no value to the Nigerian economy. Deficit spending has also contributed to the rate of inflation.

The state-owned Central Bank of Nigeria is responsible for the implementation of monetary policy. It conducts monetary policy through the traditional techniques available to all central banks—rediscounting, control over legal reserve requirements or bank liquidity ratios, and selective credit controls. The commercial banks of Nigeria are both publicly and privately owned; the Nigerian government owns about 60 percent, and foreign or local banks the remainder. The majority of the merchant banks that provide wholesale banking and equity investments are owned by the government; there are also state-owned development banks. Through the Central Bank, the government designates preferred sectors for resource allocation. For example, in 1984 commercial banks were required to put 8 percent of their loans into the agricultural sector and 36 percent into manufacturing, and merchant banks were required to put 79 percent of all their loans into agriculture, mining, manufacturing, and housing.

Monetary policy is set forth once a year as a part of overall government budget policy. The Central Bank of Nigeria implements this policy in several ways. First, it may grant assistance to the government to fulfill economic development goals by making credit available to finance government deficits. It has not only made credit available for financing government deficits, but has promoted a capital market through which funds are made available to finance government debt. Second, through the Nigerian banking system it promotes policies that increase the availability of credit for economic development. Third, the bank has control over the use of foreign exchange. It places a limit on the total amount of foreign exchange each commercial and merchant bank has to allocate among its customers. It also regulates the use of these currencies by mandating a certain percentage to specific functions. For example, in 1984, 58 percent of foreign exchange was allocated for imports of industrial raw materials.

ECONOMIC PLANNING   Economic planning represents an effort to facilitate the process of economic and social development through the creation of national goals and priorities. Financing for projects that have planning priority comes from the federal budget and from credit provided by the banking system. Some projects are financed by various international lending institutions, including the World Bank.

Since it became independent in 1960, Nigeria has formulated several economic plans, the last of which was the Fourth National Development Plan. The purpose of the plan was to provide a general guideline for Nigeria's economic and social priorities. The basic goals of the Fourth Plan were to develop Nigeria's physical and social structure and agricultural and industrial bases, so that the country would become less vulnerable to the fluctuations of the world oil market. Some 8,000 development projects were listed in the Plan, with an estimated investment of $125 billion during its duration. Most of these projects were cancelled in 1984 when the military government that deposed the civilian government of President Shagari in the 1983 military coup imposed austerity measures on the Nigerian economy.

A key policy in Nigerian economic planning is import substitution. Manufactured goods constitute the main targets of Nigeria's import substitution policy. The policy has been implemented in three ways. First, Nigerian industries, including textiles, furniture, motor vehicles, glass products, and consumer appliances, are heavily protected by tariffs. Successive increases in tariffs have produced a sharp decline in the absolute level and in the rate of increase of imports of such goods. Second, these and other manufacturing industries have been favored by tax policies including accelerated depreciation and special relief from taxes for a period from three to five years depending upon the amount of local capital invested. Third, many businesses are exclusively reserved for Nigerians. This restricts the amount of foreign involvement in local activity.

Much of the growth in Nigerian manufacturing is a result of the planned policy of import substitution. However, the process of import substitution has not helped the foreign debt problem, because it has resulted in an increase in imports of raw materials.[17] To produce at home the goods previously imported, many of the basic raw materials that have not been available locally have had to be imported.

GOVERNMENT OWNERSHIP OF INDUSTRY   Nigeria has basically a mixed economic system, with government ownership in certain areas of economic activity. Public utilities and transportation systems are owned and operated by the government. There is a state-owned National Oil Corporation and the Nigerian government has joint ventures with American and British oil companies. Coal is produced by a government-run corporation. The banking system is for the most part owned and operated by the government, and foreign banks are required to have at least a 60 percent Nigerian government interest. Seaport facilities are owned by the government, as is the Nigerian National Shipping Lines, which has the carrying rights to at least 40 percent of the freight to and from Nigeria. Communications facilities, including television broadcasting, are owned by the government.[18] The state-owned Federal Radio Corporation is solely responsible for radio broadcasting to all parts of Nigeria. Sixty percent of the Daily Times Group, the largest publishing house in Nigeria, is owned by the government, which also operates its own daily newspaper.

PRIVATE ENTERPRISE

Economic activity in most sectors of the Nigerian economy is primarily the function of private enterprise. To some extent, British colonial rule facilitated the development of a local entrepreneurial class in Nigeria. The British financed the development of railroads and port facilities. They abol-

17. A. Olaluku, *Structure of the Nigerian Economy* (New York: St. Martin's Press Inc., 1979), pp. 201-220.

18. Each state government also has its own radio station, but is allowed to broadcast only within state boundaries and only in the local language. State governments also own and operate many forms of enterprises.

ished the trading monopolies of coastal tribal kingdoms, internal tolls, and the arbitrary interference of African tribal rulers with the free conduct of commerce.[19] The British pound was introduced as the common medium of exchange. The increase in world demand for export crops in the early years of the twentieth century encouraged British firms to advance credit for the production of cash crops. This credit in turn facilitated the sale of imported goods. The expansion of export production and the increase in the money supply in the form of produce advances increased local opportunities in retailing and in handicraft and food production for the domestic market. The initial expansion of British colonial rule encouraged competition in the distributive trades.

In order to develop new export crops, traders and farmers adapted existing social institutions to regulate land ownership or use, mobilize savings and credit facilities, and recruit labor to clear, weed, plant, and harvest crops. The successful creation of export production by Nigerian traders and planters contrasted with the failure of British government and foreign company plantations. Thus, in Nigeria, colonialism enabled Africans to develop agricultural production and generally stimulated the domestic production of other goods.

British ownership and operation were limited primarily to railroad investments, banking, and mineral resources. A dual economy developed, with the Nigerians controlling farm production, trading, and small business enterprises. Nevertheless, the British controlled the economy, and Nigerian private enterprise was not allowed to compete with British commercial interests. British investments in railways led them to prevent the development of any form of local transportation system that might provide competition.

The economic orientation of British colonial rule changed after World War II from maintaining the dual colonial economy to increasing the extent of Nigerian participation in all sectors.[20] This goal was to be accomplished through government financial support of private enterprise, which the Nigerians themselves would run, but the British would control. However, increasing nationalism sharply increased the Nigerian desire for more participation and control in the development of the economy. Control by Nigerians over private enterprises increased. This participation was limited primarily to the trade and services sectors of the economy. Very few Nigerians possessed the expertise or the capital to own and manage a mod-

19. Williams, *Economy and Society*, pp. 13-18.
20. Sayre P. Schatz, *Nigerian Capitalism* (Berkeley: University of California Press, 1977), pp. 4-7.

ern production enterprise. Publicly owned Nigerian corporations began a growing number of enterprises intended to be run as profitable business ventures. At the time of Nigerian independence in 1960, state capitalism existed side-by-side with private capitalism. Political abuses of the public corporations made them largely unsuccessful, and Nigeria relied increasingly on foreign-owned enterprises for the development of a modern economy.

POST-COLONIAL DEVELOPMENT The private sector of Nigerian economy increased in importance during the period following independence. Gross private fixed investment increased from less than half of the total fixed investment in 1960 to 65 percent by 1975.[21] Most of this increase took the form of foreign direct investment. The reliance on private investment in general, and foreign direct investment in particular, has brought many government approaches and measures to stimulate private investment. The government has encouraged foreign and private domestic investment by offering financial incentives to invest in those sectors that contribute most to economic development.

The oil boom of the 1970s also contributed to the development of both public and private enterprise. Possession of oil reserves gave the government sufficient leverage over foreign oil companies to insist on joint sharing of oil revenues. In 1977, a decree was passed by the government transferring certain economic activities from public to private Nigerian ownership. Also, certain activities, mainly in small-scale industry, services, and retail trade, were reserved exclusively for Nigerian ownership.

RESULTS OF PRIVATE ENTERPRISE Nigerian entrepreneurs have established a large variety of very small enterprises. Such undertakings are easy to start, even by men and women with little education, training, or business experience, and barriers to entry are negligible. The technical knowledge is simple and many have acquired it as workers or apprentices in other small firms or through experience with large firms or in government. Capital requirements are usually minimal, and individual entrepreneurs can often operate with virtually no capital of their own, relying instead on advances from their suppliers. Requirements for skilled labor are usually negligible, and there is an abundance of semiskilled and unskilled labor. What all of this means is that there is a very large number of small enterprises in Nigeria producing and distributing in local markets. However, it is difficult for any of these enterprises to acquire the capital and technological know-how to make the transition to large-scale operations.

21. Ibid., pp. 20-27.

■ PERFORMANCE ■
OF THE NIGERIAN ECONOMY

The performance of the Nigerian economy can be divided into two time periods—from 1960 to 1980 and from 1980 to 1985. During the period from 1960 to 1980 real per capita GNP increased at a rate of 3.3 percent a year, a rate that was well above average for all of the African countries.[22] There was a decline in the importance of agriculture relative to other sectors of the economy and an increase in the importance of manufacturing and trade. Agriculture accounted for 65 percent of Nigerian GNP in 1960; by 1980 it contributed around 25 percent. Conversely, manufacturing increased its share of GNP from 4.4 percent in 1960 to 9.0 percent in 1980.[23] However, the country's manufacturing activity, which consists essentially of light consumer goods, is highly concentrated in a few largely urban centers, such as Lagos, the nation's capital.[24] The mineral extraction sector of the economy increased from 1 percent of the GNP in 1960 to almost one-third by 1980. Virtually all of this increase was accounted for by the growth of oil production, which constitutes the main basis for the development of the Nigerian economy.

The Nigerian economy began to deteriorate during the later part of the 1970s and early 1980s. Real per capita GNP decreased at a rate of −0.7 percent for the period 1973–1982. Nominal GNP fell from $77 billion in 1980 to $65 billion in 1984. This decline can be attributed to one factor—the drop in the world price of oil from $40 a barrel in 1980 to $28 in 1984. The situation has worsened as oil prices have fallen further, to $15 a barrel in early 1986. The Nigerian economy, in spite of its modernization, is still largely undeveloped and is subject to the vagaries of the world market price of oil. The problems of Nigeria are similar to those of Mexico—a large foreign debt, a rapidly increasing population, political corruption, and inefficient agricultural production. Mexico has one important advantage over Nigeria in that it does have a more developed industrial base. It also has a closer proximity to a major world market, the United States.

FOREIGN DEBT

At the end of 1984, Nigeria's foreign debt was $22 billion, which represented one-third of its GNP and was twice as much as total export earnings

---

22. The World Bank, *World Bank Atlas 1985*, p. 8.

23. Central Bank of Nigeria, *Annual Report 1984*, p. 2.

24. There is supposed to be a new capital at Abaja, but it has not been completed.

for the year. In 1984, Nigeria spent 40 percent of its foreign exchange to pay the interest on the debt, and it had to reschedule payments of the principal. The debt was incurred on the assumption that oil revenues would continue to rise, thus facilitating its repayment. The loans were supposed to go to improve the infrastructure of the economy; unfortunately, much of the money was wasted on projects of little value or was siphoned off by politicians in the form of graft. The result of the debt problem was the imposition of austerity measures by the military government in 1984 and 1985. Government spending was cut by 30 percent and exchange controls were used to reduce imports. In 1984 the government allocated only $4.8 billion in foreign exchange to the commercial and merchant banks. These austerity measures occurred at a time when the annual rate of inflation was around 40 percent.

POPULATION GROWTH

The economic development of any country depends on the quality and quantity of its human and capital resources. Rapid population growth in Nigeria has put a strain on agricultural resources. There have been reports of starvation in parts of the country. Population growth has caused deforestation, which has contributed to water pollution, and urbanization, which has contributed to air pollution, poverty, higher infant mortality, and social and political unrest. Rapid population growth has reduced the potential for saving and capital formation because production must go for consumption.

The population of Nigeria is growing rapidly due to a high fertility rate and a declining mortality rate.[25] The size and composition of the population is affected by several factors. First, given the high birth rate and declining mortality rate, it is young, with 48 percent of the population 15 years of age or younger. A young population tends to have an adverse effect on the size and productivity of the labor force. Also, population growth will increase as the female children reach childbearing age. Second, there is an enormous ethnic diversity. There are more than 250 ethnic groups with different languages and customs. Active tribal rivalries compound the problems of government. Third, the population is unequally distributed geographically. The areas of greatest population density are either the cities, which do not have an adequate infrastructure, or areas that are remote from transportation facilities. Fourth, more than half of

---

25. The population of Nigeria increased by three million from 1982 to 1983.

the population is illiterate. Only 16 percent of the relevant age group is enrolled in secondary schools and only 3 percent of the college age group is enrolled in college.

CORRUPTION

Corruption, a fact of life in Nigeria, assumes many forms. There is the standard low-level bribe, called "dash" or "chai," which is payment rendered for services performed or anticipated. It may take the form of a package of razor blades, a case of Scotch, or a digital watch. Higher level bribes include payment of money or an expensive gift such as a car. State-owned corporations are often run by political hacks rather than trained civil servants and management experts. Public projects are often not completed because politicians and contractors have appropriated the funds.[26] The tax system of the country is so inefficient that much of the revenue potential is not realized because tax evasion is widespread and tax officials are often corrupt. Conspicuous consumption by public officials, which takes the form of expensive foreign automobiles or villas in exclusive residential areas, creates resentment on the part of the impoverished and is responsible for the periodic military takeovers of the government.

Corruption carries with it many costs. There are wasteful expenditures on projects that do not get built, or, if built, serve no particular purpose. Economic development is retarded because money is wasted on projects that have little pay-off. Bribery is an impediment to entrepreneurship because it diverts energy from the pursuit of excellence in economic performance into political performance and cultivation of the right contacts. Citizens will have little incentive to work or save when they see the pay-off to corruption. Educated young people will leave at their first opportunity. When government projects are so mishandled that it is necessary to terminate them, then all or virtually all of the costs of the equipment and structures are expenses of corruption. Even attempts to avoid political corruption may affect the composition of expenditures by causing the government to avoid worthwhile projects that are prone to political abuse.

POLITICAL INSTABILITY

Nigeria has been ruled by military governments for most of the time since it gained its formal independence from England in 1960. A relatively

---

26. Olaluku, *Structure*, pp. 166-167.

stable civilian government ruled Nigeria from 1960 to 1966, when it was overthrown by a military coup. A second military coup later in the same year led to an attempted secession by the eastern part of the country under the name of Biafra, and resulted in two and a half years of civil war between 1967 and 1970. The civil war also split the population along tribal lines, with the Ibo tride seceding from the rest of Nigeria. The civil war cost at least one million lives and huge amounts of badly needed resources before Biafra was brought back under Nigerian control.

Another military coup, in 1975, overthrew the previous military government of General Yakubu Gowan. Nigeria was then organized into 19 states, largely on the basis of tribal lines. After 13 years of military rule, free elections were held in 1979 and Alhaji Shagari was elected president. He was reelected in 1983, but was deposed by another military coup at the end of the year. The military is still in power.

Political instability in Nigeria has been caused by a number of factors, not the least of which is very limited experience with democracy. Nigeria is an amalgam of 250 tribal and religious groups, each of which wants to preserve some degree of autonomy.[27] When free elections are held, political support is usually based on regional and tribal identity. It is difficult to reconcile the differences of competing groups. Corruption is a second factor that contributes to political instability. Fueled by money from the oil boom, corruption became more blatant in the late 1970s and early 1980s and contributed to the overthrow of the Shagari government. Unemployment and high inflation also led to political instability in an impoverished nation. The decline of world oil prices and a rising foreign debt created a period of readjustment in the middle 1980s. Prices and unemployment increased at the same time oil revenues decreased. The decline in oil revenues made it more difficult to import both consumer and industrial goods, and shortages of each caused prices of some goods to rise as much as 400 percent in 1984.

AGRICULTURE

Despite Nigeria's oil wealth and increasing industrial base, agriculture is still the mainstay of the economy, with more than half of the labor force employed in this sector. There is considerable underutilization of labor,

---

27. Reuters, the British news agency, announced that 100 Nigerians were killed in a conflict between Christians and Moslems in April, 1985.

given the seasonal nature of agricultural activity. The performance of the agricultural sector has been poor, in part because it has been neglected as emphasis was placed on the development of industry. The land tenure system also inhibits the development of agriculture. Control over land is vested in clans, villages, and communities. Farmers work the land as tenants and pay a portion of what they produce to the village or clan. There is little incentive to invest in land and equipment.

Agricultural output actually declined during most of the 1970s. The decline occurred despite an increase in the population and cultivation of large tracts of land that were in the area previously affected by the civil war. A drought in the early 1980s also had an adverse effect on agricultural production, with famine in several regions of the country.[28] The drought also affected the export of cocoa, Nigeria's leading agricultural export.

POVERTY

It must be remembered that Nigeria is an underdeveloped country. Its per capita GNP of $760 in 1985, while about average for Africa, is low when compared to the incomes of the developed countries. Moreover, the per capita GNP has shown a decline of $100 for the period 1983–1985, as income from oil exports has declined. Poverty and unemployment have been exacerbated by the decline in oil earnings and by drought, which has affected food production in part of the country. What Nigeria seems to have achieved, particularly during the period when world oil prices were high, was a rapid rate of economic growth accompanied by little internal economic development. There is a growing pattern of unequal income and wealth distribution between rich and poor, between urban and rural areas, and between the employed and unemployed.[29] The great majority of agricultural workers receive an income that is less than one-eighth of the national average, which has engendered unrest in rural areas. The use of government power by politicians for self-enrichment contrasts with widespread poverty and encourages social unrest.

---

28. In April, 1985, the government expelled 650,000 refugees who had come from Chad, Gabon, and other neighboring countries, saying that it barely had enough food to feed its own population.

29. William Zartman, *The Political Economy of Nigeria* (New York: Praeger Publishers, 1983).

S U M M A R Y

Nigeria is the largest country in Africa in terms of population and is also one of its wealthier countries. It was a British possession from 1868 until 1960, when it became an independent country. The economy can be considered underdeveloped, with a majority of Nigerians still employed in agriculture and an industrial base concentrated in a few relatively large urban centers. Manufacturing is a rather small source of employment, accounting for around 10 percent of total employment in the country. The oil sector has been the main source of the rapid growth of the country's economy over the last 10 to 15 years. Revenues from oil exports have been used to finance the economic development of the country. However, dependence on oil exports has put Nigeria into a precarious economic position. As the world price for oil has declined, revenue from oil exports and per capita GNP have also declined. Nigeria is in the same position as Mexico in that it has a large foreign debt and declining earnings from oil exports. However, Nigeria is less developed than Mexico and lacks the internal industrial base that Mexico has developed over time.

Nigeria has a mixed economy, with the private sector providing the bulk of capital formation. Economic activity in the directly productive sectors of the economy is primarily through private enterprise. Government investment and ownership is concentrated mainly on the infrastructure of the economy. Nevertheless, the role of government in the economy is important and extensive. It provides much of the savings in the economy, which is channeled into various sectors through state-owned lending institutions. Economic planning is also used by the government to establish priorities in resource allocation. The plans have generally stressed the development of industry, while neglecting agriculture. They have been interrupted by periodic military coups, the latest of which occurred in December, 1983. The role of the national government in the Nigerian economy is made very complex by the regional factionalism of the country, which is based on tribal and religious loyalties. Corruption is also an inhibiting factor in the development of the economy.

R E V I E W   Q U E S T I O N S

1. What was the impact of British colonialism on the development of the Nigerian economy?

2. What role does private enterprise play in Nigeria?
3. Discuss the influence of oil on the Nigerian economy.
4. The economic and social problems of Nigeria are common to the great majority of African countries. Discuss.
5. What are some of the problems of economic and social development in Nigeria?
6. Why has democracy failed to take hold in Nigeria and other African countries?
7. Discuss the impact of Nigeria's foreign debt on its economy.
8. Compare the Nigerian economy to the economies of Mexico and China.

■ ——————— R E C O M M E N D E D   R E A D I N G S ——————— ■

Balabkins, Nicholas. *Indigenization & Economic Development: The Nigerian Experience*. Greenwich, Conn.: JAI Press Inc., 1982.

Belasco, Bernard. *The Entrepreneur as Cultural Hero: Preadaptations in Nigerian Economic Development*. Brooklyn, N.Y.: J.F. Bergin Publishers, 1980.

Kirk-Green, A.H.M. *Nigeria Since 1970: A Political & Economic Outline*. London: Hodder & Stoughton, 1982.

Nafziger, E. Wayne. *The Economics of Political Instability: The Nigerian-Biafran War*. Boulder, Colo.: Westview Press Inc., 1983.

Okwudibu, Nnoli, ed. *Path to Nigerian Development*. Westport, Conn.: L. Hall, 1981.

Schatz, Sayre P. *Nigerian Capitalism*. Berkeley: University of California Press, 1977.

Stevens, Christopher. *Nigeria, Economic Prospects to 1985: After the Oil Glut*. London: Economist Intelligence Unit, 1983.

Zartman, William. *The Political Economy of Nigeria*. New York: Praeger Publishers, 1983.

PART 6

CONCLUSION
AND
EVALUATION

20
THE ECONOMIC SYSTEMS:
EVALUATION OF
GOAL FULFILLMENT

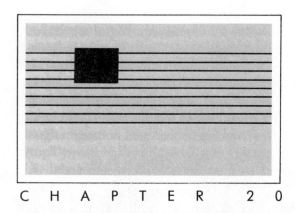

THE ECONOMIC SYSTEMS: EVALUATION OF GOAL FULFILLMENT

Full employment, price stability, and economic growth are basic goals of any economic system. To these goals, a fourth goal, an equitable distribution of income, may be added. The results of production must be shared among members of society in such a way that they feel that the system is just and equitable. However, there are also a number of noneconomic measures that are widely regarded as indicators of well-being: education, health and longevity, individual freedoms, environmental quality, and others. These may be measured under what can be called a quality-of-life index. In advanced industrial societies, as output and real incomes rise, basic wants are satisfied, and interest can be directed to the quality as opposed to the quantity of life. One quality-of-life indicator is the extent of water and air pollution and the capacity or willingness of a country to invest significantly in clean-up programs.

Governments in Western countries and Japan play a very important role in attaining economic goals. This role has taken two basic forms that have been mentioned repeatedly. First, changes in taxation and government spending have influenced output, prices, and employment. Moreover, progressive income taxation and transfer payments have been used in most countries to create a more equitable distribution of income. Second governments have also come to serve as a powerful force in the determination of productive capacity. Certain key industries are publicly owned, and there is also direct participation in the formation of capital. Government expenditures have also contributed to the health, education, and training of the labor force, and hence to productive capacity.

The centrally planned economies of the Soviet Union, China, and Eastern Europe are in a state of flux. The Soviet Union has had four leaders since 1980. The current leader, Mikhail Gorbachev, has made improving the efficiency of the Soviet economy a major goal. China is undertaking an ambitious experiment with its economy by introducing various elements of a free market system. Economic growth is a problem high on the agenda of Eastern European leaders for the 1980s. It necessitates a choice of economic policies that will not only affect the day-to-day functioning of their economies, but longer term prospects as well.

■ A COMPARISON ■
OF ECONOMIC SYSTEMS

In the remainder of this chapter, various measures will be used to compare the operating results of some of the major market and centrally planned economies. (For this analysis we will include the mixed economies in the market category.) Comparisons can be made of income distribution, consumption, employment, and economic growth. Economic systems can be judged on the basis of how well they channel the energies of producers and meet the needs of consumers. However, before comparisons are made, it is necessary to provide a brief outline of the basic differences between the market and centrally planned economic systems. There are variations in the basic institutions depending on the country, so it cannot be said that these descriptions are 100 percent applicable in all situations. Each economic system has certain strengths and weaknesses. Centrally planned economies have several advantages over market economies. They can enforce a high degree of mobilization of resources, they can ensure use of those resources, and they can direct the allocation of the resources toward the fulfillment of selected quantitative goals. Given these advantages, there is one thing they don't do well—namely, they cannot ensure economic efficiency in the operation of their system.

While most economic principles, such as scarcity and diminishing marginal productivity, that apply to a capitalist political system are valid under a socialist system as well, the economic institutions of capitalism either do not exist or are not allowed to operate as freely under socialism. For example, a capitalist system can be defined in terms of private property, the profit motive, the market mechanism, and competition, while another system, such as socialism, can be defined in terms of the modifications it would make in some or all of these institutions. Table 20-1 compares the basic economic institutions of capitalism and socialism. Probably the most significant difference between the two systems is that capitalism relies on the market mechanism to allocate resources, while socialism relies on central economic planning to do the same.

Figure 20-1 compares the operation of a centrally planned economy with that of a market economy. Each economy is divided into producers and consumers. In a centrally planned economy, production and distribution decisions are made by a central planning agency; in a market economy, production and distribution decisions are made by consumers and producers operating in the market. In a centrally planned economy, prices are set by the central planning agency; in a market economy, prices serve an allocative function and affect the consumption, production, and distribution of goods. Prices are determined by the forces of demand and supply. The arrows in the diagram indicate the flow of goods and services from producers to consumers, from consumers to producers, and from producers to producers. In a planned economy, the flow is through the planning agency; in a market economy, the flow is through the market.

TABLE 20-1   CAPITALISM AND SOCIALISM COMPARED

Capitalism
1. Means of production are privately owned.
2. Economic motivation is personal gain—Adam Smith's "invisible hand."
3. Competition promotes efficiency and innovation.
4. Freedom of enterprise, the right to operate a business or to choose an occupation, exists.
5. Profit is used as the test of whether anything should or should not be produced.
6. The price mechanism is the basic resource allocator.

Socialism
1. Means of production are owned by the state.
2. Motivation is based on the creation of the "socialist" person.
3. Cooperation is stressed instead of competition.
4. Power is concentrated in the hands of the Communist Party.
5. Economic planning, rather than the market mechanism, allocates resources.

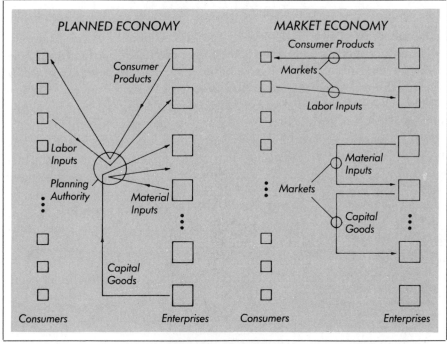

FIGURE 20-1 COMPARISON OF A PLANNED AND A MARKET ECONOMY

Source: Gregory C. Chow, *The Chinese Economy* (New York: Harper & Row, Publishers, 1985), p. 43. Reprinted by permission of Harper & Row, Publishers, Inc.

It has been emphasized that economic systems are not all alike. Just as there are institutional variations in the market economies, there are also variations in the centrally planned economies. Sweeping changes have been made in the Chinese economy, where Deng Xiaoping has permitted the introduction of private enterprise in many areas of economic activity. The commune system of agriculture has been abolished and replaced by a contract system, where the state leases plots of land to individual farmers. A set amount of the farm product is delivered to the state at a fixed price, but the remainder can be sold in the free market. Hungary has replaced at least part of a Soviet-style centralized economy with profit-oriented agricultural cooperatives and small-scale private enterprises in many areas of economic activity. Yugoslavia has developed its own version of decentralized planning, the most important characteristic of which is the workers' council, which selects factory managers and sets such basic policies as wages and production targets.

■ ECONOMIC GROWTH ■

Economic growth can be defined as the rate of increase in an economy's real output or income over time. The prime rationale for economic growth is that a constantly rising real gross national product is necessary to maintain a high level of employment and to improve living standards. This is especially true as long as a country's population continues to grow. If an economy does not grow, there is no way in which unemployment can be reduced, save for government action, and new job seekers absorbed into the labor force. Further, a country will not be able to solve its social problems and to provide the schools, medical care, hospitals, and other things it needs. A low rate of economic growth also can create social unrest among those groups that are caught in the syndrome of rising expectations.

Table 20-2 compares real per capita growth in GNP for selected market and centrally planned economies for different time periods. As the table indicates, the Japanese economy has performed the best of all economies. The performance of the U.S. economy has been somewhat uneven. In the late 1970s, the real growth rate of the Soviet Union declined, and this decline has continued into the 1980s. The economic growth of both types of economies during the 1980s has been mediocre. With the exception of Japan, no country has performed particularly well.

PERFORMANCE OF THE MARKET ECONOMIES IN THE 1980s

During the 1980s an economic malaise has gripped capitalist and socialist countries alike. This malaise represents a continuation of problems that began during the 1970s. For the economy of the United States, the long trend of good performances since the end of World War II ended in the 1970s when three major problems converged: the problem of inflation, the energy problem, and the consequences of a government increasingly incapable of controlling its own budget. The first two problems have largely disappeared, but the last one remains. A new problem is the decline in the competitive position of the United States in the world economy, which can be attributed in part to the strength of the U.S. dollar in comparison to other currencies and the status of the United States as the world's leading debtor nation.

High interest rates and the doubling of oil prices in the late 1970s had an adverse impact on the Western European economies. The rapid rise in oil prices worsened the rate of inflation in all countries. Increases in the price of oil marked an immediate, sharp check to the growth of consumption and buying power. Government policies in Western Europe had been

TABLE 20-2 REAL PER CAPITA GROWTH IN GNP

			Average Annual Rate of Growth			
	1980	1981	1982	1983	1984	1985
Market Economies						
United States	−1.5%	1.9%	−2.5%	3.5%	6.5%	2.3%
Canada	−0.2	4.0	−4.3	2.8	5.4	4.0
Japan	4.1	4.2	3.1	3.3	5.8	5.0
France	0.6	0.5	1.8	0.7	1.3	1.0
Italy	3.7	0.2	−0.5	−0.4	2.6	2.2
United Kingdom	−2.3	−1.4	1.5	3.4	1.8	3.2
West Germany	1.5	0.2	−0.6	1.2	2.6	2.2
Centrally Planned Economies						
U.S.S.R.	0.9	1.9	2.5	3.6	2.0	3.0
Czechoslovakia	1.8	−0.6	1.5	0.7	2.0	na
East Germany	2.1	2.1	−0.2	1.6	3.3	na
Hungary	0.9	−0.7	3.8	−1.1	1.5	na
Poland	−3.3	−6.3	−1.8	3.7	2.5	1.8
Romania	−2.2	−0.4	2.1	−0.1	4.0	na

Source: Central Intelligence Agency, *Handbook of Economic Statistics, 1985,* p. 40; *Economic Report of the President, 1986* (Washington: USGPO, 1986), p. 378.

directed toward pushing the pace of economic growth and the redistribution of income. These policies set in motion forces that led to the acceleration of inflation. Monetary policy was then used to reduce the rate of inflation. Interest rates increased, which constricted buying and investment expansion, putting a break on economic expansion. Slower economic growth in the 1980s has created economic and social problems; in the last two decades growth has been tied to various social objectives, particularly full employment and increased real income.

PERFORMANCE OF THE CENTRALLY PLANNED ECONOMIES IN THE 1980s

The Soviet Union and Eastern Europe experienced a transition from rapid economic growth to slow economic growth. One factor contributing to the decline in growth rates was an increase in OPEC oil prices during the 1970s, which affected market and centrally planned economies alike. The consequences to the market economies were increased inflation, restrictive monetary policies, and higher interest rates. This in turn affected the socialist countries because they had to pay higher interest rates on their external debt, but could not increase their exports to earn more convertible currency.[1] Abundant supplies of cheap energy from the Soviet Union are also a thing of the past. Agriculture continues to be a problem as the centrally planned economies continue to pay a price for neglecting it in favor of industrial development. There has been neglect of essential infrastructure investments—especially the development and maintenance of rail transport and other distribution networks.

The 1980s have presented a difficult set of problems for the Soviet Union and the Eastern European countries. In the past, there has been an economic–political tradeoff, with increased consumer well-being a substitute for political support of the government as represented by the Communist Party. Declining economic performance in the Soviet Union and Eastern Europe makes it unlikely that consumers can continue to be satisfied to the extent that they were previously. It remains to be seen whether or not economic reforms will be introduced on a broad scale in an attempt to improve economic performance. Actual reform efforts, with the exception of those introduced in Hungary, have been rather tentative, focusing primarily on the decentralization of administrative authority. Moreover, reforms

---

1. Daniel Bond and Lawrence B. Klein, "Impact of Changes in the Global Environment on the Soviet and Eastern European Economies," *East European Economies: Slow Growth in the 1980's*, Vol. 1, U.S. Congress, Joint Economic Committee, 99th Cong., 1st Sess. pp. 7-21.

and reorganization in planning, management, and economic incentives threaten various groups that are interested in maintaining the status quo.

■ UNEMPLOYMENT ■

In their critique of capitalism, communist leaders regard unemployment, which plagues market economies from time to time, as one of the most important proofs of the inefficiency of the capitalist system. Marx himself predicated the collapse of capitalism on mass unemployment, which would occur when society was split into two sharply demarcated classes: the bourgeoisie and the proletariat. The buying power of the latter would decline because they would earn subsistence wages as employers tried to wring as much surplus value out of them as possible. A social upheaval would eventually occur; and the proletariat, because there are more of them, would wrest all instruments of production from the bourgeoisie and centralize them into the hands of the state. Eventually the state was supposed to wither away, and a classless society, the proletariat, would be created. Rather obviously that has not happened.

Nevertheless, there is validity in the communist critique of capitalist unemployment, as Table 20-3 can verify. It compares unemployment rates for the major market economies for selected periods. As the table indicates, with the exception of Japan and to a lesser extent Italy, unemployment rates in the other countries have been high during the 1980s. In the United Kingdom, the rate of unemployment has averaged around 11 percent for the period. However, in the United States there has been an expansion in the number of jobs available to workers. Over the period 1975 to 1985, the number of workers employed in the U.S. labor force increased by 20 million.[2] There has been no corresponding increase in employment in the other countries.

Political leaders in the socialist countries have placed a high priority on maintaining full employment, even at the expense of other economic considerations.[3] Unlike enterprises in a market economic system, which strive for profit maximization and where problems of unemployment are left to the free play of market forces, enterprises in a centrally planned economic system are supposed to maximize output subject to the constraints of available resources. Socialist enterprises may expand employment beyond the

2. *Economic Report of the President, 1985* (Washington: USGPO, 1985), p. 268.

3. Yugoslavia's brand of socialism does not guarantee full employment. Consequently, unemployment has averaged around 15 percent of the labor force.

TABLE 20-3 UNEMPLOYMENT RATES FOR INDUSTRIALIZED MARKET ECONOMIES

	1970	1975	1980	1981	1982	1983	1984	1985[1]
United States	4.9%	8.5%	7.1%	7.6%	9.7%	9.6%	7.5%	7.2%
Canada	5.7	6.9	7.5	7.5	11.0	11.9	11.3	10.5
France	2.5	4.2	6.2	7.6	8.6	8.5	9.6	8.2
Italy	2.8	3.0	3.8	4.2	4.6	5.0	5.2	5.1
Japan	1.2	1.9	2.0	2.2	2.4	2.7	2.8	2.5
United Kingdom	3.0	4.5	6.8	10.4	11.8	12.8	13.0	13.5
West Germany	0.5	3.4	2.9	4.1	5.9	7.5	7.8	7.9

[1]Estimates.

Source: Economic Report of the President, 1986 (Washington: USGPO, 1986), p. 377.

point where profit-maximizing capitalist enterprises have to stop, as long as the newly hired workers contribute to the output of the enterprises. Their performance is evaluated with the help of certain plan indicators, and enough labor enables them to increase output performance from year to year without depending on productivity increases. The acceptance of the principle of fulfillment and overfulfillment of plan targets stimulates socialist enterprises to maximize output and employment, particularly since their wages and bonus funds are linked to plan fulfillment.

However, full employment can also be associated with a number of negative phenomena.[4] One phenomenon is overemployment, which can be defined as employment over and above the number of workers actually needed to meet production targets at a given level of technology.[5] These workers can be considered underemployed, which is an inefficient use of labor resources. Another negative phenomenon is that of labor hoarding, which means that enterprises store labor for use in periods of peak activities or to gain an advantage over other enterprises. When enterprises produce to satisfy plan targets, there will be slack periods, but as the target date approaches, there will be a speed-up of activity to meet the goals. Thus, there is a waste of working time that results from deficiencies in the planning and organization of the production process. A third negative phenomenon is low labor discipline, which is reflected in absenteeism, extended work breaks, and theft by employees. To some extent, this low discipline can be attributed to the knowledge that jobs can be taken for granted.

■ INFLATION ■

Inflation is also an important economic problem that has confronted Western governments and many developing countries. If carried too far, it can bring down governments and lead to revolutions. In Germany after World War I, inflation destroyed the savings of the middle class and sowed the seeds of social discontent that led to the rise of Adolf Hitler and the eventual destruction of democratic institutions as represented by the Weimar Republic. On a more current note, inflation, coupled with low economic growth in the 1970s, were factors that contributed to the defeat of Jimmy Carter by Ronald Reagan in the 1980 presidential election. The

---

4. Jan Adam, "Employment Policies in Selected European Countries: Poland, Czechoslovakia, and Hungary," *East European Economies: Slow Growth in the 1980's*, pp. 232-233.

5. This is also called disguised unemployment.

reduction of inflation was a major rationale for the "supply-side" economics introduced by the Reagan administration.

There is no question that inflation can have deleterious social and economic consequences for any country. In periods of general inflation, price signals are often distorted with respect to investment and capital formation. It becomes difficult to compare the profitability of a project initiated last month with a project initiated this month and to separate transitory changes in individual prices from fundamental changes. Inflation tends to bias decisions toward short-run payoffs and consumption. Contractual income from some long-term investments is eroded by long-continuing inflation, while other investments yield great rewards because they happen to benefit from inflation. For all of these reasons, inflation often causes allocative inefficiencies that in the aggregate reduce economic growth and increase economic hardships for many people.

Table 20-4 presents the rate of inflation as measured by changes in consumer prices for seven major market economies for selected periods. It should be emphasized that the inflation rate for these countries is small in comparison to such countries as Argentina, Israel, and Mexico. In Argentina, for example, the average annual rate of inflation for the period 1973–1983 was 168 percent, compared to 7.5 percent for the United States.[6] The rate of inflation in Israel for the same time period was 73 percent, compared to a rate of 4.3 percent for Japan. In the early 1980s, the rate of inflation for some of the less developed and developing countries ran at an annual rate of 100 percent or higher, while the rate of inflation for the developed market economies showed a marked decline.

According to some theorists, the possibility of inflation in a centrally planned economy is remote.[7] After all, the state controls the allocation of resources through the economic plan, which is supposed to achieve a balance between production and spending, so that price stability can be assured. The state also has control over the prices of the factors of production. Wages are fixed by the state in accordance with the national wage fund as set in the economic plan. Increases in wages are also determined by the state. The prices of many consumer goods are set by the state. Consumption can be restricted by manipulating the wage fund and social consumption on one hand and retail prices on the other. Any excess demand can be bottled up by rationing cars and other consumer goods that would require long waiting lists.

6. World Bank, *World Development Report 1985*, pp. 174-175.

7. J. Wilczynski, *The Economics of Socialism* (London: George Allen & Unwin, Ltd., 1977), p. 149.

TABLE 20-4 CONSUMER PRICES FOR INDUSTRIALIZED MARKET ECONOMIES
(average annual rate of growth)

	1976–1979	1980	1981	1982	1983	1984	1985
United States	7.8%	13.5%	10.4%	6.1%	3.2%	4.3%	4.2%
Canada	8.4	10.2	12.5	10.8	8.8	4.3	4.5
Japan	6.2	8.0	4.9	2.6	1.8	2.3	2.6
France	9.7	13.5	13.3	12.0	9.5	7.7	7.2
Italy	15.2	21.2	19.3	16.4	14.9	10.6	10.1
United Kingdom	13.5	18.0	11.9	8.6	4.6	5.0	5.8
West Germany	3.7	5.5	6.0	5.3	3.6	2.4	2.5

Sources: CIA, *Handbook of Economic Statistics 1985*, p. 42; *Monthly Report of the Deutsches Bundesbank* (October 1985), p. 72; Bank of England, *Quarterly Bulletin* (December 1985), p. 258.

In practice, inflation does exist in planned economies, though its extent or degree varies from country to country. One indication of the extent of inflation can be found in Yugoslavia, which has its own brand of market socialism. The average annual rate of inflation in Yugoslavia during the period 1973–1983 was 22.8 percent.[8] Chinese economic reforms, which have placed more reliance on free markets and the elimination of many state-controlled prices, allowed the rate of inflation to increase to an estimated 23 percent in 1985.[9] Long lines in front of butcher shops and bakeries in Poland and under-the-table bartering of goods and services indicate suppressed inflation.

Inflation, hidden or otherwise, also exists in the Soviet Union and other Eastern European countries. Hidden inflation occurs when the quality of inputs used to produce certain goods is reduced without corresponding downward adjustments in price, e.g., the substitution of inferior raw materials of domestic origin for imported raw materials. There can be several causes of inflation.[10] Artificially low prices for products can cause their wasteful use. Increased use of monetary incentives to increase output leads to increased spending power for consumers. The tendency of enterprises to hoard labor and other resources causes shortages that can also contribute to inflationary pressures.

Table 20-5 presents the average annual rate of growth in retail prices for the Soviet Union and the Eastern European countries for the period 1971–1983. These rates may actually be understated for the following reasons.[11]

1. Official price indices may not be representative of the actual basket of goods consumed by households.

2. The nature of goods represented in the official price index may change in the direction of reducing quality in order to maintain fixed price.

3. No account is taken of price developments in the so-called second economy (private markets), though their relative importance has markedly risen in some countries, notably Hungary and Poland.

---

8. World Bank, *World Development Report 1985*, p. 175.

9. *Time*, January 6, 1986, p. 35.

10. Wilczynski, *Economics of Socialism*, p. 151.

11. Jan Vanous, "Macroeconomic Ajustment in Eastern Europe in Response to Western Credit Squeeze and Deteriorating Terms of Trade with the Soviet Union," *East European Economies: Slow Growth in the 1980's*, p. 47.

TABLE 20-5   AVERAGE ANNUAL GROWTH IN RETAIL PRICES, 1971–1983

	1971–75	1976–80	1981	1982	1983
All items[1]					
Bulgaria	0.2%	4.0%	0.5%	0.2%	na
Czechoslovakia	0.1	2.1	0.8	5.7	0.9%
East Germany	−0.3	0.1	0.2	0	0
Hungary	3.0	7.1	5.0	6.6	7.2
Poland	2.5	6.8	21.2	101.0	25.0
Romania	0.5	1.4	2.0	16.0	5.7
Soviet Union	−0.1	0.7	1.4	3.4	na
Food[2]					
Bulgaria	0.6	6.2	0.3	0.2	na
Czechoslovakia	−0.1	1.2	0	10.6	0.3
East Germany	0.2	0	0	0	0
Hungary	2.2	7.3	3.1	8.2	5.6
Poland	2.9	7.5	30.3	125.0	26.0
Romania	1.1	1.0	1.7	na	na
Soviet Union	0.3	0.4	1.9	3.8	na

[1] In most cases including services.
[2] In most cases including prepared foods in restaurants and enterprise cafeterias. Alcohol is also included.

Source: Jan Vanous, "Macroeconomic Adjustment in Eastern Europe in Response to Western Credit Squeeze and Deteriorating Terms of Trade with the Soviet Union," *East European Economies: Slow Growth in the 1980's,* Vol. 1, U.S. Congress, Joint Economic Committee, 99th Cong., 1st sess., pp. 48-49.

■ INCOME DISTRIBUTION ■

Decisions about equity in the distribution of income are a fundamental starting point for comparing economic systems. Under market systems, individual preferences expressed through spending determine market demand for goods and services, but these individual preferences are weighted by incomes. The distribution of ownership of productive resources is very unequal. A large part of the population owns only its labor power. An individual with no income or wealth has needs and desires, but he or she has no economic resources with which to satisfy them. This means that individual preferences will not be properly reflected by the market. This leads to a misdirection of production because inequality in the distribution of income sharply reduces the accuracy with which the prices of various goods on the market measure the relative intensities of human desires for them.

All Western governments are now involved in altering the distribution of income either directly or indirectly. The idea no longer holds sway that incomes can be determined by impersonal market forces out of human control. As has been pointed out repeatedly throughout the book, Western governments have altered the distribution of income through the use of taxes and government expenditures. When government collects taxes it lowers the taxpayer's income, but when the money is spent it raises someone's income. Since government does not spend its money on the same goods and services that would be purchased by private individuals, a transfer of purchasing power from individuals to government yields a different set of demands, and therefore, a different distribution of incomes, from that a truly free market would provide.

A planned economy allegedly would be superior to a market economy when it comes to income distribution because the incomes of consumers would be determined so as to maximize the total welfare of the whole population.[12] Differences in incomes based on social barriers between classes would disappear in the relatively homogeneous socialist society. Basing the distribution of income on the assumption that all individuals have the same marginal utility of income, a socialist society would strike the right value in estimating the relative needs of different persons, while the distribution of income in a capitalist society introduces a class bias in favor of the rich. Moreover, income distribution in a planned economy would not be affected by the business cycle because output would be planned so cycles would not occur. Decisions to produce would not be guided by the

---

12. Oskar Lange and Fred M. Taylor, *On the Economic Theory of Socialism* (New York: McGraw-Hill Book Company, 1964), pp. 100-103.

desire to make a profit on each separate investment, but by considerations of making the best of all of the productive resources available in the whole economic system.[13]

Therefore, it can be assumed that incomes are more evenly distributed in the socialist countries than in the capitalist countries. The Marxist goal that eventually all of society's goods should be distributed on the basis of human need would be reflected in the income distribution. Socialist economic policy includes a guarantee of a minimum standard of living to everyone. Basic needs are subsidized, and these subsidies can be significant. In Poland, for example, food subsidies amounted to one-fourth of total government expenditures in 1982 and comprised 75 percent of food value at the retail level.[14] Housing and transportation are also subsidized, and the wage structure of the socialist countries is compressed to narrow income differentials between occupational groups.

Nevertheless, real income inequality does exist in the socialist countries, and some people do very well. The nomenklatura system insures that the Communist Party elite enjoy many benefits not available to the masses. Professional workers and persons who possess special skills, such as ballerinas, opera stars, athletes, and movie stars, also do quite well.[15] The distribution of income in some market economies is comparable to some planned economies. For example, income distribution statistics published by the World Bank indicate that income distribution in Belgium, the Netherlands, and Finland is not far different than in Hungary.[16] The highest 10 percent of households receive 20.5 percent of household incomes in Hungary compared to 21.5 percent in Belgium, 21.5 percent in the Netherlands, and 21.7 percent in Finland.[17] Among the industrialized market economies, the United States has the most unequal distribution of income and Japan the most equal. One study indicates that Japan has 50 percent less inequality than the United States when the earning gaps between the top and bottom 10 percent of the population are compared.[18]

---

13. Ibid., p. 109.

14. Elizabeth M. Clayton, "Consumption, Living Standards, and Consumer Welfare in Eastern Europe," *East European Economics: Slow Growth in the 1980's*, pp. 250-252. It might be added that the Polish government reduced these subsidies in 1984; they were proving to be too expensive.

15. The author was invited to a reception in Budapest to meet people affiliated with the Hungarian film industry. On the way to the reception he was impressed by the number of fine homes overlooking the Danube. Every time a mansion was passed the author asked: "Who lives there?" The answer would be a T.V. producer, a Communist Party official, an entrepreneur, and so on.

16. The four countries may be atypical. The three Western countries are advanced welfare states, and the Hungarian economic reforms have created a number of prosperous persons.

17. World Bank, *World Development Report 1985*, p. 229.

18. Malcolm Sawyer and Frank Wasserman, "Income Distribution in the OECD Countries," *OECD Economic Outlook* (July 1976), p. 14.

■ THE QUALITY OF LIFE ■

The quality of life defies easy definition or measurement; it relates to personal or societal preference. However, there are a number of measures that can be accepted as indicators of a society's will. The quality of the environment in which people live is one. Air and water pollution have negative effects on the mental and physical well-being of people in both the capitalist and socialist countries. Environmental problems are not just limited to the developed countries; they affect the less developed countries as well. Primitive farming methods can lead to soil erosion and fouled water supplies. Another measure of the quality of life is individual freedom. Included would be freedoms that Americans take for granted: freedom of speech, religion, and association. Social consumption including education and health care would be considered another measure of life quality.

THE ENVIRONMENT

Neither the capitalist nor the socialist countries have a monopoly on despoiling the environment. In fact, it is hard to say which system is worse. Los Angeles is second to few cities when it comes to air pollution, and exhaust fumes on the West German autobahns have damaged the plant life in the Black Forest. It appears, however, that the Soviet Union and the Eastern European countries have surpassed the West when it comes to environmental pollution. In Krakow, Poland, for example, the sulphur dioxide content of the atmosphere is reported to be higher than that of London, which is a much larger city. Many waterways in East Germany and Poland are polluted to the extent that they are not potable.[19] The Vistula river in Poland is regarded as the most polluted in Europe.[20] Czechoslovakia annually generates about eight tons of air pollution per person and is among the countries of the world most intensively affected by air pollution.[21] Industrial emissions have damaged approximately one-twelfth of all arable land in the country and have contributed to worker illness and absenteeism.

19. John M. Kramer, "The Environmental Crisis in Eastern Europe: The Price for Progress," *Slavic Review* (Summer 1983), pp. 204-220.

20. Ibid., p. 209. The author was told the following joke when he was in Warsaw in the spring of 1985: "Jesus Christ walked on the Sea of Galilee; any Pole can walk on the Vistula."

21. Ibid., p. 207.

INDIVIDUAL FREEDOM

Individual freedom is an important quality-of-life variable and is a composite of a number of factors. One factor is the right to worship at the place of one's choice. Another is civil rights, including freedom of speech, association, and assembly. A third factor is freedom to travel and emigrate, and a fourth is protection for the rights of minorities. These rights are difficult to quantify and to add to measures of welfare, but attempts have been made.

Freedom House is an organization that has rated nations according to the civil and political freedoms offered. A nation's degree of freedom is ranked on a scale of 1 to 7, with 1 the highest and 7 the lowest for each of the two categories. The United States, Canada, and many other Western democracies got a 1 in each category.[22] France and West Germany got 1 for political rights and 2 for civil liberties. Conversely, the Soviet Union got a 7 in each category, as did nine other communist countries.[23] Hungary received a 5 + on political rights and civil liberties. Taiwan received 5's in each category, and South Korea earned a 4 + and a 5.

SOCIAL CONSUMPTION

Social consumption refers to the availability of public education, health services, housing, transportation, and cultural activities. It is a legitimate measure of the well-being of any society. This form of consumption is collective and may be provided free or at charges well below costs by both the capitalist and socialist countries. In market economies, reliance on market forces can also provide goods and services available for social consumption. In the centrally planned economies, social consumption is financed through the state budget and through the social funds of state enterprises. There is a wide variation in the amount of social consumption provided by the socialist countries. In 1981, social consumption amounted to 5 percent of total consumption in Bulgaria, compared to 27 percent in Czechoslovakia.[24] In the capitalist countries, there is also a wide variation in the ratio of social to total consumption, with the United States at the low end of the spectrum and Sweden and Japan at the high end.[25]

22. *Map of Freedom* (New York: Freedom House, 1985).

23. A total of 20 countries received 7's in both categories.

24. Thad P. Alton, "East European GNPs: Origins of Product, Final Uses, Rates of Growth, and International Comparisons," *East European Economies: Slow Growth in the 1980's*, p. 97.

25. *National Accounts Statistics, 1970–1982* (Paris: Organization for Economic Cooperation and Development, 1983).

EDUCATION   Education is central to enhancing the quality of human resources, for it supplies the tools for learning that are basic to the process of adapting to change. The quality of a country's labor force is directly dependent on the quality of education it provides. Poor educational performance is not just an individual loss, it is a national disaster. The problem is not only finding jobs for the functionally illiterate in high-tech societies, but how these societies are to survive competitively if much of their force cannot effectively contribute. As the United States, in particular, moves from an industrial to an information society, brain-power will become more important than physical power. The Third World countries are taking over many of the industrial tasks formerly performed by the United States and other developed industrial economies.[26]

Available evidence indicates that the U.S. educational system does not score well in comparison with other Western countries. When 19 different achievement tests were administered to students in different countries, Americans never ranked first or second. If comparisons are limited to other developed countries only, the United States ranked at the bottom seven out of nineteen times.[27] Direct comparisons of the capitalist and socialist educational systems are more difficult to make. Although the Soviet Union turns out more engineers than the United States, their educational backgrounds are not as good. Modern computer facilities are lacking in the Soviet Union, and much of their advanced technology is imported from the West.[28] Higher technical education in the Soviet Union includes a large amount of classtime spent on Marxist–Leninist ideology.

HEALTH CARE   Health care is another component of the quality of life. Two measures of health care are life expectancy and infant mortality. As Table 20-6 indicates, the major capitalist countries rank ahead of the major socialist countries in these categories. The life expectancy for both males and females is higher in all of the capitalist countries than it is in any of the socialist countries. Infant mortality rates also vary considerably, ranging from a low of 7 per 1,000 births in Japan to 32 per 1,000 births in Yugoslavia. The highest mortality rate of 11 per 1,000 in Italy, West Germany, and the United States is matched only by East Germany; the rates of the other socialist economies are higher.

26. President's Commission on Industrial Competitiveness, *Global Competition: The New Reality* (Washington: USGPO, 1985), p. 141.

27. *International Student Achievement Comparisons and Teacher Shortages in Math and Science,* U.S. Congress, Joint Economic Committee, 98th Cong., 1st Sess., 1983, pp. 24-29.

28. While visiting in the spring of 1985, the author saw a West German firm installing computer hardware at a Polish university.

TABLE 20-6   LIFE EXPECTANCY AND INFANT
MORTALITY RATES, 1983

| | Life Expectancy in Years | | Infant Mortality Rate |
	Male	Female	(per 1,000 births)
Italy	73	78	11
Japan	74	79	7
France	72	79	9
West Germany	72	78	11
United Kingdom	71	77	10
Canada	73	79	9
United States	72	79	11
Sweden	75	80	8
Hungary	66	74	19
Bulgaria	67	73	17
Yugoslavia	66	72	32
East Germany	68	74	11
Czechoslovakia	66	74	16
Poland	67	75	19
Romania	69	74	28
U.S.S.R.	65	74	32

Source: The World Bank, *World Development Report 1985*, p. 219.

SUMMARY

Economic systems can be compared on the basis of how well they satisfy various economic performance criteria: employment, price stability, economic growth, and an equitable distribution of income. Other criteria that would come under the category of quality of life can also be used to make comparisons. The quality of the environment is one criterion, and health care is another. During the 1980s, there has been a general decline in the economic performance of both market and centrally planned economies in comparison with earlier periods. Growth rates for some countries were negative during the early 1980s, but have rebounded somewhat. Poland, in particular, suffered a sharp decline, and industrial production there is still less than it was in 1977. In the capitalist countries, high inflation rates have declined, but unemployment in some countries, particularly the United Kingdom, is high. Much of the future performance of the socialist countries will depend on the economic policies to be implemented in the Soviet Union.

R E V I E W   Q U E S T I O N S

1. Why should the quality of life be used as a measure of comparison of economic systems?
2. Why is it easier for the centrally planned economies to maintain full employment than the market economies?
3. Full employment can be maintained without any costs in a centrally planned economy. Do you agree?
4. Compare the rates of economic growth in the major planned and market economies during the 1980s.
5. Can inflation exist in a centrally planned economy?
6. Compare income distribution in capitalist and socialist countries. Are incomes distributed more evenly under capitalism or socialism?
7. What is social consumption?
8. Compare the capitalist and socialist countries using various quality of life measures.

R E C O M M E N D E D   R E A D I N G S

Alton, Thad P. "East European GNPs: Origins of Product, Final Uses, Rates of Growth, and International Comparisons." In *East European Economies: Slow Growth in the 1980's.* Vol. 1 U.S. Congress, Joint Economic Committee, 99th Cong., 1st Sess., 1985, pp. 81–132.

Clayton, Elizabeth M. "Consumption, Living Standards, and Consumer Welfare in Eastern Europe." In *East European Economies: Slow Growth in the 1980's.* Vol. 1, U.S. Congress, Joint Economic Committee, 99th Cong., 1st Sess., 1985, pp. 249-262.

Kramer, John M. "The Environmental Crisis in Eastern Europe." *Slavic Review.* Summer 1983, pp. 204–220.

Kravis, Irving B., Alan Heston, and Robert Summers. "World Product and Income." *UN International Comparisons Project.* Phase III. Baltimore: The Johns Hopkins University Press, 1983.

Shipler, David K. *Broken Idols, Russia, Solemn Dreams.* New York: Times Books, 1983.

Thurow, Lester C. *The Zero-Sum Solution.* New York: Simon & Schuster, Inc., 1985.

INDEX